Stoned

'El Pimpressario' by Andrew Loog Oldham

Stoned

A Memoir of London in the 1960s

Written and Produced by
Andrew Loog Oldham

Interviews and Research by
Simon Dudfield, Edited by Ron Ross

ST. MARTIN'S PRESS ⚍ NEW YORK

www.stmartins.com

ISBN 0-312-26653-7

First published in Great Britain by Secker & Warburg, The Random House Group Limited

First U.S. Edition: February 2001

10 9 8 7 6 5 4 3 2 1

· CONTENTS ·

· PREFACE ·

ALO: May 95, I'm in the James Dean suite, better known as two shoe boxes at the back of the Hotel Iroquois on West 44th Street in Manhattan, and life has definitely lost its colour. You try a few things to forget that he who is not busy being born is busy dying, to block out the thought of yourself as a wingless, hurt, spineless bird of the 60s. Another grey line – they're not even white any more – another grappa or Southern-anything-without-Comfort can bring you back to life for a few minutes, but it's not a given. Occasionally you get up from the couch and have to check yourself out in the mirror above the fireplace to make sure you are still there, and that's an effort. One could say that when life becomes too painful, the body sickens and withers and the soul departs.

Your circulation is so shot, you have a permanent drip; you can't risk beige trousers 'cause you leave sir john and ten minutes later dicky boy still isn't finished. At five in the morning there are definitely animals in the soup, the hall and your mind, and the thought of them provides the only colour in this bioflick. There's an inflamed eyesore-orange cutting through the grey death-white pallor of the door and it's as bright as the people and/or animals are real and active in the corridor. You eventually open the door, the hall is empty, and as silent and as lifeless, grey and oh-so-off-white as the lifelessness inside.

My blood feels like liquid cocaine mixed with grappa, fire without the flame; problem is it feels there is less and less of it flowing through me. My heart has to beat faster to give me oxygen and to find some remaining grimy pocket of nutrition. I've hit that point when more than half of any given day I can't answer the phone or make a call; anybody could hear the pain. I don't feel like a long-distance man any more.

I keep getting glimpses of the other side: looks okay, but I don't want to be there just yet. The seductive calm of the other side is replaced by my wife Esther's and my boys' faces and they are not calm, they just don't get it. I pull back and the other side goes away for a time. I think often of the dark Christine, who right-handed Olympic Studios through the 60s and 70s. When she decided to move on to less painful pastures, she settled all the local accounts, left not a tradesman unattended, paid her milk bill up to date and left a tidy desk, with a neat left-and-right balance sheet for one last well-planned session at Olympic. And so went off to her well-planned death.

She got in her garaged car, plugged up the exhaust pipe, and pulled from her bag a bottle of vodka and a hundred or so sleepers she'd hoarded. She sacrificed her sleep to a dream of relief, planning and styling this final roar of her broken engine. Just in case the vod and hundred nods were not enough, as the exhaust did its work, Christine smashed the empty bottle on the mahogany dash and slashed her wrists to final pieces.

I get some rest and that's exhausting in and of itself; I get up by noon and head down the block to Un, Deux, Trois for my staple grappa and espresso, followed by a good sweat and a line in the loo, after which I can hold down the soup of the day. The Un, Deux, Trois folk are kind, I'm never rude and they never embarrass me, but it's apparent I'm embarrassing myself.

It was time to get my affairs in order, so this is how I didn't do it. My James Dean suite in the Iroquois was such a mess I couldn't get it together to pack and leave; I just rented a fresh abode and moved on up to Columbus Circle's Mayflower Hotel, the move giving me the zap to put on a fresh and happy face, allowing my movie to return to widescreen Technicolor for a few moments more. I called room service, ordered a well-done steak, and limited my booze intake to a beer set-up chased by a line to aid my digestive tract.

I hadn't seen Thomas 'Doc' Cavalier for quite a while, and I recalled a long-outstanding debt of quite a few grand left over from our various recording activities in the 70s. Doc still lodged in Wallingford, Connecticut, and in a nearby town lived one Al Goodin, a champion gent I'd met some eight years ago on a jet bound for Vegas who told me a few truths about life. The magazine of the same name had done a piece on the vast number of great white unemployed in all the armpits of North America, and I had asked the obviously worldly and patriotic Al whether this was to be *The Grapes of*

Wrath revisited, the beginning of an end for America. 'No,' said Al, his 'N-o-o-o-o' so long and a-e-i-o-u-ed that it had to be followed by a prophecy of doom. 'Andy,' he said, 'the end will be when folks our age start asking for our social security and there's nothing left, and what is left over younger blood will keep for itself.'

I checked out of the Mayflower, kept the Iroquois on tap, hopped in a limo and stopped on Amsterdam Avenue to buy two-fifths for the road. Soon enough we were on the Merrit Parkway heading for Connecticut and in my memories time stood still, my heart throbbing with pain and shame at travelling the same freeway twenty-five years later – when all seemed to be moving forward save I, who had been drunk and stoned then, and still was. Though now I couldn't let myself drive.

Once I arrived in Weathersfield, I sat down to catch up with Al Goodin and thought I was putting on a good front, when he cut me down with, 'You know, Andy, you're a drunk.' I was in shock. Get the picture: I'd burnt my bridges in show-biz, and now in the real world I was just a plain old drunk. I agreed with Al's call, which felt both cruel and kind, as it came from a true American soul. I knew that if I was ever to see this man on another occasion, out of respect for his opinion I had better be sober. I'd met my worldly match 'n' catch-me-out Barnum, and Al was raking my life over his warm coals.

He was a more northern Panama-hatted Ed Begley Sr from *Cat on a Hot Tin Roof*, my mother's boyfriend Alec revisited in logic. That first conversation with Al left me in a panic and reaching for another line and a grappa. I was such a hypocrite; I frowned at him and pretended I 'used' to take coke. I was in a real spin. He had me explain what I did for a living, what I'd done, how I'd got there, where I'd been; this same story used to come out produced with the right amount of colour and echo, but now it sounded scratched, hollow and worn.

'I don't know why you bother, Andy' said Al.

I interrupted with a panicked, 'What Do You Mean?'

'I mean,' he went on, his smile carried on wings of mercy, 'that life as you know it is over, you are spinning your wheels, you're redundant. It's time to get on with change and find your new life. Your old life pays the rent, but your body and soul are spent, go to bed. I'll drive what's left of you to Wallingford in the morning . . .'

Three days later Al poured me into Wallingford: not even the coke could stop me blacking out, so I slept it off and waited for another loop of slight life to lock in. Then I called Doc and met him for my brandy-and-beer breakfast; he smiled at a man dying, trying to tie up some loose ends in his life.

'How's the family?' Doc asked.

He can see clearly now, so there's no words I can muster, just a pained effort of a 'hmm-guess-howz-my-family' grimace on my tired barbed-'n'-wired face. I libatiously limoed what was left of me back to New York and sat in a coma; my elevator had shut down, I was cringing in the basement, looking in the *Yellow Pages* for help. The Jimmy Dean rooms breathed a little, life wasn't bright but there was a ray of hope; the animals and voices in the hall had done their work and moved on to other folk. To paraphrase Jimmy Webb, the loon's a harsh mistress. I knew the ride was over, but I wasn't ready for the other side.

I finally got the message when at five in the morning on 44th Street, returning to my hotel, I saw this horse. Problem was the horse was fifteen storeys high, exiting the Royalton and entering the Algonquin. The horse had opaque white flanks through which I could see all the way to Times Square. I blinked a couple of times to try and get rid of this momentary hallucination, as I'd been up for days already, but every time I opened my eyes, in this endless moment that I can't put time on, the horse was still there, slowly crossing 44th Street.

And then I decided to get well, to survive, and I called Doc . . .

· CHAPTER 1 ·

ALO: There are three sides to every story: yours, mine and the truth.

I lost my father before I knew the meaning of loss; I lost him before I was born. World War II had kept my mother busy as a nurse by day and a nightingale by night. But she found a moment for herself with one Andrew Loog, a Texan of Dutch origin, who served in the Army of the United States Air Corps from 15 July 1941 until the day of his separation by death, 13 June 1943. Flt Lieutenant Loog, assigned to the 332nd Bombardier Squadron, 94th Bombardier Group H, was shot down over the Channel. I shot out on 29 January 1944, when Celia was admitted to Paddington General Hospital having gone into labour prematurely; perhaps she was working there already. Thus Air Medalled and Purple Hearted, Louisianan Loog left a wife and a child dependent in Texas and, perhaps, this happy, independent little bastard in London.

My birth was complicated, and I was born ill, weak and puny, a mere four pounds. I had a 'soft skull': a 'hard hat' was specially designed to protect me, and I wore it for the first year of my life, until my head became as hard as it has remained ever since. I was named Andrew Loog Oldham, in memory of Airman Andrew Loog, although on my birth certificate the space for daddy is blank.

The day I was born, Germany mounted its final offensive, the most vicious blitzkrieg over England yet. My mother and I spent many a night getting acquainted in the Underground as the German 'doodlebugs' rained down on the capital and drowned out the sound of Bow Bells, and along with them much of the life, but not the spirit, of our fellow Londoners.

My mother, Celia Oldham, has Alzheimer's, so I am telling you her story with help from some who knew her back in the day. She was born in

Paddington, New South Wales, on 11 February 1920. It has been pointed out to me that my first real employer, Mary Quant, was also born on 11 February some years later.

Celia's father was an Ashkenazi Jew named Militar Schatkowski born in Plotaly, Kovno, Russia, who fled Poland in 1916. Militar had looked across the oceans of choice and ended up in New South Wales, where he met my grandmother, whose name I've never known. Perhaps they were wed, and two years after my mother, Cecelia Olga, was born, a brother – whose name might have been Robert – joined her. In 1923 my mother's mother gathered her brood together and shipped off for England, leaving a bemused and culture-baffled Militar horizontal with drink at the Sydney race track; for him the race was over.

My mother was four years old when she arrived in London. She was schooled to conceal her Australian and Jewish lineage, socially a double whammy at that time, and grew up to become a fiercely proud, aloof and radiant redhead. I'm afraid that it is typical of my mother's reticence, shall we call it, that nothing is known of what happened to my maternal grandmother or how my mother was raised. I can presume she passed on before I was born, but I cannot commit to that as a fact. My mother never mentioned her, so there was no reason for me to reason. Why should I? It's not just that she was the grandmother with no name or face; she simply never was.

Growing up in London, Celia cultivated a certain style, which along with 'correct' behaviour mattered to her above all else. She was nineteen when what would become World War II was declared with Germany, the women of Britain playing an active part in the war effort. Many succumbed to recruitment posters that made service dress look smart and sophisticated. My uncle was drafted or enlisted into the Royal Australian Navy, and Celia joined the Women's Voluntary Services, my fashion-conscious mother opting to become a nurse. Norman Hartnell, the prestigious dressmaker, designed the uniforms.

Once, when I was about nine, I asked my mother what had happened to her brother. She gave me a look that warned me not to cry 'uncle' and went on to tell me that she had not got on with her brother very well before the war, so there hadn't been any point in finding out whether he had survived it. I was happy that she felt more for me: the only thing that was mine was my mother. Most other people's 'mys' were in the plural. I knew already that my mother had taken some cold, hard decisions as a woman on her own with a young boy child and that perhaps warmth of heart had settled for second place as a consequence.

Celia Oldham

Celia – and ain't life genetic – had already developed an opiatic cotton lair around her that prevented one from entering, as she went about the business of life. Detail was for the poor and unfortunate, and I would continue to cross over that line with Celia when, aged eleven, I worried (not for the last time) about the future prospects of my hairline and asked my mum for details of my father.

I started at the bottom. 'Where was he buried?' I asked. My mother fetched from her desk some forbidding-looking papers and showed me one letter from an American Air Force chaplain, who had written in answer to my mother's enquiries. In officialese he informed her that Flt Lieutenant Andrew Loog was interred at the Ardennes American Cemetery and Memorial, Neurille-en-Condroz, Belgium.

'What did he look like?' I continued. She smiled and went back to the good place in her heart. Her face was radiant, then she frowned and looked around the room as if wary of eavesdroppers.

'He was tall, over six foot, handsome . . . a good man,' she said quietly.

'But don't you have any photos of him, Mummy?' I persisted.

I could see from her eyes that her mind was flashing through the snaps of her life as she pursed her lips and replied, 'Well, Andy, there was a war on, we really didn't have time for pictures.'

Later in life I often thanked God that my mother, when considering whether or not to abort me, had not displayed the characteristic coldness with which she allowed the rest of her family to slip away. I believe there was a real shyness beneath her seeming self-confidence.

After the war, we were continually on the move. Celia rented a series of horrific single rooms in houses and flats around north-west London. By winter 1947, the worst for over a hundred years, the British economy and morale were at an all-time low. There were queues for everything: the country was getting worse, not better (rationing of food and clothes continued until 1949). The black market burgeoned and spivs took control of the streets, the crack-men of their time. Familiar neighbourhoods still looked like a lunar landscape, abandoned airfields dotted the countryside, and all the spontaneity and joy had gone out of life. It was a deadly dull and demanding time, and all in all I'm quite glad to have been too young to remember much of it.

Celia was as devoted to me as she was to herself, determined that I should receive the very best upbringing. She installed me at a nursery school in Sussex, far away from the destitution and disease of London. I remember my mother's visits, when more often than not a Doctor Jimmy, who'd reputedly made himself rich practising illegal abortions during the war, accompanied her. In the post-war austerity years, running one car was an extravagance that few could afford; Jimmy had two – twin Sunbeam Talbots, grey and maroon.

My mother could have stayed kept, but she opted for keeping busy, forging a career for herself as a freelance Comptometer operator (a primitive tallying machine that was a predecessor of the modern computer), keeping the books for several small companies. On this steady but small wage, the only luxury she could afford was the knowledge that her Andy was being kept at a decent school. The general post-war malaise of the British working classes horrified Celia. Despite her rather outré position as a single mother, she wanted her son to rise above the gloomy masses, just as she felt she had, though she never detailed from what to what she had risen.

By 1950 Celia was relatively settled in a one-room apartment at 18 Old Marylebone Road, close to the Edgware Road. She shared this tiny space with an old wartime friend, Joan Bingham, or 'Lady Joan' as she liked to be called, who had over-enjoyed the wartime party when each night's revelry held the promise of the final snuff-out. Joan had no one to anchor her, as Celia had me; the war had burnt her out like some tired old silent-movie star. She got straight to the point, and during my first summer holiday in London we returned home to find Lady Joan dearly departed, with her head in the oven, stone-cold dead from gas poisoning. Not a very jolly experience for a six-year-old. We think the 60s were wild, but that decade's death we brought upon ourselves. Surviving World War II, greedy for life, with no choice about death, must have been the ultimate head trip: despite the odds, some managed to grasp a post-war existence, and some – like Lady Joan – couldn't handle the return to the norm and moved on.

Celia moved out of the room in Marylebone Road shortly afterwards, finding accommodation the other side of the Edgware Road in Maida Vale at 6 Elgin Avenue. Here she rented a room in an apartment belonging to two Hungarian refugee sisters, both working as airline stewardesses to earn enough money to retire to Spain. I was growing up fast and very much enjoyed the double fun of listening to the radio in the room of the sister I fancied, while silently ogling her.

In the summer of 1951 Celia first introduced me to her steady boyfriend, Alec Morris, a man who was to play a significant paternal role in my life. Twenty years older than Celia, Alec was a successful Jewish businessman.

His company, Made by Morris, was one of the best-known manufacturers of furniture in the country. By the late 50s he had moved out of the furniture business and into private banking with Alec Morris Investments Ltd.

Pat Clayton, daughter of Alec Morris: Celia was very cagey about her family; she never discussed it, she sort of referred to this guy who she'd been married to. He was going to be a doctor but they had to pack it in because of the war. People must have wondered who the hell Celia was. 'Where's yer kid's father?' 'Oh well, he was killed in the war.' That was acceptable. But Celia knew Alec before Andrew was born, around 1942, and that's why it makes me wonder, y'know maybe . . . Andrew doesn't look Jewish, but before my dad was bald, he was ginger, and so was his father. There are a lot of red-headed Jews from Poland.

They were very hungry people. Alec said his father worked every hour God gave him, he never stopped working. That was how you did it, especially as an immigrant. You're hungry and you have a lot of mouths to feed. Jews in Britain changed their names, more so than in the States. English Jews, particularly, wanted to be part of the urban landscape. They didn't want to stick out. It was the women who carried the race and culture of the Jewish religion. The men disappeared or became 'stomach Jews': eat well on Jewish food, go to synagogue sometimes and that's it.

ALO: Alec had grown up in the East End at the turn of the century, tired of it as a teenager and in 1915 smuggled himself aboard a troop ship heading for the States. There he spent time in New York teaching the tango and foxtrot alongside George Raft, the alleged gangster, gigolo and, later, movie star. The same George was drummed out of the UK years later for fronting the Mob-connected Colony Club.

After a few years in the States up to everything, Alec returned to London to join the family furniture business. When World War II began, all furniture manufacturers had to go into war work, making ammunition boxes and wooden rifles for the Home Guard and the army. After the war, Made by Morris started to produce utility furniture and from then until 1950 the Morrises lived the good life, rolling in money – living on the right side of Hampstead and getting there in a Rolls-Royce.

Pat Clayton: My dad was flying back from a buying trip in Italy in 1948, when he nearly died and became a hero in the national newspapers: he rescued an air-hostess by jumping with her from the plane, forty feet off the ground, just before it crashed. They were the only survivors. The event may have made him a hero, but it gave him nightmares for the rest of his life: he'd always hear the screams of the people; he always heard and saw the people dying.

ALO: My mother was Alec's long-term outside affair, but he had no intention of deserting his wife and two children, an arrangement that suited all. Unlike many wayward husbands, Alec showed genuine concern for his 'second family', and lavished attention on me. He would pay for my education and for our holidays abroad – La Baule on the Normandy coast, and the Costa Brava.

Pat Clayton: My father always had a soft spot for redheads; he was also very fond of Andrew, he certainly looked after him. Everybody at the factory knew about the affair. My mother knew, she didn't really care. She did a deal: he looked after her, they had a good marriage, a good home life. My mother never really minded about Celia. Celia used to visit the house. She would bring clothes for my mother, go shopping for my mother, very strange. They became great mates.

My mother was eccentric, dotty, completely nuts, maybe she came to terms with it. Her nickname was 'Unconscious'. Celia was fun to be with, she was very good company, although she could be quite bitchy and was always vain. I don't think she had an easy time of it, she obviously should have had a better position in life, more fun. She should have had a more settled life than she did. She was quite a classy lady.

ALO: By the time I met Alec, Made by Morris had been sold and he'd invested his time and money into becoming Alec Morris Investments Ltd. As well as driving a Rolls-Royce, Alec practically lived in the Ivy, London's most élite restaurant, the moneyed showbiz haunt. His other favourite home away from home was Cunningham's on Park Lane.

Alec acted like a real father to me, and I liked to imagine he was. He rewarded me when I did well in school by taking me to dinner at The Ivy.

This practice continued for many years. When I did less well, it was Lyons Corner House, corner of Oxford Street and Tottenham Court Road.

My mother never gave up her day job or her independence and continued with her career as a Comptometer operator. To me life seemed normal, the relationship between Celia and Alec did not bother me: it was all I knew, and I felt truly loved by two people who had a great deal of apparent affection for each other. My education was her primary concern, and Alec paid for this agenda. I was enrolled at a new boarding school, the Aylesbury School for Boys.

In early September 1952, just a few weeks before the new school term started, my mother was informed that Aylesbury was 'overcrowded' and I was to be relocated to an alternative school, the Cokethorpe School for Boys, situated in the leafy Oxfordshire hamlet of Witney, in blanket country. This school would leave a lasting impression on me.

Cokethorpe to me seemed like the Oxford of *Brideshead Revisited*. The school occupied a magnificent mansion with stables and many acres of lush green fields. I was particularly impressed with the clothes of our stylish headmaster – a three-piece tweed suit and Hush Puppies made him appear to be as comfortably aristocratic as the exiled Windsor. By his side, his glamorous wife, in her tartan skirt and Shetland wool sweaters, looked like nothing so much as a 'royal'. So this was the world Celia wanted us to live in!

Since I was acutely aware of my 'illegitimacy' and dreaded the subject being brought up by my classmates, I was grateful that the head treated all of us as if we were his own sons. I recall an occasion when one boy's parents forgot his birthday, since they were too busy separating for such sentiment, and the head took him into town to the toy store and bought him a present.

Then one day a new headmaster arrived to take over at Cokethorpe. Colonel Elston was a brooding bachelor with a handlebar moustache. Customarily attired in a double-breasted blazer, he wore crisp shirts set off by the navy and maroon regimental striped tie of the Royal Guards.

Col Elston aroused much curiosity among the pupils, particularly as at midday every Wednesday he left the school in his sleek black Rover, returning hours later in the early evening. Rumours abounded as to what the colonel was up to. We fantasised that he was an adviser to the War Office or involved with the Secret Services. Seven years after VE Day, the war still provided the scripts for the comics that children devoured.

After my first year at Cokethorpe, I returned home to London for the summer holiday. Mother had moved again, now sharing a flat at 65 Eton Avenue in Swiss Cottage with an extravagant hairdresser, Harry Mizelas. Mizelas later became the André of 'André Bernard' and, beginning with the flagship salon in Mayfair, his empire eventually stretched to over twenty establishments. But he met with a brutal death: shot dead in Hyde Park during the 70s. He drove from his schlock-Regency town house down High Street Kensington, turned left into Hyde Park at Knightsbridge, steered his Roller to the right in the direction of Park Lane, then pulled over to the left, having noticed an acquaintance, who shot him in the head. I remember my mother being questioned by the police on many occasions, but to this day the case goes unsolved.

There was no fridge at Eton Avenue, so for most of the year we kept milk cold on the window ledge; there was no telephone, but Celia had bought her own radio set, which became my window on the world. I regularly listened to BBC melodramas like *The Archers*, *Riders of the Range* (whose hero Jeff Arnold also featured in an *Eagle* comic strip) and *Dick Barton, Special Agent.*

The BBC radio monopoly offered little in the way of musical entertainment that would appeal to the post-war generation. *Two-Way Family Favourites* was a weekly two-hour music show that played the requests of British soldiers still serving abroad for their families and sweethearts at home, and vice versa. Dickie Valentine and Slim Whitman were popular favourites, but I preferred my dramas.

Every morning Alec arrived in his wildly exciting silver Rolls-Royce to chauffeur Celia to work and drop me off at Pamela Marshall's, a war friend of Celia's who kept her home fires burning minding me, while her wing commander husband still served his country overseas. I would walk the neighbourhood if Pamela was detained by some errand, and it was on one of these excursions that I encountered a way of life as far from Alec's Silver Cloud as could be, just over the next block. It made me shudder and set off in me both ambition and appreciation for the perhaps austere, but well-decorated womb with a view Celia had made for us.

As I crafted my way down Crawford Street, a shell-shocked, withered-to-the-bone elderly lady in apron and carpet slippers stood, arms folded, eyes searching, in the doorway of her depressing one-up, two-down. She caught my eye and my attention, beckoned me towards her, held out a coin in her grimy, work-worn hand, and asked if I minded coming inside to feed her gas meter, which was too high for her to reach with her deformity. I was happy to return her to light and heat, but chilled by the poverty to which I was exposed for the first time, ashamed that my discomfort might be perceived by her as disdain.

Back on the sunny, well-heated side of Old Marylebone Road, Pamela kept me on a loose leash, thankfully, and I was able to explore her neighbourhood without fear of Celia's disapproval. I returned to the ABC Cinema off the Edgware Road any number of times to stare at the movie posters, and finally plucked up the courage to sneak in. Geography, psychology and anatomy were on offer at the Academy of Motion Pictures, and so pop became my favourite schoolmaster.

The first film I remember is John Huston's *Moulin Rouge* (1952), starring Zsa Zsa Gabor and José Ferrer, who played the crippled painter Toulouse-Lautrec. It was one of the first films to have been shot in Cinemascope, and I was reeling afterwards. Widescreen close-ups of chorines doing the can-can gave me my first glimpse of how art could get away with murder, as legs I might wait a lifetime to see in real life pummelled me in the stalls. I left the cinema shaken and stirred. The film experience put off any appreciation I might later have for women's legs, as in *Moulin Rouge* they just seemed like lethal weapons.

I had just returned home from Cokethorpe's spring term when Celia received a letter from the local vicar. There was 'something awfully wrong' at the school. I didn't know what that something was, but I never returned to Cokethorpe. A year later Celia and I were on a train taking us to the south coast for our holidays. She got comfy and opened up the *Daily Express* to see a photograph of Cokethorpe School for Boys on the front page, beneath a headline that read 'Four Jailed in School Swindle Ring'. My beloved Cokethorpe had been the work of confidence tricksters! The 'gang' had opened and closed seven private schools in total, including the supposedly overbooked Aylesbury School. After collecting up the tuition and boarding fees, the conmen ran up credit in a small town and then moved on without paying, to open yet another 'school' in another town. Cokethorpe was their final scam before they were caught. They'd been averaging out about £80,000. Col Elston's mysterious midweek sojourns were to a parole officer and not the Foreign Office. While my mother paced the corridor, ruing her bad luck, I devoured the larger-than-life newspaper with a great deal of interest and some delight. To me, it was an ingenious scheme, original and entertaining.

Celia next bought a five-room basement flat at 44 Belsize Park Gardens near Swiss Cottage, with financial assistance from Alec. She quickly arranged for me to attend the local Swiss Cottage junior school. At first, I was happy to be staying at home, and thrilled to learn that at Mum's new flat I would have my own bedroom at last. For Celia, the Belsize Park flat was a rung up the ladder of respectability. She had a telephone installed and, best of all, a television delivered.

Swiss Cottage state school was unremittingly grimy and depressing, all the more so after the glamour of Cokethorpe. I was frequently ill from fear and revulsion. I nevertheless enjoyed running credits for the film I hoped the day would become. The older boys ritually inducted new pupils, and on my very first day I was forced into the local sweet shop and ordered to steal something. I got caught, an early indication that I was about true romance, not true crime. I tried to make the most of our new accommodation: after school, between 7 and 10 p.m. every night, I tuned into Radio Luxembourg. The invariably bad reception annoyed my mother, who under any circumstances did not suffer imperfection gladly, but I was glad to have an alternative to the Beeb.

Television and film combined with radio to stimulate my hungry senses. Unlike most of my peers, I wanted a peek behind the scenes; I remembered the names of producers and directors as well as actors. While the major American studios such as MGM, United Artists and Warner Brothers found a ready audience in Europe, I was always attracted for some reason to the independent producers of my homeland. Romulus Films, a production company formed in 1949 by the brothers Woolf, James and John (sons of the veteran producer C.M. Woolf), specialised in Anglo-American co-productions. The films produced by the Woolfs and their Romulus atelier were most distinguished: *The African Queen* (starring, of course, Humphrey

Bogart and Katharine Hepburn, 1951), *Cosh Boy* (1952), *Beat the Devil* (John Huston's wicked satire with an all-star cast, again including a 'mature' Bogart, 1954), *The Bespoke Overcoat* (1956), *I Am a Camera* (Christopher Isherwood's memoir of decadent, 'tween-wars Berlin, later turned into *Cabaret*, 1955), and best (and worst) of all *The Good Die Young* (1954), which introduced me to the actor who would tower in my youthful imagination as a paragon of accomplishment and style: Laurence Harvey.

Both 'above the line' and on the screen, *The Good Die Young* was my kind of deal; I found it fascinating that James Woolf managed Larry, and both brothers produced his movies. James also found time to touch Terence Stamp's life, and died in 1966 at the age of fifty-three. But Laurence Harvey was his crowning achievement.

Laurence was born Laruschka Mischa Skikne in 1928 in Lithuania, and as a child moved with his Jewish parents to South Africa. He joined the Royal South African Navy at fourteen by lying about his age and was enlisted for the last two years of World War II. By 1946 he was in England studying at RADA, and at eighteen he was playing lead roles in rep. At twenty, in 1948, he had his first lead role in a film. My kind of guy, pace and life!

The British character actress Hermione Baddeley, twenty years his senior, took him under her wing. Larry, too ambitious to be swayed by the glamour of youth, made this his pattern. He married the much older West End theatre star Margaret Leighton in 1953, and her introduction to the stages of the West End and Broadway provided complementary challenges to his suave roles in films like *Darling*. He did *As You Like It* in 1953, toured with the Old Vic as Henry V on its 1958–9 tour and starred in *Camelot* in the late 60s in the West End and on Broadway. He married Joan Cohn in 1968, she being the widow of Columbia Pictures mogul Harry Cohn and, again, some twenty years Mr Harvey's senior. The last eleven months of his too-short life he was married to the model Paulene Stone, passing away in 1973 from cancer.

Laurence Harvey signed with the Associated British Picture Corporation in 1948 and remained a 'contract' actor until 1952. He was due a salary rise that year from £25 to £35. ABPC cried poverty and asked Harvey to re-sign for the same wage. That same week ABPC announced profits for the year of £3,000,000. Mr Harvey, understandably, left ABPC and was out of work for most of a year before signing with the Woolfs. Commuting between London and Los Angeles, rubbing noses with the likes of Jane Fonda and Kim Novak, Larry leapt off the screen into immortality as Joe Lampton in the 1959 Romulus-produced *Room at the Top* and the 1965 sequel, *Life at the Top*.

Laurence Harvey and first wife Margaret Leighton on their way to the Paris Fashion Show 1954

Laurence Harvey in *Room At The Top*

Messrs Harvey and the Woolfs are together responsible for remarkable bodies of work and illuminating lives. Laurence Harvey's stardom and James Woolf's management of it would inspire me throughout the turbulence of my youth and showbusiness career, and would encourage the birth of my own Immediate Records by their example. As Immediate staggered between controlling its acts and trying to remember who they actually were, I – like Larry – would remain 'happy to be part of the industry of human happiness'. To this day I am indebted to their genius, which has lighted my life even in its darkest moments.

Back in the 'real' life of mid-50s London, Hollywood-on-the-Thames beckoned in the form of Harold Lang, a B-movie gangster in many Anglo Amalgamated-produced films, who lived just round the corner from us. Although he was not in the same league as Laurence Harvey, I'd seen Harold on TV, so I went a-knockin' and the kindly actor let me in. His huge blond peroxide quiff and exaggerated gestures fascinated me. Over tea and biscuits, I barraged him with questions: 'Have you met . . . ? What's he like . . . ? Who's the best director . . . ? How do you do that?' Off-screen Harold was a nice man, not at all like a gangster. He did, however, radiate something different. The tension of an actor's life appealed to me even then, and Harold had that attractive aura of a man working in a field apart from the norm.

About this time I made friends with a young Swiss Cottage boy, Jeremy Holt. Jeremy's father, Seth Holt, was the Ealing Comedy editor who'd worked on *The Lavender Hill Mob*. For a short while I fell heavily under the influence of Mr Holt, who was tickled that I could knowledgeably discuss the work of British producers like Sir Alexander Korda and the Boulting Brothers.

Holt went on to direct Britain's first teenage angst film, *Nowhere to Go* (written by Kenneth Tynan) in 1958. He told me that Swiss Cottage was home to many celebrities, including Stephen Spender, who in 1946 had been sent to de-Nazify German libraries, and Humphrey Lyttelton, the British jazzman who, with his partner Chris Barber, launched the 100 Club.

I myself became interested in jazz while visiting my immediate next-door neighbour, Bob Carroll. Bob taught me how to listen critically to a record, to listen for the part around which the music wrapped itself: the horns, the trombone or the bass. He played me Miles Davis, Count Basie, Duke Ellington, Frank Sinatra, Nat King Cole, the Hi-Lo's, the Modern Jazz Quartet, Gerry Mulligan, Chet Baker. He showed me how Sinatra and Nat King Cole used their voices as instruments and were in fact an extension of the orchestra. I know I applied that one later on. Why Bob chose me I don't know, but he did, and I've never forgotten what he gave me. I don't remember what I was learning in school at the same time, but I remember producers and arrangers like Frank DeVol, Billy May, Gordon Jenkins and Nelson Riddle.

After one jazz session in Bob's top-floor apartment, I returned home to the basement flat and glimpsed, through an open bedroom door, my mother and Alec making love. They didn't realise I was home until they dressed and came out into the hall. I was standing on top of a chair with one end of a rope around my neck and the other end attached to the pipes running along the ceiling, threatening to kill myself. 'Come down, Andy,' advised Alec, first of the many practical men who have remained unswayed by my flair for the dramatic, 'you'll only break the string.'

Celia rented out a spare room in the basement flat to Gladys Byrne, a no-nonsense Joan-Crawford-on-top type in her late fifties who worked at the BBC. When she learnt of my addiction to television and film, she promised to introduce me to her brother, Gus Byrne. Should either of them ever have considered an operation, they had only to look at each other to guess the outcome. Gus was personal assistant to one of TV's top personalities, commentator Gilbert Harding, celebrated as 'Britain's Rudest Man'. On the radio he hosted *Twenty Questions* and on TV compered *What's My Line?*, a celebrity-panel quiz show that the whole of Britain gawked at throughout the 50s. Harding remains famous for the statement 'But I do wish that the future was over' and for breaking down in tears while talking about his mother on Britain's most provocative interview programme, John Freeman's *Face to Face*, in 1957. At the tail end of the 50s, he guest-starred in *Expresso Bongo*.

After we met and I pumped him for everything he could tell me about life behind the scenes, Gus told Celia that I had showbusiness in my blood, which could hardly have come as good news to mum.

By this time I was allowed to attend the cinema on my own. I had a new favourite every week. For a short period John Payne was one of them; his *Tennessee's Partner* starred future American President Ronald Reagan as the bad guy. I followed Payne's subsequent career, as he went on to co-write and produce his next big movie, *The Boss*. The dark *Slightly Scarlet* scored a double hit with me, due to the resemblance between leading lady Arlene Dahl and the leading lady in my own life, my mother.

I loved bad boy Tony Curtis in *Six Bridges to Cross*, and fell for Audrey Hepburn, after seeing her star in Billy Wilder's *Sabrina*. Miss Hepburn was the first of my androgynous icons, a fascination that would grow in intensity and refinement over time. Victor Mature's versatility impressed me since he was just as convincing as Samson or a gangster. And we happened to share birthdays.

As the up-and-down first year at Swiss Cottage was drawing to a close, with the summer holidays looming, I began to search in earnest for a suitable Saturday job. Even at ten I was keenly clothes-conscious and longed for a wardrobe worthy of my fantasies. Alec had given me a good start by passing down a stylish suede golf jacket and a pair of cufflinks for my tenth birthday, and I was grateful for his sartorial example, since I knew most of my role models only from the silver screen.

I landed a job at André's on Finchley Road, a refined Swiss Cottage hairdressing salon. For a month I swept up the dead hair and fetched cappuccinos from across the road for the clients. I enjoyed the responsibility and the opportunity to earn my money, play flash and buy presents for my mother. Unfortunately, a valued customer sat on a plate of biscuits that I'd left on a chair. She didn't take too kindly to me calling her a 'silly bitch' and telling her that next time she ought to look where she was sitting. Here endeth the first job.

I tried to put out of my mind the looming prospect of another year at the squalid Swiss Cottage state school. Television was a handy escape route, and the advent of the commercial channel offered a welcome alternative to the BBC. I fell under the spell of Mark Saber, a one-armed Selfridges store detective, and for a few television minutes I weighed the possibility of a regular store job, so suggestible was I to any scenario that was photographed and cleverly acted.

Mother's favourite programme was one of the few American shows going, *Liberace*, and we often watched together on a Sunday. Celia loved to hear the smiling queen croon 'I'll Be Seeing You (In All the Old Familiar Places)', while I preferred the programme that followed, *Free Speech*, a political debate show with Michael Foot for the Left and Lord Boothby for the Right.

I went to call on Lord Boothby at home one Sunday morning, knowing he'd be in, and he opened the door himself, still attired in his dressing gown. He blinked twice at the package the Lord's day had deposited on his doorstep and, thinking better of rearranging his plans for the day, gave me an autograph and sent me on my way.

ITV had hit the jackpot with *Sunday Night at the London Palladium*. This, and two quiz shows not dignified enough for the Beeb – Michael Miles's *Take Your Pick* and Hughie Green's *Double Your Money* – firmly established the alternative channel. Britain's families worshipped at this shrine of showbusiness in far greater numbers than had attended church in the preceding twelve hours.

Both Mum and I really enjoyed our new 'sideboard-style' record player, stacked with 78s by Frank Sinatra, Nat King Cole and Johnnie Ray. With a record player at home, music began to play an increasingly influential role in my life. I took to the fan magazines to learn all I could about Mr Ray, whose chart-topping 'Cry' single had won him the devotion of British fans. His concerts at the London Palladium were noted for the mass female hysteria they inspired, which led to accusations that Ray was a hypnotist. Johnnie was an Oregon-born bar and club singer discovered by CBS and developed as the male equivalent of the four-hankie movie. After 'Cry' came 'The Little White Cloud that Cried' and 'Such a Night'.

To me, Ray took music to a whole other level, for which my jazz sessions had not prepared me. With his sexual presence (and despite his sexual preference), Johnnie Ray was a *popular* star, in the same way as Laurence Harvey, but with a legion of adoring crazed female fans. From now on film, television *and* music were equally to be my escape routes from the earthiness of school life. In April 1955 I bought my first record: a single by Perez Prado, called 'Cherry Pink & Apple Blossom White'. When I played it, I was transported for a few minutes to glamorous movie sets inhabited by *femmes fatales* and white dinner-jacketed could-be villains.

Johnnie Ray was booked to appear at the London Palladium in spring 1955, and the event would be televised on the Sunday night show. I had bought his latest single, 'Such a Night' and counted down the days until the 'Cry Guy' arrived in town. I was among the hundreds of fans gathered outside the Palladium waiting for Ray when he arrived to rehearse his performance. I watched gobsmacked as Ray, flanked by ten soldiers he had befriended just that afternoon, was ushered into the venue. Then I hung around until he appeared later at the stage door to sign autographs. That evening found me at home watching Ray perform his brilliant short live set. I teased my mother by pointing out that even the country's protectors were in awe of his unique talent. I was fascinated with stars. They stopped traffic, made hearts beat a little faster and had their pictures taken when they walked through airports. They had the best lighting on offer and lived a life that didn't end up on the cutting-room floor. There was no doubt in my mind who was the real Prince of Wails.

The line had been crossed, and for the first time in Great Britain audiences were tearing themselves apart over the Nabob of Sob, who in the years from 52 till 55 recorded non-stop emotional classics as sexual as any

Johnnie Ray

careless whisper heard on the airwaves during the past twenty years. With 'Such a Night' Ray was live sex, made safe and acceptable by the vulnerability he wore like a sheath dress. He came to Britain, saw, suffered and conquered; Johnnie seared a lyric into your life, twisting the words into shameless tears, and then wrung them out over hot wax, scarred by every groove. On disc and stage he was as much a method actor as Montgomery Clift; he hurt from here to eternity – and he was deaf to boot. After reading that Ray wore a hearing aid, I got hold of one and wore it the way earrings are worn by young men today.

The 40s' Paramount-Theatre Sinatra and the 50s' Prince-of-Wails Ray set the sexual mould of pop; Ray did not have a great voice, but he acted a great song, sucking you into his three-minute screenplays of shame and pain. He affected mothers and daughters alike and was able to rule in British households because he posed no threat in the master bedroom. The subliminal awareness of Ray's sexual calling made him no competition where it counted; he wouldn't hurt your missus or your daughter – a Johnnie

Ray was too hurt himself.

By mid-57 Ray had his last bona-fide British hit, 'Yes, Tonight Josephine' and ended his UK run on a slight chart appearance with 'Build Your Love'. He didn't build any more and disappeared under the wash of Dean, Presley, Eddie Cochran, Gene Vincent, Little Richard and the after-skiffle arrival of Tommy Steele and the early Cliff Richard. I didn't think any more about him, paying the rent on the lounge circuit always miles away from the expressways of contemporary America.

During the mid-80s in New York I saw an ad in the *Village Voice* announcing a week of appearances by Mr Ray at a club in the SoHo area. By now I'd witnessed countless 'popular' artistes who had had their five minutes or five years, and when it was over they had dried up, moneyed up, bottomed out and disappeared, literally. The magic of those moments had been siphoned out of their bottle of life, faster than soda: no bubbles left, no bottle, only the sad reality of the moment gone.

The Nabob of Sob was still nervous, still hurt, but he'd grown into it; he was American pie around the waist, but in the face the man was still the Prince of Wails. He took me there one more time, and I was glad to go. He talked about appearing with Judy Garland at the London Palladium in 1964. He sang a verse, then played on the piano the verse Garland would sing. He had the ability and talent to take us back those twenty-odd years, out of that New York club and into the stalls of the London Palladium, and he showed us how it had felt.

Back to the future, with my eleven-plus exam coming up, I studied unusually hard – the result would determine whether I'd be accepted by the local grammar school or sent to the dreaded secondary modern. Summer 1955 was one of mixed emotions. I was glad to have left behind my hateful infant school, yet full of trepidation over the eleven-plus result, and all shook up by the excitement that American singer Bill Haley was generating in the UK. His 'Rock Around the Clock' single was causing a sensation among Britain teenagers, already hooked on the new rock 'n' roll craze emanating from America. I bought the record, played it endlessly and teased my hair into a Haley-inspired kiss-curl.

The eleven-plus exam result proved positive, and Marylebone Grammar accepted me. It was a rough school, situated in an intimidating five-storey

Victorian building, surrounding a dark and dismal courtyard. Had it still been standing, Stanley Kubrick could have used it as a location in *Full Metal Jacket*, which was filmed in London. Mum told me I 'just had to survive', or was it succeed? Didn't matter: I was in trouble from day one.

Over the summer I'd seen *Rebel Without a Cause* many times and James Dean was now my ultimate idol. *Blackboard Jungle*, which featured Bill Haley's 'Rock Around the Clock', was another controversial smash. Angry parents attacked the film, claiming it was a threat to the decency of British adolescents. This only served as added publicity, as we were now even more desperate to see this 'shocking' film.

At Marylebone I inadvertently estranged myself from my new class-mates. While they gossiped about the potential 'bad influence' that *Blackboard Jungle* might be having on them, I pronounced the film 'a bore', unable to admire any film where the lead character was a schoolteacher – this was not an escape from reality. I felt isolated and alienated at Marylebone Grammar, mostly because of thinking for myself. Initially the only way I could survive was by imagining I was starring in a film. Each day as I walked in through the gates I'd see the opening credits start to roll.

Walking to school one morning, they caught me singing the theme tune to *The Man from Laramie*, a James Stewart western I'd seen the previous Saturday afternoon. During the morning break, the lads trapped me in the school toilets and forced me to sing the song for the pleasure of forty braying boys. For a few weeks I toned down the effluence of my charisma.

Just after my twelfth birthday I yielded to yet another new obsession. Elvis Presley had broken into the British charts like a teenager's spots. 'Blue Suede Shoes', 'Heartbreak Hotel' and the sexy ballad, 'I Want You, I Need You, I Love You' sounded totally original to me, but more than anything I loved the 'look' of Presley. However, this only served to increase my sense of alienation: only a couple of other lads I knew could spend hours contemplating Elvis in a pink striped jacket with black velvet collar turned up, or understand that Elvis was indeed as attractive as Natalie Wood.

Derek Johnson, *New Musical Express* Features Editor 1956–69: When Elvis came on the scene, record sales went up by 300 per cent. You could sell a million singles in the UK easily. Of course, there was no competition from albums in those days. Fewer records were being released each week than are now, largely due to lack of vinyl. The market was there and the field was open. The *NME* was largely responsible for getting him off the ground in this country. That's what Elvis thought, anyway. We were writing about him when his first nationwide US single came out, before UK radio would even play Elvis.

Maurice Kinn, *NME* founder/owner: When Elvis caused a sensation, like everyone else we went for it hell for leather. From the moment Presley started to stir an interest, we didn't stop. That was our policy: if somebody was in the charts, that was our signal to give the people what they wanted. The success of the paper started when I made that the policy. We went for stars in the hit parade, as opposed to being a poor man's *Melody Maker*, making big stories outta the fourth trombone change in Teddy Cox's Orchestra. After the war the biz was easy, you didn't need experience or training. That was the trouble with most of the singers; they couldn't cope with their lives, they'd grown up in working-class conditions and then suddenly they're hitting the big time. It went to their heads and they couldn't handle it.

ALO: Meanwhile, my teachers frequently reprimanded me for my tendency to disrupt classes. My attitude towards what was being taught was blasé at best, and I was by way of grooming myself into a strident 'problem' child. Apart from English and art, I had no interest in school lessons. What could they teach me at Marylebone Grammar? There was little attempt to teach anything the least bit useful, only to force memorisation in order to gain a satisfactory report and move on.

Marc Gebhard lived on the same street as me, and attended the local private school, St Mary's Town and Country. Marc was thirteen to my eleven.

Marc Gebhard, actor: We got into trouble together, plain and simple. For instance, we met up one day and took the piss out of these kids from another prep school. We nicked their caps and slung them over a wall. We both got reported to our respective schools by the kids. We were confronted by the headmaster of the prep school, demanding an apology. We both had kinda neurotic, hard-working mothers, and neither of us had fathers.

ALO: At Marylebone, I started blackmailing other pupils with the help of a mate I called 'Big Elvis'. He did the dirty work under my direction. We would sneak up on an unsuspecting boy after school, at a bus stop or train platform, and forcibly steal his wooden pencil box. This little box was compulsory at Marylebone, so the unfortunate victim always accepted our offer to sell it back for sixpence. This scam continued on a regular basis for a few weeks, until an aggrieved pupil complained to the headmaster. Celia was summoned to the school and informed that her son was to be punished by expulsion. A kindly prefect, George Lowenstein, tried to intervene on my behalf, but to no avail.

Forced to find another school anyway, I longed to return to the 'refined' environment of public boarding school, where I had hopes my distinctive style might be more appreciated. Another plus was that I could get away with more, once removed from Celia's ever-watchful eye. I was in a funk: at both Swiss Cottage and Marylebone I'd stuck out the wrong way. The trouble I'd got into wasn't even fun. Probably due more to my mother's own sense of pride than any empathy for my individuality, I was soon placed at a private school in Hampstead which specialised in 'problem' kids. Here I studied to pass a Common Entrance exam, a qualification needed to gain entrance to public school.

Unfortunately for Mum's peace of mind, I couldn't start until the beginning of the new school year in September 1956. That was almost five months away and Celia worried whether I could be trusted to stay out of trouble while she was out at work. I argued persuasively that I was old enough to look after myself, and she had few alternatives to leaving me alone.

I was finally allowed to spend these school-free days at home. I spent hours listening to the radio or to records like 'I'm in Love Again' by Fats Domino, watching television and visiting the cinema. This was *my* idea of studying. I read about rock 'n' roll voraciously, intrigued by Gene Vincent, whose first UK EP (a seven-inch 'Extended Play', 45 rpm) had just been released. I bought the EP and wore it out spinning the lead track, 'Say Mama', back to back with the latest Elvis single, 'Hound Dog'.

American rock 'n' roll was the real thing; Britain as yet had nothing to compare. Tommy Steele, trumpeted as 'Britain's answer to Elvis', was a poor imitation of his Yank counter-numbers. Thousands of British teenage kids disagreed with me on this (as, I'm afraid, they have from time to time ever since) and made his début single 'Rock with the Caveman' an instant hit. Lionel Bart wrote the song.

Lionel Bart and Alma Cogan

Lionel Bart: Tommy Steele was my way in. All Tommy was doing was copying Bill Haley. When we made 'Rock with the Caveman', we were at Decca no. 3 studio. I didn't really write music, so I didn't have any parts. There were Ronnie Scott, Dave Lee and Benny Green in this little control

room, along with Tommy, his mum, dad and the dog . . . and no band parts.
We had a tea break and the boys, being jazz musicians, improvised an
instrumental, which was pretty good – it was all done like that. Three days
later the thing was a package and it was a hit. It wasn't easy; I was very lucky
to be in the right place at the right time. Tommy was the ticket for me, really,
the ticket to ride.

ALO: Through reading about Tommy Steele, I understood that the new
British rock 'n' roll scene was all happening in the coffee bars of Soho. Here,
young hopefuls sang, sneered and swivelled their hips. Managers plucked
them from obscurity and launched them to fame in the charts. Business was
conducted in Tin Pan Alley, where agents, publishers, managers, producers
and songwriters all worked their magic.

So naturally I decided to write a rock 'n' roll song and sell it down Tin
Pan Alley. I'd read an article which suggested that songwriters were the real
winners of the British rock 'n' roll boom – a hit rock 'n' roll record earned the
songwriter a small fortune. My dream was to write a number-one hit and
never have to return to school at all.

After a week of singing and scribbling, I completed an awful rip off of
whatever Tommy Steele ripped off. I was sure my very own – wait for it! –
'Boomerang Rock!' could be a hit.

> *Boomerang Rock!*
> *Throw it here*
> *Throw it there*
> *It'll always*
> *Come back at'cha*
> *Through the air*
>
> *Boomerang Rock!*
> *Do the Boomerang Rock!*

Soho's Tin Pan Alley was not what I had pictured in my imagination. I
expected a glitzy Mecca for fantastic-looking rock 'n' rollers, and what I (and
everybody else) found was short, shabby Denmark Street, just off Charing

Cross Road. Tin Pan Alley was an inhospitable place, full of brutish men with none of the grace of those I felt I had come to know from the world of film and television. I rang every buzzer on Denmark Street attempting to get 'Boomerang Rock!' heard and sold, and returned the next day to try again. Eventually one small company, Box & Cox, let me up to their offices, gave my song a hearing and some kind words that, summed up, meant 'not this month, mate'. Close up, the rock 'n' roll business was uninspiring at best. In fact, neither school nor commerce seemed to be of the stuff that made life worth living.

Nevertheless, I returned to Soho as often as I could – its hustling neon crassness was like a drug before drugs. I was lying to my mother, of course, telling her I was visiting a friend in the evenings, then rushing off to Soho to the coffee bar on Old Compton Street where British rock 'n' roll was being put on the map. 'The world famous 2Is coffee bar, home of the stars', the neon sign above the door proclaimed.

The 2Is had started playing host to 'live' rock 'n' roll and skiffle acts in early 1956, when Australian wrestlers Ray Hunter and Paul Lincoln took over the lease. Tommy Steele had made his name there, and since signing to Decca Records his success had brought the 2Is unlimited publicity. Downstairs, in the tiny basement that had been decorated by the already successful songwriter Lionel Bart, a regular crowd of 200 teenage hipsters danced the night away.

The coffee bar was a haven for managers and agents on the hunt for fresh talent, eager to cash in quick on the current teenage thirst for rock 'n' roll. Larry Parnes, who became the most successful and notorious manager of the 50s' rock 'n' roll scene, was a regular. Duffy Power, Georgie Fame, Sammy Samwell – all were trying their luck and, as yet, all were absolute beginners.

Lionel Bart: I got involved with Larry Parnes and all his stable: Billy Fury, Marty Wilde, Duffy Power, writing songs for these people and many more. I used to have something in the Top 10 of the *NME* charts every week for about four years. Course I could see the market in those days. I could suss out who needed what song in a couple of weeks' time. It was rather like writing for a character in a play. Larry Parnes's thing was really in the Elvis and Eddie Cochran vein. Eddie Cochran was the big icon.

The legendary 2Is

When I first saw Georgie Fame he was called something else. I picked him up in some club in Soho; he had dyed his hair white. He said he was in a rock band, just down from up north, smiling all the time. I called him Bertie Beamer. He spent a couple of days round my place, at the piano, playing all Jerry Lee Lewis stuff. I phoned Larry, who only lived round the corner, and said 'I think I've got your next . . .' Larry said, ''Ere, what's his name?' I said, 'Well, you'll sort out a name for him.' Larry named him Georgie Fame. He had a lovely voice. I used to see a lot of Georgie later on with Andrew.

ALO: I was only twelve and hadn't a farthing, but I stood for hours outside the 2Is, watching the customers slide downstairs to the 'skiffle' bar. Skiffle, according to Lionel Bart, became popular because no one could get their hands on electric instruments or amps. I was on the outside looking in, checking the names on the shining jukebox placed strategically in the window and chatting to the female doorkeeper, Nora. After many such evenings window shopping, the kind-hearted Nora took pity on me and let me downstairs without paying the usual one-shilling cover charge. Here I saw my first live rock 'n' roll shows, courtesy of Vince Taylor & The Playboys, and Paul Raven (Gary Glitter in the making). Eventually, I started lugging cases of Coke downstairs at the 2Is for two and sixpence a night.

In September I started at my new private school in Hampstead. Headmasters Welland and Wilcox, used to dealing with 'problem' children, took me under their wing. Encouraged by their concern, I worked studiously, knowing the result of my endeavours would determine whether I got a place as a boarder at a public school. I absolutely couldn't bear the prospect of having to return as a day boy to a 'normal' state school.

Another boy attending this 'crammer' was Nicholas Mason, who lived over the other side of The Spaniards Inn, off the road that led down to Golders Green. His first-floor bedroom was given over to what seemed, to my size and station, a massive drum kit. Nicholas's agenda was already set: a dozen years on he would be known as Nick Mason, Pink Floyd drummer.

The 1956 Suez Crisis was a political disaster and the final nail in the coffin for a no-longer-great Britain. The crisis provided me with my second job, at a Swiss Cottage florist, Cater's. Miss Cater was a pleasure to work for: chic, tweedy, grey-haired, stern but kindly. Her live-in companion and driver, a tough little lady named Billie, seemed less happy about the new shop assistant. I was brought in for the busy Christmas season when the country's petrol gave out, and Billie could no longer drive Miss Cater to work from their Hampstead Garden Suburb. Despite the scarcity of public transport, I delivered holiday flowers to all points of Hampstead, NW3 and 6, doing very well in the tip department from grateful homes surprised that someone had braved heavy winter snow to bring them cheer and dead flowers.

Miss Cater was kindness itself, and Billie held her butch tongue – had there been no fuel crisis I'd have been jobless, and she'd have been off in the wood-panelled powder-blue Morris Traveller, perhaps doing well enough off the tips to afford another pair of her manly brogues. I remember fondly the gratitude of my customers, but better yet, the smile of heartfelt pleasure on my mother's face that Christmas. A significant portion of my largesse went towards buying her a handsome clock, in sincere appreciation for her having had time for me.

· CHAPTER 2 ·

ALO: Billed as the 'American rock 'n' roll originator', Bill Haley became the first American rock 'n' roll act to tour Britain in February 1956. Alec bought me a ticket (at ten shillings and sixpence) for Haley's show at the Dominion Theatre on Tottenham Court Road. I went by myself, which was just fine, since most others wouldn't have understood my pre-show ritual in the men's room, perfecting my kiss-curl.

The north-east corner on which the Dominion Theatre stands is hallowed ground, home to long-running hits of the West End such as *The Sound of Music*. Earlier, on the south-east corner, the Astoria premièred impresario Mike Todd's scam-'n'-star-laden Todd-AO extravaganza *Around the World in Eighty Days*.

Bang opposite the Dominion was Lyons Corner House, where Mother and Alec took me on those occasions when my grades did not warrant The Ivy or Wheeler's. I got to know the Dominion's façade well, since I was at Lyons more often than The Ivy. The Dominion is a magnificent theatre; its stalls slope towards the object of the evening's awe like an audio-visual wedding train. It is a feast for the eyes and ears that impresses all who gather there, regardless of their taste in entertainment. And the 2,000 Teds in that beautiful old theatre were ready to rock. In their powder-grey drape jackets and brothel-creepers, they looked like royalty against the backdrop of the Dominion dress circle. Their girls appeared to be bleached, quiffed pearly queens enjoying their own version of Covent Garden opening night. Imagine how our modern British couple must have felt when their first taste of genuine American rock 'n' roll turned out to be so unsavoury.

Haley was a nightmare. There was an hour and a half by the spastic Vic Lewis and his Orchestra, then a paltry thirty-five minutes from this fat, kiss-curled housewife from the middle of America, the uncle you never wanted, Bill Haley. It gave me pause, I'll tell you, as at the end of Taylor Hackford's fabulous pop flick *The Idolmaker*, when all seems to slip away while Ray Sharkey works out what to do next. That's what happened to me at the Dominion. Confronted by the mediocrity that was Haley, I thought for a moment rock 'n' roll was over. But recalling the Then of Johnnie Ray and the Now of Buddy Holly and Little Richard saved the day, my imagination roared on intact and faith returned, replete with sound and texture.

Haley was also featured in two rock flicks that summer of 1956: *Rock Around the Clock* and *Don't Knock the Rock*. Audiences on both sides of the Atlantic danced in the aisles, ripped up the seats, and gave rock 'n' roll a reputation for mayhem to live up to. I saw the movies in the primly sterile Haverstock Hill Odeon with twenty or so uptight patrons who tutted and shifted in their seats, while I quietly tore a gash in mine. Had I dared to take the tube two stops south to Camden Town, I wouldn't have missed the party. A few years later I attempted as a newly hatched independent publicist to kindle the same reaction on behalf of Don Arden and Little Richard, with similarly controversial results. Perhaps I was making up for the lost opportunity.

Teds were magnificent specimens with an attitude way out above any station. They were the first teenagers to stand up, let it rip and be counted. Beatniks didn't count: they sat around drinking coffee and smoking Gauloises, while the Teds draped and duck's-arsed themselves into a national outrage that made headlines. They spent their newly disposable incomes taking the piss. I loved the sight of a Ted on the high street a whole lot better than the first American rock 'n' roller I got to see live.

So what if Bill Haley looked like an Oklahoma City short-order cook; there was the thrilling sky-grey slub fabric that clothed the Crickets, and the silky mohair drape-suited vision of Little Richard in *The Girl Can't Help It*. For good measure, I also fell for Grace Kelly and got a huge lesson from her duet of 'True Love' with Bing Crosby, which I applied years later when I met Marianne Faithfull. Some people like their sluts to be back-street girls, but I prefer tramps that pass for pure, and that kind – the all-too-rare Kellys and Faithfulls – you can bring home and have a good laugh with at Auntie's expense.

In June 1957 I took and passed the Common Entrance exam and while I waited to discover which boarding school would welcome the pleasure of my company, my mother offed me away to board for the summer with a farmer's family in Dulverton, near Taunton. There, I fell in love for the first time with a 'real' girl: the beautiful eighteen-year-old redhead who tended the horses on a well-to-do farm at the other end of the manor. I became suddenly and surprisingly interested in all things equine and spent most of my time helping her in the stables. At the end of the summer I was rewarded with my first real kiss. The smile was still on my face when my mother met me off the train at Paddington with the good news that I'd been accepted as a boarder at Wellingborough, a public school in Northamptonshire.

Celia took me out to celebrate, an early supper at Lyons Corner House, and for the special treat of my choice I chose the musical *Expresso Bongo*. Written by Wolf Mankowitz, this was the first ever British dramatisation of the 50s' rock 'n' roll scene and the revolution in the streets it was fomenting. 'Soho Johnny Never Had It So Good – Or Lost It So Fast' blared the billboard. Even more than the censored weekly TV shows that pandered to youth, or the increasing interest by promoters in cashing in on live rock, *Expresso Bongo*'s run in the West End signalled a coming of age for the new music, the new style, the new hustle. Even better, it owed very little to its Yank progenitors; it was Brit to the core. It would become my liturgy: a scenario where the manager was equally important as the artist. And Johnny Jackson became my object of worship.

I sat in the stalls at the Shaftesbury Avenue Theatre mesmerised as Paul Scofield brought the street-smart manager Johnny Jackson alive, before an audience that was no doubt both titillated and 'orrified. In the first run, Bongo Herbert, Johnny's wannabe star from the coffee bar, was played by Jimmy Kenney, a young blond actor I'd noted in some of the Woolf brothers' Romulus films. I learnt the basics of self-restraint that night (would that the lesson had stuck somewhat) so as not to let Celia know just how wholly I identified with this work of 'fiction'.

Just before the intermission, Bongo, an overnight sensation in the classic sense, starts to sing the ballad 'The Shrine on the Second Floor'. He allows us to think he's singing about his girlfriend, but by the bridge it's apparent that he's singing about his mother! It's her flat that's 'the shrine on the second floor'. As we're absorbing this delicious irony, huge, stained-glass windows drop down, transforming the stage into a veritable shrine and a church choir enters to take the song to its heavenly erotic climax. *Expresso Bongo* was at once so incredibly obvious and yet, oh so subtle: sex, religion, a whiff of incest (which I believe to be the rock coupling that dares not speak its name). I saw through those cheesy imitation stained-glass windows to a future where Bongos begged me to be their Johnny. And almost as important as the boost the play gave to my own aspirations was the reassurance that, despite the loneliness I often felt, I was not alone and, with like-minded fellows, anything was possible.

This new feeling of well being was short-lived. When I boarded the train at St Pancras bound for Wellingborough, smartly attired in my dark maroon blazer, and waved goodbye to Celia, I was leaving the streets of London I knew so well for a life of narrow-mindedness and sport that has tortured British thirteen-year-olds from time immemorial. I felt all I was taking with me was Elvis's latest number one and a little suitcase I packed myself.

A two-hour journey by train from London, Wellingborough was a small, quiet town between Northampton and Market Harborough. When I arrived at the 400-year-old all-boy public school, I was registered as A.L. Oldham and shown around the square mile of stately red-brick buildings that was to be my home for the next three years, then dropped off at my single bed in a row of twenty. The floors were bare and the bathroom had just two tiny tubs for all twenty boys. Interesting how the British idea of an aristocratic education resembles a poor and rather dirty imitation of ancient Sparta.

Competition with and for boys was the social order of the day for those at Wellingborough Public School who wished to 'fit in'. The four houses, Garne's (which housed me), Weymouth, Platt's and Fryer's, vied with each other at soccer from September till Christmas. Rugby and 'athletics' divided the spring term, and cricket and swimming the summer term. Marksmanship and other games of war were on for all three terms, as was the constant rivalry for the attentions of those lads one fancied. In an environment where the traditional unofficial curriculum was romancing the boys, the school establishment merrily condoned this childish lovemaking among their charges, with the understanding that not too long after one left school, one 'settled down' and gave the girls the benefit of one's experience. Of course, films like Dirk Bogarde's *Victim* (1962) reveal the dreadful consequences of this hypocrisy rather more realistically.

Our uniforms were grey suits, sweaters and shirts. A straw boater and white shirt with stiff detachable collars signified Sunday, the boaters a must for any walk into town. The wardrobe for Wednesday Cadet Corps afternoons was standard army gear, and in short order I managed to get myself into the Cadet marching band, playing drums, inside the middle of the sound, where I could either be on time or mime it.

ALO (second from right, second row) with his first band

John Douglas, school chum: Everything with Andy was: Let's try it and see how we get on. The idea of having a drum and walking around the streets of Wellingborough banging it seemed like fun. The uniforms were horrible and we were crap drummers, so we soon knocked that on the head.

ALO: That same first term I got myself into the Wellingborough School Film Society, due to my artistic talents coming to light. Films as old as Richard Widmark's *The Halls of Montezuma* from 1951 were shown on Sunday nights.

David Miranda, school chum: As Andrew was good at drawing, he was asked to design and create the poster that would advertise the latest movie. Andrew would always do a good job, good sense of colour, graphically grabbing. He was able to capture the spirit of the movie even though he might not have seen it, but he would probably find out enough about it to know how to design a good poster. He was a very talented person, he had great artistic creative abilities, very inspired and imaginative. We all used to get a kick out of the posters he did.

ALO: The Film Society members were amazed at how close in likeness I managed to make my posters to the originals. I just couldn't tell them that during the school holidays, as I lived in London and knew the six films booked for the next term, I could whoop down Wardour Street in Soho, the epicentre of the British film industry, and pester the film companies to give me the original posters. If I got them, I would trace them and they would be deemed original and brilliant, otherwise I was merely great.

John Douglas: He was very sophisticated and visually tuned in. He could do good graphics and began to cut his teeth on little projects. He'd make little projects up for himself because the school was so boring.

Garnes House (John Douglas back row 7th from right; ALO third row far right; John Elwick second row third from left)

ALO: My housemaster at Garne's was John Oughton, who only caught me out three times on an offence that warranted caning, but that was three times too many, thank you. I made every effort to stay out of Mr Oughton's way. The first assistant housemaster was a young and pleasant science teacher, E.R. Marson, who was good enough to let a select five or six devotees into his quarters on a Saturday night to watch Jack Good's *Oh, Boy!*

In January 1957 two new rock 'n' roll shows for teenagers had made their television débuts. Although the BBC's *Six-Five Special* and ITV's *Cool for Cats* were lacklustre in comparison to what was really happening on the streets of Soho, I never missed the Jack Good-produced *Six-Five Special* every Saturday. For a while I was taken with the house band, the John Barry Seven, who would later perform the soundtrack for the Hammer flick *Beat Girl*.

Cool for Cats, presented every Wednesday by Kent Walton, offered up ageing acts and treated rock 'n' roll as just one more 'teenage fad' that would quickly pass. It was evident that the British entertainment hierarchy was wop-bop-a-loo-bopped by rock 'n' roll and vastly underestimated its staying power. In time, Jack Good left the Beeb, moving over to the independent channel to create a show that defined the times, the earth-moving *Oh, Boy!* It went out in the same Saturday slot as Good's old show, which was soon axed. So too were the BBC's next couple of music shows, *Dig This* and *Drumbeat*, as *Oh Boy!* ruled during an incredible thirty-eight-week run.

E.R. Marson, Garne's assistant housemaster: I seem to recall that it was Andrew who persuaded me to let him watch television on Saturday evenings for such programmes as *Six-Five Special* and *Oh, Boy!*, with my room full of quiffed boys watching a black-and-white picture on a small fourteen-inch screen. It was apparent that he had already determined where his future lay. The threat of withdrawal of this privilege was a useful lever in encouraging acceptable behaviour.

I remember him as an energetic, independent and assertive character with strong opinions. He found the constraints of a single-sex school irksome. He was not an academic type, finding outlets for his energies on the games field and in school societies. He did not suffer gladly those whom he considered fools. A phrase which seemed to sum him up was 'rebel with a cause'. One other lingering memory is that, after leaving, he returned to an Old Boys' day in a large open-topped American car full of nubile young ladies and was a centre of great attraction.

ALO: On *Oh, Boy!*'s first show, Good introduced a fresh-faced and very British seventeen-year-old Cliff Richard, making his début with the Drifters. He performed 'Move It' (written by Ian 'Sammy' Samwell) and for me the earth stood still. The following week Maurice Kinn wrote in *NME*: 'His violent hip-swinging was revolting, hardly the kind of performance any parent could wish their children to see. He was wearing so much eyeliner he looked like Jayne Mansfield. If we are expected to believe that Cliff was acting naturally, then consideration for medical treatment may be advisable.' Sounded like a rave to me.

Jet Harris, the Drifters bassist: If anybody started it, it was Cliff Richard with that superb 'Move It'. Before Cliff, the rock 'n' roll over here was dreadful, you had Tommy Steele with 'Rock With The Caveman', Marty was trying a bit, but Cliff really started the rock 'n' roll over here and now they say the Beatles did it. I always feel sorry for Cliff, when I see these programmes on the television, *The History of Rock 'n' Roll in Britain*, and they insist the Beatles started it. We did, but they never give us any credit. We were the first line-up with three guitars and drums. We'd look at all the pictures of Gene Vincent & the Blue Caps and see what guitars they were using. When I first met Gene I was absolutely shakin', I was such a fan, it was quite embarrassing. He was an idol of ours, that's what we called real rock 'n' roll – Gene Vincent.

Tony Meehan, the Drifters drummer/arranger and producer: Jack Good was a visionary, he saw the whole thing coming and really got off on the sensation it caused. He saw it the way we were seeing it. He realised this potential and put it all together, but that's the way we were seeing it too. None of us missed an episode of *Oh, Boy!* It was *the* show. There's never been a show like *Oh, Boy!* It was the most exciting rock television show there's ever been. It was quite revolutionary when it came out. If you can imagine how it was then, it was just absolutely mind-boggling; it just blew

(l to r) Cliff Richard, Jet Harris, Tony Meehan, Hank Marvin, Bruce Welch

you away, it was sensational. Just so together and right on the nose. It was like YEAH, this is it, this is what should be happening. We haven't really moved on from then. They've still got *Top of the Pops* on the bloody BBC, if you can believe that. That's how original they are. They had Sammy Turner on the show; there was also a resident black vocal group called Neville Smith & the Cutters or something, and the Vernon Girls: white girls and black men singing together and they were backed by a white band, Lord Rockingham's XI, who were an incredible, great band, great arrangements.

Tony Hall, *Oh, Boy!* compere, Head of Promotion, Decca Records: Still, to this day, *Oh, Boy!* is the most exciting thing there's ever been on pop TV in this country. The secret of its success was actually that it was done in black and white: the lighting made it special. The lights were done by a girl named Rita Gillespie. Jack Good stirred up all the enthusiasm on the music side, and Rita made the show look so exciting. *Oh, Boy!* was years ahead of its time. Mainly because of Rita's presentation. The pilot that went out was better than any of the subsequent shows. The pilot was something else: it was evil, dirty, nasty and rebellious.

ALO: Though Jack may have toned it down some from the pilot, *Oh, Boy!* was a weekly communion of pure sex and energy, with words and rhythm that proved to me there was more to life than what was being dictated. The subversive music had sounds, melodies and words that echoed exactly how I felt. Suddenly I was not alone.

Oh, Boy!

John Douglas: *Oh, Boy!* was unbelievably influential on Andy's later entrée into the British rock scene. He somehow managed to blag his way on to *Oh, Boy!* We saw him on TV, hollering in the audience, which was a big status symbol for a fourteen-year-old.

ALO: *Oh, Boy!* was the perfect showcase for the sublime Eddie Cochran. His UK appearances so far had been brief, with small parts in two big films, *The Girl Can't Help It* and Mamie Van Doren's *Untamed Youth*. He came to London to play 'Summertime Blues' at the Hackney Empire, and the *Oh, Boy!* spots made him a legend.

Oh, Boy! also established Billy Fury. His début Decca single, 'Maybe Tomorrow', raised the stakes among the Brit rock boys. He was the only English solo star who was comfortable sharing a stage with Eddie.

Jack Good was soon promoting fantastically successful *Oh, Boy!* package tours with Larry Parnes around the UK, starring Cliff & the Drifters, Billy, Vince Taylor, Adam Faith and Wee Willie Harris, who dyed his hair a different colour – pink or green – every time he appeared on *Oh, Boy!*

Mr Marson, our benefactor with the TV, would move on to head up another house and he would be replaced by another science teacher, John

Elwick. He was a cat of a different stripe altogether. I was besotted with the man and his style: thirtyish, slim, fair, and with intense eyes and hook nose that added to his haughty attitude. Plus, he was a bachelor, which meant that his wardrobe would be more extensive and expressive than any married teacher's could be.

John Elwick, Garne's housemaster: Andrew seemed to fix on me. You knew he was listening to what you said, but he would never like to commit himself to being obedient. He always liked to do his own thing. There were always complaints, certainly every week, about his behaviour. It was endless. The main thing was that he got under everyone's skin, he didn't see that these petty rules were important.

All public schools have a core ideal that emphasises sport. Wellingborough was quite good at sport, and Andrew was a good soccer player. If he'd toned down his flamboyance even a bit, he could have worked his latent athleticism to greater advantage. He was very lithe, slim, slight and elegant. They'd all fall for that, I should think. His hair was not a repulsive red colour; he was quite attractive.

John Douglas was a very likeable person and showed it, whereas Andrew didn't straight away. He was quite cautious about showing any form of affection or friendship, although it was underlying everything. It is true they had a cult status, they were known throughout the school as more worldly than most. They'd got wit and a lot of style about themselves and were very funny together; they were a duo.

ALO: John Elwick played Himself: he was simply 'on' all the time, you never caught him off-stage, he never left the lights as he strode around the school grounds. He even managed to make watching a school soccer match, sitting on his 'horsie' saddle stick, an elegant affair. He presented himself to us each day with variations on the same sartorial theme: cavalry twill two-buttoned suits with gen-u-ine bone buttons, flared at the waist, slanted 'hacking' pockets, lapelled vest, and trousers not too tight to disturb his fellow teachers, but turned up and tight enough to impress me. White wing-collared shirt, striped tie and suede chukka boots made up the length and breadth of the man. He roamed the grounds so well dressed that even the mandatory teacher's black gown did not diminish his elegance. He wore that most antiquated and unstylish of British academic garb with a 'Blackgamma, What Becomes a Legend Most?' insouciance, walking at a pace that allowed the breeze to part the gown and reveal the haberdashery beneath.

An equal admirer of Elwick was the best friend of my Wellingborough years, John Douglas. Fine-featured and fine-looking, John had the same priorities as me, but came from a completely different background. John's Scottish father was a respected physician, who with his wife and John's sister Liz lived in what seemed to me a huge mansion opposite a park on the outskirts of nearby Northampton.

We loved to the same degree of distraction Elvis lounging poolside in *Jailhouse Rock*: his flappy black trews foreshadowing Armani, his black-and-white shoes and his tight, cable-knit dark sweater with upturned collar symbolising the triumph of rock 'n' roll in the world of showbiz. We were sure that the way he had treated Dolores Hart in *Loving You* had caused her to take the vows that ended her screen career prematurely. We loved the choreography of the *Jailhouse Rock* production number, with its innumerable Elvis clones, and we just knew He had created the routines himself. John and I shared Eddie Cochran, Buddy Holly and the Crickets, Gene Vincent, Jack Good's *Oh, Boy!* and the later *Boy Meets Girls*; Cliff Richard, Billy Fury, and Marty Wilde stalking his way through Bill Parsons' *All American Boy*, the Jody Reynolds' classic *Endless Sleep* and Thomas Wayne's *Tragedy*.

On-camera, we appreciated Tony Curtis as a wide boy in *The Sweet Smell of Success*. Curtis was hounded by co-star Burt Lancaster, and the film was co-produced by Lancaster's Hecht-Hill-Lancaster production company. *Success* was shot partly on location in New York, where the lobby of the Brill Building took a break from housing a hit factory to serve as J.J. Hunsecker's apartment block. *Elmer Gantry* and *Trapeze* were also hits from the Lancaster organisation. Another muscle-man-turned-movie-mogul whom I admired was Kirk Douglas. His Bryna Productions would deliver some of Kirk's biggest successes, among them *Paths of Glory* and *Spartacus*, inspiring young Michael Douglas along the way.

The other Douglas in my life shared my love of stars and style. I left Elvis to John, and expressed myself with a peroxide dip that I fancied combined

Jet Harris's moodiness and Adam Faith's air of displacement with the Marlon Brando of *The Young Lions*. Anything James Dean was fair game for me to cop. Apart from John and our other pal David Miranda, I was the only one who knew what film was playing at the cinema in my head.

John Douglas: The first night in Garne's house, I plonked down in the bed next to him and said 'Shall I call you "Ginger"?' My father was a middle-class GP from Northampton. I was meant to be at a highly regarded boarding school in Scotland, but had failed miserably there. Wellingborough was my last hope, the last hope for anybody, really. Academically it was the pits. The vast, literally unwashed mass had no interest in academic life; all they wanted to do was get to leaving age and go back to work on the family farm. By then the die had been cast and even at that early age our identity as outsiders was set: we were square pegs in round holes. We both had very low self-esteem. He looked in the mirror and wanted to be James Dean, I looked in the mirror and wanted to be Elvis Presley.

Chapel and Church: that whole number was the beginning of showbiz 'live and in person' for us. We used to just sit there and watch, speculating, 'That could be a good act.' From where we were coming from, it seemed strange that the majority couldn't understand why we got off on what we got off on.

We were bonded by the backbeat. We played a bit of sport, but our main recreations were wanking and listening to rock 'n' roll. We got hold of a Crickets LP, and WOW! It was the first time we saw two Fender guitars together and we spent many hours discussing the significance of this. The Crickets were the definitive band as far as we were concerned. They were cool dressers, especially in their 'Ivy League' button-down collar shirts.

ALO: Our other pal was David Miranda; he had a dark, Jewish, Tony Curtis look, which meant he was cool. Our friendship took some doing on all our parts, since fraternisation between houses was not encouraged, only competition, but David was always on the perimeter of whatever John and I were up to.

David Miranda: Andrew was always a colourful character. We were both from London, and the great majority of the other boys certainly were not. We stood out from the Midlands lads. We used to take the train back and forth to London together, so we spoke quite a bit. He was always a bit of a rebel. He didn't want to be thought of as just another ordinary kid. I think he felt that he had unique abilities and he was proud of them. It was apparent at school that he was very knowledgeable about music.

It got on Andrew's tits that there were students only a year or two older than us who believed they were obliged to crush your spirit if they felt you were being cheeky. Suddenly you were a troublemaker, and you needed to be taught a lesson. Andrew fell into that category a great deal. He was not the type of personality that was going to keep quiet. Wellingborough was very plain, stifling and unimaginative. Andrew had already been exposed to other things and wanted to explore new areas all the time, whereas at that type of school, exploration was discouraged. The relative freedom of London made Wellingborough very hard to take. In many ways, it was like being in the army.

John Douglas: At Wellingborough, among the many farmers' children, there was a small number of foreigners. We talk of the 'global village' now, but we were very Anglicised and provincial in those days. At Wellingborough, however, we had Chinese kids, kids from Hong Kong and Saudi Arabia. Because they could never become part of the culture, they were much more supportive of Andy and me. They were disenfranchised too, they weren't mainstream. When an African turned up, it was the first time we'd ever seen a black guy, so we physically examined his hair, skin and teeth. It was just naïve curiosity and he enjoyed being the centre of attention.

For us, as adolescents, there was a very strange sexual undercurrent at Wellingborough. You'd look at the choir boys and think, 'Oh, there's Grace Kelly.' No one told us about sex, or emotions, or feelings. We had to discover all this for ourselves, largely with each other. All the masters and matrons seemed to come from a different planet. We were like an undercover team, trying to nail this down, trying to understand what it was all about.

ALO: We were not allowed to mix with the local town girls. Consorting was generally *verboten* at Wellingborough, except for dance lessons and the Cat's

Whiskers fêtes we organised, at which we were allowed to exhibit our dancing prowess. But how can you learn to dance when your partner is dissatisfied with her very physical being? The girls were nervous, whether they were wearing bras or not yet wearing them. If they made up their lips, they were embarrassed, as if make-up made them tarts. It was like partying on the Planet of the Apes.

David Miranda: Andrew and I were involved in the Cat's Whiskers. We *were* the Cat's Whiskers, actually. It happened maybe once or twice a month. We'd take over a classroom, get rid of the desks, add coloured lighting and other decorative pieces and try and transform it into a nightclub. We'd invite various girls from the local high school across the way.

ALO: After my first year at Wellingborough, I returned home to London for the summer vacation. Celia, ever with her eye on the main chance, stressed that success at Wellingborough was only the first step in my life trajectory: O then A levels, university, a 'good' job. She had moved house again, and our new home was much grander than the basement flat at Belsize Park Gardens. Close to the bohemian affluence of Hampstead, 19 Netherhall Gardens was an austere two-floor flat of which Celia was very proud.

Pat Clayton: Around this time Celia and Andy moved from Belsize Park Gardens over to Netherhall Gardens, and it was a lovely flat. Dad must have helped with that, otherwise how the hell could she have afforded it? It was Hampstead after all, my dear. Celia was very concerned about Andrew. He was so much like her: he moved the way she moved, he was rather graceful with his hands, and that was Celia all over, it's amazing how like Celia that is. His stance was exactly like his mother's; she was an attractive woman and she knew it. As definite as she might have been in her social opinions, in many other ways Celia was extremely flighty. She was always a bit vague somehow.

John Douglas: During the holidays I used to go to his place or he'd come stay with my family. His mother's flat was very austere. She was dotty but lovely. She was sweet, but she was out of sync with everything. I found her very engaging, I felt great empathy with her. Although she wasn't blonde, to me, she was like the dizzy blonde. I sensed she had a private agenda, which Andy didn't even know about. Despite Celia's aloofness, Andrew in his own way was very fond of her.

ALO: Pat's elder brother, John, was an ace at water-skiing, had been on the British team in the South of France and was a flash all-rounder about town. On Saturdays, John took me to Chelsea football matches in his left-hand drive Lincoln Continental convertible. I was really knocked out. We'd come out of the football ground and sit in the King's Road, ostentatiously buzzing the canvas roof down. Everyone would be staring at us in this incredible car, I loved it.

Jimmy Greaves, Chelsea FC, was it, and only eighteen, a wonder striker, idol to me and all blue-and-white scarved Stamford Bridge lads. I was there August 58 when he woofed five goals past Wolves. Alec and John always took me to Chelsea during my school holidays, and I stayed Greaves-struck all the way to 1961, until he left for AC Milan. I think he put three away that last match. I cried: there were a lot of lumps in the throats of grown men, as well as boys, that day.

Jimmy Greaves: I was on £20 a week. You could hardly say I was a money man. I've never had money. I finished playing in 1972 and I was earning £100 a week! So I think that myth has got to be totally drained away.

When I first signed for Chelsea, I was on £8 in the winter and £7 in the summer, and then it went up to £17 a week, and when I left Chelsea to go to Milan I was on £20 a week. So I wasn't really a money man. The King's Road was out of bounds to me, it was more like the Fulham Road and the public bar and the downtown, broken-down public house. We couldn't go the other way, over the bridge – that was towards the King's Road, couldn't afford it. Not in those days.

I had no lifestyle. I can't really recall having any style or any panache. I was basically a very ordinary young man who was just fortunate enough to have the ability to play football. I might have done that with style, but I certainly didn't lead my life with any style . . .

The rock 'n' rollers were on a different wavelength to us. I think the gap's obviously closed now and professional footballers associate themselves with the pop- and film-star scene. But in those days football was still basically a working-class game and rock 'n' roll stars were in a different field, and the twain didn't really meet. I think you'd have to go towards the mid-to-late 60s, when you're talking about Georgie Best & Co., when that sorta started to change . . .

So Andrew drove to the game in a Lincoln Continental convertible. Well, I caught the train and bus, and I was the player! Myself and all the rest of the team . . . we used to turn up with the supporters and walk down the street. Only they used to go into the stands and we used to go into the dressing room . . . Nobody had cars, we all went by public transport. And how late you left the ground afterwards depended on how well you played, 'cos you didn't want to bump into the supporters if you'd had a bad game. There was no difference between the professional footballer and the supporter.

It's a totally different culture now: Beckham and Posh Spice are interlinked by their earnings, their status, by their symbolism, if you like . . . and that's happened over the last ten, fifteen years.

I got no impression at all that I was like a rock star, idolised . . . none at all, none whatsoever. And unfortunately the manager didn't give me that impression either, or I might have asked for a bung or something, but of course you couldn't. Maximum wage, you see, all you could get was £20 a week. That was it, that was your level. The only reason I went to Italy was to try and earn more money . . .

I never ever associated myself with anybody in the other forms of media. I was just a footballer who turned up and did his job, that's all.

John Douglas: Andy was nuts on Jimmy Greaves. Then, with each new month, a new public personality would take pride of place in his heart. He got taken with Marlon Brando as the blond Nazi in *The Young Lions*, so Andy became a blond Nazi. He used the bathroom detergent Vim in his hair. No one was telling you how you get your hair blond, but the Vim packet had the word 'bleach' on it, it was there and it was free, so he schlepped it on. He never liked that he'd got ginger hair, let alone the ginger tag. He went through a phase of wanting to be a blond bombshell, and Brando was a pretty good role model for that.

David Miranda: Stunts like the blond hair and the German accent got Andrew talked about too much and the reactions, from both students and teachers, could get violent. It just did not pay to stick out.

If a kid was caught smoking Woodbines for the second time, they decided to give him a good slashing with a cane. The attitude would be, 'That's good for him, that'll teach him a lesson.' It just seemed wrong. Too much power was put in the hands of students who couldn't handle it, turned them into little sergeant majors, bullies who just abused their power. Sometimes people say things to you and you say to yourself, 'I'm not going to respond to that because it's gonna get me into trouble.' It's the type of situation, if you're in the army today, where a sergeant major can say all kinds of things to you, but if you wanna have a reasonably pleasant life you keep your mouth shut and you just take it.

Andrew couldn't always keep his mouth shut. That used to get him into trouble. That was part of his personality, his character. The housemaster of Garne's used to have a cricket ball in the classroom and if he thought you weren't paying attention, he would throw that cricket ball at you. You could be sitting in the back of the classroom, maybe just tuning out, and the next thing you knew a cricket ball would be flying at your head.

John Douglas: Sartorially Andy was very in tune, so anyone whose dress was off-centre, he noticed and enjoyed. The dressing room of his mind was overflowing with clothes he'd wear once he could afford them. Laurence Harvey was a huge, huge influence. *Room at the Top*, *Expresso Bongo* and *The Sweet Smell of Success* literally shaped Andy's notion of character. The protagonists in those films became his models in life. If anyone could have directed Andy, they would have got a tremendous result out of him as an actor.

He learnt early on the value of shocking people. That became part of his currency. He understood that the first thing you had to do was get their attention. The London connection was good. He had this long-running fictitious dental work, which allowed him to go off to London for the day, and nobody sussed that out. That ability to size up the opposition and shock them into response began as a reply to the social barriers and restrictive norms at Wellingborough. Once we'd got orientated, we started to plot out what were

Burt Lancaster and Tony Curtis in *The Sweet Smell of Success*

the outer reaches of the world as we knew it, how far we could go, what we could do.

ALO: One of my continual run-ins with the authorities was over clothing. At the start of each new term, I would show up with unsatisfactory variations on the grey-flannel school uniform. I turned the standard on its head with clothes of my own design, bought with money I'd got from various school holiday jobs. When the masters would ask me just what I thought I was doing, my stock answer was, 'But it is grey, sir . . .'

My masterpieces were made at the Burton's tailoring chain in the West End. Although I lived in one of the world's largest cities, it simply wasn't done to venture far out of one's proper neighbourhood. Had I been able, I might have discovered that real bespoke was readily available in the East End, and within my means, so long as I knew my manor, my wants and my needs. I was on a strictly Hampstead to West End run, however. It just wasn't done, and possibly a bit dangerous, to go wandering about.

Burton's had made a fortune providing suits for ten to twelve guineas for the lower and middle classes, who had to be suited for work in imitation of their masters, normally just knocking off two- or three-button suits from the same pattern. I drove them berserk by taking them up on their tailoring invitation in which you picked the details. I had a dove-grey mohair suit with nipped waist, covered buttons, inverted pleat in the back of the jacket, draped trousers, slanted pockets and a paisley lining. As he took my suit away, Mr Oughton, the housemaster, said, 'I don't know why you bother, you only wore it for a day.' 'Yeah,' I thought, 'but what a day.'

David Miranda: Andrew was not exactly the class clown, because he wouldn't clown around. But he was the type of kid who would make a smart-aleck remark in class, and all the kids would break up laughing. Or he would make a very funny remark at an inappropriate time, or turn up in one of his spiv variations on the school uniform rules, and all the kids would burst out laughing and the teacher would get infuriated, then Andrew would be in trouble. That was typical.

John Douglas: We derived strength from each other, we backed each other up. We began to have cult status at the school. He had an inherent advantage because it was a natural process in his mind. Andy began to have that ability to manipulate things in his favour; occasionally his schemes would backfire, but in the main he achieved what he wanted to do. The basic love of the musical material of rock 'n' roll was the fuel which drove him further and further down the road away from everything public school represented. But Wellingborough was a damn good apprenticeship for learning to pay the price that the world demands of its rebels.

Our love affair with Eddie Cochran helped both of us to understand the mechanics of putting a record together in the most elementary sense – not understanding notes or studios, but appreciating that there were people who'd made the jump to writing their own songs, who furthermore could produce a sound of their own. Cochran was beginning to develop the rebel theme in his lyrics, so of course that struck another resonant chord with us. In Britain the nearest we had to that kind of force was Billy Fury.

David Miranda: We only had access to small portable players, and the sound was awful, but it was one of our few forms of entertainment. Even back then, Andrew was always up on the newest groups, knew the latest songs, knew all about the artists. He had a good sense of musical history, he seemed able to place music and musicians into various categories. He knew his subject well. He'd play Billy Fury's 'Maybe Tomorrow' for hours.

Billy Fury

Lee Everett, Billy Fury's girlfriend for eight years: Bill arrived backstage at one of Larry Parnes's concerts in Liverpool with songs he wanted Larry to buy. Marty Wilde or someone like that was appearing. Bill played Larry these songs, and Larry was just so excited, he threw him on-stage there and then and that was it. Billy had absolute talent.

He was very unique on-stage. An audience of girls would scream themselves silly, and at one point he used to come to the front of the stage, take ten minutes to light a cigarette, pull on it, and do all this moody bit before the curtain opened. The audience would be mesmerised, you could hear a pin drop. None of the other boys took rock 'n' roll seriously, ravin' away like loonies. Billy used to rehearse, practise his every move; he was serious about his stage act. The others, Dickie, Georgie and all the rest, would go on in a barrel, just fall on-stage.

They all smoked grass . . . it was common in the Parnes stable. Billy smoked grass from getting up in the morning to going to bed at night.

We were chased out of London. We lived in a flat that Larry Parnes bought us in Cromwell Road. The fans were nearly committing suicide on Billy's doorstep. I had to walk girls about, to bring them round after overdosing on pills, until the ambulances arrived. There were girls hiding out in the dustbins, it was just horrendous.

We bought a house in Kingston Hill. We had a six-foot fence, and they got over that. My mother had a breakdown, from the house being in a constant state of siege. You wouldn't believe the gates we had; it was Auschwitz in there, we were prisoners, and they were still coming over the wall. Then we put a four-foot barbed-wire top on the wall, but our blue-rinsed neighbours complained and we had to take it down. Because then the home of our dreams really did look like a concentration camp.

Alan Freeman, disc jockey: Billy Fury had all those hits but never a number one. I think Billy Fury had something like thirty hits over the years in the Top 10, but never made a number one ever. The UK scene was just simmering at the time. It was a period when youngsters wanted to leave home, find their own lives and their own levels. The 2Is crowd – Marty Wilde, Cliff Richard, Joe Brown – they all wanted to be rock singers and they all wanted to sound like Buddy Holly. Everybody wanted to be Buddy Holly.

ALO: You needed a lot of pocket money to keep up with Buddy Holly. The man had so many hits in his head, he could sustain a solo career along with fronting the Crickets, who had just gone number one in America with 'That'll Be the Day'. Disc jockey Alan Freed had launched them at his Brooklyn Paramount showcase gig, after which they'd broken out nationwide on a seventeen-act Freed-promoted US package tour, 'The Biggest Show of Stars' – and that it was. Our minds boggled: Buddy Holly & the Crickets, Chuck Berry, the Everly Brothers and Jerry Lee Lewis all on one bill! Decca Records had the licence to Coral in the UK and they couldn't get it out fast enough for us, the hits just kept comin' and comin'. You'd have wept, it was incredible. 'Not Fade Away', 'Oh, Boy!', 'Peggy Sue', 'That'll Be the Day', 'Rave On', 'Think It Over', 'Fool's Paradise', 'I'm Lookin' for Someone to Love'. This man's B-sides were number ones! It was a wonderful time to be in your early teens: music was life-confirming, problem-resolving, and everything that mattered started with a count-off and a look.

· CHAPTER 3 ·

Lee Everett: Larry Parnes was the first British impresario to be examined by the media and made famous. In his own way, he embodied the music biz concept, 'Artists may come and go, but Larry Parnes is for ever.' His partner, John Kennedy, found Tommy Steele – that's how it all started. The Parnes family were in the rag trade, then Larry got the bug. He went round finding boys and built a huge stable. I was in cabaret at the Bag O' Tel in Bond Street. When Larry came in, all of the girls used to put the make on him. They thought he was fabulous. The hostesses and cigarette girls were all over him, Larry was a particularly handsome man, he had great charisma, he was wealthy and he wore it well. He was also a gambler and, later on, when he was in Gamblers Anonymous, in a low-profile way he'd help people out who had gambling problems.

The 2Is was open all day, you could get up there and have a jam; if you were any good Tom Littlewood would sign you up. We all lived in the coffee bar Act I/Scene I, opposite the 2Is. That's where our agents could find us. Joe Brown arrived straight from being a Butlin's redcoat; Georgie Fame, Johnny Gentle and Dickie Pride, all waiting for the phone to ring – on one coffee a day. Norman Shake Gun used to take so many pills that in the end they took him away in a straitjacket – there were a lot of casualties before the 60s. Dickie Pride, he was very talented and our best friend; he used to live with Billy and me. Dickie was a heroin addict, one of the first people to have a lobotomy. He used to be so funny and talented, but after the operation he was just like a pod, one of those things from outer space; he just wasn't in. His death was tragic.

Jet Harris: I was a rebel without realising I was being one. I didn't think,

'Right, I'm gonna have a rebel image', I just acted as myself. I was very fond of the drink, as everybody knows, which I don't do now. I wasted a lot of years with that drink. The Shadows [A Leiber-Stoller black American group called the Drifters had started to hit, forcing the UK Drifters to change their name to the Shadows] were the benchmark at that time, and the truth of the matter is that I left the Shadows because I didn't get on with Bruce Welch. He used to get everybody nervous. He'd start tuning up about three hours before the show, he was just a maniac with his nerves. The fact is I had a stomach full of ulcers to go along with this, which made me quite moody to look at on-stage. I was in pain and people didn't realise that. They thought I was a moody-looking bloke, but I was just suffering on-stage.

Once, on a sleeper coming back from Plymouth, I was with an artiste called Larry Page, who at the time was Larry Page, the Teenage Rage, and his Pageboys. I was a Pageboy. It said 'Do Not Drink the Water' in the toilet. But I couldn't help myself. I was gasping for a drink. I got this stomach complaint from the toilet water, and from then on I got ulcers, and that's what made my face all moody on-stage. I really suffered on the road, especially in America, when we spent a month as special UK guests on the Dick Clark Caravan of Stars.

Tony Meehan: We toured with Clyde McPhatter and the Isley Brothers. I could see it then, and I was only sixteen. You actually had what were called 'Race Records': white people listened to white music, black folk listened to black music; the two didn't cross over. There was no such thing as a crossover in those days. We'd get to a place and the blacks would sit on one side of the hall while the whites would sit on the other. The black acts would play to the black audience and the white acts to the white audience. It really was very segregated all over the southern US at the time. We'd go into a white restaurant, they'd have to go into a black restaurant. I always remember being in Raleigh, North Carolina – there was a drinking fountain, a memorial to the Korean War, and there were two taps: one for white people, the other for black people. I just thought: 'How many black soldiers were killed in the Korean War?' It was bizarre, absolutely bizarre.

The blacks kept to themselves. We made friends with them as musicians and learnt a lot from them and we all mixed in the shows, but white kids came to hear Frankie Avalon, Bobby Rydell and Fabian; blacks came to hear Fats Domino, Little Richard and Chuck Berry. In the films they made at that time there was the implication that white American kids got off on rock 'n' roll music, but really it was Bill Haley they were buying. I think a few hip white kids were buying black music, but very few. Nobody had ever heard of Gene Vincent, if you can believe that, nor Eddie Cochran.

Well, it was a very disposable culture even then. Also it was a very big country – you could have a hit in Virginia and no one would ever have heard of you in New York, and vice versa. You could have huge local hits, especially in the big cities like Chicago, New York or Philadelphia. You'd meet people coming out of those urban areas, and you'd talk about southern music and they wouldn't have a clue. We Brits had a much more comprehensive idea of American music, black and white. So we picked and chose what we liked and out of that sort of amalgam came the Shadows.

The English record companies supported this musical racism. What they did was get a black record that was a hit in America and then cover it with a white artist here. White kids thought the records were the product of white English groups, but they weren't at all. They were actually coming from the Chicago south side, Alabama, Louisiana, Mississippi. Billy Fury covered a load of black records. There was never any originality in any of that. The only original musicians in this country at that time were Cliff Richard & the Shadows. We were the only people actually generating an English sound; the rest of them were all copying American stuff, claiming it, in the sense that they didn't tell anyone it came from this or that black group. Even the Beatles did 'Twist and Shout' and more or less stole it from the Isley Brothers.

The entire purpose of Decca's London-label deal in America was to poach off the black hits there. Black records weren't played on the BBC, I can assure you of that. Occasionally you'd hear something on Radio Luxembourg, and then when the pirate stations offshore started up, they played a couple of black records, but not that many, really. To this day, I don't think people in England realise just how much poaching of American music this country did. There was no English rock 'n' roll.

Don Arden, manager, promoter and artiste: I started booking acts around the same time as the 2Is was happening, but I had nothing to do with it. At that time I just couldn't see the British rock 'n' roller. To me they were a pathetic imitation of real rock 'n' roll in those days. I felt that all the Larry Parnes stable was simply pathetic.

Of course, I was managing Gene Vincent! He was the best of them all, in my estimation. His phrasing of a song was absolutely unbelievable. The thing I loved about Vincent was that nobody ever told him how to sing; he never ever spoke to anybody about his performance. He just knew he could do it, and he went out there and did it. It was born in him. Unfortunately, he was living in the wrong period to be as big as he should have been. If Elvis hadn't been so overwhelmingly huge, I feel Gene would have got more respect. The one thing I thought about Gene was that he was probably just a little fierce for the public to take to heart. He lost a lot of fans that he could have had, and should have had, because he was quite sinister. I think a lot of the girls couldn't take it.

Gene Vincent at the *NME* Pollwinners concert

Lee Everett: In those days the fans would not have anything to do with anyone who got married. It was more moral then. Girls then saw a married man as untouchable, whereas now they don't give a shit. In those days, that was it; if they found out you were married, your career was over. Marty Wilde got married and his career died that minute, and his records didn't sell from that moment on. It wasn't a Parnes law to say you should remain single, it was a law written by the fans. Parnes had to take Marty from the top of the bill and put Billy on, while Marty had to start closing the first half. 'Rockin'' at the 2Is' shows were all over England; Mickie Most was on those tours . . .

Mickie Most, artist/producer: I used to do an act with a mate of mine, Alex Murray [friend of Lionel Bart and producer of the first Moody Blues hit 'Go Now'], and we used to call ourselves 'The Most Brothers'. Jet Harris was the bass player, Hank B. Marvin was the guitar player . . . We had a very good band for that time, I suppose. I'm talking about the late 50s . . . We were on the road together for almost a year. The 2Is was a trip from about 56 to 59, then the music thing moved on to other parts of Soho: to the Flamingo, the Scene Club and the 100 Club. I was at the 2Is every night, I almost lived there. Joe Moretti used to go down there a bit, Marty Wilde & the Wildcats and that American guy, Vince Taylor from Vince Taylor & the Playboys, they were quite happening. Lionel Bart used to play in a skiffle group down there on washboard. Skiffle came out of necessity – no one could afford electric guitars and amplifiers, so the instruments were acoustic guitars, tea-chest basses that you could make yourself, and a washboard. It was kinda do-it-yourself music; this was the first stage, because this country wasn't traditionally a music country. At that time England didn't contribute musically unless it was through the classics. If you said to your tearaway friends, other teenage werewolves, at the time, 'I'm really into music and I like to write', they'd think you were a faggot.

The British record companies at that time took tremendous advantage of artists. When I was first signed as an artiste to Decca in 1957, I carried my recording contract with me in my pocket for at least a year, because it was really something . . . there were only about twelve people in England who had a recording contract. I never knew what the royalty was on my contract because I didn't care. The royalties meant nothing, I made records . . .

Derek Johnson: No matter how big the English acts might have been here, they were nothing compared to Elvis, who was always The King. I met him first when Maurice Kinn sent me out to his army base in Germany. Elvis knew which side his bread was peanut-buttered and wanted to look good in the *NME*.

He had a mansion a few miles away from the camp, where he entertained all the 'starlets' and strippers. He occasionally slept in his room at the camp so that he could have some privacy. We sat talking there till the early hours. He said, 'You'll never get a cab now, you'd better bunk down here, there's a spare cot in the corner.' I must be the only journalist to have slept with Elvis! In the morning he had an enormous breakfast: a huge T-bone steak with all the trimmings. Then he challenged me to a game of pool. He'd had two pool tables at Graceland and was used to beating everyone. He took me back to the mansion to meet his father – his mother was dead by then. Major Beaulieu arrived with his daughter Priscilla and they disappeared upstairs.

Some time later, he phoned me at the *NME* and told me he'd be leaving camp in a couple of days' time and his plane would be stopping off at Prestwick to refuel. I went there to meet him. It was the first and only time Elvis ever set foot on British soil. He said he'd be back to play some UK dates, but when he got back to the US, the Colonel put the kibosh on that [Colonel Tom Parker never had a passport and Elvis never toured outside the US]. A few years later, I went out to the US and stayed at Graceland on a personal visit – nothing to do with the *NME*; all my subsequent visits were by Elvis's personal invitation. He said he enjoyed my company. I asked him about the Stones. He said, 'As much as I like the Beatles, these boys are much more in sync with today's market.'

I started to freelance for the *NME* in 1956 and joined the staff in 1957. My bag was to write about people who were hot at the time, British artistes mostly. Benny Green used to write the jazz column. Michael Winner was the film critic. I was friends with Billy Fury, Cliff and his group the Drifters. I had a chance to manage Cliff when he was raw and playing at Butlin's Clacton ballroom.

I was promoting a series of Sunday Concerts at the De La Warr Pavilion in Bexhill for the local council. They asked me if I could get Cliff Richard & the Shadows, as I knew Tito Burns who was managing them. I went along and asked him if they'd do a couple of houses there. He said, 'Well, for you, Derek, anything for £650', which was quite a bit of money, but as far as Cliff Richard & the Shadows were concerned, it was quite cheap. They used that opportunity to give the Shadows their first ever solo appearance; they closed the first half and then returned to back Cliff. Hank said to me after the show, 'So what charity is this for, Derek?' I said, 'Well, Hank, it's not for charity, it's for the Bexhill City Council.' It transpired that Tito was paying them a fiver each and Cliff a tenner because it was a charity show. The next week they changed their manager.

Tony Meehan: Old Tito was a terrible rogue. A lot of them were; a lot of them are. That's the music business. You just have to get a philosophy about it. It's gone from being a musical set-up to almost like a fashion business now. In those days there were a lot of fly-by-nights, a lot of rogues, who just got involved because it was a way of making quick money, and if you were enough of a conman you could get away with murder.

To put it bluntly, to this day I still feel that Andrew got away with murder, but good luck to him. *Expresso Bongo* pretty much said it all; none of them thought rock 'n' roll was gonna last. It was just a fashion, something that was gonna come and go; it was shit, it was rubbish, they didn't understand it. They didn't understand, they didn't listen to it. And they thought, 'Let's just make as much money as we can as quickly as possible.' Everyone got ripped off – I don't care who it was – up until the time when groups really started to get into lawyers, and now the lawyers are ripping *everyone* off.

In those days we knew nothing, we just wanted to play, we were in love with the music. That's the way it was, and people took advantage of you. If someone said to you, 'Would you like a record contract?', you'd say, 'WOW! Jesus, I'm gonna record!' No one ever thought about advances or getting a decent royalty. If you look at the royalties that were being paid, it was totally outrageous. It was daylight robbery. That's how these people like Sir Edward Lewis were making money at places like Decca. They were making millions by offering these cruddy deals. People weren't wise to it at all.

It wasn't until midway through the 60s, up to the 70s, that the business changed even a little. People started forming their own record labels and they got smart about the business side. A lot of clever college kids like Richard Branson came out of universities; different brilliant people came along, but how much more or less honest the new guys were I don't know, it's a matter of conjecture.

Tito was an established agent, but he blew the biggest thing he ever had, which was Cliff & the Shadows. He was always trying to turn us against one another. His foolishness cost him a fortune. I think he knows that he could have had Cliff Richard if he'd just played it straight, but he didn't. There were a lot of them like that.

Don Arden: I went on my own in 1958. I'd worked in showbusiness since I was thirteen, I was Europe's most famous Hebrew singer. There were very few managers, agents or impresarios that were ever artistes. That's why I felt I had a special place in the business. If I criticised an artist, it was because I *was* an artist for nearly twenty years and I knew my profession, I knew my business. It's very hard to make the public appreciate that their idols are just gits who long for somebody to mollycoddle and do everything for them. There are very few that, left on their own, function well once they step off the stage.

I used to call myself the 'King of Rock 'n' Roll' in this part of the world. Not just in this country, but this part of the world. If there were European promoters who wanted to put on American artistes, they had to come to me because I had 'em all tied up. That's how I became a partner in the Star Club, Hamburg. The Star Club couldn't get people like Jerry Lee Lewis, Little Richard, Bill Haley, Ray Charles, Fats Domino, Sam Cooke, the Shirelles, Bo Diddley, Duane Eddy, Brenda Lee, Chuck Berry . . . They couldn't get them without me – in those days I had first call on all those American artistes. That's how powerful I was: instead of being the exclusive booker for the Star Club, I was eventually offered a partnership. That, in my opinion, was the greatest rock 'n' roll club of all time. I don't think there was ever a club in London that had that atmosphere.

ALO: After *Oh, Boy!*, the Film Society and the Cat's Whiskers, the next move had to be a band. A local boy, Vic White, was Cliff Richard & the Drifters crazy, and owned a guitar he could actually play, so we were off. I should have managed the band and let John sing, but I insisted on doing 'Tell

Laura I Love Her' at a school concert. The loudest sound in the room as I entered stage left was my knees knocking. I couldn't hit the high notes without breaking into a pig's squeal.

Every year the Wellingborough School Theatrical Society would mount a dramatic or musical work, something light and Gilbert & Sullivan-ish, wherein effort could hopefully be mistaken for entertainment. This particular year it was *HMS Pinafore*. John and I got the gig of painting the sets and backdrops.

John Douglas: Andy was a dilettante: though he'd got natural ability, he didn't stick long with things, because there was always something new to have a crack at. At one stage he'd had piano lessons and in the inter-house competition, knowing he was a duff player, he decided he would embrace all the skills and showmanship of Liberace. He actually put a small chandelier on the piano, did the bow, adjusted his seat for about five minutes, opened the piano, lifted his hands and I think he must have played three notes and then reversed the same way he came in. He won the hearts and minds of everyone and got virtually a standing ovation. He was crap at music, but he was the best turn there was.

ALO: As the Theatrical Society rehearsals progressed from round-the-table readings to cues, blocking and run-throughs on-stage, the leading 'ladies' started getting into costume. Up in the rafters, painting the sets, John and I were beside ourselves at this bizarre transformation of boys into girls.

John Douglas: We thought that was really weird. We were becoming sexual people, and they would tart up the prettiest boys and make them into girls and then parade them up on-stage. It was playing mind-games in a way.

ALO: Contact with girls, unless supervised, was an offence punishable by expulsion. Our boyhood crushes were hardly homosexual by deliberate, conscious choice, just 'one of those bells that now and then rings'. This was a world of innocence, before the terrorism of AIDS; we were working with what we had to hand. Had we been on a desert island with hundreds of young girls, we'd have gladly welcomed our fate.

At Wellingborough you'd be expelled if caught smoking a cigarette, so there was little margin for more serious breaches of conduct. Before the pill, young girls who came up with child ruined both their own and the young man's future. In view of the fear and awkwardness that surrounded all things sexual, it was safer to stay home and play. Anyway, the boys were prettier, and available.

I made a pass at the 'leading lady', a snotty but pretty little farm-boy, who belonged to the in-crowd prefect of another house. For my troubles, I got cornered on a cricket pitch one Sunday, and well and truly decked. One punch and I decided to stay down. A stretcher was called for. I acted knocked out, and was carried away to the school sanitarium.

John Douglas: That was just ugliness and I think jealousy. They probably thought we'd got too big for our boots, but because I was the more acceptable face of our partnership it wasn't me that got decked. Andy's lip was split open badly. That shook him up. Until then he'd been able to gob his way out of everything.

ALO: What was amazing was that my mother took me back to London, got my mouth stitched back up and sent me straight back to school, never mentioning the fact that I had been accused of running a homosexual ring. She was told not to expect the school to discipline my attackers. I don't think she believed them for a moment, but she understood the rules. Celia could only hope that some day I would understand at least some of them, too.

There were more lies to come. A few concerned locals had seen me being taken off the school fields on a stretcher and wanted to know what had happened. In the local paper the following week, the school explained away the incident by claiming that 'the pupil was knocked unconscious by a cricket ball'. Wagging the dog is nothing new, you see.

There was an up-side to my end-of-term misadventure. The alluring wife of the headmaster took pity on me and invited me into the mansion for tea and sympathy. I was lucky the stir this caused didn't result in another beating, and even luckier the head didn't knock me down himself.

Summer, and the comparative freedom of London, couldn't have come at a better time. I'd read an article about Shirley Bassey, which mentioned that her husband and manager, the producer Kenneth Hume, lived off Hyde Park. I wanted to meet Hume, because I appreciated the Svengalian effect he'd had on the development of substance and style in the Welsh singer's career. To me, Hume *was* Shirley Bassey. I looked up the showbiz couple's address in the telephone directory and went to visit. Hume himself opened the door and engaged me in an inspiring chat over a cup of tea, the great British social lubricant. There was a marvellous paradox in those days between the national, and even international, celebrity of many British showbusiness figures and their openness to my 'knock-knock' visits. Perhaps it helped that I was impossibly young and unbearably precocious. They couldn't believe their eyes and ears.

Shirley Bassey with her husband Kenneth Hume

In the summer of 1959 my two major passions, rock 'n' roll and cinema, collided to sensational effect in the long-awaited film version of *Expresso Bongo*. No one could have pleased me more as manager Johnny Jackson than my own Larry Harvey, who was as at home in the coffee bars and strip joints of Soho as he had not been in the society drawing rooms of his immediately previous hit, *Room at the Top*. And to prove even further that my subconscious was beginning to control the audio and video of 'real life', Bongo Herbert was played by Cliff Richard.

What really struck me was the upbeat conclusion, after a music-business tycoon and an over-the-hill floozy conspire to steal Bongo from

Johnny. Just as he's decided to get his drums out of hock and go on the road, leaving the scrumptious Sylvia Syms behind in her pasties, a notorious showbiz deadbeat repays a loan that Johnny never thought he'd see again. The movie ends with Johnny dropping his drums in the street and strolling off in search of the next Bongo. Although I may not have articulated it at the time, that attitude became one of my mantras: 'They always fuck you for the first one.'

Laurence Harvey as Johnny Jackson in *Expresso Bongo*

Johnny Jackson, in *Expresso Bongo*: The picture in the fan mag showed this gangly kid in jeans and a sweatshirt, his face contorted, mouth wide open, beating with both hands on a bongo set round his shoulder, and over it the headline 'BONGO SCORES AT TOM TOM'. The same terrible stuff, but this time it was good because it was me who dropped the deadbeat drunk columnist a fiver to run it. Because this new boy Bongo Herbert, playing nightly for the past week at the Tom Tom Express back of Frith Street, he's under contract to nobody but me. Half of the ten pounds he picks up this

Friday comes to me. Half of everything he beats out of those little bongos for the next three years comes to me.

I had wet-nursed this kid along, bought him cigarettes, coffee and sandwiches, a couple of sweatshirts with bongos painted on them, a pair of tailored black jeans and a fancy haircut. Turned him from Bert Rudge, snotty-nosed nobody, to Bongo Herbert, Britain's latest answer to America's latest solution of how to keep discs selling by the million.

John Douglas: Rock 'n' roll was our religion. If we were lost, we always went back to our roots and put on some records. Though we didn't like the place, Wellingborough brought out qualities in us. Even to this day I will cross-reference mentally and think, 'I wish I was sharing this moment with Andy.' Everything was coded, we just had to look at each other, we were very in tune. He had become aware that he could influence and control events, often by his ability to make people laugh. Especially when he was in full flow, being amusing and laughing, Andy could always capture an audience.

One of his strong points was his wit. He did it like Elia Kazan, he was a method actor, in the sense that he lived it, breathed it, drank it, fucked it, did whatever he had to do to be that for that period. He got bored quickly and moved on, but I was forever being amused to see the distance he'd go to capture the moment.

He always had a hang-up about his eyes, which I thought were one of his strong points. He thought he'd got animated but beady eyes. Andrew decided very early on that they weren't a strong feature and he would disguise them with shades.

ALO: Just before Christmas, John and I skived off school to see the Shadows share the bill with Emile Ford & the Checkmates at the Granada Cinema in nearby Kettering. Emile Ford had just become the first black Briton to have a number one, with 'What Do You Want To Make Those Eyes At Me For?' Emile sat on the edge of the stage with his feet in the orchestra pit and managed to get the whole audience to sing 'White Christmas'. This was another pivotal realisation of the possibility of rock 'n' roll as total entertainment. The hairs on the back of my neck tingled. I was in love with showbiz. The Shadows were more than showbusiness, they were life.

John Douglas: You've got to remember we were true fans and as a true fan, Andy had done this beefed-up illustration of the Shadows, highlighting his idol, Jet Harris. After the gig, he somehow managed to get backstage to present it to the Shadows. That's where I just have to take my hat off to him. He would go where angels fear to tread, and he was accepted because he was such a cheeky chappie.

He adopted whatever persona he needed to get his passport signed; that was his great acting ability. He would be what people wanted him to be – he was mobile, upwardly mobile. He got around. He quickly began to realise: if they can do it, I can do it – and better. For the mass of us in that era, at that age, we would have sat on our arses, we would have thought it was impossible.

ALO: It was 1960, I was sixteen, and I decided to lose my virginity. Regular dances were held at school to which girls from the dancing classes of Mrs Josie Marsh were invited. Naturally enough, I set my sights on the prize catch, Mrs Marsh's daughter. She was two years older than I, and, as John said, 'out of my league'.

Alexis was soon confiding that she was most unhappy about her mother's plan for her to be married to a man of Mrs Marsh's choosing. Alexis, though dutiful, was put out by the calculation of it all. I invited her to visit me at my mother's flat in Hampstead. She agreed, obviously keen on having an adventure before her mother had her way. I celebrated with John over a brandy and Havana cigar. We both vomited.

Over the Easter holiday, as promised, Miss Marsh rang me at my mother's. Could I meet her at the train station? Excitedly I changed into my finest threads and rushed off to meet the girl. Back at Netherhall Gardens, with a few hours to spare before Mother returned from work, I 'became a man'.

We performed in the front window because I knew the old people opposite, who were always peeping through their curtains, would get aggravated. But it was over very fast. Afterwards I thought, ' Oh God, this is terrible. Now I've got to see Alexis out, right back to the station.' It was not her fault, I had no idea what I was doing.

Soon after my liaison, I was devastated to hear that Eddie Cochran was dead. The car he had been riding in to the airport with Gene Vincent was totalled. Gene escaped with injuries that accentuated the limp he already had. At the time I was convinced Eddie had died for England, to light an eternal flame for rock 'n' roll in the hearts of the nation's youth.

Eddie Cochran

Derek Johnson: Eddie only did one tour of England, like Buddy, mainly because he was scared stiff of flying. He just didn't want to cross the Atlantic. I interviewed him backstage at the old Bristol Hippodrome on the final night of the tour. After we'd finished our chat, he got into his hired car and was going straight to London airport to fly back to the States. He was trembling with fear at the prospect of that flight.

ALO: I'd decided I was out of Wellingborough after the exams, although John's parents had arranged for him to stay on. No manner of persuasion or pressure from Celia could get me to stay any longer. As a capper, the school wrote her a letter stating, 'Andrew may do well . . . but not here.' But Wellingborough had indeed prepared me for the rest of my life.

H.J.C. Bashford, Headmaster of Wellingborough School (from ALO's final school report): 'He knows too much about life and not enough about how to live it.'

John Douglas: Every move Andrew made afterwards, I'd seen in dress rehearsals at Wellingborough. Okay, his scams got more sophisticated, but the basics remained the same: first get their attention, second shock 'em, third make 'em laugh, and last (if not most important) take their money. He was pretty good at that part, actually.

David Miranda: When he left Wellingborough, I thought he was going to be either a great success or a miserable failure. He could have gone either way. You could have called and told me, 'Andrew has spent the last fifteen years in jail', and I wouldn't have been at all surprised. They say about Al Capone that if he had gone into a legitimate business he would have been a great success, because he was a great manager. I think that's true of Andrew, too: what attracted him to rock 'n' roll was precisely that it was *not* a 'legitimate' business.

John Douglas: I remember him returning to shock the school in his sky-blue Chevrolet, with sky-high bodyguard and Keith Richard, literally crashing into Garne's House. Another time he drove his Rolls-Royce across the cricket wicket. The final time he returned, it was for an Old Boys' football match. After scoring a goal for each side, he blacked out. During the evening he escorted disc jockey Alan Freeman from dormitory to dormitory giving out his autograph.

ALO: It was good training for life – perhaps not the life I planned for myself, but, nevertheless, it worked. That school was like being in rehearsal, and leaving school was like going on-stage. We rehearsed a movie called 'Life', and I owe that place, the way Al Pacino says he owes Lee Strasberg. They gave me the tools. Destiny had been declared.

· CHAPTER 4 ·

ALO: Rid of the country at last and back in London, I got on with my life. To pay for my fun and to avoid at all costs more hectoring from my mother, I determined to find hire worthy of the workman.

In Piccadilly, opposite the Rialto Cinema, I spotted a notice for a part-time sales assistant in the window of Adams, a small, conservative men's clothes store. The old man who owned and managed the shop liked what he saw and heard from this smartly dressed, well-spoken school-leaver and appointed me on the spot. The window was drab; so was the clientele. They didn't get the overflow from Daks or Aquascutum, just a few world-weary travelling salesmen on their way back to Leicester.

Within a few days, Harold, Adams's full-timer, knew he had a new tuner for his fiddle. Life had more hazing in store for me, it seemed. Five years older than I and East End bred, Harold threatened to beat me up if I didn't follow his orders, which were: at closing, take a few garments into the changing room, put them on under your mufti, say 'good night' and wear them out. I coughed them up to Harold in the Piccadilly Circus tube-station men's room, long a familiar scene for illicit rendezvous. If Harold judged an item too naff to move on, he'd throw it back at me with, ''Ere. That looks good on you.' Thus I was forced to steal bread off the table of my new family, which seemed a poor exchange for remaining in Harold's good graces.

Game, set and clobber that never matched . . . It wouldn't have been so bad, had the clothes from Adams not been so – well, as Harold would have it – naff. For the most part old Mr Adams sold apparel I wouldn't be seen dead in. While rethinking my entrance into the working week, I decided to rest up for an early summer holiday, and spend some of that quality time with my mother – time that was rapidly becoming scarcer as my life became my own.

Juan-les-Pins, the then fashionable South of France resort, was our destination. By this time, I actually felt liberated by 'He may do well, but not here'. My mother's influence over me in the career department was on the wane. With a spring in my step, I would transform my dreams into reality. The film in my mind would soon leap off the screen on to the streets . . .

Oh yes, I would work hard, but I had no intention of applying for the traditional school-leaver's apprenticeship: clerking at some boring, average company, where I could only expect more dress codes, more restrictions on thought, speech and hours, more frustration. In a word, an Establishment lifestyle that disincentivised discipline to maintain the status quo. I was more than willing to overcome frustration, I already had a dress code, and I had no doubts about my discipline and grip.

While we packed, Celia expounded her objections about our upstairs neighbour, Frank Norman, who rather enjoyed being the block's leading celebrity. 'He comes home drunk at all hours with a different girl every night.' My mother's eyes shot lasers up through the ceiling to the Norman residence. 'It's not a life,' she concluded, but exactly why Mr Norman had no life remained one of Celia's secrets.

Frank Norman

I admired Frank Norman. In his thirties, he had the sort of butch, languid features that would drive Pasolini, made dangerous by the intersection of his long scar with his smile. Norman draped his tall frame in the same barrister pinstripes worn by the lot that had prosecuted him. He was an

East End ex-con, who had repaid his debts to society as the guest of numerous of Her Majesty's prisons, then turned his life of crime into a well-paid after-life in entertainment. Frank moved north-west to Hampstead to join all the other well-heeled cons on the hill. Mother was forced to share her would-be genteel neighbourhood with some of the most interesting people in London.

In fact, Frank Norman was one of the original working-class heroes of the glitterati (cf. the more unfortunate débâcle of Jack Henry Abbott and N. Mailer). He wrote *Fings Ain't Wot They Used To Be* in the late 50s, the musical comedy version of 'the last angry man'. With staging by Sean Kenny, music by Lionel Bart and sponsorship by Joan Littlewood, the production of *Fings* kicked open the doors of the West End theatre with a disregard for conventional opinion that I could completely relate to. As could John Osborne, who by now had achieved fame and was starting to look over his shoulder in anger or fear: 'Lionel Bart, booted by the genius of Joan Littlewood into soupy crash-bang wallop success with *Fings Ain't Wot They Used To Be* . . . achieved a knees-up for the nobs . . .' he wrote in his autobiography.

Upon our return from Juan-les-Pins, my final Wellingborough results were waiting. I'd got one O level in English Lit, and just in case the pen were not to prove mightier than the sword, I'd gained second-class proficiency in rifle shooting. The report hemmed and hawed about my 'ability' . . . and my 'inability' to use it; you know the rest.

Tania Sarne (née Gordon): Marc Gebhard lived around the corner from Andrew, and they were pretty good friends. I used to give them free meals at the coffee bar where I worked. Marc and Andrew were two very lonely boys, both ambitious and good-looking. Andrew lived at home and none of us had any money, so we'd go to the Hampstead Everyman Cinema, where independent art films from France played in the neighbourhood.

Andrew would start busking outside, embarrassing us enormously. He'd start singing and standing on his hands and generally making a huge exhibition of himself, but he'd always get enough money to get us into the movie; that's how we used to see films. Oh, he was a right little exhibitionist, he was shameless.

Anything he could do – whether it was cartwheels or just make fun of people, or simply stand there and say, 'Give us some money, we wanna see the film' – whatever it was, he'd get it. He was an admirable hustler.

Jackie Bisset was around Hampstead at the time, and there were a lot of French Lycée people that Andrew used to take the mickey out of. I remember we got arrested for breaking into the outdoor pool in Hampstead. We went skinny-dipping one night. I think that was the only time I've ever been arrested.

We were very young; I was sixteen. When you're young, things seem to happen around you.

ALO: Sheila was the beautiful, waifish, ethereal fifteen-year-old daughter of a well-respected psychoanalyst father and sculptress mother. They – Sheila, her three brothers and parents – lived at the right end of Frognal, on the right section of Hampstead. She attended art school in Shepherd's Bush and studied sculpture part-time at St Martin's College. She hung out with her school friend, Linda Keith, an actor's daughter who lived over in West Hampstead. It was Tania who introduced us.

Sheila Klein: Tania, Marc and Andrew were all together when I came out of the Everyman, to be confronted by Andrew rolling around in the gutter. If he hadn't been with Tania I'd have probably just walked off. I'd never met anyone like him. I wanted to be an artist but didn't have any life experience. When I saw Andrew I thought, 'Ah, here we go, here's the fast lane.' It stood out a mile. Even just walking down the street in Hampstead, people would turn and stare at him.

He looked amazing and was entertaining, funny and theatrical. I was fascinated. We lived close by and saw a lot of each other. I encouraged him. It was a period where we realised we were comfortable together. For me, I found the fact that he was not overtly sexual very interesting. I'd been jumped on by so many men that it was a relief to find a friend who was not like that. He didn't know girls well, so he was very cautious, very sweet. He was very gentle at that stage, compared to how he became later. We were very good friends, very close. It was quite a long time before we became boyfriend and girlfriend.

ALO and Sheila Klein

Linda Keith: Andrew was very funny, very quick-tempered, couldn't stand idiots, if you weren't cool or hip . . . He wouldn't suffer fools happily, he would just blow them away. There was a sort of fearlessness about him. He was a forerunner of the Mod thing in an era that was quite beatnik. He wasn't into that, it was too funky. He was never funky, he was smooth. He wore those little bum-freezer mohair suits. Everything was an opportunity; he did have such style. He had such a gift of hustling.

Sheila Klein: He used to pinch my pocket money. I think sixpence used to be quite a large amount of money then and he needed to pay his mother sixpence per shirt. She charged him to iron his shirts. I probably had ten bob pocket money. Celia wasn't around a lot. We used to go round to his place quite a bit. I think she had to struggle. She had a reasonably wealthy Jewish man friend who I think probably bought her flat. She certainly didn't work.

She was very money-orientated, she did a lot of checking out the prices in different stores to find which one was the cheapest. She made the most

fantastic Christmas cakes. As far as I can gather, she sent him off to boarding school from the word go and so he didn't have any kind of home life at all. And I think she was quite tough on him. I remember outside their flat there was a bench on the street and this old tramp used to go and sleep there. Andrew got interested and would go off and have chats with him. Celia would make a big fuss about that.

Marc Gebhard: I was prepping for RADA when Andrew said, 'Forgot about being an actor, I can make you into a pop star.' I laughed, 'cause he was quite eccentric even as a kid. I said, 'I can't sing.' He said, 'Don't worry, you've got the right look.' He was the most concerned-about-clothes person I've ever met in my life to this day. He was meticulous. He was so critical, he influenced me a lot.

He persuaded me to sign a contract. I thought, 'He's mad', but he was very business-like about it, so I began to take it a bit seriously. I signed just to shut him up 'cause he kept pestering me about it. Within a couple of weeks he got me some jobs modelling for an exclusive men's shop called John Michael. Somehow he also got me a job dancing the twist on a cinebox, which was the prototype of video, called Scopitone, a company which produced videos for jukeboxes. You put your money in, pressed your number and you got a little film going with the song. I was dancing the twist in a French version of 'Let's Twist Again', with a French model. So I thought, 'Well, this guy's got me some work, he can't be all that crazy.'

He had a way of getting things done. Andrew was the first person to tell me, 'It's all business, Marc: everything – music, acting – it's all a business.' I was quite amazed that someone our age would come out with something like that. It was only later that I realised he was quite right.

Sheila Klein: He'd make these long, dramatic speeches on Hampstead Heath, like he was in the theatre and wanted to project to the back row. That was his practice, that was where he'd go to rehearse. If there happened to be anybody around . . . well, it wouldn't have mattered to Andrew. If he'd done it today, they'd probably have locked him up; back then he was moving so fast, he was like . . . gone. He was performing all the time. A lot of performers switch off when they come off-stage; Andrew didn't. He was never off, he was always on-stage. Except when he was depressed, when he couldn't crank it up, then he'd be quite quiet, sitting around reading a magazine or watching TV. Every time he stepped out of the door, it was like, 'Wow, what's gonna happen now?' If it wasn't gonna happen from outside influences, he'd make it happen.

ALO: I felt like a thoughtful French New Wave movie, so I rolled the credits and appeared on location in Hampstead Village's thriving beatnik scene. An arty vibe pervaded the Witch's Cauldron, where the young and mainly affluent religiously posed and preened, as they drawled quasi-cultured monologues over well-nursed cappuccinos. I, of course, stood apart from this dishevelment. Their uniform of scruffy, shabby jeans worn under large and holey sweaters hid a universal preoccupation with getting (or not getting) laid.

I was trying to sell my imported Elvis singles. Thinking I would have a captive market back home, I had spent my allowance in France on forty copies of 'It's Now or Never'. It was certain to be hot, since it was as yet unavailable in England until a copyright dispute over 'O Solo Mio' was resolved. I would have turned a greater profit had I invested in Juliette Creco or Jacques Brel. I didn't sell many discs in this dalliance with retail – the bohemian punters wanted the Modern Jazz Quartet, and the neighbourhood Jewish kids refused to be conned.

Gina, a pale beatnik wraith whose parents owned a Greek eatery on

Heath Street, yanked me outta the Cauldron, away from the dregs, and up to the Hampstead Everyman Cinema to catch a Chabrol film kicking off the French New Wave season. She led; I followed.

Sheila Klein: Gina's make-up was striking. White lipstick, loads of black eye-shadow, very straight black hair plastered down at the fringe. She was like the first punk. At the time she was the epitome of beatnik.

ALO: Gina and I were slim and pleasing – to each other, and to those who wondered whether our bodies kept the same timing because we shared the same spring and smile in the night to our step. They didn't, but Gina and I enjoyed the game, the complement that our spirits were to each other, and those we did keep time with. Opposites don't always attract, sometimes they just look good together; her spirit was unharnessed, unbroken, a mod pop bundle of joy.

And perhaps more than her own Peter Meaden, whom I'd meet on another Everyman day for night, she introduced me to the space between notes that lives above gender, for that space occupies a room or two and Peter lived out on the ledge. I remember the moment we were not above it, and we could, but would not, get attached. We were on the slope that takes you away from Hampstead High Street down over Frognal and down again towards the Finchley Road, where up on the hill away from the traffic Gina lived with her family. Gina took note of the moment too; we both laughed it off. I blushed, her eyes furnaced above the pale mask she wore. My hand wondered how pale was the rest of her, as our arms clasped around each other a little tighter to preserve and bottle the moment. Laughter and love went together, and we settled for harmony; we'd both just been and felt effective jazz.

We picked up our pace and strode on up the hill towards the heath and the Everyman. I would occupy this space with several significant others in the very near future, but Gina was a first of her kind.

We walked the minute or two south towards Fitzjohn's Avenue where, snugged in the last cluster of shops, we snacked and nattered in the warmth of Gina's parents' Greek eatery. I held the cup the way I wanted to hold her hand. I had seen some leaflets on the earlier life of the Everyman and was now an expert, holding forth to Gina about how the cinema had once been a live theatre and had housed an earlier angry young person, other than our good selves and 'le bonfroglot'.

Thirty years earlier than Osborne, in 1924, the young master himself – as pop personified – had written and starred in his first number-one and controversial smash *The Vortex*. The young master? Noël Coward.

Gina and I didn't care much about the matters that weighed *The Vortex*: drugs, homosexuality and mother's little penchant for toy-boys. For me, one had been left resting on the mantelshelf at Wellingborough, the other resided in Soho, and my mother's only little penchant was for her toy-boy to get some decent work.

What gobsmacked us was the shock Coward caused, the uproar among his peers and elders – that's what it was all about – the cry to have the play removed from the stage of life, not dissimilar to a later hue and cry about the Stones. We didn't fall for the cast or the hoopla; we were both too high at the pride of our lives to be interested in the grotty malaise. We fell for the move forward in life – the arrival, the charisma of Noël Coward making his indelible mark . . . the event.

The falling-down in life to powder and flesh we knew naught about yet. We were happy, deviant free New Wave divas, and we wrapped ourselves in all things Noël, hot lemon tea and moussaka. We forgot about that blush of fate earlier on the hill. We strode back out on to Hampstead High Street, bidding adieu to that. School was now out, shops were now near closing, Hampstead and its heath alive with cars on their way home. The other kids marching on the block were different. Somehow they knew where they were going and didn't like it, whereas Gina and I did like where we were going and our stride was already there.

It was the new cinema that we were on our way to see that seduced and hooked me instantly. Springing from the political atmosphere that had inspired the New Left, it ridiculed commercial cinema. The work demanded plots and exemplified themes relevant to the struggles of reality, stirring me to dress down and attitude up.

I happily let the wave wash over me. Claude Chabrol was a man after Laurence Harvey's many hearts – he financed his first film *Le Beau Serge* with an inheritance left to his first wife. It introduced Jean-Claude Brialy, whose cynical screen personality, lively temperament and courtly manner I identified with and adopted immediately. The Chabrol style in *Le Beau Serge* and *Les Cousins* via Brialy was curiously detached and I liked it. The props were a New Wave haircut, textured clothing like Shetlands, cords and 'Le duffel-coat'. A return to brogues on the feet, the 'moouvement' of the hands to express my heart, and I had it down. A beige wool-and-cashmere driving jacket from the Adams booty proved to be a wardrobe coup for this new movie.

Jean-Claude Brialy (left) in Chabrol's *Les Cousins*

When life demanded something a little more brittle, I would change reels into Jean-Luc Godard, get *Breathless* and allow for jump-cuts and unsteady, hand-held moving shots. Godard reshaped film syntax while paying homage to the American gangster movie, as Jean-Paul Belmondo re-invented Jean Gabin by way of James Dean meets Humphrey Bogart. That role was a stretch for me at sixteen, so I usually calmed down into the more comfortable and laconic Jean-Claude Brialy mode.

I may have left Wellingborough, but I was still at school. But don't let my French New Wave languor fool you. I was hard at work, as were many others.

This underground cinema movement was radically different, philo-sophically and visually, from anything we had ever experienced on-screen before. The Hampstead Everyman, champion of the New Wave in London, was manna from heaven for my friends and me at the time, as we celebrated

'La différence'. As the 60s gathered momentum, the French New Wave would heavily influence the British arts, initially in film and theatre, by engendering the British Free Cinema, helmed by Karel Reisz, Tony Richardson and Lindsay Anderson. This trio of young British auteurs brought a new kind of internationality and sophistication to English-language films with *Saturday Night and Sunday Morning*, *This Sporting Life*, *Look Back in Anger*, *The Entertainer*, *The Loneliness of the Long-Distance Runner* and *A Taste of Honey*. Tony Richardson and John Osborne formed Woodfall Films and would later go for the whole nine yards with *Tom Jones*, winning an Oscar in the process. La Nouvelle Vague, spearheaded by Chabrol, Godard, Truffaut, Rivette and Rohmer, still makes causes and harvests effects on film-making to this day.

Its visual style trickled down into the fashion world via André Courrèges' bold, stark, scientifically precise mathematical beauty. Pierre Cardin's vision was to become the most highly franchised designer name in history. And let us not forget a little *später* pop music from the Beatles and the Stones. The French films' sparse, grainy black-and-white look would dominate early images by the beat boom's leading lights. The Stones' input came direct from *moi* via the Everyman, plus what they brought to the table, and the Beatles got their attitude in Hamburg under the tutelage of Hamburg's Star Club and their German friends.

It was at the Everyman, too, that I met the light of Gina's life, Peter Meaden, who would provide both fuel and beam to so many lives, save his own. I came, I saw, he conquered.

Tony Hall: I remember seeing Andrew striding down Wardour Street, he must have been sixteen, seventeen. He looked like a white English equivalent to a Blue Note record sleeve. Blue Note was the hip black jazz label; their record sleeves had all the latest fashions, all the buttoned-down collars, width of the ties, everything that was ultra-hip among black musicians was always on those sleeves. For his part, I always thought Peter Meaden was a genius.

ALO: Peter Meaden and I bonded on the look of American jazz style from the back of album covers, downloading life into the simplicity of the

complicity we shared, and concentrated on that. We found each other's anger
and reinforced our ambitions. We honed each other's humour, band-aided
each other's social sores and fronted the lot with the totality of that. Peter had
been out and about longer than I, so I happily fed off his learning.

He worked by day at an American-style ad agency at 63/69 New Oxford
Street (in the same building that would later house my Immediate Records
company). We began to meet regularly after work and comb the West End
and Soho. We'd check out Austin's on Shaftesbury Avenue, a clothes
emporium specialising in American imports, the best and latest in Modern
Jazz style. Endorsed by the cool and knowing of the day, Austin's was a feast
of reversible houndstooth and herringbone, staggered vent jackets, worn with
broadcloth button-down, pin-through and tab-collared shirts. Neither of us
could afford to buy anything from this style palace, but we guzzled up the
styles regardless, walked and talked a mile a minute, and were busy making
plans.

'John Michael', né Ingram, owned two hip men's shops: Sportique on Old
Compton Street and his flagship John Michael store on the King's Road. For
the most part, Sportique's fey clobber was ludicrous unless you were
swarthy, wealthy and gay. John Michael, on the other hand, with its formal
grey flannel suits, and striped or gingham round-collared, fly-fronted, well-
tailored shirts, was another fashion plate we could ill afford, but we badly
wanted. So I did starve a little for a superlative skinny wool-knit tie and
gingham tab-collared shirt.

At C&A's in Marble Arch, on a high-floor back rack, Peter and I found
a few lightweight, staggered vent suits, cheap and in amazing colours; 99 per
cent of British men's suits were still post-war grey or black. Bottle-green
mohair with a paisley lining was a visitation to be celebrated, and coupled
with side-laced suede ankle boots we had heaven on earth and thrills on our
feet.

Peter introduced me to a different form of nightlife, a different form of
life – Soho. Our first port of call was the Scene Club, behind Piccadilly, just
off Windmill Street in Ham Yard. It was run by Ronan O'Rahilly, who later
started Britain's first pirate station, Radio Caroline. The Scene was a loud,
smoky haven for the disenfranchised working class, where white-on-black
soul was the soundtrack till dawn's harrowing light. Having grown up in the

relatively rough district of Edmonton, Peter was attuned and passed for one of this crowd, while I stayed close to the edge watching the kids speeding on pills and good music, posing more than dancing, jaws frantically chewing the night away. Three-legged, legless Mod monsters, pilled to the walls of aurafide stress, bound and bonded by sound and dread of the job on Monday.

We'd move over four blocks left and right to the Flamingo on Wardour Street and a funkier, jazzier crowd. On Saturday the Flamingo was the only Soho venue serving drinks and playing music all night, giving itself up to black R'n'B, Atlantic and early Stax-type fare. An exotic mélange of Soho sex and underground sorts, gangsters really, usually crashed in late after disposing of earlier engagements. Rik Gunnell and his brother John ran the late-night Flamingo, so it was very safe, which when you think of it is the perfect atmosphere for a club: decadence without the possibility of violence.

John Paul Jones, musician/arranger/Led Zeppelin bassist: I used to hang out with Peter Meaden here and there. He was exciting, knew where all the bands were; he knew what was good to see, rather than just hanging out at the Scotch of St James . . . The Face, yeah. That was Peter. He took me to see the Who the first time down the Scene Club. It was brilliant, the Scene, smoky, loud, it was very punky in those days. One time later, Peter and I gatecrashed a party at 11 Downing Street – it was Caroline Maudling's party, we just went and blagged our way in. The Stones and Andrew had been invited, and Peter was pissed off he hadn't been.

I used to play down the Flamingo Club with Mickey Eves, who used to be in the original Blue Flames. John McLaughlin was on guitar. I was playing organ. The Flamingo was just funkier and jazzier; the Scene was all a bit white pop, more punk – what would become punk – and it was all pills. Pop music was all pills in those days. Preludin was the original speed pill, then it was blues or purple hearts, that kinda half/half colour. We used to call them blues in the jazz world but they became purple hearts in the rock world.

Peter Meaden, in *Sounds*: There is no other drug like Drynamil – purple hearts – that gives you such a bang, such an up. The high, combined with the music, gives you the energy to stay up for three days running. You feel great. You can dance, you have courage, confidence . . .

John Paul Jones: Whereas with jazz and rhythm and blues everybody was smoking, so you had two different cultures. Pop musicians hadn't really come across smoke, apart from Billy Fury, who got all that from the jazzers. Also, there were a lot of ska clubs around, like the Roaring Twenties; you'd have ska bands down the Flamingo, the Whisky À Go-Go. The ska scene was pretty big coming into 64, and Blue Beat before that. All the Mod style was from Jamaica, stingy brims and high buttons.

The Flamingo was extremely seedy, hot and sweaty, but a brilliant vibe. The music was great, everyone was into black R'n'B and some jazz. I remember the Mar-keys playing down there and a very risqué show by Sugar Pie De Santo, the music was mostly Atlantic and Stax. Brian Auger was down there, Sonny Rollins, Roland Kirk, Geno Washington, Duffy Power, Dickie Pride, Cyril Green, Georgie Fame, Alexis Korner. Basically they were all jazzers who played R'n'B. The Blue Note record label was big among the jazzers, Coltrane, Miles Davis; there was a big jazz scene that ran hand in hand with the R'n'B scene.

Which was why the Stones and the Yardbirds didn't fit in, because they weren't jazzers, they hated jazz. Andrew came up with the Stones and to us that was white R'n'B, which nobody was into at all. There was this whole little white R'n'B movement, which grew up quite separately and would evolve into the Stones and the Yardbirds.

I wasn't really involved in the white group side. We were into Otis Redding and the Mar-keys, they were all into Chuck Berry and the Chess people, blues twits really. As a musical scene they just didn't rate, really. None of those people did: the Yardbirds, it was like, 'Oh dear', it was more punk than R'n'B. Oh, it was great for that, but when you heard them play 'Little Red Rooster' you'd go, 'Oh no, please don't . . .'

ALO: I followed my leader Peter and, what with the leapers, our life was a party and I, too, was grinding my teeth down to the bone. Sometimes we'd head back to Hampstead for rest and more partying, and sometimes I'd go back on my own. I'd stop off and tell my mother, 'I'm home.'

If I was with Peter, we would bathe (he'd shave), change, collect Gina and we'd step out to the Hampstead raves. With Peter's motorbike and side-car, we'd park in the hedges of well-to-do addresses and crash the parties of wealthy Jewish, would-be arty girls whose parents had gone away for the weekend. Though more often than not, I'd leave Peter revving in Soho and head for Hampstead on my tod. I should think that when Peter finally did come home, Gina gave him a well-to-do settled look; Peter would have done well to have embraced and grown into what Gina was offering. But to Peter, home life was backstage, between shows, on the nod to Mod, and therefore not to be.

With all the partying, I never stopped looking around for places to present myself. The London *Evening Standard*, one of the two evening papers, had just started a weekly column on men's fashion called 'Mainly for Men'. It was a pioneering feature, dealing with a hitherto undiscussed-by-men subject – their clothes and their lifestyle. 'Mainly for Men' was edited by Angus McGill. I bombarded him with calls, enthusing about his clothes, my clothes, any clothes, praising the column and life in general. Mr McGill responded with an invitation to his office.

Angus McGill: He was very persistent. He wanted me to photograph him. He basically wanted some publicity, but because he wasn't working it was hard to know what the publicity would be useful for. I didn't quite understand it. I think perhaps he'd have liked a job. He was very much looking around to place his life. He was very confident, very charming and very into himself. He was projecting himself the whole time in a very pleasant way. You didn't quite know what he was on about, but he was very together, really going places. He was always talking about clothes.

Andrew was a very thin, well-dressed, very elegant figure, very ex-public school. His clothes were very smart, an adaptation of what the grown-ups were wearing, really. I didn't think of him as a 'Mod' or a 'Rocker', he seemed a cut above, a very smart-looking guy. He was wearing his school shirt, which was grey, a tie and jacket. It was the grey shirt he thought had a future. He thought this was the thing at the moment. It was grey flannel, nice actually. I did a piece about him, a short piece with a nice photograph. It was centred around the grey flannel shirt, what he said about it, what he thought about men's fashion. That was it. He was quite pleased; he had the picture, a bit of a write-up, his name in the paper.

ALO in gingham and grey flannel shirts

ALO: I had exactly that, a bit of a write-up, my name and mug in the paper, the energy to turn that moment into work. Peter and I decided to form our own public-relations company. I imagined I had visibility, the article had given me balls I had to live up to, so I'd front it and Peter would moonlight, supplying the stationery and printing out of his day job's back door. We called it 'Image' and our slogan was 'Feet's Ahead' atop a sketch of two bare feet, akin to the cover that holds this read.

Peter and I scrambled our nuts as to who we'd land as our first client; we'd sent out a hundred-odd enticers to major clothing manufacturers and stores, to no avail; we weren't in the loop. I knew that the owner of Sportique and John Michael – John Michael Ingram – lived in a cul-de-sac off the same Frognal street as Sheila. I reverted to type, knocked on his front door, hustled through it and lucked out. The first gig we got was to design the invitations for a reception at the recently opened John Michael in Bond Street.

Sheila Klein: You can imagine John Michael going, 'Who's this pipsqueak knocking on my door?' You don't knock on the doors of those houses on Frognal and say, 'I'm such and such.' You just don't do it. That's why those people live there.

Angus McGill: John Michael went for smart, casual, expensive but conventional clothes, nice plain sweaters, very nice well-made suits for wealthy young men. He started out with one shop on the King's Road, selling beautiful and expensive shirts. He was very successful.

Chris Stamp, co-manager, the Who: It was John Michael who actually began the trousers. They were like hipsters. He designed these hipsters in incredible toniks, great colours, perfect. Somehow he got the fit right, you could go in and they'd really fit on you tight, they looked fabulous. Wonderful blues and silver toniks. That was John Michael.

ALO: The invitations we designed for the fashion show were written on a shirt cuff peeking out from under a chalk-stripe suit: they were a complete success. John Michael was duly impressed and asked Image to design a brochure for his upcoming Sportique Boutique spring collection. Peter and I went to work tracking down and ripping off all the fashion spreads in recent issues of American *Esquire*, tracing and replacing the American gear with the Sportique gear. We came up with what we considered a genius story-board for the brochure. Entitled 'Sportique Takes a Holiday', the visual narrative followed a film director named 'Ted Wayne', travelling in a T-Bird, traced from the *Esquire* ads, to the South of France, picking up a young blond hitchhiker named Lance wearing 'Sportique's new denim shorts, available in pink, grey and blue at only 59 shillings and sixpence . . .'

We delivered the finished brochure, underwritten by Peter's unsuspecting ad agency, to John Michael. He was more than a tad taken back by the overtly gay sub-plot of the brochure, its drawings and text. Homosexuality was still a criminal offence, and the brochure could appear offensively mocking to John Michael's sensitive showbiz clientele. JM politely sacked us, leaving the matter of payment up in the air on Queer Street.

We may have been down, but before they could even start the count, I went chasing the King of Carnaby Street, John Stephen. He had claimed the schmutter crown when he opened up in 1958. He racked up huge sales by retailing clothes so body-conscious and sexy that it was less of a problem to afford them than to fit into them. I was granted a fifteen-minute a.m. audience.

Glaswegian sped-up elf that Stephen was, he ate me for breakfast and spat me out as he raced towards lunch at a table reserved for him alone. Having single-handedly invented Carnaby Street Inc. in a blaze of youth power, he belittled Image and me for taking up even this much of his time. Luckily, the not-to-be-denied Peter couldn't make the meet – he was attending to his day job. JS was in rapid-fire braveheart flow, informing me he'd rather use a more upmarket ad agency, one already operating in the world he was going to be a part of.

In a matter of a few short years, we would both become tycoons of teen, creators of franchises that the public adored. Stephen's empire included eighteen Mod clothing shops, of which six monopolised the Carnaby street of dreams. Wearing John Stephen's clothes competed with playing guitar or drums as a lad's first real commitment to banddom.

Chris Stamp: Stephen was the guy who took John Michael's ideas and made them successful. John Michael came up with the look at Vince Man's Shop and Adonis, the first two Carnaby Street places. They were poofy, began as gay shops. Queens have always got the jump, right! We thought Carnaby Street when it began was for poofs, it was nonsense. We liked to look slightly androgynous, but that was so geezers would think we were easy to take, then we'd kick 'em. The early Mod thing was always semi-violent and certainly not tolerant of sexual deviancy. The word 'Mod' came from 'Modern Jazz'. We sorta liked Gerry Mulligan, Jimmy Smith and John Coltrane; we weren't that into jazz – it was the look. Subconsciously we knew that blacks had no real power in the States, any more than we did, but their clothes made them look in control, on top, not be messed with. That attitude was why clothes were part of the triad with music and pills for Mods. Musically, we didn't start any revolutions: we were strictly Elvis, doo-wop, American, but not black stuff particularly. In the very early 60s, Stax and that hadn't been recorded yet. All that Tamla Motown influence was a second generation of Mods who got into scooters and rediscovered the look and started to change it.

ALO: Peter Meaden had warned me to stay out of Stephen's way, but I had not heeded him, and got a good common-sense hiding along the lines of 'Be prepared, don't insult and don't hustle a hustler' for my trouble.

Chris Stamp

We moved on to our next entrepreneurial folly. We discovered we could rent our local Hampstead Town Hall free for the evening if it we were fund-raising for a non-profit-making entity. Accordingly, we formed 'The Hampstead Literary Society' to qualify, and booked the Town Hall. Then we began advertising a 'One Night Only Rhythm and Blues Extravaganza'. This was not all-knowing Soho in the West End: this was superficial, out-of-it cappuccino land, whose gullibility I once again counted upon.

The night's entertainment was hardly R'n'B. The first act came 'Direct From Their Successful German Tour', because the bass player had just spent his holidays in Bavaria. Next up were the then Gordon and Peter, who as Peter and Gordon later hit with Lennon and McCartney's 'A World Without Love'. Peter Asher survived that round to become one of the 70s' and 80s' most consistently successful managers and producers. His work with Linda Ronstadt and James Taylor was one of the era's most high-earning, cross-cultural transmigrations.

We managed to end the evening with no R'n'B at all, topping the bill with Marc Conquest (a name that even Larry Parnes had passed on, but then we were 'not for profit'), direct from his successful engagement with Gordon and Peter earlier that same evening – the part of Marc was played by Gordon Waller. The food sold by Gina's Greek restaurateur ma and pa failed to quell the universal demands for refunds as Peter and I skipped out the back door, fifty-seven quid in hand. We moved into the Chelsea Town Hall with the same scam, but we'd forgotten the King's Road was an experienced old

whore, and the scam fell flat on its face, with our Hampstead profit disappearing down Chelsea's drains.

Back at 19 Netherhall Gardens, I tore open an envelope to get to the first
letter addressed to Image. It was from a major American clothes designer,
Emerson Mead Jr, whose first para boasted of twenty-seven retail outlets on
the American East Coast. The letter explained that Mr Mead Jr had been on
a buying trip in London and chanced upon the 'great' 'Sportique Takes a
Holiday' brochure. Were Image interested in designing a brochure for
America? Could the directors meet him in ten days' time – in Liège, Belgium
– to discuss the matter?

'Let us check our schedules,' we joked, 'we can't over-extend.' We
couldn't afford to fly, so we booked on the boat. Pete and I shivered in our
lightweight jazz suits as the bitter cold of winter kicked in on the night ferry
across to Ostend. With only half a ham sandwich and a half-bottle of brandy
to keep us warm, we caught a train to Liège in the morning, arriving in good
time for our meeting in an expensive but antiquated hotel in the city centre.
Liège was decrepit, dull and boring. It could have doubled for Newcastle-
upon-Tyne. After an hour's wait, we checked with hotel registration and
found out there was nobody by the name of Emerson Mead Jr staying with
them. The awful truth began to sink in: we'd been had – revenge, perhaps,
for all the fashion and R'n'B scams we'd pulled back home. The original
letter was a hoax.

During the cold and penniless hitch back to London, we both agreed that
the prospect of continuing as partners in Image was too much. Pete needed
to buckle down to work or risk losing his prestigious job at the advertising
company. Though at the time we were furious, lock-jawed and in to kill, we
both secretly admired the scam. By the time we went our separate ways Peter
knew almost too much for his own good. He was young but close to being
jaded, and couldn't separate the dross from the gold; reality was out of kilter
with his expectations. We said goodbye, taking leave of our good selves till
we met again in 64.

Pete Townshend, songwriter, the Who guitarist: Through Jack the Barber,
we stumbled somewhere along the way into Peter Meaden. We were called
'The Who' when he came in to work with us as a publicist. He worked for

Helmut Gordon, our manager at the time. We were ready to make it as an R'n'B band. We had leather Pierre Cardin jackets that actually made us look like dustmen, but we were a brilliant band and we were gonna make it. Meaden managed to get us to go out briefly as the High Numbers, which was what he had christened us, but he certainly wasn't our manager. Meaden was obsessed with turning us into Mods. He felt that we were close enough for rock 'n' roll, but he had a hard time convincing the other three members of the band. Because of my art-school exposure to Pop, I supported him. In fact, I became a tremendous energy behind him and with him.

Pete Townshend

Unfortunately, by the time he got to us, he was a bit pilled-out. He was still really quite brilliant but he tended to babble his ideas. He was a real holder of court: really enjoying all the loquacious high energy, all the tumbling potentialities he was dying to foist on us and the public. He was starting to get somewhat incomprehensible; he was using his own private language. Words like 'Face', 'Ticket', 'Number', which have passed into mythology – he was the only person I ever heard using them at that time. When I met Peter I was eighteen; he was twenty, I suppose, but he'd put in a lot of time already.

Peter Meaden was very much caught up in a small Soho thing. He thrived as one of the kings of that scenario. I used to walk with him from one dingy little basement full of publicists and magazine writers to another. And as we walked, he'd talk at hyper-speed: 'This is what's happening, man, this is where it's at, this is what's going on, this is what we do . . .' We'd go into a pub, have a quick drink, pop a few more pills, go down to another basement. And in this little kinda – not even square mile – square half-mile between Covent Garden and Dean Street he did all his business. He lived in a basement in Covent Garden.

ALO: Peter went back for a while to New Oxford Street. After experiencing Adams, John Michael, Sportique, R'n'B nights in Hampstead and Chelsea, demoralised by an expensive hoax, I was tired and needed to rest 'between shows'. I met up with a transplanted American teenager, Chris Harris, at a party in Hampstead – he and the attractive Susie Ornstein slumming north from their residences in Belgravia. Chris's father, Leslie Harris, had crossed the Atlantic to become manager of Incorporated Television, the company that made programmes like *Danger Man*, *The Baron*, *Ivanhoe*, *The Saint*, *Robin Hood*, *Four Just Men* and, ultimately, *The Prisoner*. I accepted Chris's gift of friendship and spent my time-out restoring myself in the womb of the to-the-showbiz-manor born.

Incorporated Television Corporation was a subsidiary company of Lew Grade's Associated Television. ATV, as it was better known, had since 1955 been part of Britain's only alternative television channel to the BBC. ITC provided all its episodic adventure needs. Lew was one of three Jewish brothers, who between them built Britain's most protean showbusiness empire. Their influence and business interests stretched above and beyond; their position in entertainment was unassailable. Lew not only owned ATV and ITC, he also owned the Stoll and Moss Empire Variety Pantomime and Summer Season and a rich theatre chain comprising the Palladium, Drury Lane and Her Majesty's, plus fifteen provincial theatres. AP Films, which made *Thunderbirds*, also belonged to Lew Grade, as did 60 per cent of Pye Records.

Lew's brother, Leslie, chose the performers for ATV's finest hour, *Sunday Night at the London Palladium*. He co-owned London Management, London Artists and the Harold Davison Group of agents and impresarios. The client list read like a Who's Who of the showbiz world: Dirk Bogarde, Albert Finney, Laurence Olivier, Ralph Richardson, Julie Christie, Noël Coward, John Gielgud, *et al*. The Davison Group acted as UK reps for Frank

Sinatra, Ella Fitzgerald, Duke Ellington and Count Basie (and soon the Animals, the Dave Clark Five, Lulu and the Hollies). Leslie also had a 50 per cent interest in Elstree Studios, which made, among many others, the Cliff Richard films. The third brother, Bernard Delfont, owned more London theatres, produced shows all over Britain, virtually monopolised the pantomime and summer-season industry and had an interest in London's Talk of the Town nightclub.

I was charmed and fascinated by this Chester Square, Belgravia, view of the world. I looked forward to meeting the Grade Brothers' debonair Yankee import, who was hired to select escapist adventure fare for our clothcap-discarding lower-middle classes, who agreed with their Prime Minister, the Right Honourable Harold Macmillan, that Great Britain had never had it so good. Chris's father looked as if he'd stepped straight off an American movie set, tanned and with immaculately styled grey hair, grey suits and 'elder statesman', striped pin-through, collared shirts. Wool ties, not silk. I slipped into my eccentric cousin Jean-Claude Brialy role from *Les Cousins* quicker than you could say 'left-hand drive' and relaxed with this well-heeled set.

Chris's gal-pal, fellow American Susie Ornstein, was the daughter of Bud Ornstein, who ran United Artists in the UK. It's a small, small world in which there are no accidents: under Ornstein's helm, United Artists would get both the eventual Beatles movies, *A Hard Day's Night* (64) and *Help!* (65). After a first marriage to entrepreneur John Fenton, Susie settled well with Neil Aspinall, who started out as a Beatles roadie and now heads up their ongoing Apple Corp. I had a crush on Chris's black convertible T-Bird and a bigger one on Susie.

Susie Aspinall: I only knew Andrew very briefly and just for that moment. I remember going out with him one night in Hampstead with Marc Bolan when we all got thrown out of a club. Then I was sent away to school in California, and he used to write to me quite a lot. The way he signed his letters was very impressive; my girlfriends in LA at my boarding school used to say, 'My God, is he a Lord or something?' Andrew Loog Oldham . . . y'know.

Sheila Klein: He loved showing off in Chris's car. There were very few cars on the road in Hampstead – maybe every street had one car in it. So to have a car then did stand out. That was some sort of prototype for him, the idea that you gotta have a car, top down, cruising . . .

ALO: Basically I was an all-American boy. From film and TV to songwriting credits, I just wanted to know the stories and motivational factors behind these creators of three-, thirty- or sixty-minute dreams. As regards the three-minute wonders, I had noticed that US songwriters – Goffin/King, Leiber/Stoller, Mann/Weil and Pomus/Shuman – had their names on the labels beneath the titles of an astonishing number of US Top 20 hits. I read up on the famous Brill Building, New York's twenty-four-hour music factory, where hits seemed to fly out the window. The table for this musical feast was set by hosts Don Kirschner and Al Nevins, whose Aldon Music was the first independent power in music publishing. Aldon had its ears on the street and had writers who knew where to put the bomp, young writers who had the talent and suss to take everyday facts and phrases of life and turn them into teen-dream reality; to take us up on the roof and under the boardwalk and create a body of work that exemplified American Pop Art of the moment.

At home, an innovative television series featured Anthony Newley. *The World of Gurney Slade* was an off-the-wall perspective on life directed by one Ken Hughes. Mr Hughes had made his reputation as a reliable director of British B-films in the early 50s. With a feel for American dynamics, Hughes often employed actors with faded stateside marquee value to light up a mundane genre. His Columbia Pictures Paul Douglas starrer, *Joe Macbeth* (1955), a mobster take on the bard, was way ahead of Coppola's later Corleone saga. Ken Hughes, with his ability to flit from pre-Monty Python mirth to Shakespearean mobsters, was a man I just had to meet.

He was in the phone book, living in a flat on Elgin Avenue. I called and he invited me by. I tripped down to his basement pad to be greeted by a bohemian, yellow-grey-haired, mad-professor, *Goon Show* boffin who invited me in for a chat, some biscuits and tea. It was a time when not everybody was a star, and Mr Hughes seemed as pleased by my interest as I was with his openness and candour about the canvas of his life. As with Kenneth Hume, Harold Lang and the others, when I recall these events I may come up short on detail, but I hope I've conveyed the fondness I have for them and the time they gave me.

It was another glimpse of how those special moments conspired to happen: a man's imagination becomes a vision, he works that vision, and his vision becomes the 'reality' of entertainment. I would hurry back to Frognal and Sheila, I would try to describe this wonderful magical world, and I probably did.

Sheila Klein: Andrew blossomed, it was quite incredible. Before, he was really uptight, but he seemed to relax after we started dating. I think it helped Andrew fill out the other half of himself, the half that he hadn't touched base with yet. You could actually see the change in his face, the delight and surprise. He was really happy.

John Douglas: The sweetest and nicest part about Sheila in those days was that she was very good for Andrew, brought to him a warmth that he never had before. She was almost always on the verge of laughter because he amused her so much.

ALO: My mother told me in so many words to shit or get off the pot. She couldn't call Chris Harris a bad influence, but she thought I was a fish out of water, gills pumping, out of my league. In my mother's book you didn't trade classes, so in a sense Mummy took the T-Bird away and Chris with it. Sheila she considered a troublesome distraction, though perhaps competition would have been a better word. It was back to shape up or ship out; buckle down, buckle up; it's time to get normal, get up, go to work, wipe the stars from your eyes and elsewhere. I told her I got the picture. I may have saluted, gifted her with lip service, but I lied. She thought I was sliding way off the rails and told me to stop spending hours with the old vagrant who'd made his abode on the wrought-iron bench outside our house.

· CHAPTER 5 ·

Philip Townsend, photographer/entrepreneur: In Chelsea, the latest chapter in British fashion history was unfolding to international acclaim. *Vogue* was the first magazine to champion the 'Chelsea Set' fashion crowd. This loose collective of upcoming designers, models, stylists, hairdressers and photographers was thought to be sparking a British cultural revolution! The Chelsea Set was made up of an extended tribe of aristocratic Antibes Algernons: John Fenton, Michael Rainey, Michael English, Nigel Weymouth (later to paint John Lennon's psychedelic Roll-Royce), Dandy Kim Waterfield, Edward Langley, Christopher Thynne and brother Valentine (sons of the Marquis of Bath), Michael Alexander (original owner of Alexander's restaurant), Suna Portman (daughter of Lord Portman), Lucia Golding and art-gallery owner Anthony Blond. Their parties and general carryings-on had won them the attention of society columnists too young to have experienced at first hand Evelyn Waugh's *Vile Bodies*. Chelsea competed with Carnaby Street as the headquarters of Swinging London, and its gilded youth was often compared to the 'Bright Young Things' of the 20s. That was the official line fed to the public in order to sell paintings, books, furniture and clothing. In fact, the Chelsea Set were really a gang of lay-abouts who pissed away time in pubs on the King's Road: the Bunch of Grapes, Markham Arms and the Australian.

ALO: Chelsea had come on to my reality radar screen. Since I'd have to appear to be following Celia's direction, I pretended to look for a regular job, 'cause who knows, with her quirkiness I could be out of house and home if I didn't get one. I had seen my mother turn on people, and I didn't want to be one of them. But 'regular' was still the last thing on my mind. It may have seemed that I was busy with the Want-Ads and *Yellow Pages*, but really I was reassessing the King's Road.

At the centre of this chinless Chelsea scene (as shallow in its own way as that of Hampstead Village) was a thriving, industrious and chinful King's Road boutique called Bazaar. Owned by Mary Quant, her husband Alexander Plunkett Greene and their partner, Archie McNair, Bazaar opened on an elegant shoestring in November 1955 and swiftly galvanised the pioneering young things that became their earliest patrons. Bazaar's fashions brought the expressive sexiness that only a few daring women would as yet act out in their bedrooms into an uptight workplace transformed by feminine youth. Mary Quant would give the New Workers their cockney-Chanel non-uniform uniform at a price the suddenly eager shoppers thronging the high streets couldn't resist.

(l to r) Archie McNair, Alexander Plunkett Green, Mary Quant

Vidal Sassoon, crimper and entrepreneur: I always said that the King's Road was Mary's atelier. She had her shop, right there on the King's Road, and it was one marvellous show. You could go to the King's Road, outside Mary Quant's, and there you had the young people – it was wonderful.

You have to remember, from a psychological point of view, what was going on with humanity at the time. We'd come out of a horrendous war. There were still enormous shortages in the 50s and suddenly . . . the 60s . . .

What was so invigorating about that 60s' thing was the innocence. There is a resurgence today of fashion, you know, with all kinds of things going on . . . very pleasant, very nice, but a lot of cynicism goes with it now. In the 60s there was a total innocence, people coming out of two decades of shortages, suddenly earning money of their own, young people with spending power. They wanted to spend it in their own way, and people like Mary were there to lead them. That was the creative part that I found so fascinating about that period, apart from the artistry . . . the artistry of course was there, and the meritocracy. The meritocracy . . . that's what came from that period.

Alexander was the most bizarre, wonderful character. A personality that was just beyond. Just beyond, an absolute delight. Totally bright, he knew exactly what he was doing. There were no accidents with Alexander . . .

However, part of the innocence, part of the charm – and I don't think anyone truly understood it at the time – was that our feelings preceded rational thoughts, and we made our choices from the gut. That's what I think London was all about.

ALO: The Quant Look came to be topped off by the strikingly functional and sexy statement that Vidal Sassoon brought to hair. Iconised by photographers Bailey, Donovan and Duffy, Quant's empire was the one true manifestation of pop in the years between the archetypal rock 'n' roll of the mid-50s and its eventual second coming with the Beatles in the mid-60s. Quant was naturally the place I wanted to be. I learnt that the Bazaar business office was at the back of Ives Street, close to Draycott Avenue. Nervously I knocked on the door; it was opened with kindness, and suddenly I was in.

When you're on, you're just blind, going through it, getting the job done, so you don't actually remember the moment, though you'd better be in it.

Vidal Sassoon   Mary Quant and Alexander
                                    Plunkett Green

That's why it's difficult to remember what I said when I walked in. Hopefully I listened, I doubt it. I can remember the rehearsal, and I can remember arriving. The next thing I remember is leaving Archie's office, and *voilà* . . . I had the job.

Well before 1963 changed the face of music as we knew it for ever, Britain had already got a pop business – fashion. This new rock entrepreneur took those established freedoms and applied them within the limited safe world of the music business, where they appeared innovative. Six months after leaving school, qualified to do zip, I was suddenly out of the slum and way ahead of the pack. I'd been very lucky. That's why, for me, Quant Ltd was such great training, because at first fashion was *the* fashion, then fashion became music. So I had a head start on those of my peers who remained in Soho.

I helped Mary dress the windows, which was my training for record-cover design. I poured drinks for journalists, which made me realise liquid can become print. I walked the dogs of famous models, which taught me how to handle stars – and I learnt how to throw parties. It was amazing to watch. The three of them, Mary, Alexander and Archie, were in total tandem. They didn't need words and when they did use them, so very well, they could finish each other's sentences. And there was love, and it was apparent. In their own fashion, the Quant trio were very disciplined, but they really improvised the whole thing. I will always thank Mary, Archie, Alexander and Vidal Sassoon – whom I spent much time watching as he changed the shape of hair for ever – for teaching me about fame, fashion, money and how to have fun getting it done.

I got my next press, following the Angus McGill piece, due to this madras suit I'd had made at Burton's and copped from one of Alexander Plunkett Greene's. I was chatting up Iris Ashley of the *Daily Mail* one day, complaining about how madras creased, and she wondered how I could afford what to her looked like a fifty-guinea suit. Was I using the same Savile Row tailor as Alexander? I explained about the Burton's deal, which put no proviso on style or material. We laughed about the argument I'd had in there when I requested my suit-to-fit be made out of madras. Eventually I'd even got them to make madras-covered buttons. She sent a photographer down to Bazaar to photograph me, and the next week it was all over her fashion page in the *Daily Mail*: 'The Boy Who Beat Burton's'.

Archie McNair: He was very pushy when he walked in. He was quite a dandy, and carried a cane with a silver top. He just didn't believe that we wouldn't take him on, which is quite a help actually. He had tremendous self-belief, I think because he didn't quite understand that there could be another side to it, that he might not be wanted.

Alexander Plunkett Greene and I started Bazaar in 1955. We put up the money between us in equal shares. After about three or four years we gave Mary a third, so we were all equal. They were engaged, but they got married after that. Alexander's passion was for jazz; he played the trumpet.

My wife and I owned a building on the King's Road, no. 128. We lived at the top of that. I was a photographer at that time so I had my studio there, and I turned the bottom part into a coffee bar. When Alexander said to me, 'I'd love to start a business with you', we looked at one or two coffee-bar ideas, then he said, 'Look, what we really want to do – what Mary and I would like to do – is to start a clothes shop,' and I said, 'Okay.'

Mary Quant: Archie was an ex-solicitor who had fallen in love with Chelsea life but still retained the rather precise and pedantic way of expressing himself that one associates with lawyers. He seemed oddly out of place in his own photographic studio, and this in itself was ironic, as it was there that the whole Chelsea revolution was conceived. It was odd, too, because it was he who rationalised the mood in the air. The coffee bars, the restaurants and even Bazaar would not have happened if he had not spotted the talent of the people who sat around in his studio drinking his coffee. Nor would they have happened without his flair for property and his knowledge of the law and business. When we first met him, he was just about to open a coffee bar on the King's Road – the second coffee bar in London, I think – and he invited Alexander to go in with him as his partner. At that time Alexander and I both thought of coffee bars as short-lived, flash in the pan . . . a craze that would be over and done with in six months, so Alexander refused. Many a time since we have regretted this. Archie's coffee bar was called 'The Fantasy' and, immediately after opening, became known and crowded every night. It became the centre of the social life of Chelsea. The whole Chelsea thing really brewed up there . . . between the Fantasy, Finch's pub and Archie's studio.

Archie McNair: I knew we needed a shop between Sloane Square and the Town Hall on the sunny side of the King's Road. When we opened, in October 55, John Michael's parents gatecrashed the opening party and went through all our labels, and as they went out I heard her saying to him, 'That's all right, no problem', because they were worried, of course. But we knew him, John Michael, as just 'the boy'; then he grew up and opened his own shop.

The King's Road was very, very quiet when we started. The Beatons had a bakery, there was a sweet shop, tobacconist, a few cosy dining rooms. It was all very local, but I just felt in my guts that the King's Road was going to take off.

We bought the place in Ives Street, our headquarters, where Mary still is, in 1958. That's where Andrew came and knocked on the door. We had two shops then, one on the King's Road and a relatively new one in Knightsbridge. We were trying to make clothes to supply both shops and we hadn't got the space. I went looking for a factory between Knightsbridge and the King's Road where we could make clothes, and so I found Ives Street.

Vidal Sassoon wasn't anything to do with us, but – rather like Terence Conran and those lovely photographers like David Bailey, Norman Parkinson, John Cowan, Brian Duffy and Terence Donovan – we were all sort of doing something and breaking the rules, and so forth. I don't know if Vidal was really part of the Chelsea society, but certainly Mary was very keen on getting her hair done there. In the end she said, 'Why don't you go there? Why don't the boys go there?' I think he was in Sloane Street then. I remember he came to have a chat with me about expanding his business.

We also owned Alexander's Restaurant. When we started, it was just a basement underneath the King's Road Bazaar and we didn't know what to do with it. We tried to make it into a restaurant and the Chelsea Society wouldn't have that, so we had to call it a coffee bar. We put in a coffee machine but it was basically still a restaurant. Everybody came to it; it was word of mouth, but all the interesting people, like the Oliviers and some royalty – they all came and we never gave their names to the press, so they respected that. We even had the Rainiers, Grace Kelly and so forth, all sorts; the Duke of Kent used to come. We sold it to the staff after three years because I got so busy I just couldn't manage it.

Roughly what we said to each other was, 'Mary designs, Alexander promotes and I do all the rest.' In fact I was the Chairman of the group of all the companies for thirty-three years. I actually planned the business; when it came to licensing, it was my idea. I had a tremendous row with Mary about it. I said, 'We're going to sell that factory' – we had two factories by this time. 'We're going out of clothes production; you're a designer and you're going to design. You can have eight machinists and two cutters and one workroom manager, and that's it.' She kept to that all the rest of our working life.

It was a very good move because we weren't doing very well; the name was good but we weren't making much money. It suddenly occurred to me that all we needed was a piece of paper and a pencil – in other words our business was based on Mary's designs. So I said to her, 'It means you can design anything you like, you don't have to stick to clothes.' So we went into cosmetics, we went into hosiery, we signed contracts with all sorts of people. I was a lawyer, so I was able to write contracts. I just sat on an aeroplane and went around the world doing that. We were the first to license goods worldwide; Cardin copied us in that sense, copied the idea – did it much better, but we started it. We used to say to each other, 'Money is the applause.' If you do something well, if you make dresses people want, money is the applause.

Mary Quant: I started agonising over the clothes I wanted to design for the collection with which we would open Knightsbridge Bazaar. Time flew. The day came. The new Bazaar was opened to the public. The day after, Clare Rendlesham stormed in. She marched around the shop, looking at everything. Then she turned on me. 'What do you mean opening a shop like this and not telling me about it? How could you do such a thing! Have any of the fashion girls seen these clothes?' Clare was working for *Vogue*. Pat Cunningham [Charles Creed's wife] was the fashion editor, but Clare used to rush around and find out everything that was new. Clare hardly gave us time to get a word in that day. At last we did manage to tell her that we would like to give a press party very much indeed, but we did not really know the right people to ask. Clare helped us. She really got us organised.

We managed to persuade nine of the top photographic girls to model the clothes for us. There are stairs at the back of the shop leading to a small sort of gallery room. The models dressed up here and as they danced – literally danced – down the open stairway, a wind machine caught up their skirts and blew them this way and that to create an even greater sense of speed and movement. This was really a development of all I had learnt at the Palace Hotel in Saint-Moritz. We had the right jazz music taped specially so there would be no gap in the music. We showed forty garments in fourteen minutes and every single minute was packed with incident. We were showing knee-high cowboy boots worn with fantastically short skirts; high-waisted tweed tunic suits with tweed knickerbockers; Norfolk jackets lavishly trimmed with fox collars. One girl carried an enormous shotgun; another swung a dead pheasant triumphantly round her head. Perhaps too triumphantly, because the poor thing thawed out in the heat of the place and blood began spurting out all over the newly painted walls, even over some of the journalists. Then we showed party dresses. The girls came whizzing down the stairs, an outsized glass of champagne in one hand, and floated round as if they had been to the wildest party or looked dreamily intellectual, with a copy of Karl Marx or Engels in the other hand.

Clare was determined that we should meet all the top fashion writers. She kept on saying, 'No one has ever shown clothes in this way before. It is revolutionary. We must let everyone know about it.' The next day she brought Iris Ashley in to see us, and soon afterwards Iris gave us our first full-page editorial in the *Daily Mail*. Alexander says it was Clare Rendlesham who inspired us, Iris Ashley who made us known to the masses and Ernestine Carter who gave us the accolade of respectability. She gave us a whole page in *The Sunday Times*. And for the next few years a whole series of pages punctuated by small pieces and pictures of our latest stuff. Her interest in us culminated in *The Sunday Times* Award, which was given to me for 'jolting England out of its conventional attitude towards clothes'.

ALO: The Bazaar shop in Knightsbridge was run with nutty style by Susie Leggatt. She had originally managed the King's Road store and was the original Quant girl, a notorious, beautiful creature. She had a quality that drew you to her: I loved her, so did the rest of our world. Susie had a heart of gold and helped make me feel a part of the wonderful Quant family.

Five months out of school, I'd jobbed up, lucked out and was in the middle of a movement. Seven pounds a week and an education. My mother was pleased, and I was in heaven. I wanted the excitement of the Quant day to extend into the evening and take up my weekends, too. It was an addiction to a rarefied air. Before Sheila could say 'no', I'd arranged an appointment for her to see a top model agency. Next came a cut from Vidal Sassoon and a photographic session with Crispian Woodgate.

Sheila Klein: Then on the morning of the appointment with the model agency, when I went round to his mother's to meet him, he'd suddenly changed his mind. He didn't want me to be a model any more. There was no discussion; he just locked me in the cupboard and he wouldn't let me out. That was the end of my modelling career. Andrew definitely was different. His way of handling a situation was very effective.

ALO: I had begun to become more aware of my black moods, relentless unexplainable depressions that would always arrive to hack into any elation at life's good turns. I made up for it with front-row seats to see the Everly Brothers, backed by the impeccable Crickets, on opening night at the New Victoria. I'd never heard anybody duplicate their records so smoothly on-stage: they may have been singing to the audience, but for me they were singing to each other. At Bazaar the next day Susie Leggatt was eager to share the juicy rumour that Don and Phil were enjoying the ministrations of the era's most notorious society quack, New York physician Max Jacobson. Despite the new liveliness I'd noted in the boys' expressions on recent album covers, I cannot say with any accuracy if the brotherly buns received the short sharp shock of Max's liquid life force. If they had, they would have been in the same club as myself, Brian Jones, JFK and Alan Jay Lerner. The good doctor's license was eventualy revoked, another 60s casualty for the list.

Mary Quant: One day Andrew confided to Archie McNair's wife, Cathy, that he could do any of our jobs standing on his head, Archie's included. Cathy asked him what he did. 'Well,' he said, 'when Mary's a bit tired, I design a few dresses for her; when Alexander is choosing stock, I chat up the press for him. I could do it just as well on my own. It's easy!'

I can hardly talk of Susie, even now. Susie Leggatt was one of the first people we ever employed. She was one of the most beautiful girls I have ever seen: she had 'the look' ten years ahead of her time; she had a terrific influence on me. Susie first joined us at Chelsea Bazaar at a time when we were – as usual – short of money. We were terribly involved with plans for the opening of the Knightsbridge shop at the time and we needed someone to look after the King's Road for us, especially as I wanted to spend most of my time in the workrooms. Susie came in to see us with a friend of ours, Peter Sterry. She wasn't looking. She was, in fact, a deb and a cracking snob! She just thought it might be rather jolly to work for a couple of weeks. As it turned out, she enjoyed it all so much, and we became such friends, that she was with us for nearly three years.

Susie was neurotic. Always handing in her resignation and prancing out; she had one hopeless love affair after another and at these times would create the most ghastly scenes. But she was so wonderful that she contributed endlessly to the building of the character of Bazaar. She just seized on the ideas I was producing and knew immediately how to wear them. She had the look and the style and the arrogance that fitted in exactly with my clothes. She was the first to wear black leather boots up to the crotch; the first to wear black stockings with our black leather coats trimmed with black fox-fur collars. To see the clothes I was making being worn by someone like Susie, with such incredible panache, gave me just the encouragement – and incentive – I needed. Susie leapt on every new idea the instant I produced it. She had the nerve to wear it straight away. She looked so beautiful wearing 'the look' that other people were encouraged to try.

She seemed to know everybody in London. Friends of hers were constantly filling the shop: some of them chic and smart and beautiful; others the worst dregs of the rich social classes. She knew all the young model girls. When we opened Bazaar in Knightsbridge, Susie Leggatt took over and had six, sometimes eight, girls working with her, mostly debs and ex-debs like herself. All these girls wore high black leather boots, black stockings and black leather coats. People began to queue to get into the shop, just as they had done on the King's Road. The girls really put 'the look' across. They developed 'the cult', helped to some extent by the very enterprising young Andrew, who called himself my assistant-cum-window-dresser-cum-everything-else. He had just left school, but he had all the confidence in the world. Archie thought he was a very bright boy and did a lot to encourage him.

Archie McNair: Andrew used to run around with the delivery van. We were always ferrying clothes from Ives Street, which was where they were all delivered and held in stock, to the shops. He just thought he could do everything, which was nice, it was what attracted me to him . . . he'd got a lot of charm. In a kind of way he was ridiculous, but he was great fun. So I warmed to him. I think I had more to do with him than anybody else; I took him on, for instance. I don't think he was actually that interested in how the business was run, I think he simply assumed that it was easy and he could do it better. He was very young, and I can well imagine how it looked to him. Well, then, everything looked like that to him. That's why he did so well; he just sort of didn't accept that he couldn't do it.

There was just something about him that made it worth while to try and understand his dream and sympathise with it. I think we all saw him for what he was, this young man who'd got this wonderful idea of himself, and it was very intriguing. He used to come to me in the evening because I always worked very late – I was a workaholic, I suppose. He'd come up and talk to me. He was ambitious . . . very ambitious. I remember saying to him, 'Oh, come on, Andrew, why haven't you done that?' And he said, 'Oh, I haven't had time. Why can't somebody else do it? Why can't Mary do it? She's only sitting in that little office down there drawing.' But he was great fun. He wasn't important, in the sense that he was quite peripheral to the mainstream of our activities, but he was important to himself and he was interesting from that point of view to us. Alexander, Mary and I, we used to say to each other, 'Do you know what he's done now?' It was a lovely dream that he had, and it was working to a great extent. We liked him very much, we all loved him. There was a sort of clown element about him, which was nice; he was entertaining. He was all over the top.

ALO and Mary Quant working on the window display at Bazaar

ALO: Working for Mary Quant and Co. was akin to being on the right movie. They knew they had recognised the right moment and turned a London 'cult' into a worldwide success, retaining control through independent production. I was getting an education and call to arms that would cause and effect my later work with the Stones and Immediate Records. It was amazing, there was a joy to work. The morning walk from Knightsbridge tube station would oft be pleasured up as I approached Ives Street to a good-morning honk 'n' wave from Alexander and Mary arriving in their brash, open two-seater gold Renault. The teacups were thin, the carpets were thick, the banter productive and life did not end up on the cutting-room floor.

After a Bazaar day I'd invariably end up pacing Soho, rather than head home to Hampstead. Sheila was studying for finals and we'd catch up with each other on the weekend. I'd forgo Soho for home when the tube showed *Johnny Staccato*, which starred John Cassavetes. Cassavetes would take his *Staccato* pay cheque and start a virtual American New Wave of his own with his 1961 directorial début, *Shadows*. Elmer Bernstein's cool Capitol diskery single evoked a stylish jazz-gangster New York for me, where private eye Johnny Staccato solved cases from his office in a basement jazz club.

Staccato-inspired, I started to hang around Ronnie Scott's, the famous Soho jazz club on Gerrard Street, taking stock of the customers and musicians passing in and out of the club. The musos were all very 'cool', oft dressed in clothes from Austin's, reeking of the influential *Man with the Golden Arm* and *The Sweet Smell of Success*. Alternative garb were African root-suits, the very best of your heritage courtesy of the Edgware Road.

I wanted in. Pete King, Ronnie Scott's partner, answered my call. I didn't bore him with the Quant details but cut to the chase: 'Was there any work available?' That's how I got everything. There was no word of mouth or anything. It was like, 'Where do I want to work?' Then I went and banged on the door.

Pete King: Andrew was our first waiter. There was Ronnie and myself, a secretary, a barmaid behind the coffee bar and one cashier, and that was it. Our club held about ninety people officially. We were in Gerrard Street from 59 to 66. Andrew just came knocking on the door. He was what we were, modernists. He was very pleasant, a guy dressed in a modern way from Austin's in Shaftesbury Avenue. Austin's used to get a small importation of the real thing – that's what Andrew liked, what we all liked. He was great,

Pete King and Ronnie Scott

Andrew. He was a very good guy to have around. Don't forget, it was new to him, but the whole thing was new to us as well.

We needed a waiter, so what did we have to lose? He could only deliver or not deliver, and he delivered. Anybody that came into the organisation came into a small family business, and he always will be part of the family, because he was in at the start. He was rather an unusual young man, but unbeknownst to him he happened to walk into a very good group of people, a group of people who had their minds set to do what they wanted to do. We had no idea that the club would last for forty years.

I remember him vividly, charging around the small room. We opened in 59 and for the first year or so we had no alcohol licence. It was obvious that we had to go that way because there was no room to dance, and people who were gonna sit down, they wanted to sit down with a drink. So to get a licence we had to be able to supply a certain amount of cooking. Before we had the kitchen going we used to advertise Indian food, so anybody who wanted a meal, we'd nip over the road and bring it back for them.

Ronnie was a prominent musician and I was in his band as a saxophone player. The band was very, very successful. It was well respected worldwide. Once we'd got around the union situation, and the problem of allowing Americans to come in to play at the club – all the paraphernalia of documentation from ministries and unions – we then proceeded with about fifteen different guest performers; the first one was American saxophone player Zoot Sims.

It was a tremendous time musically, a breakthrough for somebody who was interested in jazz music, because nowhere had there been any American jazz performers being allowed to play in England. Ronnie Scott's was a new development; there was an opportunity for Americans to play London in a club setting instead of a concert. At that stage we used to book 'em for four weeks. So for an American musician to get a gig at the club for four weeks, it was something. The word soon got around the American side, and guys who were over here would look in.

In those day I think we paid them about $300 a week. The customers would be paying about half a crown – two shillings and sixpence (about twenty-five pence). What we used to do was two shows, eighty thirty till eleven, then clear the club and reopen again from midnight till three. That was on Fridays and Saturdays. The club was opened specifically to develop our own playing. In those days there were very few musicians who could earn a living playing jazz – if any. You earned your money being in a dance band and touring. Consequently you'd play the same music every night, and that wasn't very healthy for the development of your own playing in a jazz sense. For those who wanted to be jazz musicians it was no good at all. Ronnie had seen the clubs in America and the young music which was bebop and was now coming into fashion. We as musicians had to try and study it from a harmonic and a rhythmic point of view; it was a development where we wanted to go, where we'd like our playing to go.

So the only way to do that was to open some place where we could play ourselves. That was really how the club started. The hard-drug scene came from America, got a small hold among a certain amount of musicians, some jazz players. But it moved on, it got more into the rock 'n' roll business in a very short while. So much so that now the jazz business is particularly clean, very clean.

We used to know the Rolling Stones before the club. There was an organisation called National Jazz something or other, Harold Pendleton used to run it with his wife, and they had a building in Greek Street where they used to put on these guys. I don't know if they were on as a band then, or whether they were on in different bands and just about to get together. I remember going there with Ronnie on a few occasions, just drifting in. There wasn't really much there for us, so we used to leave. Nothing much musically, we'd gone a bit past where they were . . .

Jazz had been in Soho for a long time, and rock 'n' roll came in as a new thing. So places like the 2Is . . . I used to live above the 2Is, so I knew the guys who owned it very well. Rock 'n' roll and the 2Is' music was sort of a poor man's coming into the music scene. It was rather disconcerting to young jazz players when rock 'n' roll came on the scene, and it put a lot of guys off, because there they were studying their instruments and all of a sudden a music came on the scene where, if you were game enough to learn two or three chords on a guitar and dye your hair blond, you could stand up on the stage and earn a lot of money. That was objectionable to a lot of jazz musicians because it was a put-down, really.

Soho was great at that particular time. Soho was like coming into an Italian-cum-French-cum-English small village, where there were watch repairers, greengrocers, delicatessens and the odd small coffee bar. It was not quite a red-light area, but it was a naughty area, and it was great. There were business girls on the streets, but then I personally prefer those times to now. What's happened is the small business people, like the watch repairers and the greengrocers, have got pushed out because the rents are so high that the only way rents could be paid was through the sex business, which took over for many years.

That's now been slowly pushed aside and the place is full of restaurants and coffee bars again . . .

ALO: Straight from work at Bazaar, I caught the no. 19 or 22 red double-decker bus (Upstairs Plleezze!) from the King's Road to Shaftesbury Avenue. I worked at Ronnie Scott's from seven till midnight throughout the week and till 1 a.m. on Saturdays. I checked coats on the cloakroom, showed people to their seats and brought in food for the patrons from the Indian restaurant over

the road. The music I got to hear live at Ronnie Scott's was world-class –
Ahmad Jamal, Les McCann, Dizzy Gillespie, Thelonious Monk – and one
musician who made a lasting stylistic impression.

Harold McNair was an alto flute player in his own quintet. He was so
cool, he was super-cool, with a smooth American edge to him. He simply
beamed. In his houndstooth suit he evoked and matched Miles Davis posing
in his raglan-sleeve, one-button houndstooth jacket for a fashion layout in
Esquire. Harold beamed, he was just there. He played so well and he knew
how to handle the spaces.

Pete King: Harold McNair *was* super-cool, yes, he was; regretfully he's not
with us any more. He was a West Indian, Trinidadian guy; he was a white
kinda Trinidadian guy. All the coloured guys used to call him Little G.

Mary Quant: When Andrew was working at Ronnie Scott's he'd ring and let
us know if some American jazz musician was in for the night. Alexander and
I would leap out of bed and jump into a taxi.

Vidal Sassoon: Ronnie and Pete King were old mates. We were very much
into the big jazz thing, you know, Kenny Lynch's club with Annie Ross and
Ronnie Scott's club. When I was apprenticed – and you are going back to
1942, the war was on – my Beatles and Stones were Duke Ellington and
Count Basie. Tony Bennett, when I asked him which one he preferred, said,
'Vidal, one is the sun and one is the moon.' By the time the Beatles and
Stones came along, I was in my thirties and I was well into the whole jazz
thing – very heavy for jazz, still am.

ALO: I can't even recall what the wages at Ronnie's were or what the tips
amounted to. It didn't matter, I was having the time of my life. Every night I
went to work knowing I might experience greatness, and I often did. Down
the block from Ronnie Scott's on Lower Wardour Street, Rik and John
Gunnell hosted late nights at the Flamingo. I signed on for the after-midnight
shift. John was on the door at the Flamingo and Rik's wife used to work with
me behind the burger stand. There was no drinks licence, so we'd serve the
Scotch in Coke bottles. A great old Soho character called Gypsy Larry

warned us if the fuzz were coming in to raid, though I think the police sometimes called ahead as well.

The three jobs would eventually get to me. I didn't miss a social life, for work was very social and the run proved to me that this life I had dreamt of existed. It functioned every day, it got up, it went to sleep and it was for real. It was possible. Mary Quant was just doing what came naturally; she, Alexander and Archie got up and worked at it, that's why they succeeded. Ronnie Scott and Pete King were devoted to their club and the music. None of the people I was working for gave me a headache. They stood up for what they were in front of. I was very lucky that all the people I worked for had that advantage in life. I never met anybody who moaned. Everybody was very happy. They were all doing what they wanted to do.

My mother resigned herself to Bazaar; after all, I had gone out and got a regular job, but when I added the night gigs she exploded and accused me of treating her flat like a hotel. I rented a room at the bottom of the hill on the lower end of Frognal and moved out. John Douglas, my Wellingborough partner, came down from Northampton to try his hand at London. It was only one block from my mother's house. The flat had a gas meter and I couldn't handle that – putting money in the thing for heat. Also, I could see my mother's house from the flat. After about three months I moved back. I didn't move out of home again until I moved in with Mick and Keith.

Sheila Klein: It was huge dark room with a gas fire and they had their beds separated by a curtain that you drew across, as if they were in hospital. Andrew was very keen on that place because it was near Tony Meehan's, that Shadow, who was performing with Andrew's idol, Jet Harris.

ALO: The work schedule was getting me a little nuts. I was sleeping four or five hours and going full out the rest of the day. I wanted to be able to see Sheila in my schedule. One evening I went round to her house and was angrily informed by Dr Klein that his daughter was not allowed out until she had finished the washing up. I got furious, pulled out a starting pistol I carried, shoved it in the good doctor's forehead and instructed him to 'Analyse this!' I was losing it somewhat . . .

Sheila Klein: I couldn't impress his mother – nothing was ever good enough for her, she wanted him to have a proper job. And he couldn't impress my father.

Archie McNair: As I remember his leaving, Andrew simply put a note under my office door. I'd had a meeting with him that evening. The note said, 'Sorry to let you down. I'm off to the South of France.' I just thought, 'Oh, he's abandoned all this and he's opting for a more interesting life.' He shouldn't have done that really, he shouldn't have just said goodbye to me like that, because I'd done an awful lot for him. That's youth, I suppose. I felt a bit put down. I had given him a lot of help.

It didn't do me any harm, because it was by virtue of the talks that I used to have with Andrew that I became a Samaritan. For instance, he was upset that he'd knocked his mother down some stairs, that sort of thing. We spent days on that. It was just the sort of work one did in the Samaritans. I remember Andrew being very, very upset . . . I didn't know what was the matter. In the end it came out, he'd had a tremendous physical row with his mother and he was very upset with himself about having lost his cool. I was quite interested in the whole business of trying to help someone who was having a tough emotional time.

ALO: When I first read Archie's voice, I was taken aback by his reference to my abusing my mother. I don't recall the incident he speaks of, and cannot imagine that Celia would have tolerated such behaviour and allowed me to live under her roof. I have a Polaroid in my mind of the cramped first-floor bathroom of Netherhall Gardens, which has one of us in the bath and me screaming. Did I strike her? I was certainly capable of speaking to her so abusively that violence was done. In that Polaroid I can recall being repulsed by her flesh. It doesn't surprise me that I would suppress the memory of this traumatic walk on the wild side. I do remember appreciating Archie's solicitude.

Mary Quant: Suddenly, entirely unexpectedly, we got a note from Andrew on Bazaar writing paper. It was a formal letter of resignation posted at the airport as he was leaving the country. Archie heard of him a little later when he was apparently trying to get a job on *Time* magazine and the editor telephoned to find out whether anyone as young as Andrew could possibly have done all the things he claimed to have done.

ALO: Six months of juggling three jobs had exhausted me. I was burnt out and getting irrational, rude as well. Del Shannon was number one with 'Runaway'. I guess that's what I was about. I packed a suitcase, tied a Union Jack around it, hitch-hiked and boated my way out of England, heading for the South of France. I left letters of regret and departure, thanking all and promising I would return . . .

CHAPTER 6

ALO: Marc Gebhard had sent me a postcard urging me to come to where the action was. He bragged about meeting the actress, Shirley Anne Field – and why not, so would I years later – and into this I read a life on the game, Marc's great looks giving him gigolo potential.

I'd taken the ferry to Calais and train to Paris, intending to hitch from there to the Med, but dressed in a lime-green angora sweater, jodhpurs, riding boots, a Sherlock Holmes deer-stalker hat and a Union Jack flag around my suitcase, I was attracting the wrong kind of attention. Somehow I ended up in the bad part of an Arab district on the outskirts of Paris and spent a tense few hours. I was not assaulted physically, although my costume might have said that I was asking for it. And as eyes can suggest and undress you in a most disturbing way, I was glad to find the freeway south.

It was 5 a.m. and raining, there were six lanes of howling traffic, none of it stopping for me except the cops. The policeman was kind and explained that I was breaking the law – you were not allowed to solicit rides on France's finest roads. He realised I was hungry, tired from the journey and my near-miss in the Arab section. He had a heart and drove me to his *Clockwork Orange* industrial flat-block. He woke up his wife and had her cook me breakfast, which I gratefully wolfed down, chased by strong black tea as the sun was coming up. The good *gendarme* drove me another mile to his precinct and parked me in a cell for an hour while he did the day's paperwork. Then it was back to the freeway. The cop stopped all cars going south, and to the one that was going the furthest he said, 'Please take him.' And she did, not only into her Mercedes but also to her bed, once in Lyons. And that's how I got through France.

It was a time that allowed for kindness: the breakfast, that Mercedes, that bed. It was before drugs, terrorism, sex with children and sex with the dead. Nowadays the cop could not trust me and I'd probably be stoned. Neither could the kind lady risk teaching me some *amour*, for fear that one of us had another agenda. Now not much remains that pure.

I arrived in Saint-Tropez two days after playing Laurence Harvey to my Simone Signoret in *Room at the Top*. I found Marc Gebhard living in a tent on the outskirts of town, so we rolled up the tent and headed for it. The colours, textures, people and the very air of Saint-Tropez are life-giving. They make you feel very well. But, as the light turned to night, our first reel of jet-set life was changed to a second one that was much less fun. We had no villa to hide away and rest in; Marc and I found ourselves stranded on the lonely, narrow alleyways of Saint-Tropez. We were promptly arrested for vagrancy and spent the night locked in a fish market with a police guard, as the jail was full. The stench of fish was awful. You had to sleep in this dirty tunnel with a cop at both ends. They really were teaching you a lesson – get out of town.

Marc Gebhard: We were caught because he went into a hotel to have a shit. We were picked up by the cops and spent the night in prison charged with vagrancy. We were both well-educated, middle-class boys from London; we were slung in a very ancient prison like a dungeon; there was just a bucket where you pissed and shit. Awful.

ALO: The days were great. You didn't need money – you were among it. Enjoying the play of sun and water, it's almost as if some of it rubs off. Anyway a hunk of bread and cheese was all you'd need in Saint-Tropez till the night. The second time we got locked up in the fish market, I persuaded Marc it was time to move on. I was sure we could hustle the streets somewhere else for a loaf of bread without this nightly cattle call for the hotel-less.

In Cannes, there were more Brits and we didn't stick out. Begging was part of the action; most of them drew their Picassos on the pavement for their daily bread. My art was the gift of gab, so I rehearsed a good story, then started to beg.

In my best public-school accent – even my mother would have been proud – I vultured the Croisette's circumcised and wealthy. Marc, who just couldn't allow his handsome fce to look hungry, stood off to one side. 'Excuse me, but my allowance hasn't arrived yet from my mother and I haven't eaten; if you could lend me ten francs and tell me what hotel you're staying at, I'll get it straight back to you.'

Enough people believed me for us to get by – and why not, it was true. I met an interesting bunch of characters while out on my daily schmooze: the TV-directing Adonis, Mike Mansfield; our own diminutive King of Mirth, Arthur Askey; Alex Strickland, the record-store owner, who gave me good and kindly counsel about my future in his biz. All gave me a look that said, 'You should know better', but they still gave up the price of a meal and a grin. And they all remembered me in later years when our paths happened to cross. I'd also often cop Larry Parnes and Lionel Bart cruising the Croisette, enjoying their limelight, starring and strolling successfully between lunch and tea.

Lionel Bart: Cannes on the Croisette – to tell the story I have to drop some names. I was there when I first started getting famous. I'd gone from writing hit singles to composing stage musicals, the first of which, *Oliver!*, had just opened in London. It ran for 2,600 performances in the West End alone.

Pablo Picasso was taking me to lunch. We were walking along to the restaurant and this young red-headed guy, about sixteen, says, 'Excuse me, you're . . .' He recognised me. In those days I wasn't quite used to being recognised, but he was a pretty astute kid. I thought he was on the game. I thought he was a rent boy, an English rent boy. He gave me this cock-and-bull story about how his parents had stranded him there and he needed to raise the fare to get back to England, so would I lend him money? I gave him about £30, quite a lot then, and my phone number and address in London.

A bit later in the day, I'm having lunch with Picasso. It's one of these places that have paper tablecloths. The waiter would draw on the cloth what you were eating: a fish, a haddock, a plaice. It was all very rough and ready, but I loved it. We're looking out on the big Croissette and there was Andrew accosting all-comers. Picasso smilingly said, *'Regarde ton ami'* and then we counted how much money he picked up on this scam. After lunch we went back to him and said, 'We were watching, you're doing well, boy. Can I have my £30 back? Thank you. Gimme a call nevertheless when you're back in London; you're a hustler and I think maybe you'll get on somewhere . . .'

ALO: You can only hustle the same corner for so long. Tucked behind the main drag was Jimmy's, a bar that was wall-to-wall photos of Alain Delon, Jean Gabin, Edith Piaf, Yves Montand and La Bardot. I strolled over to Jimmy's, trolled in, ordered a soda and came on coy, carefree and gay. Within thirty minutes I got picked up. Once inside the guy's apartment, he served me a drink and made his move.

He attempted to kiss me, and I smelt his repugnant, garlic-infested breath. I didn't mind eating garlic, but I drew the line at being kissed by it. I pulled away and the French guy knew something was wrong, but then I made *my* move. I worked the young innocent boy in an old poof's apartment: pay up or I'll call the law. He didn't have much in readies, and his clothes were awful and wouldn't have fit. The guy was cowering on the floor, squealing, 'Take what you like but don't hurt me.' I kicked the old poof in the stomach, left with 120 francs in hand, a bad taste in my mouth, and a cruel and criminal act on my conscience.

So many of England's finest had invited me into their homes, entertained, educated and improved me, without so much as putting a pinkie finger on my knee, and I repaid my debt of gratitude to this way of life with thuggery and violence . . . once was one time too many.

Marc moved back to happier stomping grounds in Saint-Tropez. I decided to stay in Cannes and rented a room, continuing to hustle the Croisette three or four times a week, which prevented overkill, allowed me to rotate into a fresh batch of tourists, eat and pay the rent. My new pal and room-mate was an ex-American soldier, Pete Fanning, who'd fought in Korea and was now drifting around the world. He showed me a suitcase full of marijuana, which he'd bought in Morocco. I'd seen people under the influence but I'd never seen the farm. Pete wouldn't actually let me smoke anything, but I couldn't help but get high with the help of my friend, as he sucked on his spliffs and grinned. Pete would spliff, grin and get horny, pull or pay girls back to the room, and I would be given marching orders to head for the Croisette.

On one such evening stroll, I sniffed the pungent herb that perfumed our little room. I followed the aroma around the corner, and there stood the man, Pablo Picasso, casually pulling on a spliff while checking out his own work enshrined in an art-gallery window. The artist looked totally contented with his lot and at one with his Cubist glass-arts. He cut an impressive figure, minotorial in his tight French striped T-shirt, his espadrilles hugging the kerb. It was a power moment for *moi*, and I guess if I had thus far ignored ganja due to my jazz experience, from this Picasso moment on, I embraced the idea of marijuana as another staple tool of creativity. I decided that if marijuana hadn't shut down Picasso, then when opportunity reared its bud, I'd let it into my life.

Picasso on the Côte D'Azur

I hadn't been doing too well on the Croisette of late, so I packed my bag, ran out on the rent and Pete Fanning, relocating in the next paradise of opportunity down the coast, Juan-les-Pins. Within two days of arriving I'd landed two jobs. The first was in a staid men's clothes shop, where I charmed the owner into having his shop windows dressed twice a week. Gig number two was major-domo at an English tearoom called Butler's, situated at the tip of a peninsula of buildings overlooking the lapping blue Mediterranean. I had been there before in another season with my mum for tea and scones. The Brit owner's French wife, Madame Butler, remembered Andy well, as I did her, so I set about waiting on tables and serving Brits. Here I met Jeremy Paul Solomons.

Jeremy Paul Solomons: I was a fifteen-year-old twerp from north London, in Juan because my parents had a second home on the front. I just liked to have fun, really loon and clown around, large it up. Andrew was on exactly the same wavelength. We had the same outlook. The only English-speaking place in Juan was Butler's Tearoom. Mr Butler, a character and a bit of a Fascist, very funny though, ran it. He had some fingers missing. He was a real British bulldog; serving at the tearoom, he'd always be saying, 'Would you like some more hot water?'

I invited my mother to meet Andrew. My family came to really like him and treated him as one of our own. He started water-skiing and coming out to dinner with us. He was so used to sleeping outdoors that when he came to stay at our flat for the first time he insisted on sleeping on the balcony.

He was seventeen but, like me, he had the brain of a ten-year-old: totally out of it, mental. My mother recalls she asked for a cup of tea; Andrew brought my mother hot water. My mother said, 'Can I have the tea?' He subsequently brought five pots of hot water without tea. That was his way of emulating Butler. My mother decided that this guy, without doubt, was totally gone, he was worse than I was!

He looked completely different to everyone else in Juan. In the heat, he'd be wearing a black suit, he looked like a fucking undertaker. Crazy! He loved his black suit and his black socks. He always wore black socks because if he lost one, he could always match them up. Anyway he was like a prawn in the sun, so that wasn't Juan's attraction for Andrew. The main square in Juan had four big restaurants: Pan Pan was the biggest. The tables outside spilt on to the road. People would fly by in their Ferraris. If you were seen in the Pan Pan, it was like being seen at the Oscars. Andrew wanted to be Mr Big there.

Juan was the youngest scene in the South of France. Young people came in from Monaco, Saint-Tropez, Cannes, from everywhere. Like the lyric in that Peter Sarstedt song, 'Where Do You Go to My Lovely?': 'You go to Juan-les-Pins on your holiday . . .' Juan was the place to go, all the big people's kids would go to Juan. Andrew knew that.

Andrew was always going to be a millionaire. He knew he was going to be in that league. My father had been a successful businessman: Andrew wasn't about to bum around with someone who had no idea what they were gonna do. He was very proud of his Jewish ancestry. I'm Jewish, my grand-parents were Russian. That was one of the things we used to talk about; it was something to do with roots. In the 50s there was a lot of talk about money and Jewish businesses doing very well. He wanted to be a part of that.

John Douglas: I arrived in Juan-les-Pins at the height of summer and Andrew was working in this tearoom. I think he was living by his wits, a euphemism for up to no good. He'd seen the value of looking entirely different; everyone else was in bathing costumes and pastels – he was in a pin-striped suit with his John Michael shirt, bowler hat, doing that number. You couldn't miss him.

Jeremy Paul Solomons: We used to find things to do that were wickedly funny, stupidly mad. One time we were in a restaurant: me, Andrew, my sister and my sister's best friend, who was gorgeous and whom Andrew fancied. I had very tight trousers on and this woman said behind me, in French, 'What a great bum that boy's got!' She didn't think we understood, but Andrew and I both spoke French. I stood up and dropped my trousers so that she could get a better look. Andrew thought it was brilliant, he just loved the art of surprise.

ALO: Juan was a massive film set. The lighting was incredible. They had a form of light that England didn't even know about yet. The rock 'n' roll clubs were amazing. They were all open-air, hidden behind a row of hedges. You could hear the music from the street. Juan-les-Pins was where the French rock 'n' roll stars went for the summer, because it had a younger crowd. The French rock 'n' roll stars were great. In the winter they would go shopping in America and claim they were on tour there.

I knew my French rock 'n' roll from A to Zee via *Salut Les Copains*, the glossy colour music mag that took its pop as seriously as *Cahiers du Cinéma* did film. Another plus of French pop was that they didn't truck in singles: for the most part, it was EPs, four sides at 45 rpm, packed in a glossy picture sleeve. Eddy Mitchell was the Belmondo-meets-Eddie Cochran of Frog-pop. Dick Rivers, with his Chaussettes Noires, did a young pre-crippled Gene Vincent. In France, original pop meant 'Who do I cop?' The legendary Johnny Halliday, the everyman of France, had it down to an effortless art: each year he'd clone last year's American flavour, and Halliday it up into Art. His enterprise was a family biz, with his brother, and manager, an actual part of Johnny's act – 'Ladeees an' Geentleman, my manager, Lee Halliday!' Johnny was on top, ahead of the pack. He played the Juan-les-Pins Casino. I couldn't afford the price of admission, nor did I have the white smoking duds required.

The raucous rock 'n' legend in his own mind, Vince Taylor & the Playboys, was now a legitimate star in France. He had said, 'Fuck it, if Elvis can't make Europe, then let me be first in the land of second best.' Vince moved with rockin' aplomb from the 2Is basement in Soho to greatness in the land of de Gaulle. David Bowie must have caught this incredible performance, for later he named Taylor as an inspiration for his Ziggy Stardust. The refreshing thing about rockin' on the Côte d'Azur was that in France rock and pop were celebrated, whereas in England they were merely tolerated. In England the warnings were muted but persistent: do not get above your station. In France an entertainer's success was welcomed and applauded, not scorned. France had a completely different notion of class society to England.

David Bowie, rock singer (interviewed by Alan Yentob for the BBC): I met Vince Taylor a few times in the mid-60s . . . in fact I went to quite a few parties with him. Taylor was trying to make his way in Britain . . . and he was totally flipped! I mean, the guy was not playing with a full deck at all. He used to carry maps of Europe around with him and I remember very distinctly him opening a map out on Charing Cross Road outside the tube station and putting it on the pavement, and kneeling down with a magnifying glass, and I got down there with him, and he was pointing out all the sites where UFOs were going to be landing over the next few months. He had a firm conviction that there was a very strong connection between himself, aliens and Jesus Christ. Those were the three elements that went into his make-up and drove him.

Eventually he went to France and became a huge rock star over there. One night he decided he'd had enough, so he came on-stage in white robes and said that the whole thing about rock had been a lie, and that in fact he was Jesus Christ. And it was the end of Vince, his career, and everything else. It was that, and his story, which really became one of the essential ingredients of Ziggy and his world view!

Jeremy Paul Solomons: There was loads of live music in Juan. It was hands-on, you could actually stand right in front of people like Ray Charles, whereas in London you'd have to go to the Royal Albert Hall to see them. It was like a real close, intimate thing. For someone like Andrew, it was Mecca, a trigger. The South of France was totally rockin', but you'd also see Dave Brubeck, Miles Davis, Ella Fitzgerald and Ray Charles. Even the product was better: in France you could buy all these albums unreleased in England.

ALO: The Antibes Jazz Festival was the highlight of the Juan summer season. In the pebbled park at the back of the casino, under the shadow of Hôtel Cap d'Antibes, a giant wondrous shell was erected out into the water. For a week a few thousand people were lucky enough to be able to enjoy cool music in this cool Juan locale. I got a gig at the festival gofering for pianist Les McCann, who named me 'Sea Breeze', as I was so fast and light on my feet going about my duties.

I got to enjoy the Les McCann Trio; Count Basie and His Orchestra; Lambert, Hendricks and Ross; and the absolute master, Ray Charles. I felt that if God made the world in six days, he had then decided on an encore and created the Antibes Jazz Festival. I never witnessed such a stellar music-and-people event till Monterey Pop in 1967.

One disconcerting moment in the midst of all this sheer joy was the sight of Ray Charles shivering in junkie time on a rock, looking out on the Antibes blue, clutching his overcoat around him to ward off his withdrawal shivers in the noonday sun. He appeared very lost at that moment.

I had learnt at Ronnie Scott's that there were two kinds of jazz musicians: those who did and those who did not. I had to be at the festival in the morning to help set up the stage, which is when I saw him. It's very clear in my mind. It was scary. I think he only had the problem for another couple of years. He was okay when he was on-stage, but his off-stage life appeared to be in disarray. It was a very heady image. I would later use heroin; it was sheer pain, not pleasure, that took me there, but seeing how Ray Charles behaved in France helped to squelch any regularity with which I took up the drug. If I was totally opposed to my mother, my masters at school or my employer controlling me, I was certainly not about to give up my freedom at that time to a drug. I could see clearly that Charles was not in control of his own life. When life around you was as beautiful as it was it seemed a silly thing to be shivering in the sun. It was an image of somebody who was not really up for anything. The smack was in control – which seemed a waste of a life.

Jeremy Paul Solomons: Ray Charles was doped to the teeth. He was lifted on to the stage by both arms, on to the piano – they'd literally put his hands to the keys, and then he'd fly. Then, when he'd finished, they'd lift him off the seat and take his hands off the keys and take him away. Really frightening. Andrew loved it.

ALO: I did well between window dressing, Butler's Tearoom and the Jazz Festival gig. I'd stopped sleeping out and got myself a garret on the road to Antibes, and still had enough for water-skiing lessons at the Cap. My landlady warned me not to go further, meaning be careful if I went out at night to the Cap. 'The English pederast . . .' she said – meaning the writer Somerset Maugham, who was living out his days on the Cap amid whisperings that young men went out there in the night, never to be seen again. Maugham, who was about eighty, was rumoured to be taking life-prolonging injections made from the cells of the disappearing young men. In fact the doyen author would blanket his knees for the drive to Vevey on Lake Geneva. There he dared hope that the cells of unborn lambs that he welcomed to his aged corpus via a needle would extend and rejuvenate his life. I would do the same myself some twenty-five years later.

One afternoon as I was window dressing in the glare of a harsh afternoon sun, the six-foot-four, good-bad but now ugly Pete Fanning caught up with me for skipping town and the rent on him. He threw me up against the wall, and the summer tan drained out of my face, as the bells of Wellingborough rang in my frightened head once more. I was sure I was about to get levelled, when Pete seemed to change his mind and dropped me. He told me he figured I'd got the lesson. I had. I didn't run out on the rent again. It was already September and it was time for the type of Brits who haunted Juan to be back at work. Butler's would soon let me go, the town would wind down, and by the end of the month it would be dead, so I decided to come up with a fresh start and check out Monte Carlo.

Philip Townsend: We were sitting in an open-air café in the square at Monte Carlo, Sue Ford, Peter Kinsley and myself. Andrew came over and started talking to us. He told us he'd hitch-hiked from London. He was wearing riding breeches, jodhpurs. I asked why and he said, 'It's a novel way of hitch-hiking.' He was so proud to have got down here from London in twenty-four hours. He had a polo player's short whip and a hard hat. He said he stood by the side of the road in his riding breeches, hat and whip, making out there was some sort of emergency. So anyone who came along stopped. He told them his horse had bolted and could they run him to the next town?

Turned out we both knew Ted the flower-seller [later Twiggy's driver] from outside Sloane Square tube. I was down there bumming around with this journalist Peter Kinsley of the *Daily Express*. We were stringers. I took this girl down, Susie, but I wasn't knocking her off. Andrew said he didn't really know what he was going to do, he'd just got to Monte Carlo. We thought up this wheeze. These were the days when you could make lots of money out of newspapers by inventing stories. We talked about what we could do to make a bit of money.

John Osborne was living down there, just after he'd attacked England with his 'I loathe everything about England and the English, and I'm never going back there' bit. I found out where he was living and dug up this ex-army major who was desperate to make a bit of money. I met him the same way I met Andrew, sitting on the sidewalk. I asked him what he thought of John Osborne attacking the Queen and all that. 'Disgraceful,' he said. 'I'd

love to give him a good horse-whipping!' 'Ah, funny you should say that . . .'
I said. 'Do you want to make some money?' So one Sunday morning I took
him to where Osborne was staying, up behind Nice. He knocked on the door
and said, 'I've come to give you a good horse-whipping.' I got the picture.
That was 'Photo News' in the *Daily Express*.

Somerset Maugham was living there too. I knew his boyfriend. He was
having the cells of unborn lambs injected while they were still warm, some
Swiss clinic treatment. The big people were Onassis and David Brown of
Aston Martin, had a big yacht down there. We came up with this kidnapping
story based on Eddie Langley, the Chelsea cad who eloped with a lord's
daughter and sold photos of her in hiding to the press. We thought: 'We can
make a lot of money out of this. We put Andrew up in this hotel with Susie.
He was happy, going down to the Beach Club at the far end of Monte Carlo
every day – very exclusive.

What we'd decided to do was tell Susie's parents she'd disappeared and
get them to report her missing to the police. We thought there'd be quite a
lot of excitement, because she had a good background, her father had been
a wing commander in the air force. We'd have the story and make lots of
money out of it. Susie was game for anything; she was a fringe socialite, a
party girl about London.

They both had to fill in these forms at the hotel. Andrew put down a
bogus name and we said to her, 'Don't fill yours in, dear, we'll do it.' I think
Sue sòrt of knew what was going on. She was sort of playing along. She didn't
know everything, because her parents were bound to be really upset.

It didn't get in the papers to start off with and we thought the reason was
that they'd got a D-notice. If it's a matter of national security, a D-notice is
put on the case and all newspaper editors agree not to publish. In the end
Peter Kinsley, who was much older and more experienced, phoned Ford and
said, 'I think I ought to tell you your daughter is missing.'

'No, she is not!'

'Well, can you get hold of her?'

'No.'

'I think I ought to tell you there's this young lad down here she's got
friendly with. I don't want to arouse too much worry, but they've eloped. Your
daughter is in serious trouble.' Remember this was 1961 and nice polite girls

didn't go screwing about.

He said, 'Are you serious? What should I do?'

'Well,' Peter said, 'what you should do is report it to Interpol.' Which he did. Then we started getting little mentions in the *Express*, 'Girl Missing in South of France', 'Wing Commander's Daughter Elopes'.

Then Kinsley rang Ford and said, 'We've found your daughter, she's perfectly well and she's engaged to a guy called Andrew Loog Oldham. We don't really know much about him, but through our contacts we're going to have a photograph of them shortly.' We got about £100 from the *Express* for that photo, and that was that. We probably got from the whole thing, little bits and pieces, about £300.

ALO: I may have got fifty or so quid, and I closed up the garret in Antibes for one last move-on. I was trying to stay ahead of the end of the season, so I got down to Nice. With my passable French, I worked on the door at a striptease club to get as many American sailors as I could to come in. It was a very tame strip club. There wasn't anything particular seedy about it. I saw a few of the shows, but they weren't really that interesting. The girls didn't really strip, though I promised the American sailors a lot more. There was a magician who used to perform between the girls who had these three amazing leopardskin drape jackets, tinted blue, silver and red. I really wanted one. They were the ultimate rock 'n' roll jackets. He had them specially made, you couldn't buy them in the shops.

So I stole one. It was a thoughtless and criminal move. The writing was on my wall; it was the end of the summer. I was starting to make mistakes and the back streets of Nice were no place to be foolish. I headed for the front and the English church, where I knew the vicar was a friend of Wellingborough's Reverend Pitt. I explained my circumstances in a roundabout way and walked out of there with a God-given £50. I thanked the Rev. and stepped over to the British Consulate, where I knew you could surrender your passport and be repatriated, with the consulate paying for your train ticket home. I was too tired to hitch, life was suddenly a bitch and in thirty-six hours I was home.

I bathed in the warm welcomes I got from Celia, Alec and Sheila and pondered what I would do next. I knew I'd better make my own plans before my mother started setting up some rigid rules. I put my hand on my heart and called Mary Quant and she was good enough to see me. She could not take me back, natch, but she could ring up a Peter Hope Lumley, who, from Knightsbridge overlooking Beauchamp Place, ran a thriving PR company and model agency, to see if there was something I could do over there.

Peter Hope Lumley: My uncle was the noted couturier Edward Molyneux, who dressed many members of the royal family, including the Queen when she was a teenager. I did and still do handle the PR for Sir Hardy Amies, who has dressed the Queen for nearly fifty years and who holds the Royal Warrant. My other clients included the royal shoemaker, Sir Edward Rayne, and the textile magnate, Sir Nicholas 'Miki' Sekers (both were knighted after Andrew's time). They were anchors of the fast-growing London scene, though neither was as glamorous a figure as Sir Hardy Amies.

Mary Quant telephoned me and asked if Susie and I could find a job for Andrew, there was nothing more she could do for, or with, him. She praised him highly and sent him round to see us. We did need a 'gofer' who looked okay, to buy us sandwiches and run errands. He must have been seventeen: we offered him £7 a week, which he accepted. It was all we could afford since we had already taken on a girl called Kari Shepherd as a 'booker' for our models. Kari was pretty, but to me totally 'unsympatico'. Andrew, however, coped with the work very well.

Philip Townsend: I had got back into town and was happy to see Andrew settled in at Peter Hope Lumley's. I'd opened a photographic studio with Lord Christopher Thynne on Brompton Road, bang opposite Mary Quant's Knightsbridge Bazaar. Peter Hope Lumley really got my career going by letting me use all his models free. I used to sell the photographs to the *Daily Express*, £30 a go, with silly stories like, 'Juliet was a sandwich maker, now she's a top model.' I didn't have to pay Lumley because it was publicity and practice for his new girls. I had a thing going with the picture editor – he got a £10 kick-back for every shot of mine he used and an extra £5 if he put my name on it. We were both very young and up to anything. Andrew knew lots of people; I introduced him to lots more, and he introduced me to people as well. He was full of personality; everyone liked him. Well, they didn't necessarily like him, but they took notice of him. That's what his business was . . .

There was a friend of Andrew's from Hampstead that he fell out with. Andrew said, 'As you progress in life you fall out with some people, you don't need them any more and they can't stand where you're going.'

ALO: James Dean said, 'The stage is like a religion; you dedicate yourself to it and suddenly you find that you don't have time to see your friends, and it's hard for them to understand. You don't see anybody. You're all alone with your concentration and your imagination and that's all you have. You're an actor.' I understood that, later rereading it in the preface of Terence Stamp's *Coming Attractions*. Thanks, Tel . . . I have only had the pleasure of knowing the brother Stamp, Christopher, on a first-game basis, but I have always had time for the example and aura T. Stamp has given us, both on the screen and on the page and in their parallel explanatory duties. This other half of the Stamp collection, from the early *Billy Budd* and *The Collector* through *Superman*, *Wall Street* and the priceless *Priscilla, Queen of the Desert*, has handled his lot with Zen aplomb. It's a rare man who has grasped the meaning of being one, and that's a fabric and station of life that Mr Stamp wears and tells well.

In 1961 public relations, like the advertising business, was considered slightly 'wide-boy' and not quite a career, an attraction in and of itself to me. But from his plush first-floor offices at 54 Brompton Road, Knightsbridge, Peter Hope Lumley had brought some solid substance to PR. He added the comfort of 'yesterday' to the selling of 'tomorrow', with a conviction that tomorrow could be now. His office suited him: oak-desked, deeply cushioned and carpeted, perhaps frayed but none the less providing a fitting backdrop to a man of no nonsense, cardiganed, striped-shirted and well-brogued as he was. The pace of life and texture of personality were not as fast and gleaming as they had been at Quant's, but it was solid quality and became home. I was welcomed very warmly and the stars gave me another good chance.

My Quant pal Susie Leggatt had come from Bazaar to head up Hope Lumley's model agency, simply called Model Agency. I did all sorts of odd jobs for Peter and the Model Agency. I walked the dogs, for one. Walking the models' dogs, I would attract wolf whistles from the workers on the building

sites as I cruised past with a couple of terriers and maybe a Pekinese or two.
I used to encourage, but never acknowledge, this by wearing a very stylish
gold overcoat, a gift from Alec that I'd had camped up by adding a huge spy's
fur collar.

Peter Hope Lumley: I pinched Susie from Mary. There were only half a
dozen recognised model agencies in London. Mine had been in business
since 1957. Susie was only twenty-one or twenty-two. Dealing with young,
often silly models and their problems was a constant stress. She acted as a
surrogate mother, a shoulder to cry on, often having to put the girl up for the
night when there had been a row and the model was thrown out of her home.
She took it all very personally and was adored by the models, some of them
being only a year or two younger than Susie herself.

She died a long time after Andrew left our employ. She was very
emotional and put her job before her private life; like all of us at the time.
She drank too much and it affected her health. When I told her she had to
leave me, her work was suffering almost as much as her health. She went to
Tangiers and died there of pancreatitis. We were all heartbroken, no doubt
including Andrew. The model agency continued for another twenty years.

ALO: Thus far the only good that died young had been my idols on the
screen and stage; now it was those that had been good to me in real life. I
remember her well.

I made deliveries back and forth to the Hardy Amies house on Savile Row.
Every visit I ran into the incredible-looking Amies director, Bunny Roger. If
I thought I had nerve, this apparition made mockery of the mere thought.

His idol was author and cartoonist Max Beerbohm. Bunny was
unapproachably aloof, but I learnt enough from him just by looking. He paid
meticulous attention to every detail of his appearance. Everything he did was
a piss-take and a celebration. He looked almost sixty, but he used to prance
about in the most amazing three-piece chalk-striped suits. His jackets were
so tightly waisted that they flared out like a skirt. The trousers were tighter
than drainpipes and his shirts had high, rounded, stiff-starched collars. His
lips were permanently pursed, and he always wore a grey bowler hat, pearl
tie-pin, make-up, eyeliner and a carnation.

Bunny Roger

Angus McGill: Bunny Roger was a dandy. He was a very rich man, lived at a series of great addresses and gave great parties once a year, always themed. He wore curly-brimmed bowlers, beautifully cut Edwardian suits. There was something very gallant about Bunny; up until his death in 1996 he was still dressing as this Edwardian figure, people were still turning around to look at him. He always looked so extraordinary.

Peter Hope Lumley: Both Susie and I had neither time nor inclination to go shopping; but we found that Andrew enjoyed it and had excellent taste. On one occasion, when it must have been nearing Christmas time, I gave Andrew a list of about ten people to whom I wished to give Christmas presents: clients, contacts, press and 'friends'. The list explained who the potential recipients were and what they did, with a top price that I wished to pay. Off went Andrew, to return within a couple of hours with a large box full of items from John Siddeley [later Lord Kenilworth], who had a very smart and expensive shop off Sloane Street. John and I knew each other through Miki Sekers; Andrew had selected a number of gifts like jars and *objets* on approval – something I would never have dared asked for. The box included a present for me from Andrew which I still have: a very pretty, green marbled jar for holding pens and pencils. The remainder of the goodies were exactly right for my friends, and all within my price range. He chose odd scarves for Susie from other shops, all in perfect taste.

Andrew was quite meticulous in his behaviour towards Susie and me, both personally and in his work, always very sharply and neatly dressed, 'buttoned down' would sum him up. He appeared at twelve noon one day, instead of nine thirty. He was dishevelled, unshaven and looked as though he had slept in his well-cut denim suit. He had. His mother had already telephoned me, saying that as I was the only person Andrew respected (I never knew what had become of his father), would I tell Andrew to stop beating her up?

'Certainly not,' I replied, for that was a matter between the two of them. Anyway, when I asked him why he was so late, he told me that he had spent the night in a police cell. His mother had telephoned the police in a panic – her son was beating her over the head while she was in the bath. The police came round and, although there was very little they could do in this domestic dispute, they did lock him up for the night before throwing him out with a warning. I was so angry that I ordered him out of my sight and told him to go and get himself shaved and cleaned up! I never told Andrew about the call, but he did once bring his mother to a Hardy Amies show and I had a sneaking sympathy for him!

ALO: Again, I do not recall knocking my mother about in any way, shape or form. It was not part of my lifestyle. She would never have spoken to me again, had I behaved in such a way. I can imagine using a story as dramatic as that to offset my being late for work. It would take an excuse that dramatic to cover for what I agreed was as heinous a breach of my own work ethic as it was of Lumley's. I would also not put it past myself to persuade my good pre-Sheila friend Diana to make calls claiming to be my mother. She was a good sport and would have been up for it. If you're going to be late, make it into an event.

That my colleagues at both the Quant and Lumley shops remember me as abusive of Celia suggests that there were indeed strong psychological and physical undercurrents at work between us. Certainly my position as a messenger boy in the fashion business was not her idea of job security, but I was satisfied that I had conformed more or less to her wishes, as well as my own ambitions. Her continued criticism was therefore irksome and, I felt, unfair, yet now I see that her mistrust of my new friends and employers was a reflection of her own feelings of rejection from fashionable society, which she was sure would be visited on her offspring. Perhaps, in her own way, she was trying to spare me the heartache of 'illegitimacy' and the class insecurity with which she tortured herself.

With hindsight, Celia, like most of her generation, was completely unprepared for the advent of the meritocracy so applauded by Vidal Sassoon. She didn't realise that in the world in which I now had a toehold, a hyphenated name got you no further than the switchboard if you didn't have 'it'. I would not necessarily recommend that Aquarians live together, as my mother and I were forced to do: we bury our agendas deep and our frustrations simmer coldly. If my mother changed reels on me without my permission, I may well have whacked her, *Psycho*-style, in the bath and blanked the act out. That cause may or may not have been made, yet the effect was simultaneous and these days a good deal of my time is spent studying, taking responsibility for and handling my less enlightened actions.

Peter Hope Lumley: Susie Leggatt and I had enormous respect and liking for Andrew and only dismissed him because in those days £7 a week wage was quite a lot of money for a blossoming model agency and a busy, but not overpaid, PR consultancy. He took the news philosophically, thanking us for teaching him a lot. He later remarked (to my then wife, when he popped in to say 'hello') that I had taught him everything he knew, including style!

I always dreaded meeting him later, as I was certain that he would patronise me unmercifully, having achieved fame and success after discovering the Rolling Stones. I could not have been more wrong: he was charming, well mannered and, apart from calling me 'Peter' when before it had always been 'Mr Lumley', I found him delightful, dressed to the nines in a large brown sombrero. He kissed my wife's hand and was most flattering about me!

ALO: Peter had warned me he couldn't afford to keep me on and I dutifully told my mother. She took it as an opportunity to pressure me to secure a 'proper job with a stable future'. Oh, my God!

Years after the Stones and Immediate Records, I was talking with my mother about life. She remained unimpressed by my fame and success, very unimpressed as a matter of fact. She just said, 'Yes, Andrew, that's all well and good, but when are you going to get a proper job?' Well, Mother, so far, so good . . .

· CHAPTER 7 ·

Keep away from people who try to belittle your ambitions. Small people always do that, but the really great make you feel that you, too, can somehow become great.

Mark Twain

ALO: I scoured the *Stage* for anything but a proper job. This weekly trade rag customarily listed the managers and agents of those few acts lucky enough to be working. An ad for actor Jess Conrad caught my attention. Jess was a singer signed to Decca and had hit the lower reaches of the charts with 'Mystery Girl' at the end of 1961. He was a protégé of Jack Good and had appeared often on ITV's replacement for Good's *Oh, Boy!*, *Boy Meets Girls*. Since then, Conrad's recording career had languished, and he was hoping to pick up the pace with his latest single, 'Pretty Jenny'.

Jess Conrad

Monte Mackey managed Jess from a theatrical agency owned by American film producer/agent Al Parker. When I met her in their offices just off Park Lane, she was like Lauren Bacall as the literary agent to James Caan in *Misery*. Miss Mackey was sufficiently impressed with my cheek to invite me to her home for a follow-up. Her neighbours at the Grosvenor House Hotel included Laurence Harvey and Jimmy Woolf.

Room service delivered tea and biscuits, and I presented myself as the press-cutting saviour of Jess Conrad's recording career, albeit I had no business card or private phone number. Monte Mackey was interested in the good-looking Conrad as an actor and was indifferent to the world of pop music, but she gave me a month to work my magic.

Tubing down from Hampstead to all points of the West End, I got no joy and even less print for the 'Pretty Jenny' single. I made one visit to Conrad's record label, Decca, and found that *Expresso Bongo* was not fiction: Wolf Mankowitz must have done his homework in the same tired linoed offices. The music industry had none of the creative spark and optimism of the fashion industry I had recently left, nor did its denizens dwell in the house of good manners.

Taciturn businessmen controlled Decca, with an apparent aversion to style reflected in the ruthlessly staid Decca offices. They did not even appear to like or listen to pop music – they could have been selling baked beans for all they cared. Their interest was in the tins. Dismayed by their apathy and appalled at their poor taste in clothes, I was repelled back on to the Albert Embankment whence I came. Decca had its own Press Department, thank you, and was ready and able to service the every requirement of its artistes – no need for the likes of me in this scheme. Isn't this where I came in?

Powerful agents and managers still regarded record companies as the valet parking of stardom: spaces for their cars, the stars, which might get spattered with bird droppings or come back immaculate. In those days your client warbling on the airwaves meant more money for the panto or summer season. The singer/manager combo's relationship with the A&R man was crucial: he found the song and he matched it with the act of his choosing. The UK business turned a blind eye to the reality of America. The British recording establishment wishfully hoped the Furys and Wildes would all disappear and we'd return to the pre-hula-hoop safety of lush Mantovani. We were a long way from self-contained artists who would march over the 'extended play' and demand the 'long player' to cover the things they had to say. For the progress we'd made, we could thank Cliff, the Shadows (né Drifters) and scribe Ian 'Sammy' Samwell, for 'Move It', as well as Norrie Paramor, their A&R man who allowed their will to be done. Let us appreciate Jack Good and Rita Gillespie as pioneers of multimedia with the always threatening, persuasively hopeful *Oh, Boy!* And let us remember that Eddie Cochran died for rock 'n' roll on the playing fields of England. This would have to do for the mo; the Beatles were still polishing their chops in Hamburg.

I found myself up against a brick wall: I couldn't do anything for Jess Conrad except smile a 'game's up, own up'. We met in Mackey's hotel suite, and I was mightily impressed by the all-knowingness between the singing actor and his agent/manager. I wanted more. I liked Monte Mackey. She didn't feel threatened by a kid trying to stir things up in her shop. Rather, she seemed a guiding light – a professional beauty, who loved her work and brightened her world. Her example of decorum and vitality made her world the one I wanted for myself.

My month was up – I hadn't landed on my feet, and Jess hadn't landed in the charts, so with a bow and a wave it was back to Hampstead and Celia's agenda. I might talk to the tramps but I was not about to join them. My first attempt to adhere to her agenda had me bounding down to Mayfair and the 15 Hays Mews address of an old-school PR firm, the Leslie Frewin Organisation. I managed to get in and pass an audition and was happy to return to Hampstead to report to my mother that, as of the following Monday, I would be assistant to the assistant of account executive Stuart Valdor.

From day one I realised I was not going to enjoy working at the Leslie Frewin Organisation; it was Wellingborough in a Mews setting. I was quickly reprimanded over my suit – 'too flash' – and my attitude – 'too casual'. Stuart Valdor meant well and attempted to take me under his wing, but him aside, they were all used-car salesmen putting on Heseltine airs, as interesting as the label copy on the back of a packet of fags. On the spiv food chain, public relations was the new upmarket goldmine. To put a finer point on it, at the time I regarded the press agent's lot as an honest one: you did your pitch, and you and your client were hopefully rewarded in ink. 'PR' as practised by

Leslie Frewin and Associates, spent more time assuring and shaping the client, it seemed to me, than going for the ink. PR appealed to the way an artist felt about himself inwardly, rather than the way the paying public felt about him outwardly. It was all fake and sleight-of-hand at the LFO. Their most exciting client was the British Menswear Guild, a consortium of staid UK clothes stores and manufacturers, like Aquascutum, guilded together in a boring, panicked, monolithic monopoly of self-preservation.

I found more to interest me in company founder, Leslie Frewin, than in our customers. Author of several self-published spy novels, Frewin had set up a self-contained independent production system long before 'vertical integration' was a buzzword. Unfortunately, Frewin's top-floor office was considered almost sacrosanct by his staff, and certainly out of bounds to inquisitive assistant juniors like me.

Between the rules and the catty competition, this job more than any other I'd taken was like being back at school. To progress up the ranks I would have to cultivate a patience I neither had nor wanted. My very being was anathema to all, and neither encouraged nor invited in, but I had given my word to my mother and was doing my best to keep it. However, the mutual disdain with which my co-workers and I regarded each other certainly meant my days were numbered.

Sheila Klein: His mother was really into the Leslie Frewin job. She was always telling me to encourage Andrew to stay at the job. But he had a real fear of boredom. Boredom being not being able to be, or wanting to be, somewhere else . . . 'There's gotta be much more than this.'

Tony Meehan was quite an influence at that time. He had just moved into a flat in Frognal near the one Andrew and John had shared. Tony was quite fatherly towards Andrew for a bit and gave him a few pointers on the music business.

Tony Meehan: Andrew lived in the same street as I did. When I left the Shadows in September 61, to pursue a career in the A&R department at Decca Records, the music press had it: 'A Star Looking for New Talent'. First time I noticed him, this chap sorta sidled up to me on the street. I was looking for a taxi or something, and he sort of made himself known. He was desperate to get into showbusiness and desperate to get out of the job he was doing.

I said, 'Well, what do you do?' He said, 'Well, anything!' I said, 'What is it you wanna do? What can you do? Can you play or do you sing, do you write?' He originally wanted to call himself Sandy Beach and compere rock shows. He used to pass my flat on his way home and very often he'd drop in . . . he really became sort of like a regular visitor. He was very into clothes, yes, and he was very fashion-conscious. He was very aware and very well dressed, he was a very elegant young man. If Andrew hadn't gone into music, he would have gone into fashion.

I used to collect a lot of early blues records and stuff like that, which he'd never heard before. I used to play them to him and lend them to him. Little did I know . . . These were original releases that were leased to Decca for the UK: John Lee Hooker, Bobby Bland and things like that. Decca had an office in New York, London Records, and they were picking up stuff there the whole time, which was very useful for them. They had the pick of the crop, they really did go into that, whereas EMI never really did seem to get that one together.

Dick Rowe when he was head of Decca A&R had a lot of good ideas, but he'd be the first to tell you he knew nothing about music. That was the first thing Dick used to come out with, 'Of course, I know nothing about music, but I know what I like.' He took gambles and he did try, but Decca was a very old-fashioned company, the way it was run was almost colonial. It was very hard to get things past Sir Edward Lewis and the directors and all these people who really didn't know the first thing about what was happening. Louise Cordet was one of the first projects I had at Decca. I sort of discovered her, got a song from Jerry Lordan and we went in the studio. Jerry Lordan, along with Lionel Bart and Ian 'Sammy' Samwell, they were the three best British songwriters of the era, no contest.

I had a piano in the flat, I used to work all night. I was a workaholic in those days. Stay up all night, go to the studio at ten o'clock in the morning, work all day and then come back and eat, y'know, that sort of thing: crazy, couldn't do it now. That's what I wanted to do – EMI wouldn't give me the opportunities, Decca did. Basically I think Norrie Paramor, who knew me from Cliff, of course, saw me as a threat. You weren't really allowed to push on much further and I was getting more and more frustrated because I wanted to do orchestration, which I learnt, and I wanted to produce, and there just weren't any openings. I wanted to move on, wanted to write film music, wanted to progress continually.

I was one of the first, if not *the* first, independent producers in this country, certainly along with Joe Meek and people like that, who found it very difficult to get their product placed and very difficult to get into these huge monolithic, colonial kind of organisations that were run like something from the British Empire, from the top down – it was very much one of those situations. Nobody believed rock 'n' roll was gonna last for more than six months or a year; nobody would let you in anyway, there just weren't any openings. People were simply trying to cream off what they could, and generally abuse the situation.

I worked with Joe Meek. I did all sorts of things that I wanted to do, for instance, session drumming, where you'd go in and play with an orchestra – just get a sheet of music put in front of you and you did it. It was like a test against yourself, you were running against yourself all the time. I just didn't want to be in a rock band playing endless gigs at Blackpool Empire or whatever. After you've done it for a couple of years . . . I started in 58, remember, so y'know I'd had two or three years of continual touring: we toured South Africa, we toured Europe, we toured America . . . In those days, believe me, touring was tough, you did 400 miles a day in a coach without a toilet or facilities of any kind. It was rough, very difficult. I didn't like the road, and I'd got married, had a child, and I thought this was the time to get into the music scene properly, in the way I wanted to, which was to produce other artists, to explore. It was an artistic decision; it wasn't a business decision.

Yes, I could have just sat there and become a boring millionaire like the rest of them. Well, I mean, that's really what it amounted to. Because these things almost always do end in acrimony. The Stones are probably one of the few bands that have somehow managed to hold it all together. I don't know whether they socialise any more, but certainly they saw the business side of it much better than any of us did and took advantage of it, in no small degree due to Andrew's influence. When he came along a little bit later with the Stones, he was able to . . . he was probably a bit more ruthless than I was, with regard to the record companies, and saw them for what they were.

ALO: Due to the influence of rebels like Tony Meehan, independence was becoming my mantra; Leslie Frewin didn't figure in my vision. I was moonlighting before too long – it had to be. *Cool For Cats* was ITV's midweek pop-music showcase and the programme's presenter, Kent Walton, was a minor celebrity. I was more interested in the lead dancer in residence: Peppi brought the show to an end each week, gyrating to the play-out record.

Despite Peppi's visibility, he hadn't had any press, so I figured that with beginner's luck I'd be able to get him something. I had to – the guy was on a television show every week, and a Yank to boot. Just by the law of averages I had to be able to get him five or six press cuttings from somewhere. All I had to do was get in.

The company who made *Cool For Cats*, Rediffusion, had their offices in Holborn. I stood waiting outside, among a small crowd of kids looking to see Kent Walton, or anybody. My screaming days were over, it was time to get a move on. When Kent finally appeared, I employed myself in officiously shooing back the kids and led Walton to his parked Mercedes. In that teaked beige master-car, Mr Walton moved from minor to major key before he could ignition-up as I leapt in the back seat behind him. Before Walton had a chance to protest, the surrounding fans forced him to put his car into motion.

Long before a quietly raging Robert De Niro pulled the same trick to get himself close to Jerry Lewis in Martin Scorsese's *King of Comedy* (1983), I knew the graft well. By then I was living in Manhattan, officed '*chez* Freddy Bienstock' at the hallowed Brill Building. During filming – proving that the apple falls not far from the tree – I ligged my way into a small walk-on part in the film.

To me, Mr Walton was a B-player, so I figured I could easily force my way into his affections. I was optimistic. Unlike some of the other people I pushed myself upon, I must have been a real nuisance to him. Like everybody else, I wanted something: two audience tickets to the next *Cool For Cats* – and I got them.

I took Sheila to the show and afterwards we hunted Peppi down. A nice guy, he got hooked on my attention and enthusiasm, but said he'd have to check with his manager, Tom Springfield, about taking me on as his press agent. Tom was naturally a little pissed off that I'd got to his act backstage. No newcomer to showbiz was Tom, a founding member of sister Dusty's

Springfields. Before 'You Don't Have To Say You Love Me', Dusty and brother Tom were Britain's answer to hootenanny and the Springfields had a deal of their own with Philips.

To prove that no good deed goes unpunished, Tom would later manage the 'Georgy Girl' Seekers. Dusty, of course, went solo – as she should – while late Springfielder Mike Hurst went behind the lights to discover Cat Stevens. Hurst cut both Cat and my own First Lady of Immediate, P.P. Arnold, on 'First Cut Is The Deepest'.

Peppi brought me to Tom's office for another audition. Tom saw straight through my act, smiled a knowing smile at my hoisting his client aloft into dreamland, and took me on board for a month at a fiver per week. The arrangement was too loose to give up the Leslie Frewin day job, but I took great pleasure in making Mr Frewin's org. work for my newest client. At closing time, I'd find an empty cupboard and hide away in it until the rest of the staff had left the office. Then I'd chop-chop to the company telephones and hustle Peppi till Fleet Street headed for home or the local. I kept one ground-floor window open, 'my front door', through which I could receive my client Peppi and leave each night.

The Peppi I longed to introduce to a mass public was at best vapourware, and his lack of tangibility combined with a modicum of notoriety yielded a scant few inches of print, just before the end of my thirty-day trial. Once again it seemed I'd been cause out of faith in effects: Tom and Peppi, once sceptical, were generous in their praise, but couldn't afford to waste any more money on PR. The reality was that there was to be no new season of *Cool For Cats*. The show faded from the screen and, with it, Peppi's UK TV career.

I was pleasantly surprised at what I had achieved for Peppi. The small success I'd had and the contacts I'd made raised the ante that the Leslie Frewin office was unwilling to put up: clients of my own. Later, when I had the means, I attempted a gesture of thanks, producing a single released on Decca in 1964, an enthusiastic reworking of Gene Vincent's 'Pistol Packin' Mama'.

H&R – homework and research – was my passion. British rock 'n' roll had once again reached an all-time low; performers who'd had magic moments had now become tame and lame, knocking out slushy ballads, from sex 'n' shake to slop 'n' rot, *en route* to becoming 'all-round entertainers'. In England there was going to be no new Cliff Richard. It was all quiet on the sexual front. The future offered by Harold Macmillan and Leslie Frewin was reflected in the music they all hoped I'd listen to. Yet I was beginning to meet people who wanted to make a different kind of music, with their own hands, so to speak.

Shel Talmy, independent producer (the Who, the Kinks, David Bowie, Manfred Mann, the Pentangle, the Easy Beats, Chad & Jeremy and Amen Corner): I first met Andrew shortly after I came over from America. I managed to get some PR via an article on me in the *NME*, and Andrew was one of the first to call and we met at my bedsit in Earls Court. We talked a lot about bands in general and where music was going, wished each other luck and pretty much went our own ways for the next few years.

Not to put too fine a point on it, I bullshitted my way into the gig in London. I had no idea who anybody was when I first arrived. I'd set out to see Europe with very little bread and thought if I could work for a couple of weeks, I could pay for the trip. I figured I had nothing to lose, as I had a gig back in LA as an engineer and had been offered a four-single production deal just before I left, which I was going to do when I returned.

So I started visiting. The first studio I went to see was IBC, which was the leading independent studio at the time. And one of the first people I met was Noel Rogers, a music publisher, who I was referred to by a friend of mine in LA, who set up the meeting with Dick Rowe at Decca.

I actually walked into Dick's office and did my 'brash American' bit, reeled off a whole string of hits that I hadn't done! I played him a couple of demos that my friend at Capitol Records had done and given me permission to use as 'mine'. They were Lou Rawls and the Beach Boys. Dick said, 'Thank God you've arrived, you start next week.'

The first record I did was Doug Sheldon, then the Bachelors 'Charmaine', which became a big hit and convinced me to stay in London instead of going back to LA.

Dick Rowe was one of the few people in England who was pro-American, not averse to giving young guys some kind of a chance to do something. I'm fairly sure I was the first independent producer in England working directly for a major label. I told Dick, 'I'm an independent producer', meaning: I get royalties. As far as I could tell, nobody else did. It was just unheard of at the time. All the staff A&R people were on salaries, including George Martin.

I didn't have an office at Decca and didn't want one. I preferred to work out of Decca Studios in West Hampstead, miles away from the Decca main offices on the Embankment, because I had a lot more freedom and was definitely in a better frame of mind, as the main office was like a mortuary.

The nice thing about the record biz at that time was that everybody who was A&R was a producer, unlike today where almost nobody is – meaning that there was a much better understanding of what problems come up in producing a record. I think that helped in all sorts of ways, like communication between artist and label, and the shorter amount of time it took to get on the same page.

I don't think Dick Rowe was a great producer by any stretch of the imagination, and he freely admitted it. But at least he had a good concept of what was happening. American kids were not into English artists and everybody's goal was to have an act that broke in America.

What Dick Rowe hired me for was the American sound I could provide, and which he felt was going to have an impact on English bands, and of course it did. With the additional spin that English bands wrote their own music. And so the 'new' sound from England became the British Invasion.

ALO: Shel Talmy wasn't the only newly hatched independent producer trying to shake England out of its doldrums. There was also the truly unique Joe Meek.

Charles Blackwell, arranger: Joe Meek was even crazier than Phil Spector. He would use a Ouija board to get in touch with Buddy Holly to find out whether the record was gonna be a hit. He felt the whole of the music industry was against him, that they were out to pinch his ideas – I think because when he used the sound of lightning to start up a record, EMI sent the record to their labs to try and analyse it. There was an evil about Joe. He was known to crawl around graveyards taping cats hissing, he was into the occult.

He was a split personality. He believed he was possessed, but had another side that was very polite with a good sense of humour. He was very complicated; when he was young his mother used to dress him in girls' clothes.

Dennis Preston was the first independent record producer in this country, with the Lonnie Donegan and Kenny Ball hits. He started off at IBC and then got Joe Meek to set up Lansdowne Studios for him. It leant more towards jazz, pure jazz. I was aiming to be a song plugger, working at a publishing company called Essex Music, which had made its name with a lot of skiffle tunes. 'Rock Island Line' was number one in America before 'Telstar'. I was packing up sheet music; sheet music was big business, there was a shop in every high street selling sheet music. Dennis Preston shared offices with Essex Music; his company was called Record Supervision. So I would see Joe arriving and I think he heard me play piano, demoing one of my numbers.

Basically Joe was looking for someone he could work with, who knew a little bit about music, who could play piano. We were down at his place in Notting Hill, one huge room, and we'd just try and do demos there, without actually going into a studio, in his front room – no soundproofing or anything. He recorded a lot of stuff there: West Five, the Cavaliers. It wasn't easy translating Joe's ideas because musically he didn't know what he was talking about. He gave me tapes to listen to of him singing over somebody else's track . . . really odd stuff . . . You would get this really weird demo tape, which had nothing to do with the song you'd end up doing.

To try and make something out of what Joe gave you was extremely difficult. You never knew if you were doing it right or not, and he could get angry if it wasn't the way he heard it in his head. Ivor Raymonde, Joe's other arranger, said Joe would tell him, 'I'd like three girl singers and a couple of boy singers and a kind of crescendo towards the end, violins here and there . . .' The demo tapes I remember were of him singing in a high falsetto and talking at the same time, singing, 'Da di da, da da da – strings go in here – da di da.'

Joe and I split under a cloud: he got a new life and a financial backer. He set up in his flat above a shop at 304 Holloway Road. There was more equipment and more wires, and all the wires were exposed, held together with chewing gum. He engineered it all himself to get the Meek sound; the machines were limited because he didn't have a big studio. He used to put the strings – four violins – and a French horn in the bathroom – so his records sounded a bit different, a lot of compression and echo. Later for his Triumph label stuff he used professional studios, Olympic and IBC.

'Telstar' was the turning point; I'd left him by then. He was with Robert Stigwood at that stage. Stigwood had John Leyton, Ian Gregory, Mike Sarne, all actors; he was a theatrical agent. Records were his way of promoting his actors. 'Johnny Remember Me' [John Leyton's August 61 UK number one on Top Rank] and 'Telstar' were done at Holloway Road. Joe usually used two groups, the Tornados or the Outlaws, for his sessions. Eventually Stigwood lured away all Joe's talent: Geoff Goddard, Billie Davis and Mike Berry. I reckon Joe must have hated Stigwood, because Johnny Leyton was a major talent and after 'Johnny Remember Me', Stigwood took over in the studio. It was the same with Mike Sarne after 'Come Outside' [UK number one, August 62].

Bobby Graham, the Outlaws drummer: Joe Meek was as queer as a pork chop in a synagogue. He was a nutter. He was very paranoiac, he used to say there were people outside in a van with special listening devices, stealing his sound, that his telephone was tapped. He had the Outlaws parade down Oxford Street dressed as cowboys to advertise one of our records. We got nicked for exceeding the speed limit in a horse-drawn vehicle and Joe thought that was wonderful. He said, 'This is great publicity.' Once he told me he didn't want me to play drums on the session, he just wanted me to bang the drum cases. Another time he punched me in the face. I remember once he came in screaming, 'Who's clicking their fingers?' No one would own up, we were all terrified. 'Sorry, Joe, it was me.' 'Great!' he said, 'I wanna use that. Do it.'

ALO: I went up to his studio on Holloway Road. He was recording a vocal version of 'Telstar' with this fifteen-year-old kid, Kenny Hollywood, and I was hired to work it. Joe Meek really scared me. He was immaculate but seedy. He had a suit and a tie on and more grease in his hair than you could imagine. He looked like a real mean-queen Teddy boy and his eyes were riveting. There were shotguns in his studio, shotguns in his head, even then.

The Kenny Hollywood single, 'Magic Star', sank without a trace and the only cuttings I could get on young Mr Hollywood confirmed that he wanted to go there. Later Joe said, 'Andrew Oldham had a couple of months with RGM Sound as a Public Relations officer but got bitten by the recording bug and buzzed off.'

In 1967, aged thirty-seven, on the eighth anniversary of Buddy Holly's death, Joe was awaiting trial for soliciting/cottaging in a Holloway toilet. His landlady went upstairs to confront him about making moves on her grandson. He blew her head off with a shotgun and then did the same to himself.

I started looking for another star to swing on: in the latest issue of *Melody Maker* I paused at an old photograph that had been used to launch teenage singer Mark Wynter when he was on Decca. His new label Pye had recycled the Lionel Bart-staged glossy to announce his signing. Mark's mentor, Ray Mackender, would become one of the first men in the pop field I respected enough to work for, rather than imitate. A large and imposing man's man, Ray had a lifestyle that put him at odds with the time; either he was born too late or too early to be able to be himself. His love of showbusiness was an inspiration and education to me.

Ray Mackender was as unlike a manager of the day as it was possible to be. For a start, he only handled the one act. He also kept up a day job in the City, as an insurance broker at a subsidiary of Lloyd's called Bland Welsh. Ray's double life was also marked by his desire to be surrounded by youth.

More than anything, Ray was a Cliff Richard fan. After meeting his idol during a taping of *Oh, Boy!* at the Hackney Empire, he'd started DJing. Soon Ray was ghostwriting articles on behalf of Cliff for the *NME*, coming up with crazy stories like Cliff thinking Father Christmas came on a white elephant. While DJing, Mackender came across Terry Lewis, a seventeen-year-old supermarket worker who did a bit of singing. Terry Lewis transformed into Mark Wynter.

Mark Wynter, actor/singer: I share the same birthday as Andrew, he's exactly a year younger than I am. Ray was also an Aquarian, eleven years older than me and well educated, his father was high up at Lloyd's. He was a fantastic communicator, great builder of bridges between people. On a Sunday morning he would have anywhere between fifteen and twenty-five

people in his tiny two-room flat in Chelsea having a coffee morning – kids
he'd met DJing. Ray would make coffee, biscuits, and people would get up
and sing. Ray would say, 'Mark, sing something for us', or 'Johnny Soho, sing
something.' He had this great energy and drive, he was determined I was
gonna be successful.

ALO: Ray took too much vicarious pleasure in his youthful friends to pay
mind to the taboos of the day. I realise this now in retrospect; my own
upbringing had been too sheltered for me to understand what Ray was really
about. He was a great boss and encouraged me to break away from
Establishment flackery, and to nourish the one I was with – myself.

The Aquarian magic between Ray, Mark and me worked threefold. The
Tony Hatch-produced 'Venus in Blue Jeans' would soar into the charts
eventually rising to number four (October 62) and staying in the charts, for
fifteen weeks. I quickly resigned from the Leslie Frewin Organisation: I
worked for Ray and Mark full-time now. I did this despite Mother's
complaints that I was throwing away my future.

Ray Mackender was a total league of gentlemen. He let me into his life
and taught me how to work. He gave me his press lists and contacts, his fire
and agenda. Ray's incredible respect for showbusiness influenced me
greatly. His discipline complemented my ambition. I enjoyed him setting me
tasks, and then delivering on them. Alas, Ray was a tad too early. If he'd had
the muscle of the moptops, like Brian Epstein, he would have had his day.
But Ray was too educated, too early and cared too much.

Ray gave me the names and numbers for a crew of showbusiness
journalists that covered the length and breadth of the Isles. Between them,
they appeared in almost every local newspaper from London to the middle of
nowhere. I worked the angle of volume diligently and had earned a list of
contacts for present and future use, a kind of legacy from Ray to me.

I was that close to Ray and Mark that for the first time I understood how
the business enjoyed caressing success into being by means of belief,
leavened by good manners. I would briefly debate in my mind the extent to
which Ray and I manipulated Mark, but that turned out to be a red herring.
Our enthusiasm was undeniable. I didn't have to tell Ray and Mark what I
wanted to do: I was doing it. And I could speak about what I was doing, and

feel confident it would be received in the spirit in which I intended it. Hindsight being what it is, this was the beginning of the happiest time in my life. I was in a unique position, a publicist in the world of pop 'n' rock. At only seventeen, I joined Les Perrin and a handful of others as a pioneer.

Derek Johnson: I have a favourite story about Leslie Perrin and his partner Harold Davison. In the beginning they'd take on any artist who came along, but eventually they became the UK reps for Frank Sinatra. Harold phoned me up one day and said, 'Derek, I know you've always wanted to meet Sinatra. Well, Marion and I are having a small dinner party for him tonight, wonder if you'd like to come? There's just one thing, you gotta remember how Frank dislikes the press, so you mustn't let on who you are or ask any awkward questions.'

I got there about ten minutes before Sinatra; in he came and I was duly introduced to him by Harold as the family doctor. Only trouble was, Sinatra had got a splitting headache and expected me to do something about it. I excused myself and went out into the hall where I had left my briefcase, in which I always carried a packet of proprietary painkillers. I gave a couple to Sinatra, which he swallowed with a glass of bourbon, and ten minutes later he was feeling right as rain. He thought I was the greatest doctor in the world, and we all had a great time. Frank didn't know the truth until a year later, when Harold told him. He thought it was the funniest thing he'd ever heard.

Dolly East: Les and Jane Perrin were like my parents. I went to live with them in Sutton. I used to help Les at weekends doing PR. I took Pat Pretty's job and was at the EMI press office in the early 60s, when she moved to Pye, then I went on to work for Cliff Richard in Savile Row. All we worked from were biographies. I used to know Maureen Cleave really well; she was unusual because she wasn't just a music writer, so it was a different angle she used to write from. There was a girl called Judith Simons at the *Daily Express* – the Beatles used to send her up terrible, everybody did; she always had ash everywhere, cigarettes hanging out of her gob, ash everywhere, ash Tuesday, ash Wednesday, ash all the time. Really scruffy, but at the same time, very smart. Andrew's whole image was so different from any other PR, or any other that has come since. Andrew was way ahead of his time, very bright and innovative.

ALO: Within a year my own list of clients would be impressive: Mark Wynter, Kenny Lynch, Chris Montez, Johnny Tillotson, Brian Hyland, Phil Spector, Bob Dylan, the Beatles, Jet Harris and Tony Meehan, the Little Richard/Sam Cooke Tour. Save Mr Dylan, they'd all had hits, and hits made my world go round.

The other indie press agents were all boring; worse yet, they were mostly former journalists, elbows and minds rubbed raw by booze. I was the new cock of the walk, the new game in town. I came from a different world: Mary Quant, Alexander Plunkett Greene, Vidal Sassoon, Hardy Amies; I reeked of *Vogue*, not *Melody Maker*. The world of David Bailey, Terence Donovan, Brian Duffy, photographers whose work for the New World designers, crimpers and fashion mags had already – beats and shutters ahead of rock 'n' roll, UK-style – sent a message to the world that the British were coming.

Just as Elvis begot Pat Boone, Cliff begot Fury, Doris Day ended and Monroe took the night; as later the Beatles allowed for the contrasting Stones – so the dark side of entertainment in movies and theatre of the late 50s and early 60s had reached out and hit Broadway and the art cinemas of New York City. Osborne's *Look Back an Anger*; the works of Behan, Wesker, Pinter, Norman and Bart; *Saturday Night and Sunday Morning*; *The Loneliness of the Long Distance Runner*; Bryan Forbes and Richard Attenborough's *Angry Silence* and *The L-Shaped Room* – all took their cue from the French New Wave and New Brit Theatre, scoring as art hits in the US. Then came the lighter side of the British coin, the Flash of Fashion, and I had been there and took that moment to where I moved on.

CHAPTER 8

Johnny Jackson: I'd caressed the hand to get the talent spotter from Garrick Records himself through an expensive dinner and dragged him into this hellhole to hear my talented client. His eyes showed the glaze of six brandies and a genuine dislike for this kind of music. 'What's your feeling about the boy?' I asked him. 'Nausea,' he replied. 'For me personally this kind of music is torture. I'll give you £35 for your client and the group, two sides, no royalty, one-way option to the company and you record next week. All right?'

'So you really think the boy has something?'

'I don't know, I don't care,' he said. 'These young idiots seem to want this kind of thing, so let's sell them what they want. Maybe next week, with this Bongo boy, we'll lose a few pounds. So what? The week after we find a Tommy Steele and make a profit.' As Bongo began to beat on his little skin money-boxes, I worked out how many discs at six shillings Garrick had to sell before Bongo earned me my first thousand. Assuming we got on to a royalty basis at a penny ha'penny with our second recording, it came to almost half a million. Meanwhile, take a fiver off for the skiffle beasts and the evening's work showed me and my boy fifteen quid apiece cash. Not exactly the late Mike Todd's kinda money – but I was in profit. 'In profit.' I love those words.

When I came out after the recording session, Regent Street looked mellow in the late afternoon sunshine, the traffic was soothing after the six hours of Bongo and skiffle, bad jokes and adolescent exhibitionism that we had condensed into two sides of a wax disc.

Mark Wynter: Even when I was still in the charts, I could see the end coming. This artist's life was rather a futile and short-lived existence, chugging around doing a summer season, a panto, a tour, a new record. Hopefully the record would take off; if it didn't, then y'know . . . Up to a point you could trade on your past hits; then, after a couple of years, you were really only as bookable as your last hit record was successful.

ALO: I didn't see Ray Mackender from 1965 until the year he passed on in Toronto in the early 90s. Ray, after Mark Wynter, moved on out into the world and became his own act. He stopped pretending, both by day and by night, and gave up both his jobs to travel the world. He worked in Australia and Tahiti as a short-order cook, as a tour guide in the mountains of New Zealand, and as a cruise-line social director, visiting ports of call all over the world. Ray gave up on the City and, when rock dropped the pop and tough nuts took over the town, he moved on to another berth. When I saw him that last year before he died, he still had the shine that drew me to him, that light for those with the wherewithal and the discipline to hone their talent into manna from the stalls to the upper circle.

If my recollections of the business in the early 60s make the artiste appear to be a necessary evil, I'm not exaggerating. One young record-industry promotion man decided to swim against the scum-line. The Decca office that Tony Hall set up in Great Marlborough Street became the place to go. Hall took over the third floor, had his wife Mafalda decorate the offices, and left the main area to be used for receptions to welcome American artistes. The atmosphere of the offices reflected Tony's personality: loose and cool, totally different from the Albert Embankment HQ.

Tony Hall: I pushed for a separate Decca promotion office because the contacts – the DJs, TV people, the BBC – were all in the West End. You couldn't expect a busy BBC producer to come down to the Albert Embankment where Decca was dug in. Why the hell do they wanna waste their time doing that? Decca didn't impress anybody.

The company didn't exactly approve of my methods. There was a guy, Bill Townsley, the General Manager actually, whom I used to call 'Doctor No'. Any time I came up with a creative suggestion, he'd shout 'No'.

Andrew, young and inexperienced as he was, contributed to the vibe I was trying to get going in my outpost office. His clothes always spoke volumes. For instance, he'd wear tweed of some kind, the English thing, but cut very hip. The cut was just ultra-sharp, he was wearing shades even in those days. He was the young, hip, upcoming guy and he stood out. I always had great respect for him. He was doing something different, he was fun to watch. I would tip him off as to who was coming to town.

ALO: The visiting American stars and their managers used to stay at the Stratford Palace Court Hotel on Oxford Street. I stopped in regularly to hustle whomever I could buttonhole. As most of the managers I spoke to were hustlers themselves, they appreciated my candour. It made sense to hire someone who would be solely devoted to their act, with them all the way for the week or so they were in town.

I managed to feather my nest with short-term assignments from Brian Hyland ('Sealed With A Kiss'), Johnny Tillotson ('Send Me The Pillow That You Dream On') and Little Eva, who went from babysitting for Carole King and Gerry Goffin to brief stardom with the 'Loco-motion'. The US acts were very nice, thank you: quiffed, coy, and in the Top 20. I loved the way they enjoyed their fifteen minutes over three, but it was their Yank managers who made a deep-screen impression; there was nobody like them working the music side of the street in England. These guys oozed from every pore the sweet smell of success – Las Vegas and Broadway version.

Johnny Tillotson's bloodhound, the affable Mel Shayne, was as Las Vegas as the neon sign over the Sands Hotel. On looks alone, Martin Scorsese would have hired him as a technical adviser on *Casino*. Brian Hyland's minder was Sidney Falco grows up: Sam Goldstein, renamed Gordon (as in quiet and flash), was an inventive, wiry, show-me-the-money Jerry McGuire via Damon Runyon. English managers, however competent and loathing they may have been, still felt they had to make excuses and curtsies for their lot as pimps. Americans came without shame and I loved them for it.

Andy Wickham, publicist and A&R executive: I had my own introduction to American management style through Murry Wilson, father to the Beach Boy brothers. Murry Wilson, through his own love of the Four Freshman, actually dreamt up the original Beach Boys sound. He was a wheedling toad of a man who was seriously smitten by Maureen Cleave at their interview in the Sands Coffee Bar in Bond Street. When he called her 'Mo' and started pawing her, she fled into the street for a taxi, with Murry in hot pursuit brandishing a Marathon bar at her as an inducement to return. Later, when I met the Beach Boys at Heathrow for their first British visit, I introduced myself to Dennis Wilson by saying how much I had liked his father. This was the first and only time I was ever punched by an artiste.

There was also Nick Venet, who had discovered the Beach Boys and produced their first two albums, in town to produce the Walker Brothers. His real name was Vanatoulis and he styled himself 'The Gutsy Greek'. Nik Cohn described him as a 'B-Feature Heavy' and he certainly looked the part with his camel-hair coat and monogrammed cigarettes, but actually he was all smiles and the power of positive thinking – a handsome, cheerful figure with an endless supply of witty vignettes. Not everyone took him seriously, but he had great style and went on to make a string of classic records with people like Linda Ronstadt and Fred Neil.

ALO: At the Cumberland Hotel, Marble Arch, I bumped into another American manager, Albert Grossman, a one-off among the wannabes, the calm above the norm. His young charge, Bob Dylan, was in London to play a minor role as a hobo in a BBC2 American beatnik-style television drama, *Madhouse on Castle Street*, written by Jack London. He got to perform two songs: 'Blowin' In The Wind' and 'Ballad Of A Gliding Swan'. I got a fiver to handle Dylan for the week.

At the time, Grossman was a very casually dressed, neat, grey-haired guy, nothing like the pony-tailed wild man of Woodstock he would later become. He looked like a well-to-do lawyer in his weekend clothes. His devotion to Dylan, even then, was apparent. In a world of agents it was refreshing to meet someone like that. As for Dylan, he was 'Bob Dylan' already, as he's Bob Dylan now. It wasn't an act, even if it was. He had the magic and the words of life already. But it was Grossman's singular devotion that impressed me. To be sitting in a small hotel room, giving all his time to just one artist. They were both very happy together. They acted like they knew something we didn't know yet.

Grossman was still only in his thirties, though prematurely grey. A Jewish hustler from Chicago, he was on his way to becoming the most influential American management figure of the 60s. Intuitive and gutsy, he already had a firm grip on the street-level New York Greenwich Village folk scene. Along with Dylan he managed Odetta and Peter, Paul & Mary – who in a few months would be the first of his acts to break big with a cover of Dylan's 'Blowin' In The Wind'. It was written that Grossman broke two acts at the same time: Peter, Paul & Mary and Bob Dylan. But it would be 1965 before Dylan's own platters broke through as national pop anthems with 'Like A Rolling Stone'. While I managed to secure some press for the unknown-in-Britain folk singer, Albert Grossman was re-inventing and ahead of the game, turning the quick buck into the long buck.

Soon all my English pop acts were top acts, and Ray Mackender's education in showbiz tradition was fortified by the street smarts I picked up from the Yank travelling salesmen. Their attitude towards me was not 'What Do You Want?' but 'What Can I Tell Ya?' The days were happily BRP – Before Rampant Paranoia. Everybody shared, and the shills were alive with the sound of music.

Tony King, Decca promotion: I first met Andrew through Mark Wynter. Andrew was very young, wiry, thin and sharp-looking, attentive, taking everything in, sitting in a corner taking notes. He started dropping by the Decca promotion office with Sheila and we would go downstairs for a coffee to the Café de la Paix, Hanover Square, where all the DJs of the time used to meet, before our offices in Great Marlborough Street became the place to go.

The American artistes would be in town for a week, and Andrew would go to the hotel to bump into the manager. Tony Hall was Andrew's biggest champion at Decca. He's the man who really opened the doors for Andrew there. Andrew would not have got as far as he did without Tony and Mafalda Hall; they were parent figures to the wild child. I was also grateful for Tony Hall's breakaway attitude. He was far-sighted enough to realise that it was smart to have someone who got along with artistes. American artistes were in their early twenties. They wanted a young bloke who wanted to stay out all night showing them around London. American artistes were *it*. I was in awe of them.

Tony Hall: Tony King was only eighteen and had a great talent for looking after American artistes. He liked socialising, was good at chat and liked to go shopping with the wives. It was impossible to get the records we all liked on the BBC. The early Atlantic Records, early Berry Gordy stuff, the Barbara George single 'I Know', a huge R&B hit in America; we couldn't get arrested with the likes of that in the UK and that hurt, because those records were so good.

In the mid-50s Jimmy Young would have huge million-sellers with things like 'The Man From Laramie' covering the big American record. That's what sold. The A&R man would go to the States on a song-shopping spree, bring back the hits, go straight into the studio and copy the arrangement exactly. The singer came as close to the 'original' as his gifts of mime would allow.

There wasn't such a word as marketing in those days. It'd be in the shops on Monday, and it was my job to get it on the radio by Tuesday. There was no messing around. If the record had it, if somehow there was a bit of magic to it, if you got it on the radio, it was in the shops, it sold and it was in the charts. Simple as that.

Tony King: It was very hard to get records played on the radio. One had a very small window to work in; people were waking up to the fact that the record-business phenomenon was here to stay. I was the new thing, the youngest promo man in the business. Before me, very stodgy middle-aged people ran it. Radio in 1962 was *Housewives' Choice*, *Saturday Club*, *Top Gear* and *Easy Beat*, all and only BBC. To work Radio Luxembourg, you had to go to their HQ at Hereford Street. You paid for your own shows, which played only Decca artistes, but there were lots of independent DJs working on Luxembourg who played various records, so you had to make sure they were all taken care of. Periodically you had to go there and schmooze. It was a boring hellhole.

To make matters worse, the Musicians' Union had a stranglehold on the BBC, as they controlled the musicians that the BBC needed for live radio and TV. This meant limited needle-time and a 50/50 union-dictated balance between live and recorded music. There weren't many outlets on TV, either. If you got your record on *Juke Box Jury* you'd earned your money that week.

In order to be in on the management end of things you had to be seen as part of showbiz. When you went and did these TV shows, a lot of the people who produced and directed them were from the showbiz end of the business. You had to be a part of that. Most British showbiz people made their living out of getting a few hit records and then getting a TV series or something. The record business was still growing, establishing itself; it was slightly poo-pooed by showbiz people.

Andrew was unique, he was an independent promo man, very entrepreneurial. There were other people out there, but Andrew was different – he hustled, he talked, he made things happen.

Percy Dickens, *NME* News Editor: Andrew came into the office asking for something for Ray Mackender. Andrew Oldham? Who the bloody hell is he? I looked at him, and it is still like a flash photograph in my mind's eye. My God, I thought, who's this?

He was dressed in striped trousers, a black jacket and a stiff collar, like the chairman of the board, very smart, very elegant and very well behaved. It was like a bombshell coming into Denmark Street, you can imagine. It was so sort of alien. Not many people used to wear suits in those days – the publishers, the bandleaders and some musicians perhaps, but most of us were quite scruffy. Then a couple of months later, near Christmas time, he put his head round the door, very friendly, as if he'd known me for years, and said, 'I've got a little thing for you, it's from Ray.' I noted he'd changed his mode of dress: still very elegant, but more suited to Denmark Street than the stock exchange. Andrew was a quick study.

Tony King: We'd all grown up post-war, with ration books and no access to money for clothes, working-class English boys growing up pretty poor. When this thing – this life – came along, it was an expression of one's freedom, to be able to go out and dress in smart clothes and look good. There was more money around, more jobs and more opportunity; there was a general feeling of recovery from the war. Fashion, John Stephen and Mary Quant, the importance of the mid-50s' American movies: you got a glimpse of how it was possible for young people to have fun, enjoy a bit of success and material things.

ALO: Tony King had the spark of life, still does. There was a great energy being given off at that moment. We knew we were somewhere even if we didn't quite know where. Work was given an extra kick by the two Tonys not being housed in Decca's main funeral home, 9 Albert Embankment, which held Sir Edward, Bill Townsley, Dick Rowe, a host of civil servants, plus old soldiers and pensioners from World War I manning the doors.

When I offed the elevator and entered the two Tonys' suite, I felt love and I felt at home, whether I dropped in at teatime, for a natter or a shop, or I arrived six thirtyish to a smoke-filled reception: the smoke cleared whenever I caught the gleam in either of the Tonys' eyes. There were a lot of great receptions that I and Keith Richards and others were sometimes invited to, and sometimes crashed, and on occasion it was not as amusing for Tony King as it was for us. We were the mad hatters, functioning in a world that the Albert Embankment nutters still thought quite mad and silly, but knew now was definitely not going away. I've said that the publicity-agent period, as mad as it was, also represented the calmest, happiest days of my life. Then came the Stones. Then came the real work and real madness.

I didn't see Tony King for a while; then later he joined me at Ivor Court to launch Immediate Records and promote the Stones before moving on to George Martin and AIR, Elton John, John Lennon, America and RCA, and finally full circle in recent years back with Mick and the Stones. Tony King remains a very thoughtful being whom I love, who speaks well of and to, dresses well, shops well, keeps well and laughs well. One of his gifts —whether with me, Mick, Reg or Lennon – is that Tony would only put up with the very best of you, and had the ability to help you find it.

I was now spending my time between London-American one-weekers and looking after Mark Wynter on the Larry Parnes-produced package tour of the UK starring Billy Fury. At the Britannia Pier, Great Yarmouth, I finally got to meet Billy Fury and, more significantly, Larry Parnes.

Fury was not up to the fantasy: he was not only stoned, he was bored. As David Bowie said later, sometimes it's better not to meet your idols; that way they stay intact. Billy was not intact. Parnes, on the other hand, lived up to my true pop Diaghilev image of him – a rare blend of art, money and sparkle on the job. Mr Parnes was a captain alert, while his artiste seemed to be floundering, without structure, a Nijinsky to the Maestro. I do not recommend piers in Great Yarmouth as the place to meet those who've shaped your life thus far.

Mark Wynter and ALO

Straight off the Rock & Trad tour, Mark and I headed for Twickenham Film studios. Mark, as part of the transformation to all-round entertainer, was to star in the Milton Subotsky-produced *Just for Fun* (directed by Gordon Flemying) and I was along to make sure everything went smoothly.

At Twickenham studios another film was also being shot, *It's Trad, Dad* (directed by Richard Lester, later to direct the Beatles on film), and to keep costs down many of the cast featured in both movies. Both films were poor imitations of the American rock 'n' roll B-movies, with little plot but packed with plenty of current pop acts. Among the likes of Helen Shapiro, Bobby Vee, Dusty Springfield, the Crickets, Joe Brown, the Tornados, Jet Harris and Tony Meehan, Mark was treated like a true star as he was Acting with an 'A', as opposed to miming his perhaps next hit single like his fellow cast members.

We shared the same room in a bed and breakfast near the studio. We had to be on the set at 6 a.m., and every morning Mark would go through this marvellous little routine. He'd get up, creep off to the bathroom to wash, shave, put on a little make-up and fix his hair. Then he'd get back into bed and pretend to wake up again, yawning and stretching. Eventually he'd sit up and say, 'Well, Andrew, time to set off for the studios.' He was convinced I thought he always woke up looking like that. I just thought it was great, he really was looking after his image! I loved it. If I don't think somebody's a star I have a hard job selling them. I liked the fact that Mark was on for me.

Mark Wynter at a signing with ALO looking on far right

Mark Wynter: He acted like my minder; he was a very good friend, picked up very quickly on everything. He was very aware of how things should and shouldn't be done. He knew who should be allowed to come in the dressing room. He was very clued up, very sharp, very bright. I was playing the lead, and the story was about young people getting the vote, a glorified pop TV spectacular on film. The leading girl was Cherry Roland, who'd been plucked off the street at a bus stop. We used to have heated passionate situations prior to takes. She was so nervous about filming, but our sessions helped calm her down . . . without going all the way.

ALO: In my role as deputy manager, I soaked up the glamorous atmosphere. Although press people visited the film set, I had enough spare time to be happily engrossed in the filming process, chatting with producers, directors and cameramen and watching them on the job.

My name was getting out there; it was a wonderful time of simply being and doing, when I had no concern about what others thought of me or my progress. Jean Lincoln was another doer working for the Bernard Delfont Agency, which operated out of a second-floor spread at the wrong end of Jermyn Street, above the back entrance to the Piccadilly tube. Notoriously lethal agents and managers, among them Billy Marsh, Keith Devon and Mike Sullivan, manned the agency.

Jean worked closely with Mike Sullivan, helping him book Shirley Bassey, Ron Moody and Shani Wallis. She also exclusively managed Kenny Lynch, so we met and talked about me handling Kenny's press. When I try to recall the actual meeting, all I get is lights and action – her eyes, beauty and spirit signifying that I'd met one of the big teachers and best friends of my life, whom I immediately felt I'd known in another.

Jean met Kenny in 1960 at one of his regular club bookings, Rimano's on Soho's Gerrard Street. Two weeks later she'd arranged an audition for Lynch with Wally Ridley, A&R at EMI, who signed him to an EMI subsidiary, HMV POP. His first few singles had all stalled at the lower end of the charts, but Lincoln was sure lightning would strike twice with Kenny's cover of Goffin and King's 'Up On The Roof,' a proven smash for the Leiber-Stoller Drifters in the US.

Kenny Lynch: Jean loved Andrew, they became really good friends. Any chance she had to get him in on anything, he was in! If she had a chance to push him forward, forward he went. They'd speak ten or twenty times a day on the phone, going for meetings or having lunch. He was as important to her as I was and she was living with me!

Andrew was very good for this game because he liked being Jack the Lad

Kenny Lynch, Jean Lincoln, ALO

with the stars, just loved it, which is why he was so good at it, why he got on. He made everybody feel like they were a million dollars, he had that knack. With some he wasn't that well liked, because he had that balance about him, that will, that cunningness. Though a lot of people think he was worse than he was. Oh, but he did have a lot of front, that's why people didn't like him. That's how he was, just using people up. He did it better than anybody else.

Artists get used all the time. If you're gonna get on, that's the way you gotta be, that's business. I was one of the first artists he had who anybody knew, and he never changed with me. After that Jean and I were like family to him, all through the Stones; we stayed tight – theatres, cinema, him and Jean going all over the place while I was away. Like three brothers and sisters. Sheila stayed in the background. I really liked her, lovely, nice and quiet; when she was with us we'd just talk about things of the day. I thought she was a good stabilising influence on him; he always treated her with a lot of respect when I saw 'em.

Everything was a laugh to him; if we didn't laugh eighteen hours out of a day we thought we'd had a bad day. He was a hustler, that's all he did, hustle. He had his fingers in everything. He'd come to me and start talking about somebody, some act. I'd say, 'Why are you worried about him?' Five minutes later Andrew'd say 'It's okay, I'm handling him now.'

Everybody thought he was a poof – he knew that, he couldn't give a monkey's. Andrew used that to his advantage all the time: when I'm with so and so I'll be a poof, because that's what they want. I don't mean sexually, I mean businesswise; there were a lot of poofs involved in the showbiz offices. Then with others he'd be straight as pie. He didn't dress like the Delfont/ Grade office did, but he always had a smart jacket, smart trousers, big tie, big knot. He looked like one of the Kinks, but better.

He was a real grafter. He was born to be in showbusiness. He's one of the biggest schemers ever in the business, I think he had everything going for him, except maybe the ability to steal large amounts of money. I was always saying to him, 'Why do managers steal off people when they're already earning money off them?' Andrew was like: 'The day I get it in, they'll get their whack and I'll get mine.' No one ever told me he stole money like all the other managers. He never did that.

I was a jazz singer singing in Rimano's on Gerrard Street, right opposite the Whisky À Go Go. Jean walked in with Shirley Bassey, just as I was singing a standard. Jean called me over, said, 'Would you like to meet Shirley Bassey? You're good. We think you should be making records.'

At that time I was living in Brewer Street with a mate, two beds, pulling birds. That's handy! I thought – records, party, new way of getting hold of birds. She said, 'Gimme your number and I'll try and get you a record deal.' A few weeks later I get a call from this girl to go see Wally Ridley at EMI. I was acting in a film with Stanley Baker, *The Criminal*. Joseph Losey directed it. I was portraying one of only two black guys in Pentonville prison, gambling away the time with Stanley on a mock-up location on Old Street.

I cut my first single at Abbey Road in 1960. When Jean took me on she was living with the guy who went on to manage the Walker Brothers. She said, 'I can't manage you, he'll be your manager.' I sorta got to like him; he used to steal tenners off me, it didn't matter. I was living in his house, eating his food. He was sending me up to Scotland to do a one o'clock TV game show, told me I was only getting £2. I did twenty-one shows, appeared in sketches, did the lot. He'd say, 'You're only getting the airfare, but here's three quid to spend', while he was pocketing twenty quid a time.

So I got a flat at the cobbled end of Old Compton Street and asked Jean to move in. The Greeks were fighting each other and everybody, and bombs were going off; the guy who did the C&W shows, Mervyn Conn, ran Rimano's. The Business Club was first, then came the Revolution. Whisky À Go Go was Raymond Nash – he married a princess; downstairs was the Flamingo. I knew Rik Gunnell who ran the Flamingo: he took Jean away from me because I wouldn't marry her. She said, 'If you don't marry me I'm going to live in America with Rik . . .' That's where she died.

It was Tommy Steele who got me into pop. I was singing jazz at the Style Club, with Alan Clare and Tony Crombie, in Gerrard Street. Tommy said, 'If you stop singing all that clever-clever shit, you could be a pop star.' I said, 'I don't want to sing them kinda songs.' He was right. I also knew Lionel Bart, who was involved with the second biggest agency, Jock Jacobson's, run by Peter Charleston. They had Tommy, Max Bygraves and Lionel; they took part of the shows off Lionel playing cards with him.

We were in 17 Savile Row, Cliff Richard's office and mine. Don't know why they gave me an office there, but they did. I was writing, and Freddy Bienstock liked to keep an eye on me. Mort Shuman asked me out to eat, and over dinner asked me to become his songwriting partner. I'd only written two songs, two B-sides, and they'd gone on the back of two hits, know what I mean? I couldn't believe it. I'd written two songs and now Mort Shuman, the top writer in the world, wanted me as his new writing partner. They gave me a thousand quid and a trip to America. My first time in New York at the Brill I met Leiber & Stoller, Bobby Darin, Ellie Greenwich, Barry Mann, Burt Bacharach. The Brill was the number-one music place in the world.

ALO: Kenny Lynch is a sophisticated braveheart with a great many textures: his talent, sense of humour, Shetland skin and big heart. He just fits together and lives in the comfort zone.

Jean introduced me to Roy Moseley, who handled Jet Harris. When Jet left the Shadows to go solo, he had a hit with 'The Man With The Golden Arm', a Jet-come-lately cover of the title theme of the 1955 film produced by, and starring, Frank Sinatra.

Jet had recently formed an instrumental duo with the other ex-Shadow, my neighbourhood finishing schoolmaster, Tony Meehan. They had 'Diamonds' coming out, and I got to rep Jet on the Little Richard/Sam Cooke Tour for ten minutes. Two years earlier I'd been sneaking away from Wellingborough to see the Shadows and Emile Ford at the Granada Kettering, putting Vim in my hair to have the kind of blond fun I imagined Jet was having. Jet was James Dean on bass, the man who took the bass electric and made it a star.

John Paul Jones: We all wanted to look like Jet Harris. I got into session playing through Jet Harris and Tony Meehan. Jet and Tony were my first major band. I had been in various small bands and done all the American bases. Jet was with the Jet Blacks; I walked up to him on Archer Street and asked him if he needed a bass player. He said, 'No, I don't, but they do', pointing me towards the Jet Blacks. He was leaving them, so I auditioned and joined up. Later he heard about me, swapped his bass player for me and I went on the road with them. I was seventeen and earning £30 a week with Jet and Tony, which was enormous. That's when I first met Peter Grant. He was tour-managing Gene Vincent for Don Arden. Peter later managed Led Zeppelin.

I was with Jet and Tony after they left the Shadows and made 'Diamonds' and 'Scarlett O'Hara'. They also got me into session work. Jet never played a six-string bass, it was a tuned-down guitar. He played lead and I played bass. Joe Moretti was on rhythm guitar, he played on a lot of Andrew's sessions later on.

Jet was always pretty well refreshed. I think he used to drink out of nerves, but he was a great bass player. Their manager, Roy Moseley, was a character. He would just turn up every now and again on the road, swish in wearing a long leather coat, ask how we were, be a prima donna for a while, then swish out again.

Tony Meehan: Roy was very camp. Very. He worked for Bernard Delfont and Billy Marsh. They were a big, big pair. Billy Marsh and Keith Devon were running the agency for Bernard Delfont, and Roy Moseley worked for them and took over the management of Jet Harris after he left Cliff and the

Shadows. Jet had 'Man With The Golden Arm' and a couple of other minor hits, which I played on as a session musician. The Delfont Agency booked acts. I don't think they could do promotions and all that, just book acts, so they – the Grades – just split it all up, and had people front it all for them, y'know, that sort of thing. They were all in bed with one another.

Basically there were two or three big people who carved the whole thing up. Believe me, that was it and the Grades had a lot to do with that. They really monopolised British showbusiness; those people at that time ran everything. They had their fingers in every pie. In records. In television. In radio. In films. So they had a lot of pull. They were powerful and they ran it in a very organised and austere manner. It wasn't at all flamboyant. Roy was very flamboyant because he wanted to be in showbusiness, originally wanted to act. Or something.

Jet did a tour with Sam Cooke and Little Richard on his own; that's when Andrew worked for him. Then I found this tune called 'Diamonds', Jerry Lordan had written it, and I thought: Well, this is a natural for Jet to get his act together. We made the record: it went to number one in January 1963. I'd discussed it with all the people at Decca, they thought it was a great idea. Then we went in to make our second record, 'Scarlett O'Hara', which went to number two.

Jet Harris: 'Diamonds' was number one for six weeks, it was the biggest thing. Bruce Welch was angry that Jerry Lordan gave it to us instead of the Shadows, but Jerry wrote 'Diamonds' for me. He wrote 'Apache' and 'Wonderful Land', all the big ones that broke the Shadows – you couldn't go wrong with him then.

Kenny Lynch: Jet was a raving nutter; he'd walk into the room sometimes and he'd want to fight you. Billy Fury walked into a room, the lights went out, he'd sit in a corner and hope someone would come and talk rock 'n' roll to him; a very quiet lad. Jet was pissed all the time, wanting to fight everybody. If it wasn't for Tony Meehan, Jet would be dead by now. Tony would put his arm round him and take him out to the street to sober up.

Andrew was quite an addition to this line-up. For one thing, Andrew wasn't that well liked by the Delfont/Grade people. They were jealous of him, even when he wasn't making it that much. He had more front than Selfridges. Mike Sullivan hated him. He always used to say to Jean, 'I don't want him in here.' It was like the British showbiz Mafia, but his experience at Bernard Delfont was a big help to him, because he saw it! He knew he wasn't gonna get in with these people. Jean put him right on that. From the start, I don't think he wanted to go down that road with them, he didn't want to be in the same bag, they were all family men; he wanted to be out at rock concerts. He didn't want to be a manager like Mike Sullivan, sit in his office saying, 'Yes, he's free that week.' Andrew never could have done that.

ALO: Jean was my mother, my father, my very best friend. There was nothing we didn't share as we played the game of life. She showed me showbiz – the whole block, how her world worked. She showed me where to play and where not to. She was my guide, my muse, my angel. She left for America some years later. We would end up living in the same block on Central Park West in New York, and there she died. She remains one of the faces always smiling over me.

Kenny Lynch: The people who sorta messed up the record business for the monopoly, who kind of levelled it off, were the Beatles, Rolling Stones and Dave Clark. When they started going out doing ballparks which they didn't own, that's what fucked it all up for the Grades. It became different.

ALO: The Delfont Agency didn't give a damn about the act unless they were over fifty or behaved like it. This was no happy showbusiness vibe. This was a very austere monopoly, there was nothing glamorous about it. But in the middle of this, at two formica tables, were Jean Lincoln and Roy Moseley, who both had the smile and made it worth while.

Kenny Lynch: Jean and I walked into a restaurant once in the South of France. Jean said, 'There's Arthur Askey over there.' I said, 'Oh, I'll go just over and say hello to him.' When I got over to him he was sitting with Lew Grade and his wife. I knew Arthur through radio shows, and he said, 'Y'know Lew, don't you?' Lew looked at me and said, 'I know you, I like you, I've seen you on telly, you're gonna be big; you shouldn't be messing around with who you're with, you should be with us.' I said, 'I am with you, I've been with you for two years.' He said, 'Oh, thank God for that', and just went into another conversation.

ALO: I'd got the Little Richard tour through getting up the front to tackle Don Arden. Born Harry Levy, Don Arden was once the most famous Hebrew folk singer in Europe. He'd also worked as a comic and MC, repped by impresario Harold Davison, who'd brought to the UK Count Basie, Duke Ellington and Frank Sinatra. By the late 50s Arden had retired from the stage and gone into business as a promoter of rock 'n' roll.

He'd quickly established himself as the most talked-about rock 'n' roll concert promoter of the day, the principal European agent for the whole rock 'n' roll pantheon: Gene Vincent, Sam Cooke, Jerry Lee Lewis, Little Richard, Brenda Lee, the Shirelles, Bo Diddley, Johnny Preston, Duane Eddy, Chuck Berry, Ray Charles, Fats Domino, Bill Haley, the Everly Brothers and many more, even Jayne Mansfield. Teddy boys elevated Don to cult status and the punters made him rich. Counting stubs on the many hundreds of thousands of tickets he sold, Arden had grown wildly resplendent.

Don Arden: Andrew came into the office and we did a deal on the Sam Cooke/Little Richard tour. I think he came in to see me in my Carnaby Street office. I don't know why I thought he could do it, but I did. I really don't know. I just remember him being so thin in those days, he had an overcoat on that I was sure was his dad's. He did a great job.

That was really before the Liverpool Sound took over, just before that. Little Richard was still amazing . . . when he opened for me in Doncaster he wore that great suit from the movie *The Girl Can't Help It*. And then Sam Cooke came in, joined the tour and . . . oh, he was just terrific. Jet Harris was on that tour, his first solo tour after he left the Shadows. He did quite well on that tour but he had no chance to shine because Sam Cooke and Richard were so good.

What happened was, things were going great, we were selling out everywhere. Then Andrew put an article in one of the local papers, and then in one of the London papers. It said 'This is gonna be the most sensational tour of all time. The kids are gonna go crazy, they're gonna rip the seats from out of the theatre! Come and see it!' That's what Andrew got them to print. Of course, we got a letter from old Cecil Bernstein's lawyers: he was in charge of the Granada cinema and theatre chain across the UK, that's where we'd booked the tour, and he said that unless we changed the PR guy he was gonna cancel the tour. I showed Andrew the correspondence. I couldn't afford to lose twenty dates. He understood. We were always friends after that.

He had self-confidence. Andrew and I never argued about anything. Never had a false word. He always appreciated my talent and I appreciated his. We liked each other and then he met the family. The family liked Andrew, Andrew liked them, and I think it was just one of those natural things, and we were always friends from day one.

Chris Hutchins, journalist: My first meeting with Andrew was during the period I was plotting to set up this music paper with Don Arden. I did a bit of PR work for Don, wrote his press releases, sent 'em out to various papers, no big deal. He had offices at Royalty House on Dean Street. He was really trying to be the big operator. Don hated Maurice Kinn, the owner of the *NME*, because Maurice was the big 'I Am', up there with the Grades.

Don was a maverick, he took chances on Little Richard, Chuck Berry and Gene Vincent. He wanted to set up a rival music paper to the *NME*, against Maurice. I was going around on the side getting estimates from printers, planning what we could do. I'd been at the *NME* for a year, on lowly, humble pay, £18 a week.

Don was really worried about the Little Richard tour. He said, 'I've got this guy who's gonna help you and get lots of PR for me. Andrew Oldham, he's really go-ahead.' A couple of days later I went into the office and Andrew had already sent out this press release. I don't know how he'd worked so quickly: the press release invited everybody to please stand by to rip the seats out of the floor and tear the theatres apart, Little Richard is coming to town. The release reached Johnny Hamp at Granada Theatres. Johnny and Bernstein wanted to pull the plug on the tour because of this press release. It was the most outrageous thing anybody could imagine, the most outrageous thing anyone had done.

ALO: So I was off the tour, but in Don Arden I'd made a friend for life. If you wanted to be in showbusiness you just stood next to Don. I'd had the time of my life, I'd witnessed two greats, a nightly triathlon of rock, pop 'n' stomp, fought out between the oh-so-wild Little Richard and oh-so-smooth Mr Cooke.

My dance card of life was getting fatter, richer and info'd up; people were very giving, they were competitive but the competition was not driven by fear. That's one of the courses drugs would bring to the menu, seasoned by success: a heavy toxin for most, digestible by only a few. Meanwhile 'the greatest records ever made' were being made and made again. The Four Seasons' 'Big Girls Don't Cry', produced by Bob Crewe, was at number three in the States and the Phil Spector-produced 'He's A Rebel' by the Crystals was number two. In England, Rolf Harris and Frank Ifield held those spots.

Gene Pitney: I wrote 'He's A Rebel'. I was in my car in front of a bank in my little home town in Connecticut and Phil's earlier Crystals' record 'Uptown' came on the radio. It was the first time I'd ever heard low strings in a rock song; cellos and violas, everything, it just blew me away, I loved it. I said to myself, 'I'm gonna write their next single', never thinking in a million years I could pull it off. I had this word 'rebel' and I set out to write the song; I used to try and write from a colour word, a word that had something descriptive about it.

I wrote three full versions of it. I would play piano and sing lead voice into the tape recorder, then play that back, and play guitar and sing harmony voice on top. Well, the first two versions I threw away, they were awful. So it was the third try when everything just flowed; it just hit, the wording came, the concept came . . . The people who say they wrote a song in a hour, well, this thing took me months on end.

Then Phil Spector came into my publisher's office in New York. A lot of the people who came in were A&R men who didn't exactly know what they were looking for, and they'd go out with an armload of acetates, saying, 'Yeah, well, I got this guy and I'll try this with him.' Phil came in, knew what he was looking for, he wouldn't even let the guys play eight bars of the song. They'd maybe get through four bars and he'd say, 'No. No. Next, next, next, next . . .' When they played 'He's A Rebel' his eyes lit up. He just took that thing and trucked out the door, he was gone.

Freddy Bienstock, publisher: Spector was very weird, still is. What happened with Spector was that he came from California, sent by his mentor Lester Sill, who was also the mentor of Leiber & Stoller, who later became my partners. Lester sent Phil to New York to come and see me and Leiber & Stoller. We had a small record company at that time called Big Top Records and Phil Spector produced our first record, Ray Peterson's 'Tell Laura I Love Her', which was a huge hit. He also recorded Curtis Lee with 'Pretty Little Angel Eyes', which was a very big hit. Then he went back to the West Coast and started his string of hits with the Philles label, which was Phil for Spector and Les for Lester Sill. We had his publishing in England via Belinda Music, so when he came over we put him up in a company apartment.

I had originally come to London to open a music-publishing company for Hill & Range called Belinda Music, which was to be located at 17 Savile Row. I remember I looked over across the street and there was a tailor called Anderson & Shepherd; I was told they were the greatest tailors. I thought, 'That's very convenient for me', but I was absolutely stunned when they asked me to look at patterns for what suit I wanted. Then they showed me pictures of what kind of suits they made: living most of my life in America, I said, 'No, I want to have this type of suit made. I don't want those wide lapels, I would like to have narrow lapels.' They looked at me peculiarly, then I said I would also like the trouser legs more narrow and no turn-ups. 'No turn-ups?' he said. 'I'm terribly sorry, sir, but Anderson & Shepherd make only a certain type of suit.' And with a 'Good day, sir' he dismissed me. I'd also told him I didn't want his pleats, which had already annoyed the hell out of him.

At that time I was staying on top of the Mirabelle; we had service flats, very nice. I walked down Cordon Street looking for a barber shop and I saw a place called 'Trotters', which claimed to be By Appointment to Kings George III, Edwards VII and VIII, the lot, and I thought, 'Oh, this could be the place.' But the moment I walked in, I knew I'd made a mistake. This very elderly man started asking me all these personal questions – 'How long have you been in this country?' – which I found very annoying. Finally, after more of this discourse, I was asked how I would like to have my hair cut. I said, 'Preferably in silence!'

Near the office on Savile Row I saw a place opening up called the 'Mane

Line' – a barber shop. I'm used to barbers who have names like Frank and Tom, and this thing flies up to me and says, 'I'm Mr Cecil!', so I said, 'Oh yes, I know, I know.' 'Oh really! Did you read about me or did somebody tell you about me?' I said, 'I dreamt about you.'

My first job was in the stockroom at the famous music publishers, Chappell's, in New York. Mr Dreyfuss was the head of Chappell's when he hired me as a stockroom boy. Everybody who was hired in New York had to meet him; he never thought that one day I'd buy the company, and neither did I. I eventually became a song plugger and later I was fired. I started a little company of my own, then I went to work for my cousins, the Aberbachs, at their Hill & Range publishing company in the penthouse of the Brill Building. They had the penthouse of the Brill Building for years and years. We organised a company for Elvis, and it was my job to run that company and I got to know him very well.

The way he worked was that I would get songs together and I would play them for him and then he would make his decision. I must say that in the first twelve years of his career he would never look at a song unless I had seen it first. Elvis had two companies, Elvis Presley Music and Gladys Music, named after his mother. Half was owned by Hill & Range and half by Elvis. We did the music for thirty-three films together.

I knew Jerry Leiber and Mike Stoller very well; they were buddies of mine before we became partners. I started to work with Cliff Richard in 62, 63, and then I made a deal with the Kinks, the Animals, Alan Price – a lot of the major English acts. The Beatles came to us and made an offer. My man Frank Leroy turned them down because they wanted £1,000. Later, I went into partnership with Leiber & Stoller; they'd written some songs for the Presley films – *Jailhouse Rock* was one.

We bought a number of companies together, and Bobby Darin, Tim Hardin, Doc Pomus and Mort Shuman were there on the eleventh floor of the Brill Building. Kenny Lynch came over to work with Mort Shuman, and it was a very productive time, a building full of songs and songwriters. Some of them would sell their songs many times over to the different publishers. Walter Dannison was a great early writer: he wrote 'My Blue Heaven' and sold it to three different publishers in one day because he needed the money.

When Phil Spector came over to London, we put him up at our Mirabelle flat and gave him our Rolls-Royce.

Sheila Klein: Andrew and Phil Spector looked quite alike. He had that Jewishness as well. Going to eat in Blooms in Whitechapel, they must have thought, 'Hey, we're twin brothers' or something, even though Andrew was six foot. It was almost like he'd met his other half. Phil Spector was a one-off as well. Andrew was delighted to meet someone as basically angry as himself. They shared a passion about what they were into: little tweed hats, music, you name it. With Andrew, whatever he could use, like the Jewishness, could be turned on . . . he was acting all the time, how to do the best performance to get what he wanted. He was a master of disguise; he could change the way he looked totally and he had a wonderful time doing it. It was great.

Tony King: Phil was over for the Ronettes, and I was looking after them. Andrew just started turning up, coming along for the ride, and he and Spector became very tight. Andrew was fascinated by him, taking everything in, seeing what he could use. Like the sunglasses, the whole image thing.

Andrew and Phil were a nightmare together. Andrew got hooked on Phil's generally not behaving very well. They were terrible, like two irresponsible schoolboys.

ALO: I found out the number of Mother Bertha Music, Phil's publishing company in New York, and got hold of Danny Davis who ran it. I told him I could get Phil in the British equivalent of the *New York Times*. Two days later he sent me a telegram saying, 'Do it.' It was a breeze, because I already knew Maureen Cleave was going to write about the man. All I had to do was get to the airport with Maureen and act as if I had arranged it all. This I managed to do. After Maureen's feature in the *Evening Standard*, the music press was easy.

Chris Hutchins: Andrew took me to lunch with Phil Spector and we went to the Angus Steak House on Dean or Greek Street. That was the hip place then, just the fact that you had the money and could afford to buy steak.

Andrew was the absolute fan of this man, he treated him like God. I didn't see Andrew in awe very often, never in awe of the Stones, but he was in awe of Phil Spector.

ALO: In his bright-red corduroy jacket with black suede patches on the sleeves, Phil looked more like an act than most acts, and behaved like one too, upsetting the staff at the Mirabelle. His appearance and attitude would just upset people. Little men in red corduroy jackets and shades simply did not alight from large Rolls-Royces in Mayfair. Phil set the example and I was infatuated with him. I'd spent my time till now being polite, and now I had the opportunity to model myself after a perfect little hooligan. I picked up image and energy from Spector, and used all of what I thought were his principles when I produced the Rolling Stones records. I had no idea of how he actually worked in the studio. I was very proud when Bill Wyman later said, 'Phil Spector had the "Wall of Sound", we had the "Wall of Noise".' Even though it wasn't said as a compliment, it was one.

Spector didn't just change my point of view, he helped me change my life – and, some would have it, not for the better. But he did change the way records could, and would, be made and elevated record production to commercial art. He moved the meaning and status of record production out of the back room and on to the main lot. In scale and presence he was to the record biz what Orson Welles was to Hollywood. 'You've Lost That Lovin' Feeling' and 'River Deep, Mountain High', like *Citizen Kane* and *Touch of Evil*, could not be created merely by re-creating what had been successful in the past. The pressure to repeat that one puts on oneself is almost unbearable. Phil stood and delivered for John Lennon, but that was his last call. I don't see much difference between Orson Welles at Ma Maison and Phil Spector at the Rock 'n' Roll Hall of Fame. For me it's either work or stay home, and three cheers for Steven Spielberg. Phil Spector got recognition for his craft and, one way or another, he picked up the tab.

That Christmas came as an unwelcome interruption. I did my best to enjoy a quiet break in Hampstead, dividing my time between Celia and Sheila. Celia made a fantastic Christmas cake – heavy with liqueur to ward off the bitter cold and, somewhat under the influence, I took Sheila out in the snow on Hampstead Heath.

CHAPTER 9

ALO: 1963, and the 60s as we knew them, began. Jet Harris and Tony Meehan entered the *NME* charts at number ten with 'Diamonds', Mark Wynter sat at number eleven and Kenny Lynch at number twelve. The Shadows, Elvis and Cliff held the top three *NME* spots. America was 'enjoying' a respite from real rock, with Steve Lawrence at number one warbling 'Go Away Little Girl', the number two and three spots taken by the UK's own Tornados with 'Telstar' and Chubby Checker with 'Limbo Rock'. Rock was indeed in limbo, so auld lang syne, say goodbye to the old and bring on the new.

On 13 January, two weeks before my nineteenth birthday, I was with Mark Wynter in Birmingham for his appearance on the top pop programme of the day, ABC TV's *Thank Your Lucky Stars*. Filmed live on Sundays, the show aired the following Saturday early evening. Watching in the wings, I was spellbound by a new British group making their first appearance on national television. The Beatles had landed with their second release on Parlophone, 'Please Please Me', and I wanted to know who was driving their plane. I can clearly recall the buzz of watching them rehearse. They weren't that different in appearance from the other acts – they were all wearing suits and ties. What was unusual was their attitude: they exuded a 'Fuck you, we're good and we know it' attitude. You normally didn't see that in an act making its first TV appearance. Of course that attitude was compromised as soon as they became the famous moptops, when it didn't really matter who they were but who people thought they were. Soon enough, the boys would vacillate between being obnoxiously themselves and hiding any semblance of their true personalities to avoid the hassles that followed them every-where, no matter what they did.

I asked John Lennon who their manager was. He stuck his thumb in the direction of an elegant-looking man standing in the hall. Brian Epstein radiated success in his expensive overcoat and paisley scarf. I studied this unpop-looking hotshot for a mo and quickly decided he was well worth a shot. He was obsessed and I wanted in. When I sized up the Beatles and Brian, I realised that these 60s were not only happening to me. I'd picked up on it just months earlier from Grossman and Dylan – it was hypnotic and life-giving. There was nothing calculated about artists like Dylan and the Beatles; they were simultaneously omniscient and naïve.

We took each other's measure and passed the tests: Epstein complained that Parlophone were not really helping him promote the group and perhaps, yes, I could do something for them. Maybe they did need somebody pounding the pavements for them in . . . London, which he pronounced like a man getting rid of phlegm in his throat or a stone from his shoe. Brian already had the only guy he'd impressed at Decca, PR Tony Barrow, industriously moonlighting on his behalf, but he needed someone he could call his own, and I was it. The record was great and so was everybody.

Mark Wynter: *Thank Your Lucky Stars* was the Beatles' first major TV exposure. Andrew was there with me. I rang my agent, Ian Bevan, from Birmingham. Ian had his own office in the Harold Fielding Agency and handled Tommy Steele; originally he handled Marty Wilde. I rang him and said, 'This group that are on are going to be huge. The reaction at the rehearsal was wonderful.' He said, 'I'm not interested in handling groups.' He also turned down Cliff Richard.

Sean O'Mahony, publisher of the *Beatles Monthly* and *Rolling Stones Monthly*: The only reason they got someone as well-placed within EMI as George Martin to do it was because Brian's family business, NEMS, was the biggest buyer of records up in Liverpool. He never approached the A&R department at all. He always used to go through the sales department, whom he figured correctly owed him some kind of *quid pro quo*. The A&R people all said, 'No', but Brian kept applying the leverage he had.

George Martin agreed to the recording, but EMI gave it a 'no plug' rating. The lowest rating was two plugs per week for three weeks on Radio

Luxembourg. The Beatles got zilch. The Shadows got seven plugs a week. Epstein threatened to take all his business away from EMI, so eventually somebody said, 'Yes.'

Ken East, Managing Director, EMI: I was with EMI in Australia from 1952. Sir Joseph Lockwood came to Australia and offered me a job in London as Deputy Managing Director, running the overseas division. At first I was based in Hayes, Middlesex; the record factory was there, the HQ of the company, big administrative building, tape factory, huge company. Joe Lockwood had an office on the top floor. Most of my work was outside of the UK, but I liaised with EMI Records in Manchester Square.

He was a most liberal man, Joe Lockwood, he believed in people getting on with the job. Get on with it, do it, if you don't do it well, watch out, you're fired. That was generally the way he operated. He was a brilliant man, wonderful foresight, much more forward-thinking than Sir Edward Lewis at Decca – Lewis remained in the past, couldn't see the future like Lockwood could. Look what happened to Decca Records, bought by Polygram and dead, apart from their classical label. That was one of the greatest record labels in the world. Decca US was nothing to do with Sir Edward. Decca US was owned by Universal Pictures. Bing Crosby was probably their biggest artist.

That's why Lewis had London Records; he couldn't sell Decca records as Decca in North America. Oh, it was a terrible set-up, London Records in the States. A guy called D.H. Toller Bond ran it. In his early days he wore a bowler hat to the office, bow tie, just the most remarkable man. He knew nothing about the record business but he was a friend of Sir Edward Lewis. It was Mantovani and the classical department that gave London Records their success in the States.

Lockwood could see that EMI was losing any long-term hope of staying in the American market, so he went and bought Capitol Records in 54, 55, for about five million dollars. That was a good long-term thing – the other Europeans have never moved into the North American market in the same way as EMI did through Capitol. Ironically, Capitol has never had a great deal of success in the North American market after Peggy Lee, Sinatra, the Kingston Trio, Glen Campbell, Nat King Cole, the golden era of the late 50s.

Nevertheless, it's been a mainstay base for a British company in North America.

At EMI UK there was Norrie Paramor in A&R who worked with Cliff Richard and Helen Shapiro; George Martin who did the Goons and Peter Sellers; Norman Newell who did Alma Cogan and Matt Monro . . . Decca had Dick Rowe and Hugh Mendl, they were the most forward-thinking. Dick and Tony Hall were the main men at Decca. I tried to steal Tony Hall from Decca, but he wouldn't come. We had the Beatles, Decca had the Stones. After the Beatles, British music took over the world. Prior to that we could never sell a British artist in North America; you couldn't sell a British artist in Australia, the trend there was all towards the American pop charts. The Beatles came and then the Stones and that set the whole thing going.

It was a bit like the Civil Service in the British record industry in those days. Then the independent producer suddenly came along. The majors had a stranglehold – they had their own studios, factories, you could not get records manufactured unless you went to a major company, and that all changed. There was a huge revolution and Andrew and his Immediate Records would have been a significant part of that. Independents became a significant part of the UK record industry.

EMI did have a lot of civil servants; they thought they were in a job for life. George Martin got very lucky. Decca, EMI, Pye all came out of large electronic groups. Philips the same. So the record division was just one division of a large corporate entity. The top management of these companies thought of the record industry as just 'another division', like television manufacturing, records and radio. But it was creative, you needed creative people. But it didn't have creative people, it had civil servants. That's where Andrew and his kind were different and where things got shook up.

Epstein came out of the furniture business . . . the family had a very successful record bar inside the furniture shop in Liverpool, NEMS. Brian ran the record department. He couldn't get a deal anywhere, he'd been around everybody. He said to Len Wood at EMI that NEMS was a very important account, and he really believed in these artists, and he really wanted EMI to sign them. Len talked to George Martin. George decided, 'Yeah', he could do something with them . . . and that's how it started. I suppose if he hadn't got a deal with Len, he'd have gone back to Decca or Pye and kept persevering until he got the Beatles a deal somewhere. But it wasn't like Brian Epstein had any kind of master plan, apart from his belief.

ALO: When you sat down with Brian, you knew you were dealing with a man who had a vision for the Beatles and nobody was going to get in the way of that vision. He was convinced that eventually everybody was going to agree with him. That gave him the power to make people listen. He'd say, 'I believe this', and you'd believe him, so when he said, 'I want this done', it was doable. That Brian was somewhat to the manor born gave him both a self-assurance and an entrée with the stubbornly middle-class label managers he had to deal with. At *Thank Your Lucky Stars* Brian merely stood watching his boys, yet his belief and their talent permeated the room and would soon, thanks to TV, permeate the Isles, north to south. In those early days Brian's presence, the Beatles' irreverence and their mutual pleasure all conveniently merged.

Mark Wynter: Andrew phased himself out of working for Ray and me; it happened quite quickly once the Beatles started to take off. He'd picked up a lot from Ray Mackender. He discovered his own capabilities, what he could achieve – which at the time seemed to be endless, he seemed to be able to do anything. He wasn't frightened of attempting anything.

ALO: So I moved on. Ray wanted me to work the last days of 'Go Away Little Girl', but it was time to leave Great Cumberland Place and find my own office. Walking through Covent Garden after a lunchtime pub 'n' hustle, I told *Melody Maker* scribe Don George of my need and he recommended I call on Eric Easton, who had a small back room up for rent at his Regent Street office. Easton ran a little booking agency representing Julie Grant and guitarist Bert Weedon. He also managed *Thank Your Lucky Stars* host DJ Brian Matthew and the absurd, pianistic Mrs Mills.

Sean O'Mahony: Eric Easton had been a performer, playing organ at places like Blackpool Tower, and his wife was a dancer, so he knew show-business inside out.

ALO: Eric was grey-haired, grey-suited and in his mid-thirties – to someone my age that put him over the hill, but for work space at only £4 a week I decided to like him and his fifth-floor Regent Street office, which looked out over the back of Piccadilly.

Philip Townsend: At Eric's suite, you first walked into a reception area. Eric's office was on the right-hand side. If you went through an arch on the left, there was an office about ten by six, that was Andrew's. Eric used to complain about his telephone calls: 'You really must itemise your calls because you're making an awful lot of them.'

At his desk in Eric Easton's office

ALO: I'd read somewhere that Aristotle Onassis had a recipe for success from his early days. It consisted of having a good address, be it a basement or an attic, a good suit and a suntan. I now had a good address, had had a good suit for a while, and the suntan came courtesy of some make-up.

Sheila Klein: Make-up was a wonderful way of hiding himself and his vulnerability. It was his armour. He realised that, in order to get what he wanted, he had to adopt a certain persona, and the make-up helped. He had to continually rev up the charisma and could change his look totally, so that people didn't even recognise him. He was very into that. He just loved to dress up and look completely different.

ALO: I settled into Eric's office fast, promoting every media contact I had, which now covered a wide range of publications: femme teen rags, the 'serious' music weeklies, the lightweight pop periodicals, national and provincial newspapers, and the upper and lower fashion magazines. The Beatles and Epstein came down to London once every two or three weeks, staying for two days in a hotel on Sloane Square adjacent to the Royal Court. I got them lots of ink, which wasn't too difficult. By the summer Epstein's obsession would go national and the more tuned-in among the press could already smell pop blue blood.

I scored a coup when I got them into *Vogue*, although Adam Faith had come out as a pop débutant in *Queen* magazine a year earlier. Norman Parkinson photographed Faith in a white suit, white Anello & Davide boots, and a black button-down shirt surrounded by dancing mod babes of the deb class. Parkinson's black-and-whiter was a precursor to later *Vogue* face-of-the-moment spreads, featuring Stones and Beatles draped by this year's girls. Nothing is original; it might *seem* to be, though, depending on your timing . . .

Johnny Jackson: People who don't know see a lot of pictures, headlines, blurbs and puffs, they hear a name being talked around and straight away they start counting how much money it means in the bank account of the over-publicised one. But if publicity was dough, every little starlet in town wouldn't be plotting how to marry a millionaire – she would be one. Similarly with me and Bongo. We were making a big impact, but there was still a lot of merchandising to be done before you could say that my property was a solid investment. Certainly *Expresso Bongo* was running away but, if you remember, I had sold Garrick Records the whole show outright for £35. Stupid of me – but poverty and Mr Mayer had taken advantage of both my good nature and my judgement. All the good that particular bestseller was doing us was in newspaper clippings.

Of course, Bongo was picking up television fees here and there, but booking agents just laughed and laughed when I asked them for a hundred a week for him on tour. According to them, in the provinces the public didn't watch television or read the newspapers. The reputations were made here, in London, the Smoke.

ALO: Just as one can buy a ready-made or a bespoke suit, rock 'n' roll offers two kinds of stardom: cheap, off-the-rack and disposable, or costly, custom-made, real and durable. Only those gifted with the gab of song, or manna from God's own publishing wing like Cliff, get an opportunity to tailor a career for the ages. Ignoring all the beware signs, our greatest street scribes run the red lights meant to keep pop at the top. If you're not sure about who rock 'n' roll belongs to, it surely isn't yours. Rules are there to be tested and broken, as are your mind, body and spirit. History only serves the revisionists as they realign the rules of conduct for your next fucking. The only lessons that survive are clear instructions on such matters as to how to clean your bottom. The Beatles re-created the rules of survival, destruction and rebirth. On each generation their impact was total. Their cause and effect were seen and heard on every avenue of the bop and pop boulevard; their songs were, are and always will be hits.

Down in the Smoke, Brian Epstein was rather snotty about the press so I got to be 'manager for a day' when the attractively scattered moptops came to London to squeeze in some radio shows and press interviews. The no. 31 bus provided a leisurely, pleasant and dream-filled excursion, always a good ticket to ride over its unusual route from Hampstead to the back end of the King's Road. A hop, skip, jump and nod past Bazaar and John Michael, and I'd be in that solid Sloane Square, Royal Court'd and W.H. Smith'd.

The Beatles greeted me in the lobby of a small hotel facing Smith's with the wonderful fact of that time – they were *The Beatles*. John Lennon was Everyman: I'd love to have been in Stu Sutcliffe's place for a while back then and had a mind-polish from John. As it was, I took what I could get. He was loud, rude and a lout, but we would line up on the same side of the street and shout about life to others. I never knew John Lennon very well, but the times I spent with him were perhaps a mind-mapping experience for us both. He looked, I floated; I looked, he floated. I could sit next to him in a cab or a club, and regardless of whatever war we were both fighting at the time, I found peace around him, and I think it was mutual. Oh, I had laughs with him, but in his physical presence I breathed a sigh of relief – around John, life was always easy.

Paul has always been another chapter, his curiosity was honed and skilled. He didn't, like Lennon or me, crash his way through life's high street. John and I scattered broken dreams in our wake in order to preserve our own reality. At once innocent and crafty, Paul never seemed to realise he was centre-stage, which he always was, and perhaps that was a saving grace for his sanity as the world smothered the Beatles with its approval. George was already on his journey, and Ringo was clear from the off.

We'd cab around London to visit such musical scribes as Penny Valentine and Keith Altham, or to thank Chris Hutchins for his coverage of the news that day; Paul would look at me and wonder where we were going, and John would know we'd already been there.

In Los Angeles in early March 1974, John Lennon, Tony King and I found ourselves together at Lou Adler's Rainbow Club. With Lou Adler, I was with another of life's good twins. Lennon had impulsively jetted west on what would be the start of his notorious lost weekend with Harry Nilsson. It would be the last time I saw John in physical form, and the descent into Hollywood hell had not yet begun for him. He had left New York so suddenly he hadn't organised a place to crash. As I was moving out of Lou's Bel Air guest house and returning to New York, after a nod from my host I handed John the keys to the Stone Canyon abode. I was clear that year of mind games and reasonably sober, apart from my service in the marching powder-and-pill brigade, my flair for biochemistry maintaining a reasonably psychotic Ritalin even keel. John and I wished each other the very best of love and life as we toasted with cups of coffee, enjoying the pleasant irony that neither of us was pissed at midnight on Sunset Strip.

Don Arden: If the Beatles had not had their time at the Star Club, I don't think they would have made it as big as they did. That time at the Star Club, months and months at a stretch, that's what I think developed them. I think the Liverpool Sound was bullshit. I don't think there was a Liverpool Sound, it was the Hamburg Sound . . . if you stop to think about it they were really the first group to make it internationally. In those days it was all solo artistes, you can't call Bill Haley & the Comets a group . . . the Beatles made a special place for groups for all time. To simplify it, that's what they did. When you look at the history of showbusiness you'll find that there weren't many British artists that ever made it in America until the Beatles. Forget rock 'n' roll, let's talk about actors and actresses. How many British actresses were nominated for an Oscar . . . how many British actors made it? The only time you saw a British actor make it in America was when a guy like David Niven decided he was going to pack his bags and go over to America and stay there, and live there and become part of the scenery there; that's what he did and that's how he succeeded.

Chris Hutchins: When the Beatles happened a few months later, I had unprecedented access. The *Disc* weekly was on top of the Beatles game. Maurice Kinn saw what was happening. He rang me up and offered me the job of news editor at the *NME*, for much more than he'd been paying me before. I held down that job at the *NME* for five years. The *NME* sold on its news pages. If a rock star was going on tour – Adam Faith, Cliff, Gene Vincent, Brenda Lee – you had to buy the *NME* to get the dates first. Maurice Kinn insisted it had to be in the *NME* first or it wouldn't get published. Eve Taylor was managing Adam Faith, trying to turn him into Grace Kelly. There'd never been any class in the music business before Brian Epstein, nobody bought paintings; Stigwood followed closely in that, John Reid followed . . . Epstein was the first super-manager; he wore silk scarves.

ALO: At my behest the *NME* announced that the Beatles had joined Helen Shapiro, Tommy Roe, Chris Montez and Kenny Lynch for a month-long UK Arthur Howes-promoted package tour kicking off in mid-February. Unbeknownst to me, I would get to tour the UK and see the world.

Kenny Lynch: I teamed up with Lennon. Andrew was looking after all of us. We opened the first night at the Granada Walthamstow. It was a fifty-two-date tour: Newcastle, Torquay, London, everywhere. It was gonna take months, so we started messing around with them big stage hooks to get people off-stage.

The Beatles had written this song 'Misery' for Helen; she said she didn't like it. I said, 'I like it, I'll do it.' At the Prince of Wales Theatre, the Beatles would come into my dressing room to escape from the pressure. They'd hide in my dressing room. They never went to their dressing room, not for the whole tour. They flew into Piccadilly in a helicopter. These were mad days, mad days. Andrew was about, he loved it, he was backstage all the time.

When we were near London he was there; Bristol, Aldershot – Andrew turned up every night. Only time he didn't turn up was if we were in places like Newcastle; he was shrewd enough not to do that.

ALO: After an early show in Birmingham I was woken at home by a telephone call from Jean. The tour had moved on and left Kenny's luggage in Birmingham. She was driving up there to collect it and wanted me to keep her company. I agreed on one condition – she let me drive. I needed the practice. We got stopped by the police on the M1. I didn't have a licence, the Mini had tinted windows, it was all suss. Somehow Jean managed to bluff the cops with some showbiz talk and we were waved on, but I was in such a blind panic I couldn't hit the right pedal. 'Put your foot on the left,' whispered Jean, but this just confused me even more. Now the cops were walking back towards the car to see what was wrong. I had to fake a cramp in my foot and ask the policeman to put my foot on the right pedal . . .

Chris Montez was very shy and untravelled. I didn't cop that perhaps the seventeen-year-old chicano-American 'Let's Dance' star might not speak much English. He was a very nice guy, gamely struggling on-stage to get through a 'full' set. Like most American acts reared on the Dick Clark Caravan of Stars tours, he was used to doing two numbers at most. In Britain he was asked to play a six-song, twenty-minute set.

Chris's enigmatic manager, Jim Lee, had hired me to publicise his boy for the duration of the tour, and I was now representing three major acts on the bill. Lee gave me some vital tips on the music business that would deeply influence how I would hone my potential. He sat me down one night after the show and explained that he wasn't just Montez's manager, but he'd written, produced and published 'Let's Dance'. In America, Jim Lee was also the 'independent' record company, and worldwide at the end of the day he reckoned to make about $1,000,000 from the single.

Lee had a realistic sense of life and humour, knew he'd been lucky and didn't intend to try and repeat his success. He had no desire to stay in the music business. He wanted to get out before he got sucked into believing he could turn loaves and oafs into stars and was looking forward to getting out, investing his million-dollar profit and living happily ever after. I never heard of him in the music biz again and hope he got his wish.

(l to r) Jim Lee, Chris Montez, ALO

The Beatles were fast becoming a national treasure, each new single replacing the previous one as the national anthem. Chris Montez, who had been the original headline act, was no doubt relieved when told by the tour's promoter that the Beatles were now going to top the bill. At the Granada Theatre in Bedford, I stood at the back of the stalls beside Brian Epstein, who'd been slightly apprehensive about the lukewarm reactions his boys had been getting 'down south'. This night, though, there was a tangible sense of mad hysteria rising all over the theatre, and with the arrival of the Beatles on-stage it rose to a frenzy and took on a life of its own.

The kids broke *all* the backstage windows. It was pandemonium. On-stage, you could not hear the Beatles for the roar of the crowd, and the roar I heard was the roar of the whole world. You can hear something without seeing it, in the same way as you can have an experience that is beyond anything you've had before. You don't have to be clever, you only have to be a member of the public. The noise that night hit me emotionally, like a blow to the chest. The audience that evening expressed something beyond repressed adolescent sexuality. The noise they made was the sound of the future. Even though I hadn't seen the world, I heard the whole world screaming. The power of the Beatles touched and changed minds and bodies all over the world. I didn't *see* it – I heard and felt it. When I looked at Brian, he had the same lump in his throat and tear in his eye as I.

Before he returned to California my new best friend Phil Spector had left behind some pearls of wisdom, which at the time did not seem relevant to my PR-driven lifestyle. But within a few rollin' months his cautions would prove to be invaluable. Phil had been impressed with all he'd seen in the UK and was looking further ahead for me than I was looking for myself. He told me that if I ever found a group to record, I should on no account let them use the record company's studio or sign the act direct to the recording company, but instead should pay for an independent studio session myself and afterwards sell or lease back the tapes to the record company. That way, Spector explained, you keep control and you earn much more money. Now, in my present cuffed-hand-to-big-mouth existence, I had no thought for 'real' money, but control I thought I understood. And I loved the idea. What Phil didn't mention then – perhaps he didn't know it himself – is that having this much control can alienate one from what one loves best and lead to a personal life out of control.

My lunchtime port of call was the De Hems pub, just off Shaftesbury Avenue in Soho. It had been a gangster hangout in the 20s, but was now the acknowledged watering hole of the British music business. Journalists, managers, agents and promoters would meet there to seal deals or swap gossip. For me it was the perfect place to hustle for clients over an orange juice. My main De Hems hustle was *Record Mirror* editor, Peter Jones. The burly, big-hearted journo made up in *Record Mirror* space any *NME* deficiency I might suffer. With only two-thirds of *NME*'s circulation but twice the space allotted at times to my clients, Peter's *Mirror* often saved my week in clippings. I would head for De Hems with a list of five acts and settle for getting three out of five into print.

This day, Jones had had enough already. 'Oh, Andrew, we did him last week, we can't give you any space.' He was telling me to shut up, drink up and count my blessings. Then, 'Listen to me for a change.' That allowed and given, he went on to explain that a colleague, Norman Jopling, had just written an article about a fledgling R'n'B band called the Rollin' Stones. It would be appearing in the following week's issue of *Record Mirror*, under the headline 'Genuine R'n'B'. Jones had not seen the band, but Norman Jopling's enthusiastic write-up made the Rollin' Stones sound really wild. It was unheard of for *Record Mirror*, or any music weekly, to write about a band before they had a single hovering on the lower rungs of the charts. The Rollin' Stones didn't even have a record out. Jopling's going to bat for these newcomers intrigued Jones, and Jones attempted to intrigue me.

Truth be known, I didn't give a shit. I was still smarting over the two clients that Peter Jones had refused to touch and hoped that, by listening, I would be allowed to hustle them back into his good graces. So I listened to Jones's story of a musical evolution I had yet to give two farthings about: 'As the trad scene gradually subsides, promoters were heaving a long sigh of relief that there was finally something to take its place – Rhythm 'n' Blues,' Jopling was to write. 'The number of R'n'B clubs that has sprung up is nothing short of fantastic.' I think it was all of three, but journalists are entitled to their own hypes. 'The hip kids throw themselves about to this new "jungle music" like they never did in the more restrained days of trad.'

Peter Jones, Editor, *Record Mirror*: I told Andrew, 'Look we're writing about this act that hasn't got a record out, there might be something there for you. It looks like rhythm 'n' blues will make it big soon, so why not have a look at them?'

· CHAPTER 10 ·

ALO: There are no accidents, and Peter Jones was the conduit to my destiny. I was probably forty-eight hours ahead of the rest of the business in getting there, but that's the way God planned it. I met the Rollin' Stones and said 'hello' to the rest of my life.

The year 1963 was a very good one, and a very fast one. Late 62 through April 63 had me busy, secure and content with my lot. I hoped my mother had noticed, and told Alec as much. Alec's approval was just as important to me, since if he thought I was doing okay, my mother would go along with him.

I wasn't just dreaming – I was doing. When asked, I didn't have to conjure up what I wanted to do (just as well, as I still had no idea): I could spout about what I was doing. I was a publicist or press agent in the world of pop music and rock 'n' roll, and I was in a unique position. It was a new field – that of an independent, self-employed publicist; there were only a few of us. The mainstays were all employed directly by EMI and Decca (major) or Philips and Pye (minor). The tedium of supporting a crumbling system prevented them from enjoying the incessant beat of revolution booming out of Liverpool. Best case? Guitars would disappear as fast as hula-hoops and Davy Crockett hats. They could go back to sleep over their pints after that.

Now, all of my money, save what I gave to Mother out of respect, was going on music and clothes. Each day I would spring forth anew, soundtrack intact, wardrobe mistress to my own ethical grooming, with God handling my lighting, backed up by schlapp. Broadcloth-blue, tab-collared shirt, jet-black wool tie, three-piece suit complete with cuffs on jacket and trousers, flair-waisted jacket *à la* Bunny Roger with inverted vent, spit and polished side-laced black booties: a smorgasbord of crossed cultures to fit the mood the day required. One enjoyed both the charm of Harvey's Johnny Jackson and the good spark of Tony Curtis's Sydney Falco in *The Sweet Smell of Success*. Better still, I was free as a bird with no J.J. Hunsecker (Burt Lancaster) to be kowtowed to. I had both the sense and good taste to avoid Mr Harvey's hand-rolled wing collars, ordered from a Jermyn Street establishment I could not patronise; I lived on the *via* of broadcloth tabs.

So it was fitting in and standing out that I pondered on when it came time to pick my clothes for the trip to Richmond. When would the dismal anti-fashion of the Witch's Cauldron be behind me? I wondered. I anticipated a very beat outing, slumming in the south of town. Jumper, slacks, Hush Puppies I thought did rather a good job of muting my ambition without undoing my grooming. I said 'goodbye' to my mother that late Sunday after-noon and strolled from our flat down Frognal to the Finchley Road British Rail line, which fortunately ran every forty minutes ten stops from north-west Hampstead to south-west Richmond's hilly streets. It had been a beautiful day for early April, and as I alighted from the train at Richmond the sun was lingering, loath to leave day for night.

Opposite the train station was, naturally enough, the Station Hotel. The Rollin' Stones, I'd been told, would be playing in a room that had an entrance at the back of the hotel. I crossed the zebra and headed down a long alley. On my right was the Station Hotel building, and on my left, the British Rail lines running further south-west and back north again.

For the first few strides I was alone in the alley with the sound of my mind and my footsteps. Halfway down the pathway I saw that I was not alone – there were two figures ahead of me, one with back to the wall, the other facing, arms against the wall. I got closer; they weren't discussing, they were arguing. A girl was against the wall and a boy was pressing his point.

As I passed them I tried to be invisible, looking away from them, but not quite. The three of us acknowledged each other, I by picking up my pace as I passed by, they by pausing. He gave me a look that asked me everything about myself in one moment – as in 'What are you doing with the rest of my life?' His lips looked at you, seconding that first emotion. He was thin, waistless, giving him the human form of a puma with a gender of its own; the girl was a bridge to reality. They were both very earnest, hurt and similar: pale skins, brown hair and flashing eyes. And both, very attractive in their

similarity, in heat; in the shadows of the pathway I wasn't sure who was
mommy and who was daddy.

Mick and Chrissie

I edited all such thoughts out of my mental movie and quickly put a coin
in my jukebox and walked on by. Later I found out that the Romeo and Juliet
in my path had been Michael Phillip Jagger and Chrissie Shrimpton on their
first date, first fight. I turned right to the back entrance of the hotel and
bumped into a big enough queue to make the night promising. The next half-
hour went by in a moment. I do that in queues or while waiting, I change
time. It was time for the cutting-room floor anyway.

Finally, in the dark and sweaty room, the Rollin' Stones, all six of them,
took to the stage while the nattering, half-pint-sodden, hundred-odd couples
seemed ready for what they were about to receive and went apeshit. So did
the group – they didn't seem to start, so much as carry on from a previous
journey. I was already standing up but what I saw, heard and felt stood me
up again, as the remaining air left the room from the whoosh of hundreds of
waving hands, dancing feet and heaving bodies, having sheer, sheer
pleasure.

I wasn't familiar with the songs or the sound. R'n'B to me had been
Elvis's 'A Mess of Blues' and a bunch of 'interesting' Chess 45s released on
Pye in the UK, which bubbled just inside the Top 50 for a paltry week and

so were of no interest to me. They were of much more consequence to this Michael Phillip Jagger, who regularly petitioned Pye to release more Bo Diddley records. The stuttering beat spoke of sex the instant it started a little dance in my heart.

Thinking was suddenly not required, redundant. The room was as one, the music and audience had one particular place to go, a place I'd never been to but was happily being drawn to. The Rollin' Stones were six who became one. Three were backed against the wall: on the left, one Bill Wyman, on bass, to his right a large amp I'd only seen in ads and Charing Cross Road store windows. He stood like the statue who became a celebrity, concentrated, nonchalant, picking his instrument in an upright 'shhhoulder-arrrms' army-drill position, perhaps as a result of having seen service as Bill Perks for Queen and country. He was gaunt, pale, almost medieval in a way.

The drummer appeared to have been beamed in, and it seemed you didn't so much hear him as feel him. I enjoyed the presence he brought to the group as well as his playing. Unlike the jacketless other five, he had the two top buttons of his jacket done up meticulously over a just as neat button-down shirt and tie, unaffected by the weather in the room. Body behind kit, head turned right in a distant, mannered disdain for the showing of hands waving at 78 rpm in front of him. He was with the Stones but not of them, kinda blue, like he'd been transported for the evening from Ronnie Scott's or Birdland, where he'd been driving in another Julian 'Cannonball' Adderley time and space. He was the one and only, all-time man of his world, gentleman of time, space and the heart. His rare musical talent is an expression of his bigger talent for life: I'd just met Charlie Watts.

Backstage right was an odd man out. Sometimes on piano, sometimes maracas, he had a Popeye torso, a William Bendix jawline and a bad Ray Danton haircut: he cared for his 'little three-chord wonders' till the day he died. As time went by he would pay me this compliment: 'Andrew Oldham? I wouldn't piss on him if he was on fire.' Yes, the real deal, sixth Stone, Ian Stewart.

The frontstage three took in and gave out from stools, nicely opposite to their striving audience. From stage left: black as night, hacked hair, maybe baby-hacked face atop a war-rationed baby-body channelled into his guitar. This hollow-cheeked one effected an alchemic exchange in cool hand heat with himself, and turned on a dime with alacrity.

I wasn't sure, though, which was which and who played what. Such were the six-stringed exchanges between Keith Richards and the incredible blond, hulking hunk stage right. Brian Jones's ugly pretty, shining blond barnet was belied by a face that already looked as though it had a few unpaid bills with life. His head, having forgone a neck, slipped straight into a subliminally deformed *Greystoke* body. Undeniably, one half of two with one great guitar sound. Yet, of all the six, Brian was the one whose eyes darted around the room (save Perks on the perennial pull), wanting to suss the reaction right now and not able to wait for the acclaim or applause between songs. Although he bathed in that too, like somebody having sex, rolling over, smiling and saying, 'Next time, it's your turn . . .' Our own Diana Barrymore.

Finally, centre-stage front, was the boy from the railway towpath: the hors d'oeuvre, the dessert and meal in between. On that tiny stage, when I took in the Stones' front line, I saw rock 'n' roll in 3-D and Cinerama for the first time. There had always been a succession of Ones: Elvis, Johnnie Ray, Eddie Cochran and more. Then, at the New Victoria Cinema, I finally saw an act on-stage that didn't cheat. The Everly Brothers sounded like their records, the Crickets backing them superbly. In particular Jerry Allison 'be-bom-de-boomt'ing' his way through 'Till I Kissed You' and 'Cathy's Clown'. I saw double, not for the last time: Don and Phil Everly enjoyed their forever moment of music, and oh, what a feeling, as one voice lay on top of the other, reversed, lay together, sideways-always sounding, as if the girls they sang about were a front for this Lord-approved and -given musical incest.

Yeah, I know. It's also called purity.

Mick's voice was the first of many things that struck me as I watched Brian, Mick and Keith work with, and in spite of, us and each other. It wasn't just a voice, and it was much, much more than a rendition, a mere lead vocal. It was an instrument, a declaration, not backed by a band, but a part of the band, their decree. Mick moved like an adolescent Tarzan, plucked from the jungle, not comfortable in his clothes – probably, that night, a drip-dry 'Tern' white shirt and loose black string tie, Take Six mid-weight trews around a body that was still deciding what it was and what it wanted. A positive question of opposites.

Sorry, folks, it's eyes down for a full house; you've paid your money, just turn the page. I can't be clever and experienced, subtle or oblique about this. We are talking about one of the three most proficient entertainers of the twentieth century and the group that defied time, all bets and most drugs to close out the century as the world's greatest rock 'n' roll band. I can only embarrass you, not me, and have you chuckin' up, were I to put in here an 'Oh God, how embarrassing' from Mick's child-bearing lips, or even an 'I saw how you felt, 'twas true' from Charlie. A nod from Keith would certainly be fitting and, from wherever he may be, Brian would suggest 'Enough about me, what do you think about me?' I can only tell you what I felt and attempt to take you there.

I'd never seen anything like it. They came on to me. All my preparations, ambitions and desires had just met their purpose. It was a feeling of all the elements falling into the right place and time, catching all the dualities. The music was authentic and sexually driven by the three on stools and the bottom end behind them. It reached out and went inside me – totally. It satisfied me. I was in love. I heard the anthem of a national sound, I heard the sound of a national anthem. I heard what I always wanted to hear. I wanted it; it already belonged to me. Everything I'd done up until now was a preparation for this moment. I saw and heard what my life, thus far, had been for.

The look the puma had given me in the alley kicked its heels into my life and made sense. I stopped thinking; I had no programme, no thoughts on what suddenly felt like the norm. Life was not second-hand in this moment. Yes, at the Granada Bedford I stood with Brian Epstein watching the Beatles and feeling the world. But it was third-hand, not mine. Yes, I was there, but I had no real cause or effect on their lives; I wasn't that to them, and I was never meant to be. I saw you standing there and thanks for the memory. But here I was in the eye of the storm. I had stopped thinking or, more accurately, scheming, and I was feeling . . . great.

Before the pill, when sex was still a delicacy, teenagers had it artificially inseminated through vinyl and live gigs. The audience at the Station Hotel Crawdaddy Club, getting off on the Stones, were as flushed and happy as if they'd had the real thing. As for your actual R'n'B, it didn't mean dick to me. I have always maintained that, if it had, I might have had an opinion about it and missed the totality of what hit me – I was just bowled over by that totality. Ignorance was bliss.

The set over, I didn't have the bottle to approach the act on the spot. What I'd seen was amazing and somehow I felt lacking, unprepared. I needed time to get my act together and consider my move on the band. On the oh-so-slow train back to Frognal I was dizzy from the experience, a come-uppance, considering my low expectations for the evening. I mentally bounced all over the train. I'd never had career conversations with myself thus far – I just got on with life, happy in the action of the moment it had bought me or I had grabbed. Wants and needs in order, lucky in love and at one with my life. That Sunday changed all that – I felt their force and I wanted in, I felt a God-given invitation to Jagger. I'd let the band wave over me, and got the reason for all my experience and gains; this was no third-hand, once-removed feeling. I was feeling something I belonged to. I was already theirs, and theirs was the world . . .

Adrian Millar, musician/entrepreneur: The Beatles had turned up in my life uninvited, right in the middle of my Cliff & the Shadows dream. Elvis had been long gone . . . none of us believed we could be that good anyway and, to be absolutely honest, we were left with a ragbag collection of Adam Faith's, John Leyton's and Craig Douglas's, all of 'em trying to give it some. But when you looked 'up close' . . . impostors, all of 'em – lightweight beyond belief.

All of a sudden these four geezers appeared – haircuts and velvet collars – mysterious at first, then interesting and finally fascinating. They really were the bollocks, and I definitely knew . . . this mob was unstoppable.

Shortly after I'd managed to grow my hair to 'Beatle' length and tricked Mum into buying me a 'Beatle' jacket (instead of a school blazer), five other merchants tried to crash in on the scene.

'No chance whatsoever,' I declared. 'One looks like my grandfather, and the other one looks like an uncle of mine, who may or may not still be breathing.'

'They're gonna be big,' my girlfriend told me as I fondled her tits.

'They already are,' I answered.

'No, you idiot, the Rollin' Stones. I'm talkin' about the fuckin' Stones, not my Waterford Crystals . . .'

'Yeah, yeah, yeah,' I lied, 'course they are.'

'Let's go and see them at the Country Club on Haverstock Hill, its only four-and-six to get in,' she said.

I thought: 'That's only sixpence less than the Beatles and they've already got four hits to the Stones' one . . . a bit steep really, but I always believed in giving everybody a fair shot.

Sure enough, the Three Stooges in the front line were quite good . . . but very little. We stood within a couple of feet of the stage; they looked like they were from Lilliput, not somewhere near Dartford, Kent. The Stones probably thought they were in the land of the giants . . . it was only Hampstead.

Years later, as we were passing Frognal station, I remember Andrew telling me: 'Adrian,' he said, 'I probably only went to see the Stones in Richmond because the train went there directly without my changing. If I'd had to go through that shit of changin' trains at Paddington or somewhere, I may not have bothered.'

I knew then we were talkin' 'history' here, and you don't piss around with that.

George Melly, in *Revolt into Style*: The queues grew longer outside the Station Hotel. It was only a matter of time before the right entrepreneur walked in and recognised his chance. Oldham had no reservations. Here was his ready-made homunculus. He looked at Jagger as Sylvester looks at Tweetie Pie. Oldham was calculatedly vicious and nasty, but pretty as a stoat. He had enormous talent totally dedicated to whim and money.

ALO: Now, to get acts to work you had to be an agent, and you had to have a licence to be one; an agent's licence was issued by the London County Council and you had to be over twenty-one to get this licence . . . and you had to have your own registered offices. I was not in that business. I couldn't see siphoning my enthusiasm down to a Delfont: 'Well, the boys are free the third week of April.' Climbing down from the sky, I started to mark out my next set. I knew what I could provide the Stones, but that would not be enough. The band's daily bread was live work, and I didn't arrange that kind of thing, agents did.

I phoned Brian Epstein at his home on Monday. The Beatles' manager might not have wanted to hear that his London press agent had seen God in the Rollin' Stones (having already discovered over a year before that God was the Beatles). And if Epstein got involved in the deal, I would have to play second fiddle. I really didn't want to do that, but I decided to go for polite, falling back on the manners I'd been raised to have and a sense of social etiquette that I was coming to have.

Brian was in, and out, an increasing occurrence I could neither fathom nor dwell on. I informed him I was resigning from NEMS, that I'd seen this group called the Rollin' Stones and wanted to devote myself to them, try and become their manager. 'I really think they're great,' I told Epstein. 'And when I see the Stones again, if we can agree on a deal, there are so many things I can't handle on the organisational side, like getting them work – would you be interested in coming in with me on it?'

Perhaps because Brian was already frantic from working the Beatles, Gerry & the Pacemakers, Billy J. Kramer and Cilla Black, he didn't really hear me; perhaps I wasn't that loud. Whatever – Epstein chose to pass on the offer. He thanked me for letting him know so politely about my resignation.

ALO and Brian Epstein

The good news was that I would not be leaving Epstein without a London pavement-pounder. Brian had managed to persuade Tony Barrow to leave Decca and work full-time at Eppy's newly opened London office in Argyll Street. I was relieved. By instinct I knew that if the Stones joined NEMS, then they would be following a trend, not setting one. I was pleased that Epstein had turned down my offer over this band I didn't yet represent, and I was happy to have ended my working relationship with Epstein on good terms as he wished me good night and the best of luck.

By Wednesday I was back down at the De Hems pub. Perhaps my desire to become the Rollin' Stones' manager was unrealisable. I practised on Peter Jones, to see how convincing and real I could make it sound, running all the angles past the *Record Mirror* editor. I double-checked with Jones about Giorgio Gomelsky, asking him, 'Are you sure they're not signed?' Gomelsky was the promoter of the Station Hotel gig and there was an understanding between him and the band about management, but Peter Jones thought there was nothing official or signed.

Back at the back of Eric Easton's office I was agitated as I considered what I knew was the inevitable move: the man sitting next door. Putting it off, I stared out of the office window, immune to secretary Janice's well-meaning effort to lift my obvious gloom, meditating on the high-class hookers entering and exiting a club at the top of Lower Sackville Street. I mused that Eric had treated me benignly. 'That Andy,' he'd told Janice, 'what a case he is, but a nice lad. He's trying it on today; he told me the Everly Brothers were all about incest.'

The Everly Brothers

Eric Easton was an agent, he could get the band work and he could finance the recording operation I had in mind as a must. From the Stones' point of view, Easton would seem a solid partner – together we'd look like some Machiavellian showbiz partnership. 'Yeah, it would work.' I laughed my best Johnny Jackson laugh, stopped checking out the working girls and got ready to pimp. Janice heard the laugh and flashed me a smile of relief.

'Hey, Eric, got a mo?' He did. I sat down opposite him and offered him 'the chance of a lifetime', three cheers for me. I enthused about the potential of the Rollin' Stones, cash, cash, cash. Did Easton fancy being partners with me in a proposed management deal with the band, money, money, money? Did he see how well the Beatles were doing, blah, blah, blah? These Rollin' Stones could really make it big, big, big. George Harrison of the Beatles digs them, he's been down and seen them, knock, knock, knock. They stand a big chance of becoming a big-hit outfit, get it, get it, get it. Peter Jones recommended the boys without reservation, got it, got it, got it.

'You know, I don't really like this new pop music, Andy,' he said. Easton was happily married with two children and lived in a terraced house in Ealing. His one luxury was a caravan on the south coast. I knew it would be difficult to get him to leave his house on a Sunday evening to check out the Stones at the Crawdaddy. Watching *Sunday Night at the London Palladium* live on TV was like going to mass. Easton finally agreed. 'I'm making a huge sacrifice, Andy, to be missing my Palladium show, so they better be good, that's all I can say.'

The next Sunday I stood outside the Richmond train station waiting for Eric Easton, worried that he'd become fascinated with another old-timer on the box and would not show up at all. When he did, I breathed a mighty sigh of relief and steered him towards the Crawdaddy. Inside I watched Eric watch the band. Eric Easton accepted all, smiled and said, 'All right . . .'

I went up to the bandstand after the show and asked Charlie Watts for the leader of the Rollin' Stones; he pointed me towards Brian Jones. I approached Jones and told him how great he was, and that I and this agent Eric Easton were in partnership and 'would really like to do something with you'. Then I pushed Eric forward to fill in the holes.

Easton reiterated to Jones that he was an agent, that I worked in publicity with the Beatles and that we'd both been very impressed with what we'd seen, and would Jones like to have a meeting to discuss the possibility of working together? Brian seemed keen and telephone numbers were exchanged, Brian promising to call Easton's office on Monday or Tuesday morning. I breathed a sigh of relief and left the Crawdaddy Club in raptures, convinced that Eric and I had done enough to secure the band's signature and my future.

Keith Richards, in *NME*: Andrew just turned up at the end of a gig one night at the Crawdaddy and said that he was in partnership with another guy and they were looking particularly for a new act to sign up for records and personal appearances. When you've been working backwater clubs for a year, and a recording session suddenly gets dangled in front of you – well, in those days, a recording contract was almost as remote as God talking to you. Andrew was even younger than we were; he had nobody on his books, but he was an incredible bullshitter, fantastic hustler and he'd also worked on the early Beatles publicity. He got together those very moody pictures that sold them in the first place, so although he didn't have much to offer, he did get people interested in what he was doing.

James Phelge, in *Phelge's Stones*: When the Crawdaddy emptied at its 10.30 p.m. closing time the hundreds of fans would fill the small cafés and coffee bars in the area. The club had been just as crowded as the week before, with even more people queuing outside. I had noticed Andrew earlier, but only because of the out-of-place character he was with. The man in glasses and conventional clothing resembled a schoolteacher and stood close to where the Beatles had been two weeks earlier . . . The man's name was Eric Easton.

    . . . When the Stones had finished playing, Eric returned to his home and Andrew joined us for a meal . . . 'How many of you are actually in this band?'

    'There's six of us all together,' said Mick.

    'Six or seven? I thought there were seven. There's actually six in the band? You, you, you . . .' he counted, pointing at each person.

    As he said that, something clicked in my mind and I looked at him and thought: 'He's going to say the band is too big for a pop group, there are too many members compared to other bands. He is not going to be interested . . .'

The band members seemed to like him and everyone hit it off together. When we eventually left the restaurant Andrew arranged that Brian would give him a call the next day. The consensus on the way home in the van was that Andrew was okay.

Keith Richards, in *Keith*: Andrew saw immediately that there's room for more than one act. He was looking for an alternative to the Beatles because he couldn't work for them any more. I guess Andrew's mind would work this way: if Liverpool can produce the Beatles what can London produce? Liverpool was much further away from London than it is now. There were no streets, no highways. I mean, Liverpool is . . . as far as London is concerned, it's Nome, Alaska. To a guy that's been brought up in London, it's like you'd rather go to France than go north of Watford, especially at that time. Andrew had a gig with Eric Easton, he was the PR. Easton had been in showbusiness all his life, he was a musician who'd learnt all the tricks of vaudeville, the insides and outsides of the English music and theatre business, this old pier organist who was now managing a couple of top acts. He's got a business going, he's not a big-time guy, but he's got acts hitting the Top 10. He know the mechanics of bookings, he knows more than anybody because he's spent thirty years looking for a booking. And in the process he's found out how it's done and that he's better off booking other people than himself. What intrigued one about Easton was Andrew.

ALO: Brian Jones, accompanied by Mick Jagger, came up to Eric's office as arranged at two o'clock the next Tuesday. We sat down and played mixed doubles. Eric Easton, former pier organist from up north, now a nigh-on-fortyish, unassuming, slightly greying, bespectacled, open-faced man, sat behind his desk with a twinkle in his eye. Eric had that twinkle from the time I met him, on most occasions, till sometime in 65. He got the money, I hope he got a life and got the twinkle back.

(When Sean O'Mahony called me in the early 90s and informed me that Eric would soon be leaving his body, I placed a call to Eric in Florida to attempt a closure to all our acts on this earth. Eric came to the phone, but didn't really want to speak with me – his call. But that day in 63 he was all mouth, and good with it.)

ALO and Eric Easton

To me, anybody over twenty-five or twenty-six was fortyish, including Bill Wyman. On the other side of the desk from Eric sat a furtive Brian Jones, all sham, shampooed and spotless, ready to act as spokesman for his group. Mick and I sat in neutral corners waiting for the first round of this two o'clock bout to begin. Two o'clock was a very reasonable rock 'n' roll hour; years later ten o'clock meetings would be set by the men with the money to see if one could get up and not fall over. When we'd small-talked enough, Eric cut to the chase and restated our interest in the Rollin' Stones. 'We're not promising we can do anything for you, we'd just like to try,' he told Brian.

Eric asked if there was anything contractually stopping the band from signing. Brian said that Giorgio Gomelsky had wanted to become their manager, but nothing had been signed. Gomelsky wasn't in London to defend his corner. He was in Switzerland, making funeral arrangements for his recently deceased father. 'Gomelsky will be making funeral arrangements for his Rollin' Stones impresarial career,' pimpresario Sydney

Falco whispered in my ear, as Brian let us know that the band were fair game.

I was fascinated by Brian's position as group spokesman and leader. A short year later, when my knowledge of the structure of groups had increased (i.e. I was an expert), I realised that almost every group had a manager until they had one. Meaning that, until a group had decided on management or management had decided on them – and the real deal was in to help one and all up the ladder to money, fame and fuck everything in sight that moves, (aka sex, drugs and rock 'n' roll) – a member of the group either found himself in or elected himself to the position of frontman, sounding board, keeper of the cash and Checkpoint Charlie in the world in which the group lived.

Then two things usually happened: said 'temp' manager got no joy from phoning dozy drummer Dave five times to make sure he got to the gig or rehearsal on time, or got no spurt of power from holding a few quid for a few hours and welcomed getting back to just the band and the music. For the other caste of managers-in-waiting, things weren't quite so simple and they started to get a little fucked up.

They'd enjoyed holding all the cards, even for a few minutes, from the rest of the group. They'd relished the importance of telling the other anxious band members what had transpired during the day and what might happen the next week. They were the first to hear good news, and they were bearers of needed data, heeded by default. The rest of the band gave full attention to the spokesman. Though, if he thought about it, he knew actual management was needed for the dreams and reality at hand, he would never get over the loss of power, that moment of secure importance. For some, it dimmed the pleasure of all the good things to come. So Brian sat across from Eric Easton and began the long goodbye.

Linda Leitch (née Lawrence): I met them at the end of 62 when they were playing the Ricky Tick in Windsor, this little tiny pub, their first gig there. It was my local jazz club and I was fifteen. I was what you'd call a beatnik with long black hair. There were only like twenty people in the club, so it was very close contact, we could almost touch them on-stage. I was just dancing with my girlfriend, and Brian and I kept making eye contact. I was totally blown away because he had this slide guitar, this thing on his finger and he kept sliding the guitar. It really touched me; the music went very deep inside me. They took a break and Brian offered to buy me a drink, we sat and talked.

After the show he walked out on to the high street of Windsor with me. We were just talking about the music; I'd never heard rhythm 'n' blues before. We linked straight away and had strong feelings for each other. He invited me to come up to London to see them at a club in Piccadilly. I said, 'Sure I'll come.' It was such a coincidence, because the club was just round the corner from my hairdressing school. I just went out with Brian from then on, and I'd go everywhere they played. I was just so impressed with the music and I loved dancing.

To me, Brian was the leader of the band because he seemed to organise and arrange everything. It seemed like Mick had just sorta come in and they were still kinda testing who was and who wasn't playing with them. It seemed like they were trying Mick out at that time and it seemed to work, so it went on and on. I didn't miss a single gig, travelling in the van with them with Stu driving. The Richmond gig was getting bigger and bigger.

Brian used to come visit me at my parents in Windsor a lot. We would drive ourselves to the gigs, being a bit independent from the band and the boys, meeting them there. That went on for months, with my mum washing his shirts, him borrowing my brother's things, he became part of the family basically. I was very, very close to Brian, constantly with him.

I was one of the only girls with the Stones because they didn't like the girls hanging about. They wanted to have a different girl every night, so they didn't like girlfriends, whereas Brian and I were a team. They hated it because I would turn up all over the place, I wasn't gonna be pushed out like Chrissie Shrimpton and all that lot. I remember the boys driving around in a Mini, and Brian and I driving around in the Humber Hawk, which was a big solid car my father had suggested Brian get instead of a Mini, which was too dangerous a car for his daughter to be in. He liked a good solid car if I was gonna be out there.

Andrew was just a bubbly young red-headed guy who seemed to appear from out of nowhere and take over. We were the squares . . . to Andrew and the boys, it was unhip for me to be pregnant and thinking about getting married and all these corny things. They were the really cool, hip people, and we were too normal and too much in love. We started to get bad feelings. Brian started feeling the pressure, this feeling of not quite knowing what to do, because I know he loved me but he loved his band and his music too, and he wanted to stay with the music.

Andrew and Brian didn't get on. I think it was because Brian was such a strong character himself and such a strong person. Although he had insecurities, he knew what he wanted. Mick and Keith were younger, they didn't quite know, so it was easy to manipulate them. At the time Brian was trying to write his own stuff and integrate it into the music. He'd be at my parents' house writing songs in the middle of the night when he'd come back from a gig. I'd make him eggs and bacon at three in the morning and he'd be strumming away trying to shape his ideas into songs.

When Andrew came into the picture it seemed like the focus started going on to Mick and Keith. There were lots of arguments – I'd hear Brian on the phone with Andrew going back and forth about who's doing what . . . Anyway Brian wasn't too pleased about this Andrew Oldham character coming into the picture and taking over. Mick and Keith got on really well with Andrew, so that created a distance between those two and Brian. Because I was pregnant, Andrew and the other Stones didn't really want the press and the public seeing me.

Brian was living in Edith Grove, then Mick and Keith moved in, then Charlie. Brian had a room on his own and the others just shared, so it seemed like it was Brian's flat and I would stay with him sometimes up there. Brian was quite a smart boy, and he was very clean; the other boys liked to make a lot of mess. The kitchen was disgusting, and I used to bring food up for Brian from my home.

He was just thrilled to be coming up from Cheltenham to London. It seemed he made it when he made it to London. He was blown away because he was doing things in London. London was his aspiration, not the world. It was getting to London and getting gigs in London, that was his big thing at that time. He used to go see Chris Barber and all those kinds of people in the jazz clubs, used to take me to meet them. He wanted to be like them, as far as I could tell. That was his dream. Then Eric Easton, this man in Piccadilly, became the manager. Brian used to get all dressed up to go do the business, make all the arrangements. It was Brian who put the band together, he did all the practical things.

ALO: 'Please tell us what it is you think you could do for us, Mr Easton,' Brian said, allowing a nod in Mick's direction.

'Look, lads,' Eric began, the northern lilt in his voice seeking to convince. 'We really liked you, and both Andy and I would like to manage your careers, we'd do the very best we can for you. But I have to make it clear, we'll make a real go of it, but we're not making any promises about anything to you.'

'What does that mean?' entered Jagger.

'Good one,' I thought, 'I like this Jagger.' Four words to the point and not cock-of-the-run like Jones's 'What do you think you could do for us?' routine.

'What's that mean?' said Eric, lilt travelling further north, turning towards Mick, slight pause. 'Mick, it's that neither Andrew nor I are in the business of making promises to you in order to get you to sign with us. I'm not going to tell you you'll have a hit record, or even a record. It doesn't work like that and I'd have to be mad to tell you any different.'

'Get mad, Eric,' I thought, 'get mad.' The man continued, 'I have no idea what might happen to you . . . or whether others will agree on your potential. But we'd like to make a go of it, we think you've got the potential. We think you're really good.'

Brian was back in the game with 'Eric, what is it about us that you think is good, what about us did you like, is what I'm saying?' Oh, cry me a river; even Mick squirmed. Then it was my turn.

'What we like is that you've got it – I don't know what that is but, whatever it is, you've got it. It's like with the Beatles, I remember the night in Bedford they took over. Two weeks into the tour and they'd taken over. I stood at the back with a lump in my throat, you felt what was coming; the crowd roared and you felt the world, the hairs on my hand stood up, the lump . . . It's instinctive, natural and I know that the public will demand an opposite. For every kid who wants to take his Beatles home, there's another who doesn't want to share, and it'll be you that he won't want to share. And when I first saw you, when Eric and I saw you, we knew it was you. I know you've got it, and I want to do what I can to help you get it.'

I don't remember the rest of that meeting, I was too busy recovering from my own applause.

Giorgio Gomelsky: I was producing and directing documentary films on jazz and blues artists, contributing to music and film magazines and other publications. Always interested in helping the underdog, I decided to promote the blues cause by bending everybody's ears about the necessity to return to the sources to renew the formula-ridden commercial popular music of the period. Put it this way: I was convinced the blues scene would inject some authenticity into the rather pale and exploitative music scene and I started promoting events, much to the chagrin of my jazz-world colleagues, who thought that a band like the Stones were just 'rock & roll noise'! To prove my point that there was a true possibility for changing the scene, I opened a blues – or rather a rhythm 'n' blues – club as far away as possible from the West End. This was the Station Hotel in Richmond.

Having overheard my rantings and ravings to journalists in pubs, Brian Jones knew of my dedication to the 'cause' and in turn bent my ears about his 'band', 'the best in the land . . .' as he used to lisp to me on every possible occasion. It turned out Brian and I were both Pisces, born the same day, 28 February, just a few years apart, so we became friends and I started getting involved in helping him and his band. This ended up in the residency booking at the Richmond club.

Then I was making a film with the Stones, which was meant to be a documentary about the scene that we were building at the club. It was also meant to attract the rather sceptical music writers and get some coverage from them. This worked because, as is now well known, Peter Jones, editor of *Record Mirror*, did come to the club the Sunday we started shooting and told Andrew about the place. That's how Andrew got to know about the Stones. True also that I was away at my father's funeral and equally true that, when I returned to London, Brian brought Andrew to a screening of the working copy of the film and introduced him to me as an old school chum.

Sure I was broken up about what happened; Brian's betrayal was very underhand, he was my friend, supposedly. I was also disappointed in his short-sightedness in signing away their management (and their independence really) for just a few thousand pounds, which got them into serious business trouble later on. My idea was to form a kind of 'United Artists' of the London blues bands and so keep the showbusiness sharks out of the scene, but I guess it didn't cut it with the vanity-driven mentality prevailing among those guys, particularly Brian and Mick. Too bad – it would have been a 'first' in the music scene and saved the Stones a lot of trouble.

I did meet with Easton and Andrew a few days later. They wanted to find some 'compensation' for all the work I had put into the band, but also make certain that I wouldn't throw the Stones out of my club . . . they still needed the gig. My motivation in all this had been cultural rather than business-oriented. Not so with Easton and Andrew and, frankly, I thought those two were pretty low-flying characters with no interest in blues, underdog culture or social justice! Dollar signs were pointing their way. I stayed busy helping other groups like the Yardbirds, putting the blues message out.

ALO: Stars must be killers, always striking first and last. They have to be so totally obsessed and paranoid about this year's vision of themselves that it's beyond obsession – it's reality, logical and natural. There's no remorse when they kill, no regrets when they pimp and no shame when they whore. And it's really a fair exchange: the world needs them and they need the world. A star is a star is a star, and a fixed race would be nice if you could arrange it . . .

The Stones all agreed to look at an agreement that Eric would prepare, Brian calling back and telling Easton to start drawing up the contract. I'd told Eric that the contract must be for a management and a recording deal; as managers, it would be in our best interest to create a company to supervise the band's recording sessions and then lease the finished tapes to whichever record company to manufacture and distribute.

I had a lot of reasons for this, the first being control. From catching a few minutes of a few sessions, I knew what major record-company staff producers looked like, glorified civil servants *avec* pipe. I had no truck with the swimming-pool atmosphere of 'Okay, boys, you can hear a playback, it's great . . .' A Romans and Christians pecking order obtained and, as such, an act with an opinion as to what it was about would be thrown to the lions.

This was not a conducive set-up for Stones recordings, whatever that meant. I was sure, however, that what I'd witnessed in Richmond could not possibly translate to that meat-market environment. As comfortable as the Beatles had seemed in the few minutes I'd caught of them at Abbey Road, I didn't see it working for the Stones . . . or me. I also firmly believed that stars should be stars to everybody. I wanted the record company to sell the band as stars, not as mere mortals whom they'd seen sweating in the studio for the man.

Pragmatic Eric, however, was not into my utopian autarchic agenda and was concerned by one small detail. 'Yes, Andy, but who's gonna make the records?'

I told him, 'We will, Eric, we will.'

I suggested we call our independent recording company 'Impact Sound' and Easton registered it. Later I learnt that 'our' company was registered solely in the name of Eric Easton Ltd, cutting me out. Thus Eric slid into the driver's seat, little Andy being an excited and trusting minor jumping up and down in the back seat. The northern slag next set about drafting the contracts whereby, as managers, we would take 25 per cent off the top of everything, with Impact Sound paying for the sessions, taking the larger percentage for time, trouble and 'investment', giving the remainder of the receivables to the group, which would still amount to a good three times as much as an average recording-company artist's royalty. It was not the time to debate the exact fairness of that arrangement with Eric: he'd translated my art into commerce as I'd asked him to, and we needed to maintain a united front to the unsigned group.

The band accepted me because we had the same interest. They'd listened to me because we could identify with each other. Mick and Keith, especially, could be art-yobbo layabouts in search of a good time rather than a regular job. But at the same time they were as ambitious and proud as panthers, and prepared to work at it, knowing I'd pound their beat for them. The security for the band was Eric Easton. They'd have work, worst scenario, whichever way the records and the fifteen minutes went.

The group approved and Lewis Brian Jones signed the management contract, which was to run for three years. He then had to admit that he could not sign the recording document, as the band already had a recording agreement with IBC Studios. Hitherto Jones had maintained that the Stones had nothing concrete, signed or otherwise, with Gomelsky or any other party. I was totally shocked, Eric less so, by little LBJ's revelation – this could shut down my whole movie. I wanted to throw the runt to the whores.

Brian had entered into a deal with IBC Studios in January 1963. IBC provided the band with free time and their house engineer Glyn Johns, and in return IBC had a six-month option on the Stones' tapes. IBC had unsuccessfully tried to sell the five-track demo to every label in town, and had more or less given up on the group, but a contract was a contract. The IBC deal ran on until July, and that seemed like waiting for the millennium. Even Norman Jopling's article could be turned against us if some record company woke up and went for the band.

IBC Studios were owned by George Clouston and Eric Robinson, both straight and successfully out of the big-band era and not clued up or into pop. Glyn Johns had an agreement with them that he could bring in any act he liked to demo, the tapes remaining the property of IBC.

We told Brian to ring up IBC and tell them things were not going well and that he had got an offer to join another group, which involved a recording contract and a potentially bigger future than he might have with the Stones. As Brian Jones was the only signature on the contract, this would mean that, if IBC agreed 'not to stand in the way of his new future' and let him out of the contract, they'd be letting the whole group out.

A well-rehearsed Jones went to the IBC Studios in Portland Place and explained to the studio brass, 'Look, my parents have agreed to put up £90, for the cost of the sessions, and will pay it to you if you let me out of the contract.' Clouston, with the best intentions, comforted by the promise of £90 and faced with a belligerent Brian going, 'Me, Me, Me', agreed to let Brian (and so the Stones) out of the contract.

When Glyn Johns found out, he felt he'd been run over. Brian, or the group, told him they were going to be recording for Impact Sound and he opined that Andrew Oldham couldn't produce juice from an orange. He refused point-blank to engineer any further sessions for them. Eventually reality and talent would prevail and, happily, Glyn got over it to engineer my later Small Faces hits and other Immediate acts, become an Immediate act himself for a short while, and record the Stones again when we returned to recording in England in late 66. Glyn enjoyed a good relationship for a while with the group after they and I went our separate ways, but that's a lot of orange juice under the bridge of hits.

Philip Townsend: I remember one Sunday going to see them in this London club. Glyn Johns was there and Andrew said to him, 'I'm sorry about the contract.' Glyn said, 'What contract?' Andrew said, 'Well, the contract you've got with the Stones is no good because they've signed up with me now.'

Glyn said, 'No, they're signed up with me, it's all been decided.' Andrew said, 'No, they're signed up with me.' Glyn said, 'Well, I'll have to go talk with them.' Andrew said, 'Yes, you will, won't you, but it's all done.'

John Douglas: I caught the Stones early. They seemed accomplished and rather like art-school nice guys, no posturing; they were almost like jazzers, into pure rhythm 'n' blues. They were gauche, naïve, friendly and generally without any charisma, they were just doing their music. Andrew developed the driving sex and anti-Establishment thing – it was like falling off a bus for him. He was desperately looking for a vehicle, having seen what was happening with the Beatles. Though he obviously had the chemistry going with Mick, Keith was just like a boy with his train set allowed to play guitar for a living; his persona and strength and that touch were yet to come; he was just so pleased to be playing his Chuck Berry riffs. I think they were all pretty gobsmacked by the fact that Andrew had worked with *the* Beatles and by then Andrew was sprinting pretty hard, he'd got a lot of angles they'd not seen before. The first jump to get them moving and to introduce sex and attitude was very Andrew. With Mick there was such a huge change after Andrew got involved . . .

Peter Noone, Herman's Hermits: The guys at my school who were into R'n'B and Big Bill Broonzy and all that were not twits, but they wore cardigans and shit. There were the cool guys who bought black pop records by Sam Cooke, and then there were the strange guys with Bill Broonzy records who wouldn't ever loan them to anybody. 'It's a fucking record, man, let me borrow it.' 'No, no, I don't want you touching it . . .' There was this whole team of R'n'B people, they'd say, 'Oh no, this is not for you', but at the same time they had these dodgy Joan Baez albums going on. I didn't like that lot, we were into rock 'n' roll . . .

ALO: The IBC deal was done, the Stones signed with 'us' and it was time to go to work on getting recorded and released. Their job was to pick the five songs out of their entire repertoire that were the most commercial; I left them to it. They were supposed to know their part. That Thursday afternoon at a Wetherby Arms rehearsal, I was happy to inform the Stones that we'd booked time at Olympic Studios for Friday 10 May. Nobody discussed how the sessions were actually going to be produced, we just sort of mumbled our way through that one – less said the better, till D-Day. We eventually chose three songs to record, one being an obscure Chuck Berry number, 'Come On', which had never been out in the UK.

Sean O'Mahony: The deal was a bit strange: the first records were recorded at Olympic with a blind owner who didn't really know what was going on. Giorgio Gomelsky was the chap who had the Stones under contract, but Eric negotiated the buy-out of that. The record came out and I wrote about it in *Beat Monthly*, as Johnny Dean, so that helped. Peter Jones wrote about it, we all helped to get it away.

Roger Savage, engineer: I heard about the Rollin' Stones at the Station Hotel in Richmond. I went down to see what they were like, with a view maybe to contacting them and recording them. When I was down there I bumped into Andrew – very sharp and interesting – who was there basically for the same reason. I said to him, 'Well, if you want to do anything, let me know.' Oh, I was absolutely knocked out when I heard them, they were doing that Bo Diddley song . . . It was something quite extraordinary. I don't know whether they would have done anything with me or not. I assume they would have, if it didn't cost 'em anything.

Andrew contacted me a couple of weeks later and I agreed to record them one night without payment, because he didn't have any money, so we sorta crept into Olympic late one night. It was sorta an illicit session, really just a favour to Andrew without any strings attached. It was one of my first real recordings. At that time there were only really four places to go seriously: Abbey Road, IBC, Olympic and Lansdowne.

ALO: I picked Olympic, got Eric to book it: Eric telling me how little money we had; Keith Grant, the studio head at Olympic, recommending 'young' Roger Savage as being suitable for the Stones; and us trying to get as much as we could done in three hours on forty quid. I hadn't checked out the place. The control room was upstairs, and I didn't like that because it's like a machine-gun turret – one is literally talking down at the act. The session was cold.

Paying the cab fare on the way to the studio

Roger Savage: Mick Jagger arrived with an armful of books, I think he'd just come from college. We set up and did four songs quite quickly. The main thing I remember was that Andrew told me to turn Ian Stewart's piano microphone off; he obviously didn't want him in the band because he didn't look the part. I was a bit embarrassed about doing it, but that was Andrew. When they came up the stairs to the control room to play back there was no piano! Nobody said anything. I felt a bit strange about doing that. Brian was the one who was the most vocal, he was the one who was suggesting things more than the others. The sound on 'Come On' was pretty conventional. It was a clean recording compared to the later recordings which they did at Regent Sound. Their own sound was more of a mess, looser, with less separation between the instruments.

Andrew couldn't really get his head round the mixing, from four tracks down to one track, he didn't really understand how that was gonna occur. None of them had any experience of recording, so basically they sort of left it up to me. We would have overdubbed something, tambourine and I think vocals; there would have been overdubs. So I would be controlling the mix, telling them what was going on or what was happening with the process. At the time four-track was pretty unusual, we used a big Ampex machine that stood as tall as a person.

ALO: It was 'time's up', five minutes to six. I thought we were done and Roger Savage asked me, 'What about mixing it?'

I said, 'What's that?'

He explained that the basic recording had been made on four channels and we now had to reduce them to stereo and mono for public consumption. I said, 'Oh, you do that. I'll come back in the morning for it.' Because I figured if I wasn't there I wouldn't have to pay for it. I also floated the idea that I thought the electric guitars would be plugged straight into the studio walls, so that nobody would ask me to pay for an amp. A year later I was an expert and nobody was going to stop me divining exactly how four channels would be pared down for public consumption.

At that time none of us knew a thing about recording. The entire process was a new, mysterious experience for everyone. The recorded results fell somewhere in that flawed middle ground between what the Stones wanted and what I wanted. Quite simply it would do. It wasn't Willie Dixon and it wasn't the Ronettes. Now we had to get the product out, get a record company. The most logical place was Decca: after all they'd turned the Beatles down, so maybe they'd panic and sign us. I didn't believe in knocking on ten doors. I believed in picking one and kicking it down – Decca was it. The Rollin' Stones didn't have to perform to get a record contract; Eric and I did.

Dick Rowe, in *Starmakers and Svengalis*: Andrew always knew what he was doing; it was written all over him. Unlike Epstein, it was all he had, therefore he had to be more aggressive . . . It's very difficult for me to say a nice word about Epstein. I just didn't like him. He was too conscious of the fact that he'd been well educated and fancied himself as a gent . . . It's unfortunate that I didn't get on with the person I should have got on with the most.

Sean O'Mahony: The Stones came in on the back of that situation. When Dick Rowe heard about the group, Eric was implying: Here come the next Beatles, you mustn't miss this one! The story is that Dick Rowe left a board meeting to talk about it. He was so anxious, he was desperate to sign this group. Eric Easton set that deal.

The music industry then was much smaller, more parochial, not at all big-time, but the companies were like little castles – to get in there was very difficult, to get them to do anything was impossible . . . all the hits came from America.

Don Arden: Dick Rowe was my closest friend. Of course, they criticised him because he turned down the Beatles; the problem was the Beatles became the biggest attraction in the world and Dick paid for that. But the true facts are that everybody turned the Beatles down.

ALO: In the 80s I met Dick Rowe's son, he was a lawyer at Sony. I asked him how his father was and he said, 'Dead.' And that seemed to be that – no great loss, or perhaps he just felt it was none of my business. I asked him why he'd become a lawyer and he replied, 'Look at my father . . . that's why.' I felt I had to remind him that, in my life, Dick Rowe was not the man who turned down the Beatles but the man who helped me to my great break, the man who signed the Stones. Don't let the pipe or the self-deprecating remarks fool you, Dick Rowe was good at his job for a very long time; anybody can have a hit, but can they have another, and another? I've never seen George Martin work, but like you I've heard it. With his other acts – Cilla Black, Billy J. Kramer and the like – he was your competent producer. With the Beatles he was obviously so much more: the glue, the guidebook, the translator, the subtitles to brilliant foreign ideas. The only time the Beatles ever contradicted what they were all about was when they wrote 'You Can't Do That'.

Dick Rowe enjoyed a remarkable run and held an exemplary track record, starting in the early 50s with David Whitfield, the Beverley Sisters, Winifred Atwell, Jimmy Young and Dickie Valentine, all huge long-term sellers. When rock 'n' pop showed up, he still came to the table, signing Tommy Steele and Billy Fury. Rowe did two of the first tape-lease deals in England for the Eden Kane and Joe Meek product, including the Tornados and 'Telstar'. He also signed Tom Jones, Engelbert Humperdinck, Jet Harris and Tony Meehan and, of course, the Stones. That is some track record; plus he was a good guy who didn't attitude me, happy with who he was, thus having no need to rain on this upstart's parade.

Eric was already dialoguing with Dick Rowe, who'd recently had his ear bent about the Stones by George Harrison when they were both on some talent panel at the Philharmonic Hall in Liverpool. The die was cast, and I cemented it by phoning Maurice Clark, who ran Jewel Music out of Chappell's and had the Chess Records publishing catalogue. I told Maurice that his catalogue was the meat and potatoes of the Stones' act, which it was. Why didn't he be a sweetheart and call Dick Rowe, tell him he'd seen the group, they're the best thing since sliced bread and Dick had better move fast, as EMI was hot for them?

Chris Stamp: He had us totally beaten there, we didn't even know about that shit. When Andrew got that tape-lease deal, no one had a tape-lease deal. Like two other guys had a tape-lease deal – it was visionary. Literally, tape-lease deals were just not done in England. Somehow he knew that and got that. That was amazing.

ALO: Dick Rowe moved, the tape-lease deal was, in principle, agreed upon, then came the bombshell. Decca had a weekly product meeting and it had been decided that 'Come On' could be recorded better. Dick Rowe suggested to Eric that the Stones go back into the studio with a 'perhaps more qualified producer', Michael Barclay, whose Eden Kane empire had started to dissolve into a one-trick pony and was now being gold-watched by Dick Rowe.

The following Saturday, the Stones went in to record at Decca's West Hampstead studios, a little pissed off at having to record the song again. I didn't attend, I stayed home biting my nails. On the left hand, I wanted the best for the band; on the other, and I'm right-handed, I wanted the best for myself. After the session Mick called me at home and reported, 'It didn't go well, in fact it's worse than the Olympic session.' Phweww . . .

Dick Rowe took both versions of 'Come On' into the Tuesday product meeting at Decca. In the afternoon he called Eric to tell him that Decca preferred the Impact Sound version. 'Come in and we'll sign the deal,' Dick said. It was a huge relief to have everything back on again. The Stones were now on Decca via Impact Sound and 'Come On' was scheduled for release on 7 June 1963.

I've always had my doubts about the whole re-record soap opera and feel that Dick Rowe was doing his best as a company man to get the group signed directly to Decca. With Impact Sound out, Decca would have paid a much smaller artists' royalty to the Stones. I just cannot see these suits sitting around their old oak table at their product meeting deciding that 'Come On' could be recorded better – top weight, they'd be wondering why it had been recorded at all. Meanwhile Easton set about trying to book gigs for the band and arrange radio exposure around our release date: 'I've got these lads, and Andy seems to think they've got a future.'

Late in the day, after a liquid lunch with Peter Jones at De Hems, we took our last orders-marching orders and I headed north for Old Compton Street in the afternoon sun on my route back to 93/97 Regent Street. It was still a different Soho in the early 60s: the hookers kept their shrines on the second floor, not on the pavement and in your face, and the streets were reserved for characters, cappuccino action, nerve, real verve and chat, most of it about music. The streets reeked of chutzpah, and skiffle was dead – long live pop. Alex Strickland's Record Store on the corner of Dean and Compton blared the future, while now it just blares upfront sex and 'marital aids'. Oh, there was Johnny Danger on the third floor holding life's markers – evil indeed lurked behind the façade, but what a façade! When they filmed *Absolute Beginners* they forgot the rum in the punch and, alas, it was all façade. I passed the 2Is on my left, still squeezed between a deli and Heaven and Hell. I even managed a fond nod in the direction of Sportique. Walking the streets of *Expresso Bongo*, my heart went boom as I crossed that room, ghost riders in the sky. I blinked to keep my eyes dry, sussed I'd taken the long route in order to wave goodbye. I was on a final lap of honour, but it was time to get on with it and, as I crossed over Wardour Street, I said goodbye, thank you baby and amen.

The other side of Regent Street, five quiet floors up, Eric called me into his office. No offer of tea, just a sigh, as he told me he'd learnt that our lads had failed their BBC radio audition. Mick Jagger's singing voice had been deemed either 'too black' or 'just not good enough': take your pick. To Eric, this was a death-knell to our progress – to line up live work he absolutely needed the tag line, 'They're on the radio in three weeks.'

Due to union rules, for the BBC to consider spinning a new home-grown platter, the act had to be worthy of playing live on the radio, hence the audition. Easton, cigarette perennially in gob and a suit that matched the colour of the ash, was anxious that the Rollin' Stones should pass BBC muster. I ashened in demeanour when Eric suggested we might have to sack Mick Jagger.

If they did not appear on nationally popular BBC radio shows like *Saturday Club*, the Stones single was certain to be rejected as well. Eventually the BBC had to have them: the press I was getting for the group, the buzz, fuss and belief building around the scruffiest band in the land, along with an orchestrated barrage of letters from disgruntled fans, forced them to schedule a token second audition. Was this the birth of hype or a miscarriage? I'll live with it.

On the subject of Mick's adequacy as a vocalist, Brian and Eric had already had a summit powwow – oh God, how fast we all become experts – and decided that nothing should be allowed to get in the way of this 'great opportunity', including Mick. Ian Stewart, who overheard the conversation, told us that Brian agreed with Easton, noting that Jagger had always had a weak voice and 'has to be careful if he wants to sing night after night, we'll just have to get rid of him if necessary'.

Radio was that important, your fella, your never-let-you-down date. For me as a manager-wannabe-producer, live radio was a grating necessity, a ludicrous opportunity to prove that your records were manufactured and not real. I realise that my opinion was singular, in a definite minority. Fandom loved to hear its fave in all shapes, sounds and less than perfect condition; for me it was akin to putting laddered nylons on the runway. A few recordings made in radiolandia remain tip-top and magical, but the odds at the time of pulling that off were stacked against you. You entered a drip-dry world of wool ties, cloth ears and malicious Civil Service disdain. Oh, there was an occasional producer with a glint in his eye for the music as well as the hopefully gay young thing who emoted it. One met an occasional open-minded engineer, facility intact, of good heart and open ears. Given that rare combo, some real gems managed to get on to tape.

Many of the BBC studios were no better than the servants who toiled in them, but a few of the broadcast sites were gold, structured to capture resonance and kiss the sound of music straight to the stalls of your heart, then piped by pure tubular technology to your hearth and home. Old concert halls that had been Henry Hall'd, Vera Lynn'd, Ted Heath'd and Ambros'd; Camden Town vaudeville halls that had sheltered war-torn Londoners and offered them good blue belly laughs; theatres that once had amplified his master's voice, when Noël Coward polished up the worker's brain, rinsed it with wit and camaraderie, verve, nuance and aplomb. Mr Coward addressed the chore of war over the sound of sirens, rationing and being poor, crafting for everyman an edutainment, as he did his best to put food and warmth on the table of thought. Most of these wonderfully sound acoustic centres were by the late 50s electronically bankrupted by the advent of nickelodeon sight and sound, and some had been taken over by the BBC's motley crew. It was on those ne'er visible boards that the Stones stood, while beatdom hovered between doubt and fame, and against the staffed odds a lot of good shit did shine through.

Back at the offices of Impact Sound, the Cinemascope was on the wall of battles to come, but this time Eric had not thought it through and backed off when I snarled, 'So Brian sings?' I'd already heard Jones's backing vocal attempts and the Big Bopper could rest in peace. Easton, in what would become his familiar line of attack, accused me of 'caring too much', suggesting that I was too influenced by one of the guitars and the vocal refrain. When you are at a certain age you see everyone who is above that age as old. To me, Eric Easton was old; he seemed set in his way and eager to be a successful part of the Establishment and, in his world, you didn't go out with the act, you told jokes about them.

Kenny Lynch: One day Andrew said to me, 'Come and see this group, we'll manage 'em.' I said, 'I'm an artist, I don't wanna go managing groups, I don't know anything about managing groups.'

But, to help them out, I took him to the Delfont Agency. Mick and Brian were in their usual gear and when Bernard Delfont saw them he said, 'Get 'em out of here, we can talk about 'em but get 'em out of here!' I took 'em to the Piccadilly café in the tube station, which was right underneath the offices. Andrew told Jean he didn't want to go with Easton, but he couldn't get anyone else to pay for the record. Later he played me 'Come On'. I said, 'They're 'orrible!' Ask me now and I think they're better than anything I've ever heard.

ALO: Sean O'Mahony, using the *nom de guerre* 'Johnny Dean', launched *Beat Monthly* in March 1963. Sean was an old PR contact of mine. I liked the man: he had a wry, composed mind and was not put out by the new beat in town; in fact he welcomed it. I introduced Sean to Eric Easton and the two contemporaries became close friends as they conveniently lived a mere half-mile apart from one another in Ealing. I thought Sean would be good for Eric, and a good sounding board for my relationship with him.

Sean O'Mahony: Initially I thought it was an excellent partnership, a very good combination. Andrew was the young go-getter with loads of good ideas for promoting groups and giving them an image, very good at getting publicity, incredibly enthusiastic, with the right feel for the sort of music the Stones should produce. Eric was this rather conservative showbusiness agent, a very straightforward businessperson who had the necessary practical knowledge, knew how contracts worked, knew how to do bookings, knew that side inside out.

Eric was vital, the key to making the whole thing work. Eric was looking at it like a normal showbusiness agent would at the time. They didn't appear at every television or radio show or go on tour with the artist. It wasn't the way it was done. They booked a summer season in Margate and maybe

popped along once. Eric could be quite sarcastic. He had a go at me once. I'd only just met him and I was expounding my views to him on the pop business. He turned round to me and said, 'If you know so much, why aren't you rich?'

ALO: It soon became apparent that Decca were going to do very little to help me promote the single. They took out one advert for 'Come On', a quarter-page strip in the *NME* devoted to four groups. 'One week and you're on your own, my son' was the Albert Embankment motto. The fact that I had not delivered a national anthem was neither here nor there in my book – belief was the thing: here's my kill factor, now show me yours.

Decca's basic attitude was, 'Well, we've got them, no one else can have them.' Records or acts didn't get launched, they just got thrown against the wall. There were no adverts proclaiming how great the first Rollin' Stones' record was. There was no build-up by the record company. There was no support from Decca. It was just another group. You didn't even get three weeks' devotion. With a single you got a week, and the next week they had another batch of singles to bash against the wall. As Tony Hall had it: if you had the magic, you got the airplay. We had the magic, but we hadn't got it on vinyl yet. All of these hard facts helped the Rollin' Stones become what they were and are.

Now I needed to feel good and have the band feel good, so I got the Stones ready for photos by doing what I did best: I took them shopping for free gear.

Philip Townsend: Crispian Woodgate took the first set of serious photographs on the Thames Embankment. We went round to Edith Grove, and they'd just got a card from the Beatles, saying, 'Well done, you'll be up here with us soon.' The Stones said they were really hungry, 'We haven't got any money.' So I popped down to the chicken barbecue and bought them a couple of chickens.

ALO: I made my first visit to the infamously rank and scummy Edith Grove flat to prepare the band for the Embankment snaps. The worn, dirty lino in the kitchen and the gas meter in the hall appalled me. There was no telephone and the place smelt like a never-ending fry-up.

I had met photographer Crispian Woodgate on an earlier PR episode. In 1963 it was traditional for pop groups to pose for publicity photographs frozen, bland and blank, all uniform, rigidly smiling in a soft-porn-lit studio. Down at the Embankment I put the Stones, minus Ian Stewart, up against a grim-looking wall near the river. The group were 'sorry' to have forgotten their recently acquired apparel and wore their own clothes.

That look, that 'just out of bed and fuck you' look – the river, the bricks, the industrial location – was the beginning of the image that would define and divine them. Word got out: the results of the Embankment photo session were 'disgusting'. The Stones were unkempt, dirty and rude. I loved the photos, got the picture, the penny dropped. I thought we were all in the same biz, that the press and photogs had seen it all before. I was wrong, they hadn't seen anything yet. I went home, put the kettle on, drew a bath and soaked in the reaction.

Keith Altham, *NME* Features Writer: Originally Andrew put them in the houndstooth jackets and leather gear so that they had some uniform presence, contemporary to the Beatles. Gradually he realised that it wasn't gonna work and they weren't gonna wear them. He saw how the Stones rebelled against conformity, in contrast to how the Beatles were controlled by Epstein. And he saw the value in letting them have their heads. Then – and this was both his genius and his Achilles' heel – he saw it could be exaggerated, taken a step further and made to look as though they were working-class heroes. They weren't – yet. They were middle-class kids rebelling against a middle-class background.

Pete Townshend: They were an unbelievably brilliant band, electrifying in the early days. I'd see 'em in the street, and rumours were rife, all the girls wanted to fuck 'em. One day I saw them all walking past Ealing Broadway tube station; I was stunned at this collection of ragged guys who none the less looked incredibly cool.

The Who supported them on their first ballroom tour of the UK and several times around London. They were stupefyingly good; they were without doubt the best band I'd ever seen. They swung like hell. Brian Jones was a real Paul McCartney heart-throb figure in the band, much more than Jagger. Jagger was sexy and girls loved him, but he appealed to the homosexual boy in me, he was very, very androgynous – something about him, you wanted to get inside him, and be him, if you were a boy.

There was a lot of sexual ambivalence and confusion around in those days. The whole Mod thing was a blending of sexes, the girls looked like boys and the boys looked a bit like girls: even though they wore suits, they wore make-up. I remember Marc Bolan with full make-up on working as a rent boy to buy clothes, in and around the Scene Club. He was about fifteen.

It was something to see Brian Jones – with his great long, blond, floppy, overwashed hair, he was a good-looking man – and all these Mod girls who looked like boys were screaming at him.

Keith went out swinging his arm to limber up as he went on and I thought it was his trademark, so I just stole it. I was such a fan I stole it. We played with them again about two weeks later in Forest Gate and he didn't do it. I went up to him and I said, 'What happened to the arm swinging?' He said, 'What arm swinging?' I said, 'The arm swinging!' He said, 'I don't swing me arm!' – so I had it, but it came from him.

Sheila Klein: The first time I saw the Stones, they looked like punks from another planet. I was wearing these men's trousers from John Stephen, and that was one of the only times Mick Jagger said anything nice to me: 'I like yer trousers.' Bill was thick; Charlie was with Shirley; Mick, Keith and Andrew were the lads. Andrew would test people all the time, people would get used up if they couldn't actually match up to his ideal. Like a child, he'd test and test and test . . .

Derek Johnson: When the Stones were just beginning and had just released their first single, I went to meet Mick Jagger. Andrew was hovering there to make sure that Jagger said the right things. He introduced me to Jagger, and Jagger's greeting to me was, 'Nice to meet you, sir.' Can't imagine him saying that to any journalist these days. Still, he was striving for fame and I suppose anybody who could help him up the ladder was somebody he'd got to play up to. It was one of the few occasions I met Andrew; he had sort

of a hypnotic spell. You felt almost obliged to listen to what he had to say and take very close note of it. He also had a great deal of charm when he wanted to exercise it.

ALO: Mick Jagger asked me to define this 'fame' I kept talking about. I was taken aback. Specific objective questions will do that, and out of respect require succinct actual answers, from the heart as opposed to random bullshit. 'Fame', that gift God gave to a few until the 60s, by the 70s had been appropriated by all. I breathed deeply and said, 'This is how I see fame. Every time you go through an airport you will get your picture taken and in the newspapers. That is fame and you will be that famous.' I silently thanked Laurence Harvey for the line, Liberace, Lana Turner and the late Johnny Stompanato for the proof, and moved on.

I finally had to buy 'Come On' into the charts. What you had to do was convince the record company it was doing business, because the record company falls in love with you twice. Once when they sign you, and the second time when you sell. So I bought the records myself. This was before and above corruption, so no one was checking up on you. If there were 5,000 retailers, all we had to know was which 450 were being reported to the charts. The trick was to send the fan-club girls in to buy all the records on Thursday or Friday. Then you send the girls back in on Saturday, but the shops have no stock left, so on Monday morning the retailer calls Decca and orders five more Stones records. Suddenly the record company believes in you, and the record is in the charts. That's how it worked.

Sean O'Mahony: The business in those days was very incestuous, it was who you knew and if you didn't know the right people you were in trouble. You needed the contacts to get on television – television was the key media, massive; one little airing and you could sell an awful lot of records very quickly. That's how Eric got them on *Thank Your Lucky Stars*, he was close to the producer and managed the compere, Brian Matthew.

ALO: I had two more tasks on my agenda, so I met with Mick and Brian and told them that from now on, they were 'the Rolling Stones'. I'd informed Decca that 'Rollin'' was gone: they were not an abbreviation, they were not slang. I said, 'How can you expect people to take you seriously when you can't even be bothered to spell your name properly? You've taken away the authority of the group.'

Then I went for the home run: 'Look, from the first time I saw you, I've felt . . . I can only see . . . five Rolling Stones.' I told Brian and Mick that it was okay for Ian Stewart to appear on records and do live radio, but their ivory thumper could not be seen in photos or on TV. I compounded the cruelty, adding that he was ugly and spoiled the 'look' of the group. Plus I was convinced that six members in a group was at least one too many. The public would not be able to remember, much less care, who the individual members of a six-piece band were. For me, six was not synonymous with success or stardom. Five was pushing it, six was impossible. People worked nine to five, and they couldn't be expected to remember more than four faces. 'This is entertainment, not a memory test,' I concluded.

James Phelge, in *Phelge's Stones*: That night the band played again at Eel

At the Crawdaddy Club

Pie Island and the fast-moving Andrew was again in attendance. Although I was present as well, I didn't hear his bad news until the following day.

I was in the lounge of the flat I shared with Brian, Keith and Mick, when Brian and Keith entered the room, both looking tense. Seeing their faces, I asked Keith, 'What's up?'

'We have to tell Stu he's out of the band,' said Keith, who looked very unhappy.

'You're kidding!' I replied, shocked. 'Why?'

'Andrew doesn't think he can do anything with the way he looks,' Keith said. I knew of course what that meant and visualised Stu's face with its prominent chin. Stu dressed differently as well.

'What are you going to tell him?' I asked. Surely they were not going to tell Stu that directly. It looked difficult.

'We don't know yet,' said Brian. 'We don't know how he's going to take it or how to tell him.'

'Andrew said that Stu could stay on as road manager or something,' said Keith. 'It's just the image thing.'

'What's gonna happen if he doesn't?' I asked both of them. I couldn't see Stu taking to this idea and, if he left, they would lose his van too.

'We'll have to see what he says,' answered Brian, but he sounded as if his mind was made up – the Rolling Stones would go on without Stu.

[When the time came] everyone was trying hard to act cheerful – the boys knew how upset Stu would be feeling. Brian then began to promise things.

'You'll still be able to play with us on occasions,' said Brian. 'We'll work something out, won't we, boys?' The others made conciliatory noises in agreement.

Then Brian said to Stu: 'Don't worry about it, we'll see you all right, we'll make sure you get a sixth of everything.' With that he put his arm around Stu's shoulder and hugged him.

'. . . I'm sorry to hear about this, Stu,' I offered genuinely.

He took his hands from his pockets and turned his palms limply outwards as a token of hopelessness.

'I expected something like this might happen.' He sounded upset and said it so sadly. I looked at him and thought he was going to cry – if I had not been in the room I felt sure he would have done so.

Ian Stewart

Cynthia Stewart Dillane, Ian Stewart's then wife: Stu just thought it was Andrew who was responsible for the decision. Stu was deeply hurt, because he wasn't good-looking in the genre of the day. I don't think he felt anything except hurt. Stu was very honest; he was painfully shy, but he always said what he thought.

ALO: Hurt was not in my vocabulary, but perhaps it should have been. In the spirit of the day, everyone was superficially too busy and too young for slop. That was a luxury for our elders, and I had a job to do. And that meant including Stu, not excluding him altogether. Far from it: Stu had the van and he played great. I took him out of the picture, I didn't take him out of their hearts. That move would have had to have been the group's . . .

Philip Townsend: Andrew was thrilled when, thanks to the loyal few and his buying sprees, the single made the lower reaches of the charts. He used my telephone to send a telegram to the Stones, saying, 'Congratulations: you are 49 in the Top 50. This is the start of big things.'

ALO: Suddenly I didn't have time to listen to records, I was selling them. Cliff Richard was enjoying his first prolonged spate of ballads, the worst of Buddy Holly was being reissued, and Del Shannon was failing to follow up 'Runaway'. Only Roy Orbison and the Crystals gave me the spark. I didn't have time to go to the movies, I was in one. And the first reel was going slow. For the next month Eric and I fought tooth and nail to increase the group's profile, get the band gigs and push the record up the charts, thwarting the sceptics who predicted the Stones' early demise.

Thanks to Eric, a *Thank Your Lucky Stars* date was firm – we needed it. In my mind the record would then look bigger than it was to Decca. But, more importantly, the word of mouth I had carefully fomented would be made flesh by the five Rolling Stones, a feeling in search of a product. The single had reached number thirty-eight in some charts and, 'fan support' or not, was not going higher. Neither was I. I was tired, a recurring black mood was giving me its warning knock, and I didn't know how to rise above it. I needed time to regroup in my own mind. The last thing I wanted was for anything to be boring. I decided to call 'time out' and headed back to the South of France, to Juan-les-Pins, where the stars always came out at night.

Jeremy Paul Solomons: I walk into Butler's Tearoom and there's Andrew. A guest now, not a waiter. He was raving on about the Rolling Stones. 'They're gonna be bigger than the Beatles,' he said. He was staying in a little hotel in Juan. He told me all about 'Come On' and we went absolutely berserkio. Andrew and I cut out the charts from English papers, circled the Stones, put the clippings on our noses underneath our sunglasses, and walked around the beaches like we were selling peanuts, pointing to our noses, showing everyone. I was going to spend six months in Paris to finish my education. 'Whatever you do,' Andrew insisted, 'write songs; whenever you've got a spare minute write songs; it's in your blood, you'll need them.' I thought he was giving me sound advice and using me as a warm-up.

Philip Townsend: Andrew came back in time for the *Thank Your Lucky Stars* show. I took them up to Birmingham in my Ford Capri. Jagger didn't say much, Brian and Keith were the two talkers. On that show Helen Shapiro was headlining, and there was this Irish show band in light-blue uniforms with lots of gold brocade on their arms, matching peaked caps. Keith walked past them and said, 'Oh, the Irish fucking navy.' They all turned on him. The rest of us had to pull them apart, it was brewing into a major fight.

The producer came up and said, 'Look, boys, let's pull together.' Keith said, 'Well, they shouldn't be in the fucking Irish navy, should they, cunts!' Andrew broke it up. He did his best to relieve the tension and nervousness that the group felt about appearing on television for the first time. While the guys stood around on the studio stage, allowing the cameramen to block off shots (if you've wondered why the cameras are always on the bass during the guitar solo, it's rehearsed that way), Andrew waltzed about the studio as if he owned it, came to life and worked his magic. The Stones relaxed visibly at the sight of him ordering a stagehand to move the drums a quarter of a foot to the right, 'Daaaarling'. Then they mimed 'Come On' just the once, to check the angles over. They all complained the playback wasn't loud enough. The director lied, saying it'd be turned up for the show.

ALO: Back at the office on Monday morning I was racing. The Stones had their first, and possibly last, national television appearance on *Thank Your Lucky Stars* recorded, ready for transmission the following Saturday. We had a national television show. Now we needed the endorsement of a national newspaper.

The *Daily Mirror* was the biggest newspaper in our Western world with a five-million circulation. Patrick Doncaster's Thursday Pop column was the most-read musical page in the country. On my own I could probably get a sorry paragraph, hidden between the pop-star summer-season news and the Beatles. I wanted more, so I telephoned Leslie Perrin, the Patron Saint of Pop PR, and honestly explained my predicament. Experience teaches that it is often more productive to channel our neuroses than to attempt to eliminate them: my obsessive-compulsive tendencies worked well for the Stones in those early days. My manoeuvres allowed the boys an unprecedented measure of spontaneity while ensuring that their press was anything but random. Doncaster was beyond my reach, however, and my respect for some forms of showbiz tradition served us well when I approached Mr Perrin cap in hand.

As much as I needed Leslie's good will at the very beginning, his stature and poise would become far more essential to preserving our gains a lifetime later in 1966. By then the gig was to keep the Stones out of the papers – a challenge that Leslie had met for the likes of Frank Sinatra – my intuition telling me that our publicity had become rather too much of a good thing. Leslie's loyalty to his clients far transcended the income he derived from them, and when the Establishment decided they'd had quite enough of the Rolling Stones and sought to imprison them, it was Perrin who literally held Mick's and Keith's hands as they ran the gauntlet that left me too terrified to act effectively.

In those far more innocent days of 1963, an overcast Tuesday morning got brighter when Leslie arranged a lunchtime meet at Doncaster's regular pub off Fleet Street. I'd never met your man Perrin, but he'd heard of me and invited me down with an open heart to raise elbows and play with the big boys. I skidded off the no. 19 bus in Holborn and happily hopped my way to the meeting. Leslie, enjoying the hustle, smilingly introduced me to Patrick Doncaster, laughed and departed, saying 'You're on your own now.'

Fortunately for me, Pat was as much a gentleman as Leslie, and was equally amused by my forwardness. Although good form dictated my leaving Mr Doncaster to nurse his half-pint once I'd made my pitch, I was feeling Sonny Bono's songscribed needles and pins in anticipation of whether or not I'd succeeded in piquing his interest. And, once again, I got a life lesson in the art of relationships.

'I've really enjoyed meeting you, Andrew,' he allowed graciously. 'I've heard a lot about you, about how young and persistent you are. I know that you called Leslie to find out the best way to handle me.' He gave me a steady look as he let that one drop. I might be getting what I wanted, but I wasn't controlling the situation.

'Usually I don't decide till the deadline what goes into the Thursday column. But I'm going to make an exception for you, Andrew. When Leslie called me about you, we both laughed and said you should be able to get into the column on cheek alone, so . . .' he said putting his hand on my arm and slowing me down, '. . . you can relax, I think you'll be very pleased with next Thursday's *Mirror*.'

When the column came out, I had to admit I couldn't have written it better myself. We had the headline to ourselves! And it read: 'Bad News is Good News for the Stones'. The better part of an entire page was devoted to singing our praises, and my sigh of relief could be heard in rock 'n' roll heaven.

That Thursday, when the Rolling Stones rolled over England's breakfast tables and bus queues with Doncaster's stamp of approval, the nation – had it been listening closely – would have heard the sound of distant thunder. The Rolling Stones had sort of arrived . . .

CHAPTER 11

Leslie Conn, in *Starmakers and Svengalis*: I was the only guy in the music business who started at the top and worked my way to the bottom. I was talent scout for the Beatles, and I was David Bowie's and Marc Bolan's first manager. I was a producer at Decca, but got fired for bringing in Elizabeth Taylor as a co-producer. Before that I was the first ever record promoter in the business. I was the pioneer. I started the whole ball rolling. I made Frankie Vaughan and Petula Clark stars – ask them.

When Andrew came to my office, with Mick and Keith, he said, 'Leslie, you know everybody, could you recommend a co-manager?' I made a big mistake, I recommended Eric Easton, who really screwed 'em to the wall. Eric had no idea whatsoever about what kind of monster they'd turn out to be. From the very beginning of the whole music business Andrew was number one. In my estimation Jack Good and Andrew Loog Oldham were the two geniuses in this business, they had their fingers on the pulse. He was an amazing character, I'll never forget him: he saw in the Stones what I saw in Bowie and Bolan.

Philip Townsend: Eric's attitude was that his other clients – Mrs Mills, Bert Weedon, Julie Grant – were going to last many, many years, but there was a good chance the Rolling Stones wouldn't. I remember him saying to me once, 'If this popular-music business collapses, I'm not terribly worried. I've got a nice little income guaranteed; I hire out twenty organs to Butlin's.'

ALO: Eric managed to book a hard-working ballroom tour that turned out to be a fact-finding mission. I didn't venture out to a lot of these gigs. I had a lot to do, plus most places north of Luton were Beatles territory, so I just left it to the band to try and clobber the aliens any way they could. Anyway I'd been to the ballroom-tour opener in Wisbech, and somewhere between the agony of riding in the back of Stu's van and what passed for toast the next morning in the B&B, the band applauded my effort and support and happily waved me back to hustle in the Smoke.

Nik Cohn, in *Awopbopaloobop Awopbamboom*: In due course, trad would die its death and, after a seemly pause, R'n'B took its place. The Rolling Stones were the major sponsors, of course, and Saturday-night Soho used to be jammed tight with mean boys and moody girls, all long-haired, singing infinite choruses of 'I've Got My Mojo Working' and blowing mouth organs out of tune.

Like you'd expect, most of our home-grown blues men were lousy. They'd come out of Surbiton, their hair down in their eyes and their Mick Jagger maracas up by their ears, and they'd sing their blues, dem lawdy-lawdy blues, all about those cotton fields back home, the Dagenham Delta.

ALO: If this was the future as seen through a rear-view mirror by keen Cohn, then I needed a detour. I don't knock the copy-pop movement, but we needed to rise above it, and fast, or sink with it. I had a band without songs: we were akin to an aeroplane without parachutes.

Tony Meehan: The Stones were in one studio, and I was in another doing some mixing, the first time I met them. They looked very sort of wild, like beatniks. They were having great trouble tuning up. And I said to Andrew, 'That's out of tune . . .' He looked at me and just laughed – his inimitable sense of anarchy. He said, 'Yeah, great, isn't it?' He couldn't give a shit. It was 'great', people were fooled by it. It was the image – he was selling an image and he did it very well. It was almost like punk.

I started in Irish traditional music, then jazz and then pop. My background was very musical, so I was quite horrified when he sort of laughed and said, 'Great, isn't it?' because it went against everything that I actually stood for. I stood for what I thought was musical validity and as much perfection as you could get, and of course he was this anarchist who wouldn't know a crotchet from a hatchet, producing this bunch of yobs in a studio and getting away with it. If you actually listen to some of their early records, they are so appalling. They really were. He faked it. It was incredible. It was a great con.

I don't think Andrew's musical background was very wide; how can I say it, he wasn't very deep into music as such, he was into image. Andrew was more like an impresario, somebody who was producing an image rather than the music. I think many musicians at that time asked each other, 'Have you heard the Rolling Stones? Aren't they dreadful?' Of course the public bought it lock, stock and barrel: there's gotta be a message in there somewhere for all for us. That, if you sell something hard enough and strong enough, people get taken in by it.

ALO: At the Stones' first photo opportunity a half-dozen pop picture-takers shared generously their mutual disgust at their subjects. The lens lizards whispered in my ear, 'Are they really that dirty?' I quietly let on that they were. I now endorsed the anti-image, so that the Stones could copyright a come-as-we-are appearance that proclaimed they were already their own men.

That day I bid farewell to that revolting, fried-up lino pisshole Edith Grove. On my few 'rise-and-shine' missions to the lair I don't recall Brian Jones ever being at home. I later found out he was busy procreating in the suburbs. But I do remember Charlie Watts and Shirley soon-to-be Watts sharing each other in a single bed; thankfully some things remain the same. Charlie and Shirley Watts still share the same bed. One of life's achievements.

The first single arrived through a combination of wishful thinking and ignorance. I was unjustifiably optimistic about the group's ability to marshal its own career, musically. You'll recall that 'Play me the five songs you think are your most commercial' was the only command I'd issued to produce 'Come On'. Fortunately, I was saved the masochism of delving into the Stones' idea of their next fave five. The God that looks after Soho and its children deemed that the Rolling Stones' second single would be scribed by John and Paul, 'I Wanna Be Your Man'.

The Stones were rehearsing in Ken Colyer's Studio 51 jazz club in Great Newport Street off Charing Cross Road. There we had been introduced to that reality named frustration. Cover records of Leiber & Stoller's pussy-driven black-face vignettes would neither do their black masters justice nor ally me with a star of the magnitude I wanted. It was about two-thirty on a dark London afternoon, dark more so for me as we ploughed the fields and scattered the Stones' repertoire right and left for that hit.

In the studio recording 'I Wanna Be Your Man'

Then two good seeds lent a hand. When in doubt, leave the room and take your gloom away from those who have their own row to hoe. I hopped out of the basement, flicked right on the street and headed towards Charing Cross Road. I started to walk between and against the traffic, daring the cars to hit, run or pause; it was all the same to me.

The two beams of light and ale emerged from a taxi in front of Leicester Square tube station. They were a slightly wobbly John Lennon and possibly slightly tipsy Paul McCartney; at least, John was swaying visibly as he counted out shillings for the cab driver. His eyes met mine as the driver 'thank you, guv'd' him, and they waved me over. I hurried in their direction, little thinking that this chance meeting would be yet another signpost to the top of the pops. This was the first time I'd seen them since I'd left their employ.

I didn't think they knew me well, but they did. I'd also forgotten what perceptive buggers they were, as they came straight to the point and asked me what was wrong. They'd just left a Variety Club luncheon at the Savoy at which they'd been honoured and wished well, and they wished me well enough to stop me drowning in my dark afternoon. 'C'mon, Andrew, what's up?'

The Beatles and Harold Wilson at the Variety Club luncheon

They were in their sartorial Sunday pop best, but freed from the pressure of the press John had already loosened his tie. Though they looked like they'd just stepped off the stage of the London Palladium, their casual charisma was very much in evidence, and they seemed slightly embarrassed to be caught wearing such finery in broad daylight. A liquid lunch helped to make the event go down easier – the first stop on the honour chain that would come their way for contributions to Queen, Country and Apple Corps.

I explained that I had nothing to record for the Stones' next single. They smiled at me and each other, told me not to worry and our three pairs of Cuban heels turned smartly back towards the basement rehearsal. Beginning with our Anello & Davide Beatle boots, we were the epitome of upwardly mobile youth style: I was wearing my customary John Stephen blazer over a gingham shirt and grey flannel trousers, while John and Paul were fabulous in their three-piece, four-button bespoke Dougie Millings suits. With Paul in lighter and John in darker shades of grey, their gear was a Mod variation of the classic Ted drape jacket, set off by black velvet collars, slash pockets and narrow, plain-front trousers.

Once downstairs, the boys quickly got to work teaching the Stones 'I Wanna Be Your Man'. Yeah, they gave us a hit, which was certainly my oxygen, but more than that they gave us a real tutorial in the reality they were forging for themselves; lesson of the day from John and Paul. I went from downed to reprieved to exalted as the two Beatles ran through their gift for the open-mouthed Stones.

James Phelge, in *Phelge's Stones*: The band was in between numbers on the stage at Studio 51 when in walked Andrew. At first glance it looked as if he had two well-heeled businessmen in dark coats and suits following behind. The pair were in fact John Lennon and Paul McCartney. Andrew had met them by chance in a nearby Soho street and invited them over to the club. The few privileged onlookers watched with surprise as the two Beatles and the Stones greeted each other like old friends. With Paul looking on, John explained that they had a song they'd written for themselves but not yet recorded. They would be happy to let the Stones record it instead as a single, if they were interested. Everyone's faces lit up at the prospect . . . The whole procedure probably took about twenty minutes and the result was that the Stones no longer had a problem regarding their next single. Then John and Paul had to be on their way to another engagement and left the club with Andrew.

ALO: It was a match made in heaven – the north and south of musical life, rampant youth colliding, and I knew I'd hear the country cheering. It was scary; this was the beginning of home. At that rehearsal, an inspired Brian Jones added the roar of his slide guitar, John and Paul enjoying as much as the Stones and I the spontaneity of the moment. The unfinished bridge was finished there and then in front of everybody, pro scribing in your face. 'I Wanna Be Your Man' would make 'Come On' sound limp by comparison. The force of the title and the writers would demand attention, and the power of the collaboration and execution of same would guarantee the hit.

I let the oncoming black mood I'd tried to ward off take over and flew to Paris that eve, leaving the recording to the Stones and Eric Easton. I'd already heard it in my head and that was reality, and when I returned from Paris it was done. I was experiencing one of my first claustrophobically painful periods of depression. I didn't understand this mental takeover. My only cure was to get out of town, to be alone with this madness, to try and calm it down, make it a friend. I couldn't get over the fateful fact that, had I gone for a walk five minutes earlier or later, I wouldn't have run into Lennon and McCartney, and the Stones wouldn't have got 'I Wanna Be Your Man'.

This time the let-down was overwhelming. I could not afford to be seen, I just had to go. It was so very hard for me to understand why such a happy 'up', career-propelling event would leave me so down. These were the first recognisable symptoms of severe manic depression – which I would suffer from, and deal with unsuccessfully, for the next thirty years. It was so confusing and scary, yet I knew I wouldn't scream for help.

Something in your brain is broken, your clock's overwound. Depression is a sly mistress, she offers numbness in exchange for feeling, and scolds you for staying away so long. Years before success drove me mad, I'd look at my mother and know she knew, but my mother was too busy keeping her own hounds at bay to throw mine a bone of comfort. But she saw it and she recognised it. Perhaps that's what she felt sorry about – the passing on of this flat and unprofitable inheritance; perhaps it was not about my wasting my time. Sheila I couldn't talk to – my call – my bottle was on empty and I might have killed her, had she known and let me know at the wrong moment. I may well have on a later date when she dared to care, or scorn, and pull rank on this almighty and was rewarded by being thrown from a moving car. There may well have been two of her at the time, she could have been pregnant. The scream inside me could drown the sound of the Underground, and the platform would scare you because you can only associate it with an invitation to jump.

Thus I became a self-educated psychiatric pharmacologist in my driven efforts to put the pain down. When I exhausted the biochemical overdraft of self-medication, I allowed myself to believe that other 'care-givers' knew me better than I knew myself. Thus I endured shock treatments that resembled those of *A Clockwork Orange*, without the distinct advantage of being able to dog-ear the page and close the book. I will never enjoy the pain that is my legacy, but I now realise it doesn't have to define my mission.

Eventually, I returned to form, all positive, all 'up' and all front. But this lack of control over fate and my moods alarmed me, and this first in a series of career highs, followed by uninvited and unexplainable lows, left me unnerved and dumbfounded.

Sheila Klein: He was a manic depressive and his putting on an act was his way of avoiding dealing with it. He'd be really hyper and really, really up and then he'd be incredibly down.

ALO: My head was clear when I returned from Paris a few days later; I was back to my old self. My abrupt mood swing may have mystified the Stones, but I offered no explanation for my absence. All I wanted to do was hear the result of the recording session. It sounded great. For the B-side the group made its first stab at constructive plagiarism with a bluesy instrumental called 'Stoned'.

While I had been away, Eric Easton had done more than handle the recording session. My co-manager and partner had made a move on his own to handle the disposition of the B-side composition. Eric had explained to the band the obvious fact that 'Stoned', as an original song, needed a publisher to collect royalties due to it, and recommended that the band publish the song with 'some good publishers' he knew over on Denmark Street, Southern Music.

Eric Easton was in fact acting duplicitously and had forgotten to mention

to me or the Stones that he already had a joint-publishing company with
Southern, called South-Eastern Music (which would co-publish 'Stoned').
Easton would have Mick and Keith assign a few more songs into this
arrangement before the three of us put a stop to it early in 1964. The actual
details of the inter-company arrangement between Southern and Easton
emerged years later when the other shoe dropped. Despite his seeming so
straight, Eric was just plain criminal at times, representing that 'Southern
are a good outfit, lads, they'll make sure you get paid properly . . .'

The publishing scam nailed the coffin of my relationship with Eric
Easton shut. No doubt to distract me from his own bad faith efforts, Eric
constantly needled me about my personal relationship with the band. He felt
I could not be objective about their career as long as I was under their
influence as friends. He was asking me to make a crucial choice between him
and the band, as if a long-term partnership with Easton could fulfil my
lifelong aspirations. All I had to do was dream, and Eric would worry what
scheme I was up to. There was never any real trust between Eric and me, and
those days in which I was winning the trust of the group were indeed
perilous.

Still, for the moment Eric and I presented a united front to convince the
media and teenagers of the British Isles that they needed the Rolling Stones
in their lives. It was not time to fight openly with Eric, and remember, at the
time I had no real evidence of wrongdoing: only the prejudice I had against
who he was and what he did, and a suspicion that my commitment to the
Stones was not taken altogether seriously.

Meanwhile the Rolling Stones themselves were struggling with the
physical and emotional demands of their first tours: if the Stones thought the
ballroom trek with its alien and indifferent audiences was an ordeal, they
were about to find out the real meaning of hard work. On 29 September they
embarked on the Everly Brothers' theatre tour. The schedule was exhausting, with two shows a night and only three travel days off in a relentless
thirty-two-day schedule. The tour with Don and Phil was, to the young
Stones, what Hamburg had been for the even younger Beatles, and it is hard
to see how they could have become the most durable touring band of all time
if they had not suffered this thankless first rung. Night after night they fought
to win over audiences that at best found them a poor substitute for the

Beatles. I may have emphasised the Stones' roughness, but it was the road that brought out and hardened their toughness.

Don Arden: I had six shows on the road in Europe at the time and all of them died a death; I lost every dime that I ever made. The one show that appeared to be a huge success was the Everly Brothers. I'd booked them as stars of their own show and had a bunch of unknowns with them. We took in an average of £15 advance sales at each theatre – that's when I realised it was all over for the American stars. The Beatles had killed them. It was just as though the Beatles had poisoned them.

The Everly Brothers had definitely had it. I phoned up Little Richard and said, 'Richard, you've gotta come help me out.' He said, 'Okay', and we went from no bookings to very good bookings. We were still miles away from selling out, so I put in Bo Diddley, whom I got for a very reasonable price. One of the supporting groups was the Rolling Stones. I knew there was an enormous buzz, that's why I put them on for £40 a night. They weren't yet a draw outside of London, but everybody felt it was gonna happen.

Little Richard backstage on the Don Arden tour

ALO: The Stones rose to the occasion and started to shine the metal that has been the underlying strength of their career. Every night the band learnt new tricks from the more accomplished performers they played alongside. They were determined and dedicated, and they never let us down. Winning the audience over was their mission, and they took the stage unintimidated by the stars who followed.

Don Arden: Mickie Most opened up on that tour. He worked on all my shows and eventually I got criticised for it. The critics said, 'What's Don Arden putting this man on for?' They were hinting something was wrong. I knew that he could produce because I'd seen him in South Africa with Gene Vincent. That was how it all started with me and Mickie Most.

Mickie Most: When I returned from South Africa the 2Is thing had disappeared. There were a few more chords around than the three I left behind: there were five or six now, it was a bit more musical. Also there was a great interest in Chicago blues. I made a few hit records in South Africa and earned enough money to buy a Porsche, which I had shipped back with me. It was pretty out there to be driving a Porsche in 63, no one else had that.

Since I and the Stones were in the first half of the show, we could piss off as soon as we came off-stage. If we were in firing distance of London we went back. Mick would be going out with Chrissie Shrimpton, and I'd call my wife and say, 'I'll meet you for dinner.' Then we'd go on to a club with Mick and Chrissie, that's how it was. We'd rejoin the tour the next day. I'd drive him back up there in the Porsche.

Andrew made sure the press came to see the Stones in London, where he had all the girls – all the girlfriends and all their girlfriends – rush the stage when the Stones came on. That was the only place they ever did it, Andrew sorted that out. Of course the *NME* never went up to Liverpool or Newcastle but, thanks to Andrew, they saw the stage being stormed in London, where it counted.

ALO: I was far from getting the press reaction I wanted to 'I Wanna Be Your Man'. The *NME* dispatched the single with one line: 'the latest group to try their chart luck with a Lennon & McCartney song'. Though nobody agreed

Mickie Most, ALO and (back to camera) Tony Calder

with me on the eventfulness of the Rolling Stones' second record, I did manage to convince several magazine editors to feature the band.

While the Stones were on the road learning their craft, I took steps to learn mine. I formed a new 'postage stamp' company named Andes Sound. I needed recording experience if I was going to become indispensable. Decca wouldn't give me the free studio time I asked for, so I scraped together a few pounds and found an artist to experiment with in the studio.

James Phelge, in *Phelge's Stones*: George Bean was one of the hardcore Stones fans and a former drinking partner of mine from the early days at the Ealing club. How Andrew had come across him I have no idea, but for some reason Andrew decided to record George as a vocalist. I had stood drinking and chatting with George many times, but remained completely unaware of any musical ability. As far as I knew, he never played an instrument or sang and his main talent seemed to be wearing smart, fashionable clothes. He always looked well turned-out, complementing his polite and friendly disposition towards everyone. Maybe he was another dark horse like Eric Clapton, or Andrew just liked the image he projected.

Andy Wickham: Andrew's Ivor Court office was a magnet for no-hopers who hoped that a little of the magic would rub off on them. There was sour, sunken-eyed James Phelge who might have been a road manager or could have been a dealer. There was a Mick Jagger lookalike called Doug Gibbons who couldn't sing and never made it into the studio. There was a plump, smart, well-spoken boy called George Bean whose group was called the Runners and who put out a couple of singles on Decca.

Bobby Jameson was a blond double for Paul McCartney, a boy of few words and an almost girlish beauty, who always wore black and was accompanied everywhere by a polite but sinister young Italian-American manager. You would find them at the Ad Lib or the Scotch, always quietly on the fringe of the Stones' circles, eclipsed by all the fame and glory. He never happened but he made some great records, notably a song called 'All I want Is My Baby', written for him by Andrew with Keith and produced by Andrew in the vein of 'Rag Doll' as a sort of homage to Bob Crewe.

ALO: George Bean was a friend of Chrissie Shrimpton, and with all due respect to the late Mr Bean, I would have recorded just about anything. But George was one of the good guys and game. Mr Bean, mark 1, had his own group, but I wanted to experiment in the studio with musicians, arrangers and arrangements, and George signed with Andes Sound as a solo artist. I booked Olympic Studios and hired engineer Roger Savage and arranger Charles Blackwell for the session. We happily recorded a slightly R'n'B-flavoured version of the old Doris Day standard, 'Secret Love'. The song sounded terrible. I had no idea how to pick the right key for the singer and no idea whether the song was even in George Bean's range, for that matter. Too late, I found out it wasn't.

Roger Savage: Andrew must have conned someone. He was in no position to have underwritten the session. I do remember it being quite a big session, it wasn't just a group; I'm sure it had strings on it and everything. It was a Phil Spector attempt. It may have been the time he was wearing his black cape with red lining. Knowing him at the time, he was pretty sharp, he would have got around that small problem of not having any money.

ALO: I presented the disc to Dick Rowe at Decca, who took it into the Tuesday product meeting. He called back and informed me that, although Decca were prepared to release the record, perhaps I should reconsider having my version exposed because Decca had just recorded Kathy Kirby singing the same song. Kirby, managed by bandleader Bert Ambrose, had just had a minor Top 20 success with 'Dance On' and was about to get the big push from Decca. Even after Dick had kindly played me the Kirby version (which had smash written into every groove), I foolishly demanded my day at the races. There was no contest: Kathy got into the top three, and I did not. Mr Bean and his group, the Bean Runners, went on to be featured in the 1967 Paul Jones/Jean Shrimpton beware-of-pop flick, *Privilege*.

I determined that it was just a matter of time till I got it right, and turned my attention back to the Stones. With the release of 'I Wanna Be Your Man' less than a week away, I looked forward to the final dates of the Everly Brothers' tour in the London area. The record reviewers destroyed us: *Melody Maker* wrote that Jagger's vocals were 'lost', 'which may have been the intention but not a good one'. *Disc* claimed the recording was 'fuzzy and undisciplined, complete chaos'. In *Beat Monthly*, Johnny Dean wrote that the single would be 'a Top 10 chart entry – all in all a great double side, well produced by Eric Easton. The Stones are rolling again.' This last review, however, did not mean much to me even though I agreed with it, Johnny Dean being Sean O'Mahony, Eric Easton's new best friend.

Despite the poor reviews, we were in high spirits at the Hammersmith Odeon when, on the last night, the Stones received their best reception of the entire tour. Though they still played in their usual early slot, something was in the air, the month-long graft on the road had paid off, and for the Stones it was almost a 'welcome home' as they bathed in a reaction usually reserved for the headline act. A turning point had been reached: the compere, Bob Bain, had to stop the Everlys' performance to plead with the audience to stop shouting for the Stones.

Sean O'Mahony: At Hammersmith the bouncers dragged girls out of the audience and parked them along the wall backstage. There were about seventy girls sprawled on the floor showing their knickers – it was an appalling sight.

ALO: The tour had knocked the group into shape and given them focus. They were now the hottest band south of Liverpool. With the timely help of our teeny-bopper shoppers, 'I Wanna Be Your Man', which had got a good reaction in the show, was propelled into the Top 30 the week of its release. The single was given real legs as the group set off on a continual run of ballroom one-nighters, which would see them flogging 'I Wanna Be Your Man' through the New Year, with only five nights off. Putting further distance between 'group leader' Jones and his merry men was Easton's foolish decision to cave in to Brian's unjustifiable demand for an extra fiver a week, as payment for his now-imagined management liaison duties. He would also distinguish himself as a team player by staying alone in hotels somewhat nicer than the dumps the other Stones were booked into, and arranging his own transportation to avoid Stu's overcrowded VW bus.

But most of the news was good, for a change. Television was falling into line; it was certainly a better medium for what the Stones had to offer than radio, at least for the moment. The single's chart activity earned a second turn on *Thank Your Lucky Stars* and a first on the new pop programme, *Ready Steady Go!* We met Gene Pitney, who was promoting 'Twenty-Four Hours From Tulsa' on some of the same shows. I'd admired Gene's musical taste and ability since his Phil Spector-produced 'Every Breath I Take' and the Dimitri Tiomkin movie theme 'Town Without Pity' – defining moments in suburban street symphonies.

Gene Pitney: Andrew signed on as a publicist with me, so we knew each other very well by the time we did *Thank Your Lucky Stars*. Andrew was one of the absolute characters at that period of time, there was no one like him. He was skinny as a rail. I went into his office one day and, whatever I had on for a jacket, he wanted it. So I said, 'All right, but I gotta have a jacket, so we gotta swap.' So I gave him my jacket, and he gave me his jacket. I've still got it in my wardrobe, it's a Harris tweed, a beautiful jacket.

He used to stop traffic on Oxford Street with his strawberry act: y'know, strawberry ripple, cripple. He'd limp across Oxford Street in the middle of rush hour and everybody would stop; he'd make it across the street while everybody else was waiting for a light to change. That was the way Andrew was, he was a fireball as far as getting things done and just living the life, having a great time. He was very, very good at what he did. I had success in England, but it had to be validated for a period of time after that and a lot of the stuff he got done was extremely helpful in my career.

ALO: The long, unorthodox hours I was working left my mother feeling I'd been treating her home like a hotel. I was away for days at a time, only coming home to change clothes, and then heading straight back out to the job – or lack of it, as she saw it. Celia was very proud and we were hardly speaking. In Stu's van, on the way back from Birmingham following the Sunday taping of *Thank Your Lucky Stars*, I asked Mick and Keith if I could move in with them. They said, 'Yeah', and I moved in lock, stock and wardrobe. Brian Jones had gone to live at his girlfriend's house, which he'd persuaded they rename Rolling Stone. Charlie Watts was in Wembley and Bill Wyman at home (in what I snobbishly dubbed Formica Avenue) with his first wife, Diane, in Penge, Kent.

So 33 Mapesbury Road gave birth to the Rolling Stones as you know them now, then a little dimmer but always with a glimmer, as I forced them to write songs. No. 33 was a circa 30s' house on a peninsular corner that had become part of bedsitter land. The terrible three – Mick, Keith and yours truly – now had rooms in the left-hand corner of the second floor. The living and sleeping arrangements were frugal, practical and cramped enough to require a civility between us that might have seemed out of character with the image. In the morning, I would leave Mick and Keith sleeping off the previous night's gig and, in my best and only £7 John Stephen blazer (bone-buttoned by my own tailor), over the fly-fronted, John Michael four-guinea gingham checked shirt from my Peter Hope Lumley days, I would head to Willesden tube station for Piccadilly and my £4-a-week office, courtesy of Eric Easton.

Now there was no distance to complain of, and three of the Rolling Stones' leading lights beamed as one. I talked to Mick, and Keith listened, though on occasions Mick had begun to confide in me in a manner that would have given Keith only amusement. Mick and I were as close for a while as two young men could probably become. These days I enjoy the same with my dog. I love my dog, we have the same goal in mind – her food and love. Substitute what it was that Mick was looking for and you'll find between us as fair an exchange. I gave him what he wanted and got what I'd decided I needed.

Tony King: Andrew and Mick's relationship was always very volatile. Somewhere along the line something didn't go right, and it's not something that's ever been mended. Maybe they'll both get older and calmer, bump into each other in an airport, sit down and be able to have a good laugh about it all.

Artists will always survive. The ones that stay at the top are tough; there's a lot of bodies littered along the way to their success. That's why they are where they are. Mick, Elton, Barbra Streisand, Diana Ross . . . they move right along.

If you look at the managers of the period: Epstein died, Kit Lambert died, Peter Grant died and Robert Stigwood ended up a recluse on the Isle of Wight. They were all sensitive guys who found it very hard to cope with enormous success and flipped out.

ALO: From the safety of the suburban R'n'B circuit to the trial-by-fire early ballroom and cinema tours, I watched Mick find out. He would put out his hand in a gesture to the audience and watch it come back empty. He would rue it, get over it and work at it. Then he'd go out there again, put his hand out again and it would come back full.

On the home front, this growing charisma of Mick's, and his obvious enjoyment of it, was giving Chrissie fits, which she vented in outbursts that were both verbal and physical. When Chrissie slammed the door on him, Mick would ring me at my mother's. He'd walk from Edith Grove, we'd meet at a bench on the Embankment, and he'd shout and wail at the Thames and me about the confusion of being in love with oneself, one's girl and one's life. All I could be was a good listener and manager; I was not well versed enough in the avenue of the heart to tell him how to sing that song. I was working out for myself how to commit to Sheila without feeling overwhelmed or obligated. I had my own scarcely acknowledged fears that she might throw me over.

'She shouts at me all the time, Andrew,' Mick complained.

'They all do,' I replied.

'But she hits me,' he rejoined.

I had no answer for that one, though it occurred to me that there was only a small difference in our teenage angst between a hit and a kiss.

By six in the morning London was moving again and Mick had tired himself out. Since I was the sounding board for his anguish, we were both very tired. We'd walk off the Embankment, he'd stop being a victim and I'd manage us into a fresh day. We walked north with a rude nod to Number 10, a smile at the statues as we picked up the pace, got some rhythm of life and strode on to Trafalgar Square. South of Shaftesbury Avenue, east of Cambridge Circus an all-night taxi-stand café served us tea and a fried-egg-and-bacon, white-breaded saviour and we'd walk three more blocks to Jean Lincoln's edge-of-Soho flat. She'd awaken with a smile, put Mick to kip on the couch with a hug and a kiss, and a cuppa for me. Jean and I would sit in the kitchen over more tea and smile at what life had given us – especially each other – and laugh about what it would give us next. She'd get dressed and made up; I'd cold-wash my boat race and iron my shirt fit for the day. We'd leave Mick to sleep off his night's young agony, to kiss and make up with his gal, before we'd finished our day's work and he began his. And with that, Jean and I would bound down the stairs: she'd turn left to Piccadilly and Delfont's and I'd move on to Eric and Radnor House.

When it was my turn to wonder, I'd complain to Mick about how Sheila didn't understand my commitment to work and the Stones and resented how little she now saw of me. Knowing me was becoming much harder, and I wasn't giving her the chance to catch up. Life became insular and single-minded; if you weren't prepared to contribute to the subject at hand – us – then be prepared to be left out of our lives. In a superficial way, the early dramas would flatten out for a while during this halcyon period: we would attain an easy rhythm as casual domesticity and dating went hand in hand with our careers for a short while. Later, after we'd toured America, we all jumped gradients too fast and a certain madness would set in.

But during our London-based run-up to world domination, Mick, Keith and I all committed to the adventure, as Keith readily took up the life he still pretty much leads years on: basically, 'Let me know when I have to play, and in the meantime I'll work on this writing thing.' I don't know if Michael Phillip had made his deal with fame as yet; I don't think he did until we hit a few strides in America and the economics made sense to the boy's mind and training. He did maths and I did airports.

So, in the Mapesbury days, a dream come true was our reality and for the 'unholy trinity' it was fun getting it done.

Linda Keith: Mapesbury Road was very shabby, it had no décor or anything, it was just a place to sleep, pile your clothes up in the corner sort of thing, keep guitars. It had two bedrooms. Andrew got on brilliantly with Mick and Keith: they were three naughty boys, three tearaways, three lads out on the town. Andrew talked in a way that made him sound like he really did know it all and was right in there. He was real Hollywood.

Charlie Watts, in *The Rolling Stones in Their Own Words*: Andrew was very clever and very American. He's a classic example of someone who was very influenced by America. Andrew just observed how we looked and how we lived. He just manipulated the way we were.

Sheila Klein: I think I only went to Mapesbury Road once. That was a period where our relationship was very dodgy. The problems really started when he got involved with the Rolling Stones. I had to shout louder and be more obvious than Mick Jagger to get his attention.

Tony King: Andrew, Mick and Keith were like a three-headed monster. They were always together. Andrew and Charlie were close. Bill had nothing to interest him, nor did Ian Stewart. Brian was a cunt, very difficult for anybody to get on with: a fallen angel, with a golden halo surrounding an angelic face, but the soul of the devil.

Pete Townshend: The Beatles had set this trend – you had to write your own material. The Stones had not proven they could write; their first record

ALO, Charlie Watts and Keith Richards on the set of *Ready Steady Go*

was a Chuck Berry song, and I think there was a lot of panic that they might not be able to do it.

Keith Richards, in *The Rolling Stones in Their Own Words*: It had never crossed my mind to be a songwriter until Andrew came to me and Mick and said, 'Look, how many good records are you going to keep on making if you can't get new material? You can only cover as many songs as there are, and I think you're capable of more.' We had never thought of that. He locked us up in a room about the size of a kitchen and said, 'You've got a day off, I want to hear a song when you come out.' 'Who does he think he is? He's got to be joking,' Mick and I said. But in his own way Andrew was right. We walked out of there with a couple of songs. But it was a mind-bending experience for me. I was a guitar player. A songwriter, as far as I was concerned, was as far removed from me as somebody who was a blacksmith or an engineer, a totally different job. I had the mentality of a guy who could only play guitar; other guys wrote songs.

ALO: I had this thing that whatever I decided people could be, they became. I got nothing but moans and groans from Mick and Keith. They were too tired from the gigs to write songs, and at the end of a few weeks, nothing had been written. One evening I told Mick and Keith I was going to my mother's to eat – I was locking them in the flat and when I came back I expected a song, and they'd better have one if they expected me to bring them any food. It was not a real threat, it was the kind of threat you can voice to those for whom you have a great deal of affection, to let them know how deadly serious I was about the need for songs and my belief in their ability to write them.

I got back from my mother's, quietly let myself in the downstairs front door, tiptoed upstairs and listened outside the flat door. I was happy to hear that Mick and Keith were inside working. I could hear a guitar, a voice and a conversation; to me that meant a song.

I went downstairs again, slammed the front door noisily, went upstairs and unlocked the flat door, smiled at Mick and Keith and said, 'What have you got?' Mick, who was pissed off and hungry, told me they'd 'written this fucking song and you'd better fucking like it'.

Keith Richards, in *The Stones*: Andrew literally forced Mick and me to start writing songs. Andrew showed us. Andrew presented the idea to us, not on an artistic level, but more money. That was the pressure of business. That was a very astute observation of Andrew's. It was very obvious, once he put it to us.

ALO: Music publishing had come into its own with the advent of the piano as a piece of furniture and became an even more lucrative business when the audiences leaving vaudeville venues like the Metropolitan in the Edgware Road were able to take home sheet music of the songs they'd heard inside. Publishing evolved to promoting live radio performances; the sheet music was sold to all the local bands and to well-to-do homes with pianos in the sitting room. By 1964 you could make a mint selling sheet music of hits like 'Please Please Me' to ballroom band leaders all over the UK. The Beatles, with their growing catalogue of original songs, helped to create an important new revenue stream that became a rushing river of income, as each spin on the BBC, live or disc, earned the songwriter a fee; publishers collected and distributed the royalties and kept half for their trouble.

I'd discovered a cheap recording studio used for voice-over jingles, which both the Stones and I liked and felt comfortable in: Regent Sound on Denmark Street. It was a mono studio and, after our haphazard, unnerving experience in a four-track studio, everyone agreed that recording in mono would be better. Mono had the element we needed; what you hear is what you get.

Shel Talmy: Regent Sound was a shithole, it was an awful place with egg boxes up on the ceiling for sound baffling. It really was a horrible place. I don't think it'd been cleaned since the day it was built; there were stains on the stains. It was no more than a demo studio, it was a place I avoided recording in. Its location on Tin Pan Alley was convenient for songwriters to knock off quick piano/voice demonstrations of their songs to place with A&R men. Phil Spector had Gold Star, Oldham had Regent Sound.

ALO: Regent Sound was magnificent. You'd pass a small reception and be straight into the studio, which was no larger than an average good-sized hotel room. The control room was the size of a hotel bathroom, but for us it was magic. The sound leaked, instrument to instrument, the right way. You'd hear the bottom end of Charlie's drums bleeding though Keith's acoustic, and vice versa, Keith's guitar delay bleeding through the drum track. Put them both together and you had our wall of noise. It was our version of direct-to-disk recording, where the placement of the instrument defined the sound that you got. We would record all of the first Rolling Stones' album there.

When I'd decided I wanted to record properly there, the house engineer, Bill Farley, gave a little more, because for the first time he was making master recordings. Farley was bemused at the Rolling Stones' ambition: an Eastender in his late twenties, Farley did everything he could to get the right sound, and put up with my style of direction, which requires that an engineer be more familiar with proven hits than with notes and knobs. With my 'I want it to sound like . . .' approach, Regent Sound entered the major leagues.

(l to r) Phil Spector, Gene Pitney, Brian Jones, ALO, Keith Richards, Charlie Watts, Bill Wyman, Mick Jagger

This was another indirect benefit of the production company/tape-lease approach we were pioneering. If you went into Decca studios, by contrast, you were given a very strict, usually short, amount of time to do just the songs A&R had agreed to. You had to leave on time, because another artist was doubtless waiting in the wings for their turn in this expensive-to-run facility.

At Regent, on the other hand, because it was relatively cheap and they were glad to have us, we could stretch out a bit, experiment and learn from our mistakes. I have no doubt the feel of those early Stones records was due in no small part to avoiding the major studios, and the lessons we learnt would be unconsciously applied over and over by anyone trying to build a recording track record from the ground up.

Before setting off for that night's ballroom gig, we demoed Mick and Keith's first batch of songs at Regent Sound, including 'Shang a Doo Lang', 'My Only Girl', 'Will You Be My Lover Tonight?' and 'It Should Be You'. Not 'The Last Time', certainly, but a start in the right direction.

America mourned the assassination of President John Kennedy in Dallas. In England the spirit of Christmas raved non-stop right on through to the early months of the new year; this was the beginning of the good times. An Aston Martin DB4 Vantage would provide you with advantages indeed for £3,746, and suddenly the purchase was not out of the question. With all the hard work, politicking and close calls, we still had time to enjoy our new status as pop stars.

Philip Townsend: I got the Stones a gig at a deb dance in the caves down the Cheddar Gorge somewhere. It was a party for a girl called Bunty Lampson, whose mother was Lady Killearn. There wasn't enough electricity so the band couldn't play, but all the girls around them didn't seem to mind.

Robert Wace, Manager, the Kinks: I first heard of Andrew at the end of 1963. Bunty Lampson, a society hippie, was Deb of the Year and her coming-out party was being held in some caves in Somerset. I was trying to get the gig for my own band, or rather the band that my best friend Grenville Collins and I had found to back me: the Boll-Weevils, aka the Ravens, soon to be the Kinks, from Muswell Hill. Bored with working for my father's printing company, I came up with the idea of being a pop singer, 'Society's' answer to Billy Fury! The 'Boll-Weevils' backed me at débutante/society balls. In return they had a spot for their own music, and we would give them most of the money. It worked well for a while, but after three months I realised that I didn't enjoy performing, found it degrading and disliked singing for my supper. The group asked us to manage them, and we did until 1971.

But that night Bunty had her mind set on another group. I drew a blank.

'The Rolling Stones are going to play,' Bunty said. 'They're really groovy. I've never heard of the Boll-Weevils, I'm going with the Stones,' she concluded.

Philip Townsend: After Bunty's hop broke up, the Stones didn't want to go back to London. Andrew said, 'Let's go to the coast and have an early morning swim.' So I said, 'I've got this friend whose parents have just bought a castle.'

We drove there in my Capri to this castle belonging to Aubyn De Margary and got there at around two in the morning. We started banging on the door. Aubyn said, 'You can't come in, it's two in the morning.' We said, 'C'mon, we want a drink.' He said, 'You can't have a bloody drink, piss off.' Andrew said, 'What a cunt! We'll give him something to remember us by!'

They had a row of cottages outside the gate and they were having an extension built. There was actually a drawbridge over a moat to get to the manor. We gathered up the bricks from the cottage construction and spent a couple of hours building a wall across the drawbridge. When Aubyn's daddy tried to go to work the next morning, he couldn't get out! We all hid and watched him try to leave his house. Then we went to a castle and started having fights along the battlements with swords we found, and were having a rare time for ourselves until the police came and moved us on.

· CHAPTER 12 ·

ALO: People say I made the Stones. I didn't. They were there already. They only wanted exploiting. They were all bad boys when I found them. I just brought out the worst in them.

Sean O'Mahony: I started the *Beatles Monthly* and sold 330,000 copies a month five months after its launch. Later, we did the *Rolling Stones Monthly*. The Stones and the Beatles had quite different fans. The Beatles were thugs who were put across as nice blokes, and the Rolling Stones were gentlemen who were made into thugs by Andrew.

ALO: I had to find a home for the songs that Mick and Keith were writing. So what if they were soppy and imitative to begin with – they had to come to the process of songwriting through trial and error. That takes a lot of balls and front, as you find out what it is you really want to say and develop the confidence to believe that others will want to hear it.

The novelty of their first loves – Chuck Berry, Bo Diddley, Muddy Waters – had provided an edge early on, which, now that they were recording artists, could hold them back. The entire teenage population of the British Isles could not be expected to relate to the needs and wants of middle-aged blacks.

They had already learnt the language of R'n'B and now they had to create a language of their own to speak to the masses. 'There is a rose in Spanish Harlem' is a wonderful and total concept; 'You can turn off and on more times than a flashing neon sign . . .' is an example of Mick and Keith beginning to get it right in their own idiom.

The two outstandingly successful publishers of the day were Freddy Bienstock and David Platz. I feared Freddy's sophistication and worldliness and assumed he would eat me for dinner. I don't know why, I had no experience on which to base this reservation. So I picked the quiet, seemingly unassuming, all-business, not-enamoured-with-the-show-of the-biz Platz.

John Fenton, entrepreneur: David Platz started before anybody, basically. He was an office boy in our Tin Pan Alley, then he was recruited by Yank Howie Richmond. They set up Essex Music on a 50/50 deal. It was all kinda like a little Jewish Mafia, the people who controlled the whole publishing business. If you weren't Jewish you weren't in the publishing business; it was like dealing in gilt-edge securities, that's where all the money is in music, always. You have a hit record that goes on and on and on until seventy years after the writer's death. David had this knack of attracting people to his flagship, not because he was particularly hip but because he exuded this feeling of stability, which later turned out to be an illusion.

ALO: The Stones and I formed two publishing entities, Mirage Music Ltd and Nanker Phelge Music Ltd, and assigned the administration rights to Essex Music. David was born in the wrong place at the wrong time – Germany in the 30s – and the resulting murder of his family, which David so narrowly escaped, left him deeply troubled and permanently out on ethics. He would come to feel I did not deserve my good fortune, as if it was any of his business, and he took and allowed things to be taken from me.

Chris Stamp: He seemed a nice enough, charming, pipe-smoking sort of guy, quite astute. He seemed to be very keen to offer us what we wanted. He also seemed to be honest, he told you what publishing was . . . or so we thought. We all got along fine. At one time Kit and I created a record label for him called Fly Records, which became Cube Records, with Joe Cocker and all those people. When we found we didn't work well in the strict business format that he required, he paid us off and we got out of the game.

He became very strange at the end. A conman has always got the best angle on you, hasn't he, because you don't know where he's coming from. A conman will always win because he never declares his hand. It was very simple: Andrew, Kit, myself and Brian Epstein were very different from the rest of the business because we had a belief system about the value of what we did and how we did it. We weren't looking to make money and leave it at that; money was part of it, but it wasn't the bottom line. We loved the music, we loved the thing that was happening, we were dedicated to change and the bigger thing.

Ken East: The Beatles had broken through, and now the Stones were set to take the new scene to another level – there was a great enthusiasm throughout EMI that these things were happening. We would get Pink Floyd through David Platz at Essex Music; we also got Joe Cocker from him. Platz was a good deal-maker and a good spotter of talent: he had Denny Cordell, who produced Procol Harum and the Move. Later Platz said, 'I want my own label.' I said, 'Well, you can't have "David Platz Records", but I'll give you an EMI label', so I revived Regal Zonophone. All those records from Essex Music came out on Regal Zonophone.

Tony Calder: David Platz gave us four aces we thought comprised all those in the deck, but he kept another ace up his sleeve. Even if Andrew was operating more on instinct and luck than suss, the deals the Stones got on paper were absolutely sensational – they had the greatest deals, fair to this day. The Beatles were on a shit deal, probably because they came first. The pioneers always get the arrows in the back. It was another twenty years before they got their deals changed. Epstein never used the leverage with EMI that he could have used: 'Hey, you're not getting a new album until we renegotiate.' He didn't do that, he thought that was wrong, 'a deal was a deal', so he didn't ask for things. He was just so pleased he was able to keep going that he forgot to look at how far they'd come.

ALO: A song has many potential sources of income: sheet music, the pennies paid every time you hear a song on the radio, the 'mechanical' royalties paid to the writer and publisher for the use of the song each time a recording of it is sold. It all adds up, and if you have a national anthem, you are talking a lot of money; even a minor hit is going to put food on your table.

In the old world a pound would come in, the publisher would take 10 or 15 per cent off the top for collecting the money, an 'administrative charge'. The remaining 90 per cent or so would be divided up 50/50 between the writers and publisher. So the publisher's total take would come to 60–65 per cent of the income.

In a system in which writers and singers needed the artists and repertoire manager to marry them, the publisher earned his keep by being a matchmaker. The publisher was indeed doing the writer a favour by agreeing to publish and represent his work; the publisher had all the contacts and all the data on which A&R man was looking for what kind of song for which act. Without a publisher and his connections, no song – no matter how commercial – would ever get recorded.

The 1958–63 run of rock 'n' pop in the UK did not do much to change the business of songwriting and music publishing: those few artists who did write their own material did not do so with enough consistency or proficiency to empower them against the publisher-label Establishment. Nor were most pop careers at that time hurt by the artist's inability to find his own voice. The greatest of them all, Cliff Richard, did not write. His performances transcended his often hand-me-down material, with a few exceptions like the Anglo-urbanese masterpiece 'Living Doll', by the ever hit-bound Lionel Bart.

The beauty with a brain, Adam Faith, sulked to a pithy background of pizzicato strings that frequently obscured the artist's originality with musical clichés. Billy Fury, when he wasn't bird-watching, occasionally put pen to paper for the odd flash of smoked realism, but we know consistency wasn't Billy's strong suit. To move his career along, he depended on Goffin-King covers and adequate local product. Marty Wilde did have the gift and mastered the art of song, as shown by such structurally savvy ditties as his 1960 smash 'Bad Boy'. Unfortunately for Marty, by the time he had it down, he'd got married. As a groom, Marty no longer had anything to say that a fickle, blemished serial fan wanted to hear. He bounced out of the Top 10 with his final hit 'Rubber Ball' showing poorly against the Bobby Vee import, itself not the finest hour of Gerry Goffin and Carole King.

And then the Beatles changed the rules – not the rules of engagement and payment, but the total package they delivered of songs, sound, ideas and attitude made them as self-reliant as recording artists as they were on-stage. George Martin was able to discover new pop depths within his own considerably broad musical range, although doubtless his experience with Peter Sellers and the Goons helped him to get the most out of John and Ringo's looning. And the overflow from their jacuzzi of bubbling writing output helped Brian Epstein to become more than the king of pop managers; with his stable generously supplied with Lennon-McCartney tunes, he became the emperor! I would be more than happy if Mick and Keith could just provide unto the Stones.

Don Arden: This is how the Beatles' publishing deal came about: Epstein invited himself into Dick James's office on Charing Cross Road. Dick had been a singer, on the boards the same time as me, called himself 'Britain's Romantic Singer of Songs'. He did the theme from *Robin Hood*, a tremendous international television series starring Richard Greene.

Dick used to wear these terrible fucking wigs that he bought from Woolworths, the worst wigs you've ever seen in your life. We all used to stand on the side of the stage making fun of him when he came on singing these love songs. Despite his horrific barnet, he managed to be quite well known.

Epstein told me that while he was trying to do business, Dick sat eating sandwiches out of a brown paper bag. Unbelievably, he gave him the Beatles' first album for nothing. Epstein had just done the deal with EMI, I think he'd signed for eight or ten years. Epstein was the kind of guy who, if you stuck

by him in the beginning, stuck by you. Dick James got the Beatles for
nothing, he was more or less a fucking doorman, if you really want to know.
He was a guy on his own just starting up.

ALO: We were past the stage where we needed a publisher to get us
recordings; I just needed one to collect. Many publishers were loath to say
goodbye to the good old days and the lion's share of the money. Platz seemed
forward-thinking and ready to play it my way. He and Essex Music would get
15 per cent off the top for collecting, the rest being divided between Mick
and Keith or the group as writers and the two publishing companies we had
formed to cover both events.

We allowed Essex 50 per cent on foreign cover versions, meaning that if
they got Johnny Halliday in France or Enni Boddi in Italy to cover a Stones'
tune, they got a larger slice for racking up extra income for us in that
territory. Alas, I was not well versed in the local foreign law that entitled you
to get 50 per cent on the lot, Rolling Stones' version as well, if you got a local
cover version. Essex had a little demo studio and whacked off cover versions
of everybody, but especially those songs they published, and thus they had
legal right to 50 per cent of everything . . . and I mean everything. A franc
would come into the French kitty, half would stay there and half a franc
would cross the English Channel to be divvied up yet again. Nice work if
fucking is your way of life.

I hope I've made this trail of deception clearer to you than it was to me
when it first raised its hooked and ugly head. It took me a long time to digest
and learn to live with the impious suppression of talent and youth that the
publishing business believes is its rightful occupation. I'm still working
on it.

Years later I was told the story of two record companies bidding for a
new contract with an artist of some recent success; it may have been either
Bobby Darin or Tommy James & the Shondells. One company was corporate,
with audited restraints on what they could pay out in royalties. The other
company was rumoured to be Mafia-financed and run: they offered eight
percentage points more than their rival, and the act signed with them. At an
industry conference some months later the legit record man ran into the
connected one and asked, 'How can you pay that much for an act? You can't

be making anything on them after you pay them.' The connected one smiled and replied, 'Just because I promised him eighteen points doesn't mean he's going to get paid it.'

Malcolm Forrester, publisher: I was fifteen on a Friday, and on Monday started work at publishers Campbell Connelly as a trade boy. This term would most probably have different connotations today. Trade boys made up the sheet-music orders for wholesalers and retailers around the country. These wholesalers were very important; we thrived by selling sheet music, an extension of the old vaudeville piano-on-a-truck salesman.

I was poached by Belinda, Freddy Bienstock's company, to work in the trade department at 17 Savile Row. The head of promotion was Franklyn Boyd, who made me a plugger. The first catalogue I worked was Vicki Music, the London publishing end of the American indie, Big Top Records. So Del Shannon's 'Runaway' was the first record that I worked on. That record did not get into the charts based on radio play. Initially we got the public interest by the bands we got to cover it on the BBC. Franklyn was a ex-band singer who at one time managed Cliff Richard.

I was considered fortunate by my pals because I worked records. Some of my friends had to work the Palm Court string quartets and resort organists like Max Jaffa and Reginald Dixon, before they were even allowed to plug the band leaders of the day. The education was that we were all working songs, even if some of us were selling a record. I still believe that the cover-version plugs that we'd get by the various band singers were as important as the one or two record plays, the BBC air time for music being less than 50 per cent needle time. All of the pluggers had to get a certain number of plays per week; performance income had become the new revenue stream, not just the sale of sheet music.

Most of the other publishers, like Chappell, were still stuck in the world of old showbusiness, pantomimes and summer seasons, but Freddy saw that this pop business was going to grow. He started out very unpopular in the UK biz, 'cause basically people of a certain age disliked Yanks, a holdover from the war when Yanks had money to spend and Brits didn't. I can't remember what my salary was, but my Christmas bonus was £300, which was great money.

My passions were big-band jazz and bebop. I thought this rock 'n' roll thing would pass. It was the smartly dressed black guys in the big bands that influenced my generation's dress sense. We all went to the tailor Gerry Friedman. He made our mohair suits; this cloth had to be pressed every day and, if you were going out in the evening, pressed again. Around 1960 I left Freddy and went to work for David Platz at Essex Music. Dolly East got me the job. Platz had a good British catalogue but it was a different kind of music publishing, working on show tunes. I fell in love with my wife at this time, and all of a sudden money became important. I'd made a big mistake going to Essex; my Christmas bonus was one week's salary, £23.

Freddy's publishing deals were 50/50 limited companies. A writer would sign exclusively for five years, with a five-year option. Sub-publishing arrangements were not as important then, as there wasn't much life for English songs outside of England. But you'd give a sub-publisher a better break if they got a cover. David Platz started the 80/20 collection deals and he just administered the catalogue, but he collected his ownership through Europe. So, in the end, his deals were the same as Freddy's, except that Freddy was upfront about it. David started out okay, then when the rock money came along, he became dissatisfied with his lot and he wanted everybody else's.

During this period Dick James got the Beatles' publishing and went from nothing to becoming the biggest player with Northern Songs. That's when it all started changing: writers started to question agreements and managers challenged the publishers' very existence. The Beatles were like Pearl Harbor, and a lot of ships got blown out of the water. Everything about the music business changed, and if you still had a shirt to call your own, you were a lucky man. It was as if the entire business changed in twelve weeks.

ALO: Now that I was a full-fledged manager, I was taken by the idea of becoming a record producer. I understood this new role to be both a want and a need: I wanted my own version of the celebrity and madness I had glimpsed through Phil Spector; I needed the Stones' musical destiny to become as self-determined as possible. The God that looks over Soho would probably not be providing any more Beatle-arranged-and-tailored smashes. Mick and

Keith's hits would have to be recorded by someone, and I was sure I wanted to become Phil Spector and not Eric Easton.

I have often been accused of being a hustler, a bullshit artist, etc., because many of my most ambitious projects have appeared to vanish before the ink was dry on the press release. However, to my mind, a prophecy of success is always the first step in making it reality, and as I am essentially honest and sincere about my work, predicting an outrageous outcome is the surest way I know to commit myself to delivering it. So it was that I acknowledged my agenda for 1964 to the *Record Mirror*: 'Andrew Loog Oldham predicts he will be the most successful independent record producer in the country by autumn.' Now I had a deadline, driven by the hard reality that any fool can have a hit, but could he have another, and another, and another . . .

I summoned the Stones to Regent Sound within the first few days of January and set about fulfilling this prophecy. The band grumbled about recording the day after performing 'I Wanna Be Your Man' on the première of the BBC's new pop programme, *Top of the Pops*. The Stones had another ballroom date that evening and wanted an afternoon off.

But my own timetable was bringing out the manager in me: I planned to use the Stones as session musicians for a single I was producing with Cleo Sylvester. The eighteen-year-old black beauty from London had once auditioned to become a backing vocalist for the Stones (in one of their previous incarnations before meeting me). Although the group quickly abandoned the idea, Mick Jagger had stayed in touch with her, and it was Mick who suggested I record her.

On the promise of a couple of quid each, the rest of the Stones agreed to play on the single. I was now doubly grateful, as I couldn't afford to pay the seven-pound fee that real session musicians commanded, on top of the studio time that I couldn't avoid paying. 'Put it down to experience, we could all use it,' I told them.

I decided to record Cleo singing a version of the Teddy Bears' 1958 classic 'To Know Him Is To Love Him'. I remember thinking literally that if 'To Know Him Is To Love Him' had kicked off Phil Spector's career, it was good enough to kick off my commitment to 1964. I teamed up with musical arranger Mike Leander to stack the deck and eliminate any possibility that

Decca could refuse the record. Leander, although only twenty-three, had studied orchestration and conducting at Trinity College of Music. He was on the staff at Decca and admired by Dick Rowe. He had also apprenticed with American songwriter/producer Bert Berns, who seemed to make all the Atlantic hits not recorded by Leiber & Stoller. The results of the Sylvester session were good enough, thanks to Mike Leander's contribution, to convince Decca that 'To Know Him Is To Love Him' should be rush-released, and this tribute to my master's voice became my first solo independent production. We got into the charts at number forty-eight, and a week later I was ready to try again.

The B-side of the Sylvester single was a weird instrumental called 'There Are But Five Rolling Stones'. The 'Andrew Loog Oldham Orchestra' performed the song – in actuality the Stones – with writing credits attributed to Leander and myself. I was copying Spector's infamous B-side *modus operandi* for good luck: apart from not sharing the B-side revenues with the artist, I was shamelessly using the situation to promote the name of the group and my own.

Meanwhile, we all needed to earn our keep by staying busy on the road. The Stones were booked on their second UK package tour as co-headliners with Phil Spector's latest bestselling bad girls, the Ronettes. Promoted by Aussie wannabe Robert Stigwood and billed as 'The Group Scene 1964', the tour kicked off on 6 January.

Don Arden: I spoke to Eric Easton and said, 'Look, I've given them their first tour, I want them for the second tour.' He said, 'Oh yes . . . mmm . . .' which was not what I wanted to hear. Of course I found he'd done a deal with Stigwood, and Stigwood was kicking back to Easton behind Andrew and the band's back. I didn't want to do that, because I didn't think Easton deserved it. Why should I give him money on the side when I gave him their first tour? The Stones wanted more money, which I accepted, but he wanted a personal kick-back.

When I agreed to put the Stones on the Everly Brothers, Little Richard and Bo Diddley tour, I mean he grabbed it, absolutely grabbed it . . . I was giving them their break. So, in return, for the second tour I should have had an automatic yes. I was willing to give them whatever the average British star was getting, but Eric wanted this kick-back scene, and I think he stayed with Stigwood because they had this thing going until Easton was fired. I have no doubt in my mind why he was fired: I think Mick Jagger found out he was on the fiddle.

Sean O'Mahony: When I first met Andrew I was working for Robert Stigwood. Stigwood had deals going with Dick Rowe at Decca and also at EMI. He was very friendly with Sir Joseph Lockwood . . . I left Stigwood in 1962 and eventually, a couple of years later, he went bankrupt and had to start all over again . . . That's the business, isn't it? The fiercest shark wins the fight . . . The power eventually resides with the artist, if they keep on being successful.

Don Arden: Stigwood went bankrupt because of me. I'd brought over Chuck Berry for the first tour he'd ever done in Europe. I'd been negotiating for a year, not with Berry direct 'cause he was in prison, but with his manager – I forget the guy's name; he's dead now. I went over to the States the day Berry was released from prison so that I could get his signature on the contract. I had a verbal contract with him for $10,000 a week. But I was fucked by interfering people who said to him, 'You're being screwed, you're worth $10,000 a night', so a week before the tour I ended up having to give him $10,000 a night, which was unbelievable money in those days.

To make matters worse, he only sold out in the London area; the further north you went, the more people didn't want to know. I told the *NME* and the *Melody Maker* that we were selling out all over, 'cause all they did was come to review the London shows and they were packed out. I went over to New York to negotiate a second Berry tour and Chuck said to me, 'Well, Don, thank you very much for the first tour, but you'll have to outbid Robert Stigwood for the second.' I said, 'No fucking way. If Stigwood wants to pay you more than I paid you, good luck to both of you.' Of course, Stigwood outbid me and I think he paid him close to $15,000 a night and waddyaknow, he went bankrupt, so indirectly I brought him down, and it couldn't have happened to a nicer fellow. I phoned Bob up and said, 'You want Chuck Berry? God bless ya', because he had no idea Berry would play to half-empty houses in places like Stockton.

ALO: The success of 'I Wanna Be Your Man' spread the Rolling Stones' name throughout Britain, and on the 'Group Scene' tour they were treated to their first real dose of girl-adulation. The audiences on their first package tour had largely been made up of Little Richard-loving Teds and staid Everly couplets. On the 64 tour the crowds were out of their heads, thousands of teenage girls going ballistic. The group travelled back to London each night after the first few dates with the Ronettes, so that during the day I could record them in Regent Sound, before they set off for another frantic gig in the evening. Despite what I may have wanted the press and the older generation to think of us, our work ethic was never in question.

These were highly charged, innovative sessions, and I was adamant that they should include as many commercial pop songs for the looming first album as possible. Towards this end, I suggested Marvin Gaye's 'Can I Get A Witness?' When it became apparent Mick didn't know all the words, I called Freddy Bienstock, who published the song, and Mick ran from Regent Sound to pick up the sheet music left in reception at Freddy's Savile Row office. Everyone else had a leisurely cup of tea and caught up on gossip, and when Mick returned we recorded his vocal and the guitar overdubs. And that's the reason the vocal on our 'Can I Get A Witness?' sounds so breathless.

Dave Berry: I did two tours with them: the Ronettes, the Swinging Blue Jeans, the Hollies, the Stones and me. The Stones and I were playing the same style of music in the very early 60s. Even before they recorded for Decca, we did gigs together. The Stones seemed to me to be just like all the other bands at this time, young guys into their first year of success. We'd stay up and have a few drinks; we were all just starting out. That's how I was touring with them, I was playing all the same music: John Lee Hooker, Muddy Waters, Bo Diddley, all our sets were made of that music. Chuck Berry, Fats Domino and Screaming Jay Hawkins, that's what I grew up with. I've always thought music should be theatre.

On that tour I was travelling with Andrew in his car. He had this little machine in his car that played singles. He kept playing me the Crystals and the Ronettes, day after day. He just kept saying, 'These are the best things anyone has ever done.' Andrew was very much a Rolling Stone; he didn't play, but obviously he was one of the Rolling Stones. Anybody who was around at that time knew this, but as the years have gone by people have forgotten.

On the first Stones album, before the Stones started to write, Andrew used to get thirty-five tracks together, then ring the music publishers and say, 'Give us 15 per cent of the song, or it's not going on the album.' He may have got away with it a couple of times, but most of the time they'd say no. And he'd say, 'You can have 100 per cent and it won't be on the fucking album.' I thought that was marvellous, it was unheard of. Brian Epstein didn't do that; he was too straight.

It was happening for everybody, life was packed out with people our own age. It's very hard to imagine what it was like in the early 60s. It was very like a family situation. Every single I had out, not just me, every artist, we were all on *Ready Steady Go!* You didn't have to fight to get on.

ALO: The Ronettes' dates continued apace. It was a good thing our dreams were now our daily reality, because between the tour and the recording we were on the job twenty-four hours a day and literally had no time to dream up new ones. It was obvious from the reaction the Stones were getting that 'I Wanna Be Your Man' had cracked open a whole new market for them. To capitalise on this, and knowing the band didn't have another single ready for release yet, Eric and I persuaded Decca to rush-release an EP. Made up of four as yet unreleased tracks, the eponymous 'Rolling Stones' EP proved to be a masterstroke. The record stayed in the EP charts for the rest of the year! It also crashed the singles' charts, rising to number eleven.

This was truly amazing. EPs cost twice as much as singles, and for that reason were expected to sell fewer. The Stones' EP would outsell both their previous two singles! The most celebrated track on the EP was their version of Arthur Alexander's 'You Better Move On'. While R'n'B was still a cult, the BBC got behind the Stones' version of 'You Better Move On' because it was a ballad. The song enjoyed the same heavy radio exposure as Dusty Springfield's 'I Only Want To Be With You' and Gene Pitney's 'Twenty-Four Hours From Tulsa'. For a second time, the collision between my pop opportunism and the Stones' R'n'B purity had ended amicably in a hit.

The angry breach-building between Eric and me came to a head while the Stones were away on tour. Easton told me that the Regent Street office was now so busy with the Stones' business that my space would be needed and I would have to find a new office. Sure . . . In fact Eric was just totally pissed off. He'd had it with me, my style of personal management and the publishing arrangements I'd made, not behind his back, but in his face. He thought, regardless of any apparent results, that I was spending too much time with Mick and Keith, and not acting as a manager should. He just did not get that this was not a job . . . it was a way of life. He was saying, to any ear he could get, that I was having a bad effect on the rest of the group. But to me, the only ones having a bad reaction were Eric and Brian Jones. And so Eric demanded that I move out of his office, and thus began the real beginning of the end of us.

Sean O'Mahony: Eric was vital. Andrew knew nothing about the business side of it; he didn't have any contacts on that side, he didn't know about contracts, how to organise or negotiate them. He was young and very green, so he needed someone who had all that information.

Nobody expected a British act to become an international star worth millions of pounds. A hit record then was worth £3,000, not millions like today. That's why a manager thought in terms of having several acts . . . the idea was that, if one took off, you immediately started working on him. The Beatles were treated this way. That first LP they made was made overnight to cash in on the success of the single.

Andrew was one of the new breed of very young pop entrepreneurs and Eric was a typical showbusiness agent. He knew showbusiness inside out. There always must be a certain amount of resentment between a person who's a bit older and knows a lot and a young person who turns up and thinks he knows everything.

ALO: I was not entirely alone in the ranks of precocious young upstarts: on a bright and brisk early spring afternoon in 1963 I had waltzed out of the Decca Promotions offices, with not a care in the world but caring for everything in the world. As I marched past the Great Marlborough Street Magistrates' Court, I thought I saw somebody I recognised. It was Tony Calder, whom I'd met on the Twickenham film set with Mark Wynter. Calder had under his wing a young London artist, Steve Marriott, whom he'd just accompanied while the cockney tyke pleaded 'fair cop' to a petty offence. It was a serendipitous meeting – both Steve and Tony would become a large part of my future.

Tony and I are indeed a strange lot, enjoying our share of mutual good fortune while carrying each other's luggage for much of a lifetime. Tony is an engaged, passionate and handsome man, qualities that would catch Sheila's attention for a while in the 70s after Sheila and I were separated. In the long haul I cannot hold Sheila against him; he didn't take anything that was not offered.

The nature of the game is that there are many who have spoken ill of and ridiculed Tony, who genuinely thought they were doing me a good turn, and there are others who did not want me to have the benefit of him. I gave him the best and worst years of my life, and the best and worst of all was our Immediate Records, whose story can be told later. Although Tony might claim 'it was only business', the depths to which I would sink over the long while would have pained him; the waste of opportunity and talent would

(l to r) Tony Calder, solicitor Timothy Hardacre, ALO

surely have put him out. We dived into the fray with enthusiasm, and we definitely changed some of the rules of engagement. Had I assimilated some of his passionate pragmatism for the game and the players, I might have saved myself some bruising.

Tony Calder: My first impression of Andrew was that he had more flair than I did, and he was more interested in the publicity. We both realised that we could do something together. Our attitude towards the business was fuck 'em all, they were all old men, they were sad. We'd finish each other's sentences; that's when we knew we'd get along.

While I was working at Decca as a trainee I had met Jimmy Savile, who took me to Leeds where I saw these fantastic lunchtime sessions with 2,000 kids paying sixpence each to get in. From then on I worked at Decca by day and Mecca by night, as a DJ. I did Jimmy's 'Off the Record' evening sessions at the suburban and provincial Mecca dance halls in Ilford, Streatham, Purley.

Jimmy Savile had a great idea: pay the band not to work! The Musicians' Union had an absolute fucking stranglehold on everything, not just the radio, but everything. It's very hard today to comprehend the control the MU had; they believed that if you were playing records in clubs you were putting musicians out of work. So you had to employ musicians in the dance halls but the kids just wanted to hear the records. Jimmy paid the band not to play. He wasn't breaking the rules, he was making them and he never got the credit for it. All the clubs today owe him a monstrous thank you.

I decided I couldn't keep it up working night and day. I had also set up a publicity business, which I really wasn't interested in; it was all too much like hard work. Then Andrew said, 'Why don't we do the publicity business together?' and I said, 'Fine.' I was promoting 'Love Me Do' and Brian Epstein was chasing me around the desk. Andrew didn't have NEMS, Andrew didn't have the Beatles: I gave it to him. I got a call from Tony Barrow, who was still working at Decca and working on the side for Epstein, and he said, 'Can I do a press release and organise the interviews?' I said fine, they came down for the day from Liverpool and I had half-hour interviews with them everywhere. All the journalists treated the Beatles very badly.

Epstein came down to London and I said, 'Why don't you deal with Andrew? He's much easier to deal with than I am.' That's when Andrew and I started talking about going into business together.

Meanwhile, the relationship with Eric Easton was worsening. Eric cut his lifeblood off, wouldn't give Andrew any money. I'd say, 'Be nice to Eric, ring him up and ask for some money.' Andrew'd ring him up and Eric would scream at him, call him filth, say he didn't deserve it, say Andrew hadn't done any real work. So I'd try and talk to him, I was the barrow boy. Eric said to me, 'Don't you interfere, it's my fucking act.' He made Andrew's life hell; Andrew's forgotten about it. Nasty was not the word. Eric was an exceedingly unpleasant human being and he controlled the purse strings.

It was pathetic. Eric's secretary used to feel sorry for Andrew and nick him money out of petty cash. By now the Stones had started to take off and Andrew was starting to realise he'd been shafted by Eric, really shafted.

Sean O'Mahony: Most people in showbusiness would have been annoyed if their partner walked in stoned. Andrew had a different view of it and said, 'Why not?'

Sheila Klein: Andrew was smoking dope for a long time before I knew about it. We weren't together all the time, we had a lot of space. I was doing a lot of other things, too. We did manage to see each other every day when he was living near Frognal, but after he moved in with Mick and Keith, I saw much less of him. He was still very gentle at that stage, compared to what he was later.

ALO: I was scared of Sheila, so I suppose I gradually started pulling away. I had not grown up in an environment where relationships were a given; intimacy was not the daily bread and happenstance that life revolved around. Regardless of how much love and deep affection there might have been between my mother and Alec, it was still love on the side. I was very shy and only confronted people when in character, so I was a very busy actor. Sheila offered a wonderful opportunity to which I was slowly saying 'No'.

I still recall the first time Sheila invited me to make love: both the totality and the details of her comfortable first-floor bedroom in Frognal. Her bed offered the world, and I sank into it in slow, treasured motion. I can relive that freefall, isolate her body and its possibilities, the gentle dew on the window-panes, the smell and texture of the fresh sheets and our new skins that kept the world out and allowed us to concentrate on this – for me – new journey.

Bodies till now I had groped with on life's dare, as doorknobs to be turned, some dicks not yet hung to be pulled on boys who did know better, and entry attempts made on young girls who didn't. A first failed stab at immortality with Alexis, the dance instructor's daughter, had left me bruised of ego and cock robin. But I hadn't got the time or the will, let alone the nerve, to examine myself and live with what I found, that ground-swelling, earth-moving physicality that seemed to be part of this glorious invitation that Sheila extended to me when she gave me her love.

I wanted it, but I could not afford to give in to such an unknown and potentially commanding passion. I would back off, putting down the wand. I didn't work on the magic, and things between us would cease to be magical.

This love demanded an exciting but scary journey that asked too much of a self I hadn't the time or inclination to develop or know. I was in the business of 'other', of others. I was empowered to move, making their earth move, showing others their potential and, through that route, realising mine.

So I loved, feared, said goodbye even when we wed. Unfortunately I was so attracted to Sheila's beauty, but so in awe of it, that I completely forgot to get to know her. We cannot love others, so the mystics and wizards would have it, unless we can love ourselves. At that time infatuation with myself and my potential, and a grand faith in my ability, seemed sufficient; true love would have to come into my life later. With Sheila, doors opened, bells rang and doors closed at the very same time.

Sheila Klein: It was a very fast lane. I wouldn't say he used people, he just used them up. There was nothing left after Andrew went through them, me included. It took me ten years to recover from our relationship; at the end I couldn't actually speak.

· CHAPTER 13 ·

ALO: An American visited Picasso in his Paris studio just after the end of World War II. 'Picasso,' he asked, 'how does it feel to be *Picasso*, the master of the art?' The maestro said, 'Give me a dollar bill', which he pinned to his easel and then painted over. Picasso then removed the painted dollar and handed it back to the astonished American. 'There,' said Picasso, 'this dollar is now worth five hundred dollars, *that* is how it feels to be Picasso.' Now that my two little glimmers were no longer dim on the topic, I looked forward to them painting their first bill.

It was a pivotal moment in Regent Sound when Mick and Keith presented their first wares for the Stones to record. They say that writing is like opening a vein and studying the blood. I am finding this to be true as I write – it is also akin to tearing off scabs and watching them fester and infect your hitherto accepted view of events, while mental termites gnaw at your very pillars of existence. In those young days, perhaps it was like having your zits ripped off and raw. One word out of place, one smirk, and lesser talents would have zoomed into abort, but Mick and Keith counted off a part of the rest of their lives with, 'One, Two, Three, Four – Keith? De-Deder-De-Dum . . . Dhum De-De de-Dhumm . . . Dhummm . . . I-ey wantchu back a-gaayne.' Now, that's an admission that most of us would have trouble speaking, let alone singing.

Tony Calder: The move was very fast. I think I moved into Maddox Street for a few weeks, but it wasn't big enough, one room . . . if we had a bloody meeting in the fucking room, there was me, Mick and Keith, Peter Meaden and Andrew. You couldn't bloody breathe . . . I couldn't take it. Andrew had Peter Meaden around, poor fucker. Then he got rid of him. Meaden kept falling off the chair, he was always out of it.

ALO: I loved Maddox Street, it was my first real own office, with my own entrance, my own front door. The arranger Mike Leander knew of my problem with Eric and suggested I try his manager, publisher Freddie Poser, for office space. Poser was to the publishing world what Eric Easton was to the agency world, an outsider trying to get on the inside track. Poser let me move into his spare room on the fourth floor of 44/46 Maddox Street and I said goodbye to Piccadilly and hello to an abode off Bond Street.

I liked being on the top floor, and sparked up my small office with a painting by Peter Meaden, who'd now left the advertising job and figured that if Andy could turn a trick and earn a penny in the music biz, then there had to be room for him. And so there was, and for a while Peter moved into the Maddox Street digs. I was pleased to have him back in my life and workplace. But Peter and I never were the best combination in a business setting.

Philip Townsend: Andrew got fed up with Peter Meaden at his Maddox Street office, and I kind of took Pete over. He was really a clone of Andrew, without Andrew's determined discipline. Meaden and I started doing these concerts together. He got a group of eleven black guys, an African show band, and we put on shows at Edmonton Town Hall.

When Andrew grew out of Peter, Peter really turned against him. To get back at Andrew for the rejection he felt, Meaden put up 5,000 cards in Soho call boxes suggesting: 'Ring Madame Loogy – Regular Sex and Otherwise'. Andrew's telephone never stopped ringing.

ALO: There was no furniture in the Maddox Street office and the carpet was worn, but the place was decorated beautifully by my girl-Friday Annabelle Smith, an attractive young lady on the fringes of the music business via her recent marriage to composer John Barry. The Stones were at home in my new office and enjoyed the lack of formality, as Annabelle lay on the floor answering the phone.

Phil Spector flew into England a few days before my twentieth birthday to bask in the light of his incredible success with the Ronettes. I was there to meet him, more than happy to revisit the Spector school of thought, pick those brains and engage him as an accomplice in the rise of the Stones. The

Ronettes had closed out the year with 'Be My Baby' and were now about to release 'Baby, I Love You'. Phil was buoyant throughout his stay in London, assuming the role of hip hobgoblin that the US media, particularly Tom Wolfe, had created for him.

Phil Spector at twenty-three was the most significant person in the American recording industry. Fifteen hits in a row – and if that's not genius, well, what is? The Spector Sound had sold nine million records in the last eighteen months. It wasn't hard to have the London press interested in the arrival of the American Mozart. The first interview by Maureen Cleave of the London *Evening Standard* took place in the back of a limousine that carried us from Heathrow Airport.

'I've been told I'm a genius,' he said to Cleave, 'what do you think?' Cleave was a stunner, in print and in person. Phil liked her, I liked her, everyone liked her.

Angus McGill: Maureen was a features writer on the *Evening Standard*, a remarkable lady. She was very young, the same age as all these kids. She started interviewing pop groups and she sort of gave them the same place and the same serious consideration as an actor or politician. She was the first person to do the big pop-star interview.

ALO: Phil loved London, and London returned his affection. 'My records are built up like a Wagner Opera,' the diminutive thug-tycoon of one-man teen anthems told Maureen Cleave. 'They start simply and they end with dynamic force, meaning and purpose.' No one had spoken like this on pop-record production, and Phil elevated the role of producer to fame in the UK. 'It's in the mind. I dreamt it up. It's like art movies. I aimed to get the record industry forward a little bit, make a sound that was universal.'

Tony Calder: I think Andrew encouraged him, just as Phil encouraged Andrew. It was just a game to be . . . you see, we would call it weird now, but at the time it was not weird. They were camping it up, they were taking unlawful substances, and they were just talking nonsense and sending people up. They were having a giggle. Andrew and Phil considered each other to be oddballs. I think Phil admired in Andrew the fact that he really did break the rules, and he knew how to deal with people. And for Andrew it was near to the point of worship, in respect of Phil's ability to produce a good record.

Andrew used to have a pillbox with every different colour under the sun. I'm quite sure he gave Phil something to take him up a little bit and something to calm him down a little bit, and something not to make him over-anxious, and after a half-dozen of those there's another pill to make sure you don't black out!

Phil Spector and George Harrison with the Ronettes

Tony Hall: The Beatles wanted to meet the Ronettes and I gave a special party. Andrew and Spector just floated in, then they disappeared and returned about six hours later in various states. Lennon took one of the Ronettes upstairs that night, I can't even remember which one. Somebody told John I was an expert on R'n'B, and at about three or four in the morning he tried talking to me about it. I don't know what John was on, probably black bombers. I was tired, nearly asleep on the floor and he kept on and on and on. After a short while I realised that what he called R'n'B and what I called R'n'B were two totally different things. He was much more into the past, into guys out of Chicago. To me it meant Sam Cooke, Jackie Wilson, much more sophisticated commercial things. It was rather a depressing conversation, 'cause it went on for ever, and he just wouldn't let up. All I wanted to do was go to bed; I didn't want to talk about Blind Joe Somebody.

George Harrison and Ringo lived across the street from me, literally right opposite. Because of all the kids hanging around outside his house, if George wanted to cross the road to my place, he would have to phone for a taxi, jump into the cab outside his place, go around the block, change cabs and come back home the other direction – I had to be waiting in my doorway to let him in.

I have one memory of Andrew passing out cold at the party and being carried downstairs by the rest of the Stones, then being carried out by them to a car, literally out cold, and that's at a very early stage in his career; he started the way he intended to go on . . .

ALO: Back on the road with the Ronettes, the northern leg was going well and the Stones were now as popular on the Beatles' own turf as they were in London. The Beatles had just conquered America, giving us all something to think about, but not at this moment. Our working reality was the UK and, if one got lucky, the cold and grey northern tips of Europe.

The US was a mind-boggling, exciting challenge to our secure womb at the top. It scared us, Johnny Britain. The moptops had taken the States; the moptops had taken everywhere – they were the gold rush, the tea chest, the opium beat for the masses.

One night early in 1964, the Stones were in either Halifax or Crewe, and the Beatles were returning for one night to Liverpool, their first gig at home since taking over the world – rule Britannia. No need to tell you which gig this boy opted for.

I trained over to Liverpool, leaving the Stones somewhere over the Pennine chain, so that I could catch the event of the year. A celebratory Liverpool rang in its own day of the locusts, proud of its native sons made good, bells and hearts ringing out and screaming for the four lads who now belonged to the world. The concert was a smile expressed in sound and song.

The physical presence of the Beatles was irresistible. I remember Paul grinning from start to finish. The lads just beamed at each other over the screams, as they distilled into thirty-five minutes the story till now. They rolled over Beethoven, but could have just as easily triumphed by playing 'Chopsticks'.

I went back to see them after the show. 'How'd you get over here?' asked Lennon.

'By train,' I replied.

'Leave the Stones on their own, did you?' Lennon smiled.

'Yes, I did,' I smiled back.

'Want a lift back to town?'

'You bet,' I said. And what a lift it proved to be. John had his spanking-new black Rolls-Royce Phantom V limo and the seal was delivered. Somehow being able to share in that acquisition was a wonderful moment of cocksure arrival. I sat on the beige jump seat opposite John and Paul. We laughed and hooted at life as the Roller headed down the M6 and eventually purred on to the M1 for town.

The humour took a macabre turn as John and Paul started to trip on what would happen if the windows of the Phantom V zooming south suddenly shattered and splintered in their faces, turning them into unacceptably scarred and disfigured moptops, unable to carry on as part of the Fab Four now recognised the world over.

'We'd have to put on monkey costumes. We'd be a fucking vaudeville act,' whooped John.

'We'd have to have bear suits or masks . . . nobody could see us,' Paul harmonised.

I watched and listened to this thrust and parry between the two writers and found it a little bit chilling to realise just how much they relished the idea of anonymity. To the point of almost welcoming a shattering shower of glass that would splinter the Beatles and force them from the spotlight. It was apparent that, for all the triumphs of that breathtaking past year, symbolised by the very Rolls-Royce that we now rode in, part of the dream was already over in early 64. The eventual end of the Beatles was even then on the agenda of their informal bored meetings. The conversation in that most exclusive emblem of British excellence felt surreal enough: it's more than possible that John and Paul may have given me my first tab of acid to raise my consciousness even further. It doesn't really matter; it certainly felt like it. I slept long, deep and sound that night, once back in the Smoke. I awoke aware more than ever of my responsibilities to the Stones, feeling very protective towards my lads, and it all appeared a little daunting, awesome, even unnerving as I played back the ride back's acid chat. By the time I hit the phones mid-morning I was putting it down to an apathetic hard day's night and had moved on.

As manager and producer of the now second band in the land, I knew how to have fun but I still had my eye on the ball. The Stones had cracked the Top 10 with a single and an EP. So far, I had bought the records, our fan club had bought the records and the hardcore R&B mob had bought the records. The scream machine we were revving up had bought still more records. Our next order of business remained recording an out-and-out smash – tens of thousands of plastic platters that were bought even if you didn't like the Stones. Bought because one couldn't help but buy, bought because it was a great fuckin' record.

The first week of February I returned from my daily West End jaunts and hustles to the Mapesbury and found Keith exactly where I'd left him that morning – fag in mouth, guitar on knee, singing bits of Buddy Holly's 'Not Fade Away'. He was injecting an acoustic Bo Diddley riff into one of our favourite songs. I heard our next record. I could actually hear the record in the room. The way he played it – you could hear the whole record. It was less pop and more rock. It was a magical moment for me.

Tony Calder: Andrew was the first to see the song's potential and has often been quoted as saying that, so as far as he was concerned, Keith had written 'Not Fade Away'. This, of course, is rubbish. It was a Buddy Holly song. At the time Andrew thought the quote would grab a few more column inches for the Stones. Anyone who had heard the Buddy Holly original would know that the Stones version of the song is almost identical. The Bo Diddley feel is a suggestion in Buddy's version and a call to arms in the Stones'.

ALO: Two days later I called engineer Bill Farley at Regent Sound, and we went into the studio to get 'Not Fade Away' down. It wasn't easy: the group were tired, not getting along, showing the strain of five solid months on the road. The atmosphere was getting sour and despondent. Our hit was slipping away from us. I needed help.

Charlie Watts

Gene Pitney: Phil and I were in Paris and we stopped for one day in London. Andrew called me up at my hotel from Regent Sound and said, 'You gotta help me, these guys have gotta have a follow-up release.' He said, 'Decca are screaming for the follow-up release.' He told me that not only wouldn't the Stones sing together, they weren't even talking to each other.

So I made up this story: we had five fifths of duty-free cognac, so we brought in a bottle of Courvoisier and told everybody it was an old family custom that everyone had a glass of cognac on my birthday; it was just a fabrication. Actually it worked, it broke the ice. Then through the door came Phil, driven up in Freddy Bienstock's big black Rolls-Royce. The only reason we played anything on the session was because they didn't have a B-side, they came in with only the one song. Andrew said, 'Let's just do blues chords, twelve-bar blues, to get another recording, to get another side.'

So I played piano; they gave credit to Phil as playing maracas, but he was actually playing an empty cognac bottle with an American half-dollar. It didn't feel odd at all because there were no definition lines at that period of time between different performers; it was just fun. You should have seen the booth at Regent Sound: oh, the booth was so small, it was like two people would have to have their back against the wall to stand up in it.

Keith Richards, Mick Jagger, Brian Jones, Honor Blackman

ALO: The Stones now had a friendly audience – they had to perform, it's in the blood. They soon settled into a groove and within twenty-five minutes everybody was happy. The Stones nailed the A-side, glued down by Keith's acoustic guitar. Spector's maracas and Charlie's back beat leaked nicely into everything. We had a perfect pre-mix and quickly added vocal, harp and electric guitar on the one-to-one pass and the record was ready for the nation's living rooms; a sure-fire hit.

Once I knew we'd got it, I'd invited down Graham Nash and Allan Clarke of the Hollies and Peter Meaden. Spirits were high and flowing reasonably, but now we needed a B-side. Mick Jagger and Phil Spector headed for the staircase outside the studio reception, and in ten minutes flat they polished off the lyrics to a song they called 'Little By Little'. In another twenty minutes the lyrics were captured on tape, over a simple twelve-bar blues structure. So far all this had been a movie in my head, now it was real life. The Rolling Stones finally knew how to make hit records. They were self-contained.

The recording degenerated into a hilarious, quasi-drunken free-for-all. The Stones, prompted by Spector, recorded a tribute to me, 'Andrew's Blues', which remains one of the most bootlegged of unreleased Stones tracks. Phil joined Jagger on vocals, impersonating Decca boss, Sir Edward Lewis, singing about my 'qualities'. I was honoured then. I still am.

> *Well now, Andrew Oldham,*
> *Sittin' on a hill with Jack 'n' Jill,*
> *He fucked all night,*
> *'N' he sucked all night.*
> *'N' he sucked that pussy*
> *'Til it taste just right.*
> *Come and get it little Andrew,*
> *Before Sir Edward takes it away from you.*

Gene Pitney: It was one of those days where the Stones all hated each other, and I realised why Andrew was the best thing they ever had going for them. He had the nice ability to get them to put things out in the studio. Left to their own egos, they always had problems with each other.

Tony Calder: Andrew kept Spector to himself, 'cause he was enamoured with him. Spector wanted Andrew to get the Stones off Decca and on to Philles Records, Phil's company, for America. I arranged meetings for them at Decca but it didn't go anywhere. That's why Spector made 'Andrew's Blues', which goes on about 'Fuck Sir Edward' after he'd turned Phil down. That was one of the first rap records . . .

ALO: I may have gone to a meeting with Phil at Decca, I don't remember. If I did, not all of me attended. I do know that Decca would never have considered letting Phil have the group for America. Although 'I Want To Hold Your Hand' was a smash by the Beatles for Capitol in the States, EMI had let the previous singles go to Swan and Vee Jay because they didn't think the Beatles would fly in America. So Decca weren't going to be caught in the same trap; they were still smarting from having turned down the Beatles themselves. They were being very careful; if their doorman had started whistling they'd have signed him.

Anyway, although Phil Spector was an educative influence on me as a record producer, he didn't have the wherewithal or sensibility as a record-company head to deal with an act. In his world he was the act. I was reared on Irving Thalberg, Alexander Korda and MGM and, compared to their creative collectives, Phil's record company was a one-man band. However, he did predict we would soon outgrow what Regent Sound had to offer and suggested that we think about recording in America. Easier said than done: we had to get there first.

In the meantime 'Not Fade Away' was to be released late February, and it was back on the road for the Stones, promoted by Eric's new pal Robert Stigwood, with a lacklustre assortment of Stigwood acts. Only Jet Harris and Dave Berry added any spark of life to this lame bill. Unfortunately Jet was functioning at half-spark, his hit-making partnership with Tony Meehan having just ended.

Jet Harris: We did a recording, Andy and I, that never got released. It was called 'The Verge Of World War III' and the other side was called 'Daddy Wouldn't Buy Me A Bren Gun'. We did it at IBC, that's the very last time I saw him. He brought in Keith and Bill Wyman; I think they'd written the tunes I was supposed to be doing with Andrew. It was a nightmare because we didn't know what we were doing, to be quite honest, and then we came out with those outrageous titles. I don't know what happened, I think we were all a bit stoned at the time. Apparently the BBC didn't like the titles, so Decca wouldn't release them.

ALO: I spent too much time enjoying Jet and raising elbows at the local. I'd ignored the fact that Jet was already signed to Decca, and when I presented the results to them as an Andes Sound production, Decca told me, 'You just cannot record whom you like, not when they are already under contract to us.' I thought they would be delighted at the collaboration, but my track record at guessing their reaction to my manoeuvres was 50/50 at best.

Gene Pitney and I collaborated with far more success, since Gene was master of his yard and captain of his ship. Jet, sober as of late, I'm happy to say, was at that time in no shape to set sail. Pitney had the gift of adapting his unique vocal style from producer to producer, writer to writer, a have-gun-will-travel professionalism I greatly enjoyed. Gene had not yet decided on his follow-up to 'Twenty-Four Hours . . .' and I pressed his ears to Mick and Keith's songs in the hope we'd get lucky. He was drawn to a yarn named 'My Only Girl' that I'd recorded and failed to get released. Pitney felt that a rewrite would be a good way to thank his British fans for their loyal support by way of acknowledging our native talent.

Gene Pitney: I knew that they had recorded the track 'My Only Girl' with a guy named George Bean. Mick wasn't really very pleased with the recording, but he liked the song. When they played it for me, I loved the instrumental track. I told Andrew the melody didn't fit the type of thing I was having success with at the time, so I asked if we could change it? So we kept the lyrics and I redid the melody to feature some big notes and the harmonies I was known for. I loved the big, crashing sound of the track so I just went and did it.

ALO: Olympic was booked for the Pitney session, and duly paid for by Pitney's people. I booked the musicians, as well as Charles Blackwell to arrange the musical charts. Pitney allowed me to co-produce with him, and I was happy to be his pupil. Gene Pitney, like all great vocal stylists, was successful because he knew who he was and what was good for him. For me, it was a unique experience to watch Pitney shape everything for the style of his voice. Not only did he change the melody, he also retitled the song and chorus: 'My Only Girl' became 'That Girl Belongs To Yesterday'.

Charles Blackwell: I was quite hot in the business when Andrew called me in to arrange 'That Girl'. Andrew was really shocked by what I did to the track; I completely changed the formula. The demo was just a track with Mick Jagger singing and Keith Richard playing guitar. I did four tracks for Andrew in a three-hour session. He was already suss enough as a producer to make sure he had a good arranger, engineer, a well-written song and good musicians. He'd let you do outrageous things; he was very eager to discover new and different sounds.

He was very like a film producer or director, actually; making a record involved a script and actors in his approach. It wasn't that Andrew had specific knowledge of music or engineering, but he always knew what he wanted to hear going in. And, if something wasn't right, he could tell you why.

ALO: Working with Gene remains one of the outstanding pleasures of my formative years. He hired me as his publicist, he encouraged Mick and Keith as writers, he attempted to help Brian Jones find his voice as a writer, and he took me under his wing and gave me them as a producer: he was inspirational. He made possible my first Top 10 UK record outside of the Stones.

Sean O'Mahony: Andrew would always try to get other people to finance his recordings. I financed the Gene Pitney session, but of course there was no contract, and I couldn't get my money. Andrew would book the studio and tell them to send the bill to you. That was his way of doing business.

ALO: Sean O'Mahony must be thinking of a different record: he may have financed the George Bean recording of 'My Only Girl' and lost his investment because it went unreleased. True, that song became 'That Girl Belongs To Yesterday', but the recording we did with Gene owed nothing to the Bean record. Anyway, it doesn't make sense to have had him finance the Pitney session. Gene was signed to Musicor in the States and distributed by EMI in the UK. He was already a hit artist, and the session costs for whomever Gene approved would have been happily paid for by the labels . . . unless I really was that good.

'That Girl Belongs To Yesterday' was scheduled for a March release by EMI. It would become Mick and Keith's first entry into the UK Top 10 as songwriters. Now that I looked to Mick and Keith to provide material for recording, the other Stones – particularly Brian Jones – often felt somewhat redundant and unappreciated. Both Charlie Watts and Eric Easton told me that Brian had songwriting ambitions, but he was too scared to put his songs forward.

Jones did not have the firm foundation I required to build a Brill Building hit-machine; on the one hand he was obsessed with duplicating the stardom of the Beatles, while on the other he remained a blues 'purist' and obstructed our efforts to reach the widest possible audience. As Keith

Richards would have it, Brian would have played Duane Eddy's Greatest Hits to make it, but in actual fact no one was asking.

I was bored senseless by Brian's endless theories about 'subliminal themes in search of a juxtaposition', his bleating about the potential of half-finished melodies that by no means deserved completion, how many syllables Brian employed to worm his way into and out of any given point, complicating things for his listener beyond all caring! God knows Linda loved him and Brian always had his own following among the legion of Stones fans, but I could not find somebody to love in there. He resisted the symbiosis demanded by the group lifestyle, and so life was becoming a little more desperate for him day by day. None of us were looking forward to Brian totally cracking up.

In the amenable Gene Pitney, I thought I might have found a practical solution, which would help bring Jones's ideas to the table in some kind of usable form and provide an objective professional opinion on Brian's potential as a songwriter. He kindly agreed to spend two afternoons with Brian at his London hotel, with the aim of getting a couple of songs to the point where they could be demoed at Regent Sound. Regrettably, the results remain best unheard, even by Stones' completists.

Gene Pitney: What Andrew had asked me to do proved to be very difficult because Brian was such a moody guy and hard to get through to. He was having difficulty with his life across the board: with the group, with himself and with Andrew. He was a very, very emotional guy.

ALO: I realised that Brian did not love pop music, therefore he could not write it. You can't write down to anyone. He didn't respect the pop-song structure and thought it involved little more than rhyming 'Moon' with 'June'. Mick and Keith knew there was more to it than that, and appreciated how hard it was to keep things simple. They were prepared to work on their craft. They knew that Fats Domino had titled his hit 'Blueberry Hill' because he had to find something that rhymed with 'thrill'.

Writing songs means one must pay attention to life, and Brian was loath to pay attention to anything but himself. One who is not interested in life ceases to be interesting. His condescending attitude towards pop music meant that he could never satisfy his addiction to success. You can't look up or down at fame. You just have to allow for it.

'Not Fade Away' quickly rose to Top 5 status; another first for the Stones, who finally had, for want of a better phrase, a genuine piece of plastic. I called my shoppers off the retail run when the single reached number thirty-eight. It was obvious by then that the single had legs of its own. Now we were reaching those record buyers who weren't yet Stones fans, just fans of pop music. The Stones brought home their Silver Disc, signifying sales of 250,000.

Robert Stigwood alleged that he had gone bankrupt and couldn't pay the Stones their share of the tour profits (about £16,000). Stigwood must have known he was going bankrupt while the Stones were on the road. He could have done the right thing, but he didn't; the Stones had been swindled, they were the coffee and dessert of Stigwood's first run. Stigwood returned to become rich and famous as manager for Eric Clapton (from Cream through to the first solo albums of the 70s), the Bee Gees, and Andrew Lloyd Webber and Tim Rice. His fortune came together most rewardingly when he signed John Travolta for a three-movie deal and produced *Saturday Night Fever* (from a Nik Cohn story), *Urban Cowboy* and *Grease*.

When Keith Richards finally caught up with Stigwood at the Scotch of St James Club, he made sure the bankrupt Australian got a physical, if not legal, payback. Keith instructed Mick, me and *NME* journalist Keith Altham to block the stairs against the helpless Stigwood's retreat. Keith proceeded to pummel him in the balls and many of the other soft parts of his body, to the tune of '£1,000' – bang, '£2,000' – wallop, until the £16,000 was paid back according to the law of Keith Richards.

Aggressive and tireless Stones fans, dozens of them day and night, now besieged Mapesbury Road, wielding scissors with which to clip a keepsake if they didn't lobotomise us first. We could afford a move up, so it was time to move on. Mapesbury had served its purpose well and should have a plaque on its wall: 'Mick and Keith first wrote here'.

I moved to a furnished room in Haverstock Hill between Belsize Park and Chalk Farm. At £18 a week, it was one of the many new abodes subdivided and redecorated for young people with a disposable income. Mick and Keith moved to a larger space on Holly Hill, just north of Haverstock Hill.

I'd also outgrown the Maddox Street office, now that my re-formed Image PR business with Tony Calder required space as well. Though I was burning my candle at both ends already, managing and producing the Stones, and could have lived without another job, I needed cash. I was getting tired of knocking on Easton's inhospitable pawnbroker door for what was rightfully mine. But it was better to start another independent business than to rock the Stones' boat in a public pond. We were doing so well by all outward appearances that now was not the time for taking on muddy water.

Tony Calder: Andrew had just produced Gene Pitney with 'That Girl Belongs To Yesterday'. We looked at an office on John Adam Street just around the corner from EMI, but that fell through. Celia Oldham had found it for us. Then we came across Ivor Court at the top of Gloucester Place, and moved into no. 147.

Busy as we both were, we pulled the PR business together. Danny Betesh of Kennedy Street Enterprises called us and took us to lunch. He was to Manchester what Brian Epstein was to Liverpool. He had Wayne Fontana, Freddie & the Dreamers, Herman's Hermits, Dave Berry. We got them, and got so busy that within a couple of months Andrew couldn't stand the bustle, so he took 138 Ivor Court as well.

By that time we were hanging out with Lionel Bart and Alma Cogan, driving around in Lionel's Facel Vega. Somewhere I have a memory of going to Noël Coward's house and he was singing from the gallery, some house in

Belgravia – I thought: Who the fuck is this guy with his Mad Dogs and Englishmen?

Li Baby, Noël Baby, Bart and Coward baby . . . I wasn't interested in that scene. That's when Andrew started hanging out with John Lennon and first met Sean Kenny at Lionel's. I was more interested in: I've got to be up by nine o'clock dealing with Manchester and all the acts coming to town that we had to get press on; people were coming in like crazy. We pulled Andy Wickham in to handle the extra work; we got him from the press office at EMI.

Andy Wickham: I was nineteen years old and had been working in the press office at EMI for a year when Tony Calder offered me a job at a new publicity company he was forming with Andrew Oldham, called 'ALO IMAGE'.

In 1964 there was no such thing as player power, and record companies ruled. EMI was a safe but stifling environment. My job was to edit *Record Mail*, an EMI pop freebie distributed to record shops, and to get press for American artists who were considered too far away to make a nuisance of themselves. The Beatles had started to take hold, but they were choirboys in stage-suits, and EMI was still dominated by Norrie Paramor and the Big Ben Banjo Band. Heaven help anybody who fell down promoting them! But nobody really cared about Johnny Burnette or Dick Dale, though they meant the world to me.

Calder, who reminded me of Sidney Tafler, came on like a dog-track bookie. From Southampton, he had a confiding manner, hand-on-the-knee sort of thing, and he sported a dark Caesar haircut, glasses with outsized black frames and a rolling Hampshire burr. He seemed to think only in terms of deals, and he reeked of danger. I accepted his offer immediately.

Our offices were at 147 Ivor Court, the Marylebone penthouse which Andrew had vacated – having selected black-and-white tiling for the floors, he hated it once it was installed and moved his personal quarters to 138 on the floor below.

We handled publicity for many prominent artists who were attracted by the Oldham name. Through Danny Betesh, we landed the Kennedy Street account, which gave us at a stroke most of the big Manchester groups. Of these, my favourites were Freddie & the Dreamers. 'Andy,' Freddie would say as his sales began to dwindle after a flying start, 'you've got to do something about this Bob Dylan – he's killing us!' The times they were a-changing and sadly there was nothing I could do.

We also looked after Wayne Fontana & the Mindbenders, Herman's Hermits, Dave Berry & the Cruisers and Graham Gouldman's first group, which was called the Toggery Five after a Mod shop in Stockport. We had the Migil Five, who sang 'Mockingbird Hill', and we looked after the Hollies. We did the campaign for Marianne Faithfull, who was spoilt and affected but was actually a singer of some range and ability as she later demonstrated on her folk records with Jon Mark. As Andrew began to look towards America, we started to take on American clients and it soon became my ambition to emigrate to California.

The office comprised Tony and myself and three girls. The girls were all glamorous in the Mary Quant fashion – big bangs and little skirts. My secretary and Jagger's girlfriend was Chrissie Shrimpton, who had less elegance but more sparkle than her famous sister. Tony's secretary was the daughter of a King's Road photographer. Her name was Linda Churcher; she had saucer eyes and the plums came tumbling down from her mouth. Andrew's secretary was a bummy, debby type called Sassa Perkins whose father was a general. These girls shared a flat in Barons Court and one night the others ganged up on Linda and evicted her *en déshabillé*. She found sanctuary in the office and greeted us for work the following morning in knickers and boots.

Tony ran the business side of things and bills were rarely paid. Furniture was always about to be repossessed, electricity to be cut off, phones lines to be disconnected. The girls kept us afloat by fending off our creditors with charm, ingenuity and the occasional favour.

Journalists would come in all the time – Maureen Cleave from the *Evening Standard*, Judith Simons from the *Daily Express*, Pat Doncaster from the *Daily Mirror*. They would come to talk to Andrew, or to the Stones, or to any of our more exotic clients, especially the Americans. We represented Dick Clark from American Bandstand, Murry Wilson, father of the Beach Boys, and ultimately the Beach Boys themselves.

In 147 we didn't see an awful lot of Andrew, who was spending an increasing amount of time in the studio. Though we all found him intimidating, he was actually a generous and inspiring chief. He only ever pulled rank on me once. A gormless, spotted group from Liverpool called the Mighty Avengers (with whom he had just cut a wonderful version of 'Blue Turns To Grey' prior, I believe, to its recording by the Stones) came in drunk and were disgustingly sick all over my desk. Revolted, I refused to accompany them to *Ready Steady Go!* Andrew materialised and in his most prefectorial manner ordered me to carry out the assignment. It was the only time he ever ordered me to do anything.

I knew the Stones through Charlie Watts, whom I met in a West End advertising agency where we had both worked a couple of years previously. I lived in Richmond then, and after Charlie left I met him on the train one day. He told me he had joined a blues group called the Rolling Stones and that they had a residency on Eel Pie Island and that I should come and see them.

Though the Stones clearly had something special, their personality and attitude owed everything to the turbulence of their mentor. When I went to Eel Pie Island what I saw was an efficient blues group with a charismatic singer with good James Brown moves, but nothing all that different from, say, the Yardbirds. Andrew used them as a conduit for his angst and thus created the first group with a seriously anti-social stance, irritating the Beatles in the process. In a famous interview John Lennon castigated the Stones for plagiarism, but was unable to disguise his envy of their sinful image, in contrast to the bourgeois foolery of his own crew.

Chris Hutchins: The Beatles when they lived in Hamburg were what the Stones became. The Stones were a group of middle-class people, really; they didn't come from the housing estates like Paul McCartney, John and Ringo. Mick Jagger was a Dartford lad, Brian Jones was from Cheltenham. What we saw as their anger and frustration was Andrew's to start with. Andrew was rebellious; when things went wrong, he would come back twice as hard. A lot of people in the business didn't like him. I never knew anyone in the business to be as unpopular as Andrew.

ALO: I was promoting the idea that the Rolling Stones were 'the group parents loved to hate', based on my belief that pop idols fall into one of two categories – ones you wished to share with your parents and ones you did not.

The Beatles were accepted and acceptable, they were the benchmark and had set the level of competition. The Stones came to be portrayed as dangerous, dirty and degenerate, and I encouraged my charges to be as nasty as they could wish to be. At last, we had a genuine hit and I leveraged that mileage daily to embed the Stones in the psyche of the British press, like a grain of sand irritates an oyster. I was relentless and I was right. I was like a pit-bull terrier that won't let go. I got a lot of permanent messages across, a lot of press and a lot of enemies.

Chris Hutchins: John Lennon became obsessed with Andrew. He always believed the Stones had hijacked the Beatles' 'original' image. Brian Epstein made them behave, conform, perform, wear suits, be polite, made them do Royal Variety Shows. That really left the field open for Andrew to say, 'Fuck that, the Stones don't do that.' As Lennon so correctly observed, Brian left the way open for the Stones to occupy a very large vacancy.

ALO: John was so very attuned to the notion that if the music business was bollocks, it would be his bollocks, and so you never lied to Johnny Lennon. He was very fast with an opinion (an approach I was no stranger to) and it scared a lot of those he wished to scare. 'I'm looking through you' was what John Lennon did – he invited you to walk on eggshells. His directness always brought me back to myself and he appreciated that my life and agenda were not about Alfie.

We were all so good at publicity that when John said, as he might, 'The Beatles are bigger than Jesus', I'm sure he meant that – should the good public wish to slander him and his way of life – they might consider that he was as close to a man of integrity as their offspring were likely to get. It's really one of the most elegant remarks anybody has ever excited the press's haemorrhoids over. In John's highly sensitive presence you knew exactly who you were and that is quite a gift to be hauling around.

Partner Paulie came down on the side of 'It's all a show, so let's show off together', and Kansas City here we come. Party boys that we were, I don't know what Paul was like behind closed doors with his joint rolled and carpet slippers on. If he doesn't get enough credit for being a well-meaning geezer, blame it on the Stones.

But John would roll the joint and watch you smoke it, wear cowboy boots to bed and carpet slippers to meet the Queen – any of them. He watched where life and the music took you, and if you were standing in clear present time he applauded you. He dared you to have airs and to be stupid; he was always hungry for a fool. He'd ask you a question and watch you contemplate, edit and realise the futility of a less-than-total-truth answer, and this led to a rarity in the air not often breathed – a truth-only encounter. One strike and you were down with a barrage of venom, a lewd adjectival spew that many a wit and playwright would wish upon his page. Being with Johnny Lennon was like a verbal exposition of the famous chicken-race sequence between James Dean and Corey Allen in Nicholas Ray's *Rebel Without A Cause*, or the Russian-roulette sequence in Michael Cimino's *The Deer Hunter*.

Chris Hutchins: Brian Epstein was regarded by the Grades as the big new thing in the business. Brian saw himself coming up in there, going up the same ladder. He didn't realise he was on a totally different ladder. Andrew did. Epstein rang me to say, 'Christopher, Bernard Delfont's just been on the telephone with a wonderful offer for the Beatles.' I said, 'Whatya talking about, you've got them, you don't need Bernard Delfont.' 'Well, it's such a marvellous amount of money,' he said.

Brian would be very impressed by that. Andrew had the style of management Lennon would have liked, no question about it. Brian used to take John away on little trips to Spain, just to talk him round again and convince him everything was okay.

ALO: For my part, I was working the press harder than I was 'working' the boys. I didn't have to tell the Stones how to behave, I just had to let them be – they did the rest. I may have realised that, on a subconscious level, their extra-long hair and mix-and-match gear strongly hinted at rebellion and degeneracy, but the group were doing what came naturally and I was running with it. The Stones just had to open their mouths to compound what may have begun as misdemeanours into headline-grabbing felonies.

Keith Altham: If the media reacted contentiously, if the national press, TV and radio got uptight about slovenliness, there could be a virtue in it. What sells is attitude. If kids find something that they can empathise with, similar to their own dissatisfaction with their elders, then they'll go along with it. The Stones' early success was not merely founded on hype, though. They were a better live band than the Beatles ever were.

Chris Hutchins: Andrew's style of management was revolutionary; he was the best that was around at the time. Andrew lived with the act. When you talked with other managers, you knew they went home to normal lives after six o'clock. With Andrew, he lived with them. If you wanted to see his artists, you just stayed close to Andrew.

Lionel Bart: Andrew defied all the traditions, broke all the rules; he took a little bit from Colonel Tom Parker's attitude, a little bit from other people in America, like Phil Spector. Larry Parnes didn't come near the sort of outrageous approach Andrew employed. The whole PR thing he did with the Stones was very novel, it was new.

Judith Simons, in the *Daily Express*: They look like boys who any self-respecting mother would lock in the bathroom. But the Rolling Stones, five tough, young London-based music-makers with door-stop mouths, pallid cheeks and unkempt hair, are not worried about what mums think. For now that the Beatles have registered with all age groups, the Rolling Stones have taken over as the voice of the teens that don't wish to share their now and future.

Keith Richards, in *The Rolling Stones in Their Own Words*: Andrew was a genius at getting messages through to the media without people knowing, before people really knew what the media was. He always made sure we were as violent and nasty as possible.

ALO: A Hit is a Hit is a Hit. I was no longer fighting for mini-inches of press clippings, plugging upcoming Stones concert appearances or record releases. Fame was a-growing daily and although the Stones were not yet being snapped going through the airports of the world, the high streets of England would do for now.

Melody Maker repeated word-for-word my press release: 'The Stones' role in music is a powerful one. They have the anger of the parents on their side. Young fans now realise that their elders groan with horror at the Rolling Stones. So their loyalty to the Stones is unswerving.'

Another *MM* headline was a great example of everlasting meaning via product placement. I had dreamt up the line 'Would You Let Your Daughter Go With A Rolling Stone?', which would be translated into 'Would You Let Your Daughter Marry A Rolling Stone?' by the high priests of Fleet Street, who wished to avoid the ramifications of the word 'go'. I'd come up with it in response to something that either Ray Coleman or Jack Hutton had said to me during an interview; it got the headline and became one of the many slogans wrapped around the Rolling Stones for life.

It wasn't that hard for the Stones, they were natural: in the long run the public doesn't buy fakes. To this day people place themselves in relation to the 60s in terms of whether they liked the Stones better than the Beatles. Your answer was your identity; it stated who you were.

Pete Townshend: The Stones were a truly broad machine. They, better than the Beatles, properly straddled the two worlds that were being discovered at the time and became what rock 'n' roll is today, what pop music is today. The Stones finally cemented the huge fucking wall that we wanted to build between the previous generation and everybody who was to follow.

· CHAPTER 14 ·

Peter Noone: Andrew handled our publicity in the Hermits' very early days. I was only fifteen. He was the most happening guy I ever met back then. All the other guys were wannabes; he was actually doing it. He was a creator, he had this pompous gay thing going on, but he was getting away with it. People were like, 'Oh, there's a cool guy.'

Every time Andrew said something, you could count on it happening, which was totally unique. That was unusual in those days because most people were full of shit. There was a guy with him, Andy Wickham. I was very impressed with them both. Andy Wickham was unusual because he was into surfing music.

Andrew was very good at his business; he was a very aggressive childlike man. He had these strange, insane sort of people like Reg King working for him, who'd smash people's windows outta the car as they were driving along. I was very impressed. When you're fifteen you like guys like that. This is more like rock 'n' roll than the Hermits, who are going home to Mum tonight.

We were just a bunch of lads up from Manchester – y'know, where's yer bike clips? We just looked at Cliff Richard & the Shadows and thought: Let's try and do as good as they did. We were with Kennedy Street Enterprises, you had to be because there was nobody else. That was Manchester. We were a band and they were an agency; they didn't have any creative input.

Suddenly people from Liverpool with money were acceptable. Before that, if you didn't have the right accent in England you were fucked. But after the Beatles it was suddenly cool to be a friend of the common people. I thought Andrew was a typical public-school arsehole. All the people I ever met who'd been to public school were pricks. You know, Andrew was a prick, shouting at people who couldn't protect themselves, at the side of the stage picking on the sound guy. He treated everybody like they were the infantry. Take that hill . . . He had this whole team of people who knew the Krays and stuff, sorta in the background so you never wanted to mess too much with Andrew.

He wanted to be a pop star worse than anybody; he would give it all that in a restaurant. All those record producers suffered from that thing. They used to be invisible and suddenly they all wanted to be stars like Phil Spector. But nobody noticed, they'd say Mickie Most? Where's Minnie?

Alan Freeman: I was one of the first DJs to play the Stones on the BBC. I loved the Stones, because they were total rebels, or so-called total rebels. Whether Andrew engineered it I don't really quite know. I think Andrew was very fired by a challenge to the Beatles.

I was thirty when I arrived in England from Australia in 1957. I was doing a nine-month trip around the world; all Australians did it. London was like Alice through the looking glass: Big Ben, black taxis, red buses, a fairy tale . . . Even if I hadn't got into the business I'd have stayed. I wouldn't have cared less, I would have worked behind the counter at Austin Reed. The 2Is was the hubbub. It was the centre, the Mecca for youth. The UK scene was just bubbling. It was a period when youngsters wanted to leave home, find their own life and their own levels.

I was given a show called *Pick of the Pops*, 4 p.m. Sunday, the Sunday highlight. We had an audience of fifteen million people. This was before the pirates. That was when it was called 'Light Entertainment'. The other contender was *Saturday Club* with Brian Matthew. One play on *Pick of the Pops* was vital. It helped send a record, bang, crash, wallop. There was the BBC and then there was Radio Luxembourg, which was in the Grand Duchy.

The great thing about Andrew was that he was a sincere fan of pop and rock music. Whenever he landed up in my pad, he'd say, 'You gotta hear this, you gotta hear that.' He'd drive me insane, but always with great stuff. Stuff that I'd finish up playing. He was just very exciting, and he excited you about the music. He never once plugged the Stones to me. He just waited until I got into it, liked it and played it as a new release.

He was a lad of the 60s, generating excitement all of the time, with his flamboyance and his total honesty. He was the epitome of flamboyance and you could not help but take notice of him and what he said, his prophecies. I would imagine that a few of the more staid people in the industry would have been very wary of him. Here was this very, very young man, who thought differently and recorded people differently.

Andrew presented the Stones as rebels, and that had to be. He was managing them, he was travelling with them, he was their mother, father, companion, the lot. It was the transformation from the 50s to the 60s that was very interesting. The 60s started in the 50s and lasted from 1956 until 1966.

Of all the personalities in the 60s, Andrew was the most outrageous – totally – a winner by five million light-years. He was always the great exhibitionist. He always delivered and people took notice of him when he said something. He was in a league with the greatest rebels of all time. When Andrew said something, people listened.

It's always the song. Telly came in, but it's still always the song on the radio. All kinds of promotion are good, but I think at the finish, at the end of the day, it's the radio that wins. It's your constant friend, your lover, your companion, which filters records out to you incessantly until they get locked in the subconscious – that's why radio wins. The others are subsidiaries and they are important, but radio wins.

I was virtually holding in my hand the fate of a lot of people who were trying to become stars, to make money, whatever. The responsibility that one had was absolutely enormous. It's so easy to bend down and pick up nothing.

Sheila Klein: Andrew's real creative force was inspiring an artist. A lot of people just couldn't keep up with his pace, which was 150 per cent all the time, and if he had an off-day he was 150 per cent off; he wasn't just slightly under the weather. Don't believe your own publicity, they say. It was very difficult for him to separate his role in the script he was acting from the karmic causes he was actually making. Basically what we're talking about is idolatry. That's got a very specific karma. He must have realised it was all bullshit. In fact, that's what the problem was. If only he could have believed it was true, then he would be a lot happier.

If you see 'You're a genius' written in the paper, and you know how easy it is to get something in the paper, what must it feel like on the inside? 'What a load of bullshit! Am I really a genius inside? If I am, how come I can't keep it going?' If he got depressed, that's what it was about.

ALO: Style I had a good grab on. It is not as superficial as it first appears: it does not come from an undisciplined character, and mastery of it can keep you out of harm's way much of the time. It is the public face of grace, and fame is something else certainly. Fame was going to turn into a many-headed monster and, with most of them, I was happy to grapple.

I had provided a ready definition of fame for Mick Jagger, but time and its moves were suggesting that perhaps I would be better sorting out an answer for myself. I had only grasped a little bit of it in my mitt – not enough to bow to, hardly enough to savour, not enough to call a friend – yet I was already saying, 'This is good, I like it. Show me where the poison is so that I can start killing myself. Show me where the window is so I can start jumping.'

You have a great first run, the poison tricks you, you think it's working for you, you don't feel the drip that will eventually kill you. Drip drop . . . thank you, Dion. The window fools you. You are many floors higher than you thought; the drop will be long, while you whizz by the penthouse padded by that same success. It could fill another book, and it will.

I did not realise it at the time, but I'd already started to play with the loaded gun. I thought I was just flaunting my entitlement. If you are continuously jumping into a swimming pool that has a leak, eventually you'll be belly-flopping into a pool with no water. But why worry now, we'd only just begun.

I had flash readies, meaning toy money, not the real thing. Not being interested in bricks and mortar, I preferred a statement in wheels and chrome. Never dreaming the taxman cometh, I made my statement and offed the £2,000 I could lay my hands around on a powder-blue Chevrolet Impala, with a midnight-blue roof and matching dual-blued leather interior. A car that would keep me on my road – my own America. And to go with this superb king of the highway came my very own spiv, minder, driver and bodyguard, the wonderful Reg King, named 'The Butcher' by Keith. Reg was much needed, as although I drove I had not yet got a licence.

Reg hailed from the East End. He was sheer charm with a snarl, a pit-bull terrier dressed as a poodle. The diamond on his pinkie reflected the permanent twinkle in his pretty, killer baby blues. High, starched white collars; broad-shouldered, discreet bum-freezer suits; dark silk tie, tacked by a pearl. His personality was warm; he had a heart of gold. His persona lay somewhere between the gay end of the Kray twins and *Priscilla, Queen of the Desert*. I met him through Lionel Bart, who told me Reg was just what I needed.

Reg 'The Butcher' King

Lionel Bart: Reg King started working in a minor role for Brian Epstein, but that only lasted a couple of weeks. Reg was way too over-the-top for Eppy. Then he came to work for me, but I thought he'd be better off with Andrew. Worked out for a while, it did: Reg gave Andrew a good laugh when he needed it. The Stones had to be getting a bit heavy, all that Eric nonsense . . . he gave us Jews a bad name. If it hadn't been for Andrew he'd have been pumping organs; he was really mean to the lot of them. The Stones and Andrew, they were all still kids. I helped where I could, got 'em David Jacobs the lawyer; he helped Andrew with Marianne.

Andrew had to do a lot of babysitting. Mick could be a bit of a chick, y'know, what with the moaning. Had to get on Sheila's tits, cause her some bother. Keith and Linda were a lovely couple, Keith is a gem. Reg had a good heart, he was a well-meaning bloke. He's gone now, went off a cliff in Thailand with a couple of kids on the back of his bike. He just gave Andrew another room to play in, a kind of distance from all that other nonsense.

ALO: Reg ended up getting me into more fights than I would get myself into. I spent too much time dealing with driving offences and assault charges, and I didn't even have a driving licence. For a while I didn't complain. I welcomed it, as I welcomed Reg. He'd come up and say, 'Don't move, there are eight people behind you.' 'Reg,' I'd say, 'we're at a concert. We're in a crowd, there are bound to be eight people standing behind us.'

Andy Wickham: Once Reg grabbed me by the throat, balled his fist and asked me eyeball-to-eyeball if I had any gold teeth. When I gasped that I hadn't, he said, 'Oh, well then, you're not worth killing, are you?' King was tremendous fun so long as he was inflicting hostility on someone else. The names elude me, but Andrew once dispatched him to 38 Something Street to cosh an enemy and, when King returned, he looked curiously at Andrew and said that he really didn't like beating old people. When Andrew protested that the intended victim was not old, Reg looked doubtful. 'You *did* say number thirty-six,' he said, 'didn't you?'

Keith Richards, in *NME*: Andrew wanted to be Phil Spector overnight. And the minute Andrew made some bread off the Stones, it was the Chevrolet – and in England you didn't see many a Chevy convertible, metallic blue – with some hard guy called Reg, the driver. Andrew would sit beside him and say, 'Go for it, Reg!' There would be like three fucking trucks coming down the tube at you and Andrew'd say, 'Reg, hit the fucking tube, slide job', taking almost a suicidal glee in making it.

Sheila Klein: The Butcher gave me the absolute horrors. He was a really nasty character. I think Andrew at that time found it useful to have these thugs around. I don't know if he needed them for protection or just to make him look good. But he always seemed to need a gofer or three.

Andrew pushing people on the street as Reg drove close to the pavement: that terrible gangster image he cultivated was such a turn-off for me, but in retrospect I think it was necessary. Reg took Andrew to a level where he was comfortable with his fear: we're all-powerful, nothing can hurt us, let's take it as close to the edge as we can, be as ugly, as rude and as confrontational as possible. I didn't like being witness to it sometimes, but I agree it was needed because everything was so stale. But Reg was a disaster; y'know, he died driving off a cliff. It was pathetic.

ALO: One writer who loved to hate the Stones was Richard Greene at the *Record Mirror*. Rock 'n' roll has its rules of conduct, same as La Cosa Nostra or the House of Commons. Richard Greene was clearly not a man of honour. If he didn't like their sound or records, fine; or their image and look, fine and understandable. There was much to dislike about the Stones: I had seen to it. Anyone's perception of how unkempt we were was fair game. But Keith Richards' complexion had nothing to do with it.

When Greene mouthed off for a third time about Keith, I threw down the paper in disgust and shouted for Reg to bring 'Boadicea's Chariot' around pronto. The Chevy made it to the *Record Mirror*'s Shaftesbury Avenue office from Gloucester Place in twelve minutes, running a few lights, jumping a few kerbs and just missing a few people.

Reg and I leapt out of the car, leaving it parked illegally half on the pavement, half on the street, ran up the office stairs four at a time and crashed into a previously quiet reception.

'What can I do for you . . . gentlemen?' asked a startled, beehived receptionist. I was already cutting through the door, having seen Greene holding court down the hall in the entrance to his office.

The ever-polite Reg was allowing himself to be asked if he had an appointment.

'Does it look like we need one, dear?' Reg asked rhetorically in his best bemused-gangster mode.

'It's okay, Reg. He's down here, follow me,' I yelled, champing at my bit. The two of us charged into Richard Greene's office, power-driving him back into the wall. Reg kept his arm pressed into the scribe's Adam's apple, waiting for the word 'Kill'. I got my breath, pretended to relax, took the measure of the room and smiled laconically.

'Reg, get his fuckin' hands on the window ledge.' Reg did so, warning the now green-at-the-gills Greene that if he moved his hands from the sill, Reg would throw him out of the window.

'What's all this about?' blustered the writer, and his hands moved.

'Attack!' I screamed to Reg.

'Don't fucking move your hands!' commanded Reg.

He didn't. We'd already caused a commotion around the offices, but nobody was brave enough to come in and find out what was going on. I was glad that Peter Jones was not in the vicinity; this would not do and he could definitely call the meeting to order. I moved towards Greene as Reg held his hands on the sill with one hand, as the other held the window ready to bring it suddenly down at any sign of movement from the writer. It was time to bring on-stage for the first time, save mirror appearances, my Burt Lancaster as J.J. Hunsecker in *The Sweet Smell of Success*. Oh, I loved it! I'd done Tony Curtis's Sydney Falco for so long that I grabbed this new part and made it mine.

Alexander Mackendrick, Director, *The Sweet Smell of Success* in *Tony Curtis, The Autobiography*: The stars had this neurosis which goes right to the edge. You have somehow to use this to get performances from these deep-sea monsters. There was an enormous difference between Burt Lancaster and Tony Curtis. Tony had a fantastic vanity, but no ego. He could act Lancaster off the screen, but he lacked Lancaster's granite quality of ego.

ALO: Face to face with the flack, I shook my head with a disappointed sigh.

'Richard,' I said quietly, 'what is this about? You don't know? You don't proofread your own copy? You're a good writer. Your musical taste may be a different matter, but you're a good writer. Why do you have to be so vindictive? Hate me, hate my act, hate their music, but . . .'

I paused. Richard still had no idea what was going on. It was time to up the ante to make this scene plausible.

'Richard, I got a call this morning from a very hurt and upset Mrs Richards. You don't know her, but she's Keith Richards' mum. She said, 'Mr

Oldham, can you do anything to stop what this man keeps saying about my boy's acne? I know you can't stop that rubbish about how they don't wash. But Keith is a sensitive boy, even if he doesn't say so. Please, Mr Oldham, can you do anything?'

It was so good I believed it.

'So, Richard, this is the story. If you ever again write something about Keith that is out of line, that is hurtful to his mum – because I'm responsible to Keith's mum – your hands will be where they are now, but with one big difference.' My voice got louder, I rolled my eyes and twitched once. 'Reg here will bring that fuckin' window crashing down on your ugly hands, and you will not be writing, you malicious fat turd, for a long fucking time, and you won't be dictating either, you cunt, 'cause your jaw will be sewn up from where Reg fucking broke it.'

Reg and I acknowledged each other with a wink. With Reg ahead of me, we brushed past the gathered onlookers. Always with a care to his manners, Reg murmured a few 'Excuse mes' and 'Good day, dear, I hope we didn't startle you' to the receptionist. I followed Reg's orders to avoid eye contact or words with anyone, and we bolted down the stairs five at a time out on to the street.

A policeman stood inspecting our car as we approached the vehicle.

'Is this your car, sir?' he asked. Reg took over – this was his job.

'No, officer, it's Mr Oldham's car,' he said, looking in my direction, as did the copper. 'He is the manager of a group you may have heard of, the Rolling Stones, and he was upstairs in that building attending to some business with a journalist, when the journalist collapsed on the floor. I came in and we thought that the journalist might have had a heart attack, so Mr Oldham told me to go double-quick and get his car – this car – in case it might be needed to take the writer to the hospital. I brought the car around and left it like this, on the pavement. I thought that was safer for the other motorists, and I ran upstairs. It seemed that the gentleman who had collapsed was better; he just hadn't taken his medication, and after all didn't need to go to the hospital.'

'All right,' said the policeman, satisfied or bored by Reg's spontaneous and imaginative scenario. 'Be on your way. Next time, call an ambulance, that's what they're for, you know.'

We 'Yes, officer'd him in unison, got in the car and left, hooting and shrieking with glee as we illegally right-turned north into Wardour Street.

Sheila Klein: It would be to excruciating for me to watch *The Sweet Smell of Success* now.

Pete Townshend: Reg King was a killer; the story was that he'd murdered several people, and managed to get away with it. He carried a huge cut-throat razor with him. There were lots of stories about Andrew making deals and saying, 'Well, if you don't do what I want, I'm gonna send Reg in to turn the tables over . . .' There was a kind of reign of terror. Peter Meaden loved this idea and he hired himself Phil the Greek. Tall, dark and handsome, Phil wasn't Greek at all. He was an unbelievably vain and a spectacularly refined Mod. Phil the Greek was very, very dangerous indeed. It wouldn't surprise me if he were in jail somewhere now.

Chris Stamp: I found Andrew's reputation as a heavy fairly ridiculous because I knew gangsters. Andrew had around what I call 'disco gangsters', like half-baked tea leaves, they weren't exactly what you'd call gangsters. Reg King was a joke; he would have loved to be a gangster.

Steve Inglis, graphic designer: Andrew had this 64 Chevy and he'd leave *Ready Steady Go!* with the Stones on board, Andrew out of his brains, leaning half out of the car and punching people, making Reg drive close to the other cars, so that Andrew could sock the other driver. Reg was so frightening that it cost more to keep Reg out of jail than it did to pay his wages. Reg was totally crazy, completely fearless. I don't know why he drove like he did, but he was the kinda guy who would overtake on a hill, gambling on the fact that nobody would be coming the other way. Andrew loved living on the edge like that.

Andrew in those days, on the outside, appeared very straight, very professional, a man seriously playing God – he thought he was better than God. But he was absolutely taking the piss, and if you saw Andrew in his having fun mode it would wig you out. One minute he's there, the next minute he's passing out. Not that he's gone, it's just a reaction. We'd be at the fancy receptions, he'd get bored and suddenly he'd be playing on the floor. When you're at a level where you're creating half the world around you, you're slotting in with 50 per cent of it and the other 50 per cent you're creating because you have a licence to do it.

Chris Hutchins: The first time I ever got threatened as a journalist was by Andrew and Andy Wickham. I wrote an Alleycat in the *NME* which mentioned Andy Wickham and I was told in no uncertain terms it had to be Andy 'Wipe Out' Wickham. They were really menacing, really threatening. I always thought Wickham was a wanker.

After that I got a lot of anonymous phone calls from heavies at three in the morning. I knew it was Andrew putting the money up. He suddenly became very powerful in his own mind . . . He frequently came on the phone very angry; he wanted to say what went in the paper, how it was arranged, this is how you run the story, this is how you write it. He'd got balls, but a lot of us thought he was crazy.

He was the first person I came across who lived for the day. Didn't matter if everybody died tomorrow or everything went up the wall tomorrow, he lived for today, and today had to have every bit squeezed out of it. He had no fear of financial insecurity, while everybody else was terrified: would they be able to hang on to the couple of hundred quid they made the week before? Andrew threw caution to the wind. When everybody else wanted to go home, he wanted to go on, a creature of the night. But sure enough when you got to your desk – and I used to get to my desk at the *NME* by 9 a.m. – Andrew would have been on the phone already. He was a great grafter, had enormous drive, fuelled by anger and resentment which all came from frustration. The world wouldn't listen to what he was trying to teach them. He didn't want to tow the line, which even Spector did to some extent. He didn't just have arguments with people, he had World Wars.

Dave Berry: Andrew used to create situations. It was that time leading up to 'The Crying Game'. Because I'd got a bit of a weird act – I wore one black leather glove – we thought up a story that I was a Buddhist. It was always supposed to be theatre. So I did the usual thing that most rock 'n' roll people do, and probably still do. I read a few quotes and found out the main names to drop. It was anything to get a few more inches in the paper. I knew how Andrew worked; in other words, 'Fuck 'em.'

Tony Calder: Sid Posta, this wealthy guy in the furniture business, wanted his daughter to be a star. We saw the chance to earn a few bob, maybe a grand, and we made this dreadful record. No one fancied her, so we threw a party.

ALO: I didn't think the record was that dreadful. I gave it my Phil Spector best. Mick and Keith rewrote 'He's Sure The Boy I Love' for the occasion, and I was able to adhere to my decree that, if they wrote, their songs would be recorded and we'd eventually hit the gravy train.

We convinced Sid Posta to pay for a launch party for his daughter. Because, at that time, launch parties were strictly for visiting Americans, so the label wouldn't pay. The British industry thought it had nothing of its own worth 'launching'.

Adrienne Posta was a pretty little girl whom I believe we met through Steve Marriott. Steve studied with her at the Italia Conti Stage School. Her record was going to be released at the end of March on Decca, and the party was set at her parents' flat off Seymour Place, bang next door to 50s' crooner Dickie Valentine, which I took as a good omen for all. It was at this party that I met Marianne Faithfull.

I let the Chevy cool down after a hot week with Reg at the wheel, and drove to the Friday-night party in a new car I'd taken on spec – 'on spec' meaning that I was scrambling about for the money to pay for it. I think it cost £800, a maroon Sunbeam Tiger convertible with a V8 engine. I didn't have Reg on the weekends because he terrified Sheila. The car fitted us like a glove.

The party was all go by the time we arrived. Paul McCartney and his then girlfriend, the actress Jane Asher, greeted me. Her brother Peter Asher was also present; the last time I'd seen him was when Gordon and Peter were playing at a Meaden/Oldham-produced 'R'n'B' evening in Hampstead.

Now, having reversed the name, the pop duo were in the charts with a Lennon and McCartney ballad, 'A World Without Love'. So far a star-filled night, pop was definitely enjoying its own, and here I was, a rebel without pause, smack dab in the middle of it. It would be a nice night off, or so I thought. It was not to be. Peter Asher had invited his friend John Dunbar, accompanied by his fiancée Marianne Faithfull.

Marianne Faithfull

Marianne Faithfull, in *Faithfull*: According to pop mythology, my life proper began at Adrienne Posta's 'launch party' in March 1964. Adrienne Posta was a teenage singer whose single had been produced by Andrew Loog Oldham, the Rolling Stones' flamboyant manager, probably a scam involving her parents' money. He was staring at me from across the room, whispering conspiratorial asides to his partner in crime, Tony Calder. I didn't give a damn about Mick or the Rolling Stones, but the urbane and exotic Andrew Loog Oldham was altogether a different kettle of fish. Him I liked instantly. Andrew was all edge, he exuded menace, shock, razor-blade hipness. I'd never met anyone like Andrew before, he was genuinely weird. All manner of mad schemes, from fashion to movies to pop art, bubbled out of him in garbled, lightning asides. Andrew would say things you only hear in films, like: 'I can make you a star and that's just for starters, baby!' Or: 'You don't need to audition, I can see the charisma in your eyes, darling.'

Sheila Klein: Andrew's camp persona was more like an affectation or a part of his boarding-school experience. It wasn't in his soul. It was to do with creativity, it wasn't his driving force, and it wasn't predominant in any way. It was a helpful tool, another persona he could switch on.

ALO: The moment I caught sight of Marianne I recognised my next adventure, a true star. In another century you'd have set sail for her; in 1964 you'd record her.

Tony Calder: When Marianne walked in, it was like someone turned down the volume slowly, the place went into a hush. Andrew said, 'I've got to have her,' Mick said, 'I've got to have her.' Chrissie Shrimpton says, 'No you fucking don't', and Sheila says, 'Leave her alone.' Andrew says, 'No, I'm talking professionally.' It was one of the most stunning sights seeing this girl come through the door.

Diana Vreeland, Editor, *Vogue*, in *Edie* by Jean Stein: Only twice in this century has youth been dominant. The 20s and the 60s. Youth came through; the language changed; the music; the humour. The writers and the painters produced something totally different from the years before. In the Fitzgerald era, Prohibition was on; everybody was as wild as a March hare; everybody had great Stutz Bearcats, and Mercedes – great enormous cars roaring through the night; youth was wild, rich, extravagant and marvellous . . . though unfortunately it added up to very little . . . I think the 60s will add up to much more.

I don't call it a violently sexy period. You might say, 'Well, everybody slept with everybody like kittens.' It was just possible. Don't forget, the pill had changed the world. Certainly, though, it was a very intensive moment of the beauty of the body. No question. Every girl thought every other girl was beautiful; every boy thought every other boy was beautiful; every boy thought every girl was beautiful; every girl thought every boy was beautiful.

ALO: I approached Marianne through her fiancé John Dunbar, mumbled something along the lines of 'You have something, I want to meet you, and can you sing?' That 'Shang a Doo Lang' party was on a Good Friday, and a very good Friday it was: I had new maroon Tiger wheels, Sheila was happy and we were a foursome, having fixed Keith up on a blind date with Sheila's chum Linda Keith. I thought it was time that Keith went out with something other than his guitar.

Linda Keith: Keith was shy, so Andrew fixed him up with me, it was an arrangement. I was in on it, but it was an arrangement: 'See if you can wake up this chap' sort of thing. I'd seen a couple of gigs, but I'd never taken any notice of them on a personal basis until that night when I met Keith and started talking to him. The big excitement of the evening was Marianne, sitting at a piano very coyly; that was her thing, to be this coy, sweet child.

Andrew lived an incredible lifestyle. I don't know where the funds came from, don't know if there were any. Sheila had immaculate style, a great stylist. She was an enormous influence on Andrew and the way he viewed other people. Sheila would counteract Andrew's vulgar, flashy wide-boy image. He was definitely the leader of the Stones, their guide, their mentor, definitely, no doubt. They felt indebted to Andrew for his ideas, for his promotion of them, the way he was there for them, the way he would take care of them. They were all part of one team. Later on, when Andrew and Sheila were married, Keith and I would hang out more with them because they always had great homes.

Sheila Klein: Keith was so sweet, ordinary and innocent. Linda Keith was pretty multi-dimensional, and Keith was on an even keel. Linda was all over the place; he had trouble keeping up with her. They were great together.

Andrew was smoking so much dope before I knew about it. We had one big argument in that period before we were married. I was in a fury and chased him all the way down Netherhall Gardens, shrieking at him. Some man leant out of the window and asked if he could help. He thought Andrew was having a go at me. He was, it was about the dope.

I discovered I was actually a good fighter. One time he flipped out and he tried to kick me. He had his high-heeled boots on and he was on top of the stairs, and I just gripped the heels of his boots. Sent him flying.

Reg was psychotic. Andrew liked that. How do you get the same feeling you get when you have a number one and everywhere you go it's on the radio? You probably feel like driving on the wrong side of the road, and that's what Reg and Andrew would do. Anything to get out of the 50s. It was awful, Doris Day and petticoats . . . It was like being in a straitjacket, a pink-sugar straitjacket.

Michael Lindsay-Hogg, Director, *Ready Steady Go!*: After Reg, there was teenage Eddie, who drove Andrew. Floppy blond hair, looked sixteen, was probably nineteen. We were driving in the biggest Rolls-Royce to Wembley for a *Ready Steady Go!* rehearsal with the Rolling Stones. Andrew had just put some little *cadeaux* of Beach Boy delights that Brian Wilson had sent him on the built-in record player, when he pressed the button for the electric window separating us from Eddie.

'Could I have the box, please, Eddie?'

'Here you go, Andrew,' he said, handing a large Asprey's silver cigarette box into the back seat.

Opening it, Andrew said, 'Sheila rolled them herself.' Sheila was Andrew's very attractive first wife and mother of his son. 'Take one.'

I took out one of the thick, perfectly formed joints. He lit it for me and we Phantom V'd it out to where we did the work. I loved it so much – the joint, the giddy good humour, the time dislocation, the smell and taste of it – that I asked Andrew if he could get me some more. It was due on Friday, the day we shot the show, and I was looking forward to the delivery. I was paged to the telephone and, rather blithely under the circumstances I thought, Andrew said his connection hadn't shown up and so no stuff. When I hung up from getting this news, I had a revelation which was that I'd been looking forward to it so much that, if I'd got it, I wouldn't have wanted to leave it alone. This was the period of early drug problems, someone not turning up for a gig, the occasional topple over on-stage, but no real casualties yet. So, in a sense, I have Andrew to thank for my personal lack of a drug problem. Although a few years later, after breakfast somewhere, he gave me a little hit of cocaine, which made me very bad-tempered as I was rehearsing a play later in the morning. That was the same day Andrew showed me the ring he had of two people fornicating.

ALO: On leaving the Posta party, Keith bet me I couldn't drive the four of us all the way back to Hampstead on the wrong side of the road. Apart from the crossing of the Edgware Road, I did.

Two days later Marianne Faithfull turned up at the Ivor Court office with a friend and an acoustic guitar. She auditioned for me by singing a couple of Joan Baez-type folk numbers. Technically, Faithfull couldn't sing – still can't – but she reminded me of Grace Kelly, or rather Kelly's voice in the duet she sang with Bing Crosby in the 1956 film *High Society*, 'True Love'. I loved the record, I loved the image and for me it was Grace Kelly's magic bridge that helped send the record to number one in early 1957. Kelly was almost speaking her parts in a captivating and sensual monotone. It was not unlike Crosby's later 'White Christmas' duet with David Bowie playing Princess Grace. The microphone fell in love with Kelly's voice, the way the camera had fallen in love with her face. I hoped they would do the same for Marianne Faithfull.

Through Lionel Bart I'd met the maverick Irish stage designer Sean Kenny. Kenny worked closely with Lionel as stage designer on many of Bart's musicals, such as *Fings Ain't Wot They Used To Be*, *Oliver!* and *Lock Up Your Daughters*. Kenny was also the resident art director at the Mermaid Theatre, whose utopian message for drama – 'Let us rebel, fight, break down, invent and reconstruct a new theatre. Let us free the theatre from the cumbersome shackle of outmoded traditions' – was an example of Kenny's position. There was no one more vociferous about the new British theatre than Sean Kenny. We got on so very well.

Judy Geeson, actress: Andrew was somebody I met with Sean. He was a good friend to us. I know he loved Sean very much. He would name his first son after him. Certainly Sean had a great love for Andrew.

Sean had an unusual combination of abilities: he had the creativity to dream up a design. But he also had a brilliant engineer's brain, so he didn't only dream it, but he knew how to make it. That was the major thing. The two together are incredible. Once you know how to make things happen then

Sean Kenny

your imagination can go even further. I think that's probably what attracted
Andrew to Sean. As well there was a part of Sean that was really a rebel. He
had a great sense of humour. But he was a very quiet person. Sean was a very
good friend, especially to Lionel Bart.

Tony Calder: Terrific fella, Sean Kenny, he was really nice; huge, good
influence on the right side of Andrew. The best relationship he had was the
one he had with Sean Kenny. Sean was the most avant-garde stage designer
of his time in the late 50s and early 60s, he did all Lionel's stuff. He was just
a visionary; he saw new ways of doing it that are still used today.

Around Sean and Andrew, you had to drink, you had to consume as long
as you wanted to listen to the conversation. When Sean's ideas really became
outrageous he found in Andrew a sounding board; if two of those ideas got
through, Sean had at least one of those ideas in motion and on the drawing
board by the next noon. That's how he came up with the Immediate logo, out
at night and on the page the next morning. He was a very bright and lovely

guy, so way ahead of his time. He saw then that computers would be what they have become and be reduced to what they are. He saw the future, the chips, the megabytes. He and Andrew tried to develop this device for the theatre that would allow the audience to manipulate the plot. Sean Kenny was a true visionary.

Sheila Klein: Lionel was special, he was experienced in a theatrical way, lots of glam friends, he was very sweet and fatherly to Andrew. I found him a very charismatic person, wearing his heart on his sleeve. Sean Kenny, too.

Lionel Bart: I put Andrew with Sean, my designer, the Irish leprechaun, a genius. He was a hundred years ahead of his time. We had one of the only composer-designer-author relationships ever. We swapped drawings before I even wrote a note of a show. We had a good thing going. Sean's attitude was 'It can be done'. I'd do a drawing, he'd do a drawing, he'd write a three-line poem which would set me up to do a huge momentum song that would travel through four different sets inside one number on-stage. In *Maggie May* there was a song that started out in a pub, went on to the streets, went on to the Mersey Ferry, the pub became a ferry and then the ferry went across the Mersey and then we'd be on the other side of the Mersey, all inside one number. We were the first people to show the back wall of the stage, show the stage lighting, show all the changes. He didn't hide anything, it was all happening. This was a huge innovation.

ALO: Sean was my man, my muse. As I entered the rock 'n' pop end of showbusiness, he was like someone God had sent down to tap me on the shoulder and say, 'By the way, there's all this as well.' Sean made me realise that there's more to it, and more I could bring to it. As well as the angry young man, there was the angry young musical. He showed me social responsibility in practice as a living art form and imbued me with a work ethic that cut wider than self, a making of the 'you-can-do-it' emblem available to every man who could dream it. At a time when my business was about trampling myth and tradition, he reminded me to engage also in building hope and awaking spirit and vision. You'd go out for the night, solve the world's ills and wake up in the morn, as I did, in Sean's bed, with the master, a lithe

British actress and an Afghan hound. And you'd still be God's children and all would be right with the world.

Sean was a great mate and education, and his ethics and talent emboldened me even as I didn't practise them. I now needed money to finance recording Marianne, so I went to Lionel and suggested a joint venture. There was no way I was going to let her be signed to Decca direct for the sake of a few hundred quid.

Lionel Bart: Oh, I got jumped on with that one, absolutely. Well, he got this schoolgirl out of a convent. Because he was a minor, he needed support and couldn't legally manage her or them, so I became the official manager of Marianne and the Stones for a short space of time and I was their publisher. It was a family. Even when he got married to Sheila I had to be the guarantor for that.

I remember helping out with the lyrics of 'As Tears Go By' with Mick, and on 'Satisfaction'. He helped me do the opening song of Act II of *Maggie May*, called 'Carrying On', but Mick didn't take credit on that, it was a family affair. When Mick started having his power thing, he always used to get me into his sessions, sit me down in the control room and often I was really out to lunch on various whatever. I remember him ripping off some terrible song and Jimmy Miller said, 'What's Bart doing here?' Mick said, 'Lionel's just given me three notes and you're gonna do 'em.' There was mutual respect there.

ALO: Lionel and I were cruising down Bayswater after a night at foot-tapper Lionel Blair's, when we chatted about our big dreams and my empty pockets. With a heart of gold, on with the dance of life, Li agreed to fund the venture. He was a gem, a real rhythm of life. We formed two companies, Forward Sound to handle recording projects and Forward Music to handle the songs, Marianne to be the first Forward artist. Lionel had this song 'I Don't Know How' that we agreed would be one of the recorded songs – the fact that Marianne wouldn't be able to sing it didn't get mentioned.

Earlier that month I'd gone into Kingsway Studios. Regent was booked to cut some demos of Mick and Keith's latest batch of songs, and among the musicians was ex-Wildcat Big Jim Sullivan on guitar and former Tornado

Clem Cattini on drums. I was now using session musicians on their demos. I couldn't ask Brian, Bill and Charlie to work for nearly free on their few days off. We quickly put down two or three songs. There was really nothing special there, the main point was the exercise.

Keith for some reason wasn't there and the session had been a little lacklustre and not the best note on which to continue the day. While the musicians packed up their equipment I asked Mick, 'You didn't have anything else? I didn't hear that ballad I heard you working on.'

'No, that's it.' Mick wasn't pleased with the day's work either.

'Let's get it down anyway.' I turned to Big Jim Sullivan. 'Jim, I've got fifteen minutes more of your time, haven't I? Could Mick just sing this song to you – it's simple – and then we could knock it off with just the two of you?'

'You can have all the fifteen minutes you want, Andrew, my son,' said Jim and then, to Mick, 'Okay, sunshine, come over hear and let's listen to this song of yours.'

I think that Big Jim knew that Mick was not in a compliant mood and his relaxed tone got the song to the table. Fifteen minutes later I had them both down with 'As Time Goes By'.

A couple of days after Marianne had come up and done her Joan Baez warbling, Tony Calder and I sat down when everybody had left the office and talked about songs for her to record. We both ignored Lionel's song 'I Don't Know How', neither of us owning up to the fact that it wasn't a song for Marianne, unable to insult Lionel or, perhaps more to the point, afraid of 'fessing up and losing our backer. Lionel had the readies and our moral balls were locked in a greedy vice of deceit. We crossed a Jackie De Shannon song and a few others off our shortlist.

'Well, there's this song of Mick's I didn't play you that I cut at the "Sleepy City" session,' I offered and then whacked the seven-and-a-half-inch tape on to the reel-to-reel.

Tony was with me when I talked to Mick. Tony wore a matt dark-grey, one-buttoned blazer and Anello & Davide 'slippers'. I wore a blue herringbone, double-breasted sports jacket, grey-blue, high tab-collared, broadcloth shirt and black string tie. And Mick wore a checked, tab-collared shirt without a tie, with mock Prince-of-Wales checked John Stephen trews, a combo of patterns that only he would have attempted to pull off.

Tony sat on a chair, swaying back and forth, hands clasped, moving his thumbs back and forth. Mick stood in front of me, at my desk going through everything that was on it.

'Mick, that song, "As Time Goes By", it could be great,' said I, also meaning: Get your hands out of my things or learn to read backwards.

'I don't think so,' he replied.

'I've got someone in mind for it; I'd like to look at changing the title.'

'Do what you bloody like with it, it's finished as far as I'm concerned,' Jagger closed as he continued to rummage through my papers.

Marianne Faithfull, in *Faithfull*: The Lionel Bart song was awful. It was one of those songs that needed the proper register. My voice was just plain wrong. We did take after agonising take. The musicians were becoming restless, but I simply could not do it. In desperation Andrew got me to try the song that had originally been planned for the B-side, a song that Mick and Keith had written called 'As Tears Go By'.

Tony Calder: We made the Marianne record with Lionel Bart. We had no money and we thought Lionel had money; he didn't, but he had a couple of grand so he could pay for a real orchestra. Andrew had been off every night working on the B-side, originally 'As Time Goes By'. He was actually really into doing a Phil Spector, like Phil would take a Jeff Barry and Ellie Greenwich song and rework it – at least that's what we thought happened. Andrew worked it into 'As Tears Go By', gave it the new title – all-important – cut the lyrics down, took the soppy ones out, some of the original lyrics were real dogshit, but Andrew changed all that. Then he got together with Mike Leander to arrange it, which was another week of working every night.

The recording at Olympic was a three-hour session. The Bart song was the biggest piece of dogshit you've ever heard in your life, so they went for a break, came back with twenty minutes left of the session and started on 'As Tears Go By'. Then the cor anglais comes in. I said, 'It's a smash'; he said, 'Don't tell Lionel.' Decca knew he was serious; she caused a sensation, just the pictures alone – that famous picture with the ankle socks on, everyone wanted to fuck her . . .

Marianne Faithfull, in *Faithfull*: Andrew was a great fabricator of selves, and once in the studio he transformed utterly. An agitated and distracted maestro Loog Oldham strode up and down like a manic Ludwig Van on a handful of leapers. He did what I would later recognise as his Phil Spector imitation: dark glasses, Wagnerian intensity, melodramatic moodiness. It was all a game, but before you knew this about Andrew it could be quite unnerving. Mick and Keith also came to the session but they were as quiet as mice. It was Andrew's show and they said not a word.

ALO: The musicians sighed with relief when I announced that we were dumping 'I Don't Know How' and moving on to 'As Tears Go By'. The frustration of countless takes of poor Marianne sounding like an inbred hyena gave a great impetus to their playing on 'As Tears Go By'. They didn't play it like a B-side, they played it with feeling, relief and life; they were happy to be 'on structure' again and you could hear it and it glued. It was a magical moment. A few takes to sort out the loose change and we were home. I congratulated Marianne and told her she'd got herself a number six.

Marianne Faithfull, in *Faithfull*: Andrew had played me a demo with Mick singing and Big Jim Sullivan on guitar. This was the first song that Mick and Keith had written. Andrew had locked them in a kitchen and told them, 'Write a song, I'll be back in two hours.' Andrew had given them the sense and feel of the type of thing he wanted them to write – 'I want a song with brick walls all around it, high windows and no sex' – and they came up with a song called 'As Time Goes By'. Andrew knew a lot about the construction of songs, and although it was still in a very primitive state, he knew he could fix it. There was another problem: the title. It was the title of a very famous song, the one Dooley Wilson sings in *Casablanca*, so Andrew renamed it 'As Tears Go By'.

Maestro Andrew's only piece of advice to me was to sing very close to the mike. It was an invaluable piece of advice. When you sing that close to the microphone it changes the spatial dimension, you project yourself into the song.

There was about a two-week delay in cutting the B-side now. We were no longer doing Lionel Bart's song. The new B-side was 'Greensleeves' (now credited to Andrew Loog Oldham rather than to Henry VIII).

ALO: I didn't need Lionel now, so I carved him out of the writing picture and dumped his song. There was no doubt that 'As Tears Go By' was a smash, and I wanted to be on the B-side; remember, a writer receives the same money riding on the back of a hit as having written the A-side. I was greedy, in money and ego, therefore Lionel had to go.

Another practical reality was that 'I Don't Know How' would have given the game away and been an insult to those who'd bought 'As Tears Go By' to find this hyenic rendition on the back; this was a hit and I needed a B-side that partnered, not degraded. This round-robin move would rebound on me; years later, when I stopped to take breath and count a few figures, I found that David Platz had appropriated my B-side to one of his own crew – he just figuring I'd be too busy to notice, and I was. One part of this man definitely did not survive the holocaust; he just figured I was not entitled, and used a law I was not familiar with to appropriate the money to somebody he thought was. Hitler played God with his life, and Platz played God with my money.

If you are a moaner and you can't take getting fucked and screwed the first few times out, then find another business, for the hauling over is your entry fee and part of the territory.

I got an appointment to see the legendary Sir Edward Lewis to play him the finished 'As Tears Go By' and get the money for a different Faithfull B-side. This was becoming an expensive session. I had never met Sir Edward over the Stones, I was nervous and wondered if he'd heard about 'Andrew's Blues'. He hadn't: life was smaller and a different shop. We had not reached the stage where everybody was a star – that would come later. Right now it was a divine right given only to a few, those few who had begun those 60s; the rest of you could seize it later.

We sat in Sir Edward's sweeping office overlooking the Thames. He was sixtyish, a fossil, neat but scruffy in a worn, well-made double-breasted suit. His eyes were shiftier than mine but when they did make contact with you they were grey, all-knowing and quite kind. I'd never studied ears but now, looking at his, I realised it wasn't just the poor and old but the rich as well who had hair growing out of their ears. It seemed very strange that day; now I know better about fossils and hair.

Marianne Faithfull, in *Faithfull*: 'As Tears Go By' was like a Françoise Hardy song, really. Maybe that's what Mick picked up from me when we met. Slightly existential, but with a dash of San Remo Festival – the Europop you might hear on a French jukebox. Or, rather, it's what Andrew saw in me at the party and told Mick to write. Andrew's always been into that, 'The Andrew Loog Oldham Orchestra Plays The Greatest Hits Of The Rolling Stones' sort of thing. Everybody did those albums, even Keith made one. It was by working on dopey projects like this that Keith learnt to produce records.

Andrew really was out there at the time. I was intimidated by the cool, mystifying jive-speak of his that passed for chat. I had no idea what he was talking about most of the time. He was too hip for me, he was too fast. Despite the fact that he was inevitably right about everything, I was having problems with Sir Andrew. On top of everything else, to have the Mad Hatter as your manager – it was all too much.

But the most disturbing thing about Andrew was all the wild *Clockwork Orange* stories, confirmed by the unnerving, ever-present Reg, that role-playing, criminal chauffeur of his. Andrew loved to put stories out about breaking people's fingers or hanging recalcitrant club owners out of seventh-storey windows by their ankles. It was all pretend, a boy's game of cops and robbers and old gangster films, but I didn't know that; he scared me to death. I felt trapped, he was too much of a Svengali, I thought, with too much control over me. But control is always reciprocal; it cuts both ways. It took me years to realise that he was just a sweet thing.

ALO: Another A-side with the Andrew Oldham Orchestra, 'Three Hundred and Sixty-Five Rolling Stones (One for Every Day of the Year)', that I penned with Mike Leander became the main title-theme for two years' worth of Rediffusion TV's *Ready Steady Go!* That was a nice honour and a few pennies. The B-side was a tongue-in-cheek piece of reality called 'Oh, I Do Like To See Me On The B-side' written by Charlie Watts, Bill Wyman and yours truly.

A few months before, I'd persuaded Decca to release the Andrew

Oldham Orchestra, and I set about recording *16 Hip Hits* at Regent Sound with the unflappable Bill Farley engineering, John Paul Jones playing bass and arranging, and Jim Sullivan and Jimmy Page on guitars.

When Impact Sound and the Rolling Stones signed with Decca, Eric Easton did the signing; I was a minor. This time out, I was still a minor and my mother did the signing. I was pleased. She wouldn't fuck me, even if I'd made the mistake of interpreting one of her few physical showings of affection for me when I was about twelve as a sign that she had wanted me to. There, that didn't take fifty minutes and a couch, did it?

Anyway . . . How many nineteen-year-olds had their own orchestras? How many producers? None or not many: the orchestra didn't go on the road, it was in permanent workshop. I was paying my way through the Regent Sound Producer's College, and I invited all of my friends to join me. Oh, we made some huge mistakes, but one started to learn where sound sat. On 'Da Doo Ron Ron', which we balladed down, Mick Jagger came in and sang, and I added a couple of cellos. My budget was tight, it was my money – not even I had the lip to get a backer for this trip, that would have been completely over-the-top and not done. 'Excuse me, mister, could I have some money for my orchestra?' As if I really took it seriously, which from another point of view I did. Anyway, we added the two cellos with the tapes going mono to mono and the track just disappeared, couldn't handle the register of the cellos. You can hear the gaff today, but you learnt from it all, you learnt.

I recorded instrumental, quasi-vocal and vocal versions of songs by Bob Dylan, Chuck Berry, John Lennon and Paul McCartney, Phil Spector, Jeff Barry and Ellie Greenwich, Burt Bacharach and Hal David, Jack Nitzsche and Sonny Bono. 'Alley Oop' creator Kim Fowley and I rewrote 'The House Of The Rising Sun' and called it 'The Rise Of The Brighton Surf' in homage to the Mods and Rockers rumbles in Brighton. Wouldn't you have?

Big Jim Sullivan: The first thing I did with Andrew was Mick's demo of 'As Tears Go By', then I did some of his orchestral things. He was always very active in the studio, moving about, expressing himself, full of energy. It's all down to atmosphere; Andrew made everybody feel comfortable. Some of the sessions we were on, the producers were arseholes. When somebody like Andrew comes along, you get guys doing their best for him.

Clem Cattini: The name Andrew Loog Oldham was a selling point, it would sell records. The fact that it was an Andrew Loog Oldham production had a lot of weight – like, at the time, a Joe Meek production carried a lot of weight. I came from the rock 'n' roll era and Andrew was a rock 'n' roll man himself. Andrew was similar to Joe Meek in the studio, they were both inventive and innovative. Andrew would do things that supposedly you couldn't do. Maybe within the business compared to other producers he was crazy, but among the musicians . . . I never thought he was crazy. I thought he was clever. If you walked in and it was Andrew, you knew you were gonna enjoy it and have a good laugh. Andrew would ask for contributions from you, whereas a lot of other producers wouldn't: that's what's written, this is what I want and that's the end of it, so all you really were was a musical navvy. With Andrew you could put forward ideas yourself, which obviously, as a working musician, is good for you. You feel you're a part of something, you feel like you've contributed something as opposed to being a machine. Plus with Andrew I always knew I was gonna play with Jimmy Page, Jim Sullivan, John Paul Jones and Nicky Hopkins. Let's face it, you can't not enjoy that.

ALO and Jimmy Page at Regent Sound

John Paul Jones: The sessions for *16 Hip Hits* were pretty riotous, they were very funny. We did all the tracks really quickly in Regent Sound; it was done really cheap, although I'm sure the bills were quite high. Then we put all the orchestral stuff on in the Decca studios. Mick Jagger did the vocals on 'Da Doo Ron Ron' – we were pretty drunk by that time – and there's Andrew running around like a madman putting vocals on 'I Wanna Be Your Man'. I don't know how he came up with some of the songs he came up with: the B-side to 'Baja' was some Stones track. I wasn't even on it. 'Baja' was my first single as a solo performer. Andrew produced that and got it released on Pye. 'The Lonely Rocker' was one of Andrew's songs, instant sort of in the studio. He was pretty spontaneous. I was up all night arranging.

I started doing arrangements for Andrew when Mike Leander became a staff producer at Decca. Andrew Oldham established me as an arranger, which is what I wanted to do rather than just be a session musician. He was great in the studio. I was very grateful because he trusted me with these sessions and all these musicians. He gave me a chance to do all these weird things; he kinda let me get on with it, but he had a very clear idea of what he wanted. He really didn't want to know anything about music in case it compromised his feeling for what it should sound like, what it should be – I remember him saying that. At the time he had this idea of a House of Music, where he would have arrangers, musicians, songwriters and producers . . .

We were the only people making American records in England. It had a great feel about it, that widescape sound. Regent Sound was very small, mono, it was great. At the end of the session it was mixed, it was finished. His sessions were always fun, everybody used to enjoy going to them, he was always funny on the talk-back mike. So many sessions were run-of-the-mill, banal, mundane, very boring, you couldn't wait to get out of them. But Andrew's sessions were always fun and they were always interesting, he'd always want to try something different. All the old string players were really nice; they used to do whatever we wanted. He'd get them tapping their bows on the backs of their violins, all sorts of stuff. They must have enjoyed themselves because they were a pretty hard bunch, the orchestral musicians. It was either porno mags or the *Golfing Times*. It was amazing if you got them to take any interest in the session at all, but they did seem to be interested in our sessions and I was allowed to write them nice, interesting little things, especially for woodwinds – we'd always have a couple of oboes or French horns.

He obviously cared whether the records sold, but basically we just wanted to make records. I wanted to arrange, he wanted to produce, and neither of us was very choosy. There were different scenes then: the group scene which was happening more or less after the Beatles, and then there were the singer/songwriter/publishers, 'Let's get a bunch of people together, get a song, make a record' type of scene. The group scene was, 'Oh, we're a band, we write our own stuff and you'll want to record us.' Andrew had a foot in both camps.

Andrew used to camp it up with make-up, eye-shadow . . . he was all a bit ambiguous, ambidextrous, nobody really cared, that was part of the fun, shocking all these people. The records we made were really pushing what music could be; it was more the underground really. The very fact that they didn't sell actually gives you a certain freedom; you can do what you like, having a good time getting paid for it.

I always thought Tony Calder was a bit of a suit; I didn't know what he was doing with Andrew. I used to like Reg – he was supposed to have had this dodgy past, but you never knew with Andrew. Neither Andrew nor I had passed our test, so Reg used to pick me up in the Chevy. It was unusual but it was all part of that American front. Andrew had acquired this gun from somewhere and he kept firing it off the top of Ivor Court.

Andrew was an innovator and a great scam-merchant too. He actually made it exciting and dangerous, you just felt like you were out there . . . there was a sense of adventure in dealing with him. The hype was all part of it, and the fact that he felt he was putting one over on the Establishment, who richly deserved it, I have to say. That, and the fact we made good records . . . I thought he was a larger-than-life character. I was in awe of him – he was great. He used to tell me how he'd stitched this person or that person up, stitched up some suit somewhere, and I'd go, 'Yeah, fuck 'em all, I wish I could do it 'n' all!'

· CHAPTER 15 ·

Simon Frith and Howard Horne, from *Art into Pop*: For the youthful Oldham, just as determined to be a star as the Stones themselves, the packaging of the Stones was an art – his art – to be celebrated for its cunning and cleverness. The Stones, unlike the Beatles, remained 'authentic' artists, not because their music was more rootsy nor because their image was more rebellious, but because they were clearly in charge of their own selling-out process: not only did Oldham write the headlines – 'Would You Let Your Daughter Go With A Rolling Stone? – but it was obvious he did. While the Beatles had become superstars as part of a press love-in, the Stones rode to fame in a series of gleeful games with the media . . .

The Stones were, then, the first pop group to draw attention to the peculiarities of the pop process itself, leaving behind a wake of discomfited DJs, TV producers and journalists behind them, and Oldham was the first manager to bring sophisticated advertising ideas to their imagery. He used David Bailey, for example, to take photos for their first LP, using no other identifying information (much to Decca's dismay). Bailey's photos carried all the messages necessary in themselves – partly by 'secret' reference to Robert Freeman's cover for *With The Beatles* (the Stones looked noticeably scruffy and real by contrast), partly through a use of close-up composition and half-lighting that made the group look at once both near and out of reach, decadent and vulnerable.

For both Mods and bohemians the Beatles were too clearly a part of media showbiz to be interesting. The Oldham-directed Stones, by contrast, suggested a style of success that, though just as dependent on commercial calculation and teen appeal, had an artistic validity – the Stones could be taken (as Pete Townshend took them) as a gratifyingly successful example of Pop Art.

ALO: From January to March 1964 the Stones were on the road, and I promoted them, ran my shop and recorded the Andrew Oldham Orchestra. Nearly every day they had off we recorded the first album at Regent Sound. Chuck Berry, Willie Dixon, Muddy Waters and Holland-Dozier-Holland were among the writers from whom we culled the covers we recorded for this razor-sharp and earnest first LP outing. It was a first and a great pleasure for the group to have that much space to express themselves (albeit not that much time to do it in!).

Thirty-five years later this fact may be overlooked in a world where, if a talent appeals to a recording company or producer, they are usually given the long-form compact disc to display their wares to the world immediately. We were not given the world or the long-play record form, we earned them. First, a début single, then the follow-up. Then, if you were good boys, you were allowed the four-song outing of an extended 45 rpm with picture sleeve – wowee . . . something tangible for Mum to hold! Then, if your life and sales were constantly going up, you were allowed the big one, the LP. Around that time you may have some product released in France, Scandinavia or Italy, and about two years after that you may get paid . . . something.

Dave Berry: Europe was France, Germany, Belgium and Holland; that was pretty much it. I had great success in Belgium. I did the same thing as Andrew; you only needed twenty-five people to rush the stage and try to climb on. The photographers, they're not interested if they think it's set-up, are they? But they got the shot of these twenty-five women trying to climb on to the stage and wreck it.

ALO: On the first Stones' LP, or our later work, I was never Mick's voice teacher or director. He found himself and got in character, out of it or lack of it, and did it. I would just help him find or remember the possibilities.

His voice is a finely tuned instrument, as is his being; I often thought that I talked to him and Keith listened; but any time we went to work it was apparent he'd heard what he needed to. He plays many parts in as many songs. He started with straight, respectful-to-the-form, R'n'B interpretations. He still does that, plus so much more, from the near-cockney on our later 'Mother's Little Helper' to the glimmered street nigger of his much later 'Some Girls'. When Mick sang about love, sex and the women who were under his thumb, obsolete and out of time, he was totality personified, that moving violation that separates the men from the boys.

As a member of the public I would say, 'Mick, in those first verses you got me. I believe you. On the next verse could you confuse me, give me doubt, lie to me . . . then haul me back in?' And he'd do that, or the appropriate equivalent.

Great stars rise above their given medium, their chosen thoroughfare. They succeed in the world at large. Such is Mick Jagger, Nureyev, Monroe, Dean, as is the head gamekeeper, Keith Richards. Keith was the trackman, bagman, wonder to behold. He was to the recording studio born. Everybody, including me, had their nervous asides, either brought with them or acquired in the anxiety of that rock 'n' roll moment when somebody asked you what you thought. With Keith, you didn't have to ask, his body told you. Sometimes he nodded, sometimes he smiled, but that was just taking time up for Keith – valuable time, between the next and last note. If you ever wanted to know if the track was done or in the bag, Keith told you and he didn't often use words. He was the seal of approval. I was later asked by Allen Klein, who was educating up on who did what, 'Andrew, who makes the records?' Without hesitation I replied, 'Keith does.'

Keith Richards, in *The Early Stones*: Andrew learnt record producing at the same time we did. The only reason he's sitting there is because we were on the other side playing the stuff. I mean, Andrew knew nothing about recording except what he thought he wanted to hear, which may be the purest way of producing, because he's not going to turn to the engineer and say, 'Wait a minute, I want more blah, blah, blah.' It must be maddening when somebody does that. But in those days it didn't matter because it was all in bloody mono. It was like you were going for a certain sound and a lot of the time Andrew was right. I mean, he was trying to make records that *he* wanted to listen to and so were we, and most of the time he was right with all his enthusiasm and so on. And he was quick to learn. I mean, when he found out how to do something that worked with the Stones, he didn't forget it. He was very resourceful.

But [later] we started to learn more than Andrew did, and all of a sudden, Mick and I figured that possibly we had more of an idea what this band could do than Andrew did . . . Andrew just wanted hit records; we wanted great ones. But Andrew should get a lot of credit. He was very smart. He got us one of the best engineers around, Glyn Johns.

Actually, it was Johns who recorded our very first session even before Andrew was involved with us, and Andrew, as I say, was no dummy. He would always make sure he had the best people around him.

Andy Wickham: Andrew's skills as a record producer have been submerged in the overall context of his Svengali relationship with the Stones. He was a great record-maker in the tradition of his own heroes and friends, men like Bob Crewe, Phil Spector and Bert Berns. In those days he mostly recorded at Regent Sound in Denmark Street with Glyn Johns as engineer. I didn't go to many of his dates, but I remember him as always being totally in command, issuing instructions in clear public-school tones and unmusical language. Yet the musicians knew what he wanted and loved working for him. His greatest production for me is 'That Girl Belongs To Yesterday' by Gene Pitney, but he also made wonderful records with the Mighty Avengers ('So Much In Love'), Bobby Jameson ('All I Want Is My Baby'), the Nashville Teens ('This Little Bird') and, of course, Marianne Faithfull. And the early Stones records – 'Tell Me', 'Under The Boardwalk', 'Play With Fire' – were beautiful, *produced* records. One of the last he made, 'Paint It Black', remains unsurpassed as a production thirty years on and still sounds electrifying and totally up-to-date on the radio.

ALO: The début LP was rounded out by the first Keith-and-Mick composition that the Stones recorded, 'Tell Me (You're Coming Back)', and it stood out with its echo-drenched sloppy blues puppy-in-love feel, and carried the space of a blues traveller resting his head in a commercial place. I loved it!

The recording complete, I next embarked on what at the time was natural and obvious to me and is now looked back on as great career strategy. I did

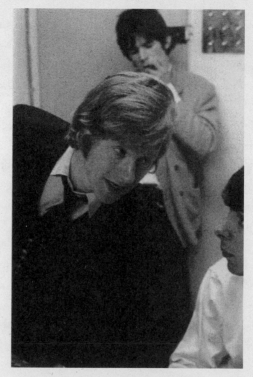

ALO, Keith Richards, Glyn Johns

not want the Stones' LP to have some inappropriate title. My attitude was 'Everyone knows who they are, that's why we don't need their name on the cover.' The idea came to me one night and was a permanent must-have implant by the next morning . . . The Rolling Stones' LP would have no title and no name, just their moody mugs staring out atcha. Decca balked, I held the tapes; Decca balked in the press, so did I; I still held the tapes. Advance orders went up – in fact doubled – during this stand-off.

The real title was embedded in my sleeve notes on the back of the cover: 'The Rolling Stones Are More Than Just A Group, They Are A Way Of Life'. If you stood with 18,000 Americans in Madison Square Gardens in January of 1998 – all trying to recover a moment to which they were not entitled in the first place, a moment the Stones lent them – then you'll know that my message is still true. So I stood my ground and I won. Bill Townsley at Decca relented and the group's first LP went out untitled, unrelenting and unforgiven.

Tony Calder: It doesn't matter how much you do, if you do the right thing at the right time. That's what pissed Eric Easton off. Like me, Eric would work five days a week, ten hours a day and Andrew would come in and do one thing, make one call, change one person's opinion and make the whole fucking thing work. Where do you apportion the credit? He got the credit and so he should, for the story about 'Would You Let Your Daughter Go With A Rolling Stone?' I think that was the thing that really made them in the UK, plus that pissing in the gas station bit. It was Bill Wyman who did the pissing, but Andrew was there to twist it, make Mick the star. From that moment the world was open to him. The Rolling Stones Are A Way Of Life, the album with no name, that was brilliant, still is . . .

Adrian Millar: I'm constantly told that the Stones and Beatles 'got good' after the mid-60s . . . what a load of arseholes. I'm not convinced on that one – the magic was in the beginning, not the bleedin' end . . . Businessmen make great businessmen, not showbizmen. Andrew was a great showbizman, he simply made the other copyists look awkward and tacky, low-budget and sub-standard.

Nik Cohn, in *Awopbopaloobop Alopbamboom*: Towards the end of 1964 Andrew had a group called the Poets. I was working for the *Observer*. He'd already got a reputation as the English Phil Spector. I was quite interested in the Poets, so I went to one of their recording sessions and I quite liked the cut of Andrew's jib, I liked his outrageousness. I thought he was an interesting person, I liked his power of self-invention and humour. I wouldn't have said any of the Stones as individuals were particularly interesting to talk to, whereas Andrew was. He was a major creative force in image and music-making.

Oldham, without doubt, was the most flash personality that British pop has ever had, the most anarchic and obsessive and imaginative hustler of all. Whenever he was good, he was quite magnificent. What he had going for him was mostly a frantic yen to get up and out: he loathed slowness and drabness, age and caution and incompetence, mediocrity of all kinds, and he could not stand to work his way up steadily like anyone else. Instead, he barnstormed, he came on quite outrageous. He slabbed his face with make-up and wore amazing clothes and hid his eyes behind eternal shades. He was all camp and when he was batting at nothing at all, he still had hit-lines and always played everything as ultimate big-time. The great thing was the way he pushed himself; he could either clean up or bomb completely. He couldn't possibly get caught by compromise.

As manager, what Oldham did was take everything implicit in the Stones and blow it up one hundred times. Long-haired and ugly and anarchic as they were, Oldham made them more so and he turned them into everything that parents would most hate, be most frightened by. All the time he goaded them to be wilder, nastier, fouler in every way and they were – they swore, sneered, snarled and came on cretinous.

All this time Oldham hustled them strong: he was hectic, inventive and he pulled strokes daily. Less obviously, he was also thorough; he worked everything out to the smallest spontaneous detail. Well, the Stones were really his fantasy, his private dream-child and, healthy narcissist that he was, he needed them to be entirely perfect.

Anyhow, the Stones were obviously just his meat. He struck up immediate contact with Mick Jagger, who was greatly impressed by him and became almost his disciple, his dedicated follower in the ways of outrage. The weird thing was, Jagger on-stage wasn't like Jagger off-stage, but he was very much like Andrew Oldham. Andrew Loog Oldham. I mean, he was more a projection of Oldham than of himself.

I found the managers to be more interesting than the bands because they were more articulate. Andrew was certainly enormously flash with the office and the drivers. Within a year or so it was commonplace, but in 1964 it wasn't. When I saw the Stones in the office or in the dressing room they were young, fairly inarticulate lads, lots of in-jokes and so on. It was Andrew who had the articulateness, the sharpness, the flash and above all the outrageousness. He did much more of the living that the Stones were meant to be doing.

In general the Stones were mumbly in public, and one thing you could never say was that Loog Oldham was mumbly. He came right out with it all, he was absolutely in people's face, with the make-up, the hair and everything. It was his golden period; he was really the only person in London who would have talked that way at that time. It took guts because he was a skinny callow youth, and people would have given a great deal of money to thump him and break him in two, and he ran the gauntlet. I thought it always took more guts to do that than to get on-stage and do a sort of stylised rebellion. People now fantasise about the swinging 60s, but in 1964 England, apart from 200 people, was unbelievably conservative, grey and grim. It would be easy to act outrageous in clubs, because there you were safe.

What impressed me was that he had enormous rage and arrogance and wouldn't allow himself to be restrained. He would be walking down the street saying things that were absolutely obnoxious to most of the people he was passing, in a very loud voice, with enormous gestures and to do this was to risk getting duffed up all the time. At the time London was a drab city, it was another winter of discontent, endless strikes, the way that England is. Andrew's quality was that he was enormously vivid; he was deliberately obnoxious but he had the talent to back him up. I think his talent and impact have been very, very underestimated. In Andrew's wake, he made life a lot easier for people like Kit Lambert to be outrageous with the Who.

ALO: Initially the Stones, away on those hysteria-swamped one-night stands all over the country, were as concerned as Decca over my album design. Mick and Keith loved the whole thing, pushing me on the way Stamp would Lambert, 'Whoa, he's off again.' Eric Easton and Bill were worried that I was going too far and my antics might deplete from sales and, yes, be a career curtain-closer, not raiser. Charlie smiled in time to the pedal of his life.

Brian took it hard and angsted on it, but he was slowly moving into his own cul-de-sac. Here I was selling this would-be serious musician as a freak.

However, all complaints and concerns about my actions and screaming matches down at Decca were soon forgotten. On 17 April 1964 the Rolling Stones' début album was released and within a week it had knocked the Beatles' *With The Beatles* off the top of the album charts with advance orders of over 100,000. I ran around town, cock of the walk with a vengeance, gleefully crowing to all that the Stones were number one and going higher. I forgot to mention that the Beatles had held the number-one spot for a year and were just taking a rest before their next number-one LP.

Melody Maker's review of the Stones' début LP concluded, 'A final word of praise to Andrew Loog Oldham who recorded the sessions. He's living up to his boast that he'd be the top independent recording manager in Britain by November.' 'Top of the World, Ma!' I heard Jimmy Cagney yell from inside me.

Keith Altham: The album reviews in the *NME* were really very lightweight at the time. They weren't very serious. The editor, Andy Gray, was a big golfer, he knew very little about rock, he started off a review of guitarist Duane Eddy's LP with the line, 'Duane Eddy's never been in better voice.' Nobody took it really analytically. Andrew was the Stones' producer, but a lot of us didn't really know what production entailed.

Chris Hutchins: Decca just thought he was crazy, that he was gonna go up in a puff of smoke. They would only dole out money on the basis of, 'Well, that's what they're worth next month, they may be finished by the following month because they've got this mad manager.' The men at Decca went home to Weybridge and such, their houses in the stockbroker belt, very nine-to-five people. Suddenly there's this guy tearing into their company demanding all these things. Even when he pulled it off, they'd say, 'Well, he got away with it this time.' That's what gave him a lot of strength. The Establishment fought him, which made him fight back.

Tony King: Andrew was very unusual in that regard; a lot of stories went around about Andrew, that he would thump desks, make lots of angry noises in label manager Bill Townsley's office if he didn't get what he wanted. That style of management was unheard of in the UK. It was very much: have a nice three-course lunch at Isow's, drink a couple of bottles of red wine and shake hands, 'Okay, old boy, we'll have your act on next week.' Andrew was going into Decca saying, 'I want this, I want that' – it was a bit of a shock.

ALO: 138 and 147 Ivor Court, at the northern tip of Gloucester Place, was an interesting building that was supposed to be residential until Calder and I moved in. By early 1964 its tenants included us, Charlie and Shirley Watts on the floor below, and Kit Lambert and Chris Stamp a couple of floors below the Watts. It was a small great world. Our first flat, 147, was basically undecorated Ideal Home Exhibition to suit Tony Calder's taste, but 138 was 'done' by the interior decorator Mafalda Hall, then wife of Tony Hall.

Mafalda was what was known as an 'outrageously great lady' which she was to all of us. She was responsible for the great church lectern from which I held forth, and great wild silk wallpaper in the halls leading up to the custom-made marijuana wallpaper in my office. There was a lot of smokin' going on and it blended in well.

By now I was having a job remembering not where I worked but where I lived, so I often slept over. There was no chance of Eric Easton dropping by. His disdain of my fight with Decca over the Stones' cover had shovelled more dirt on the shallow grave of our partnership. I was now living with Sheila overlooking Primrose Hill. Sean Kenny and I had already been hauled in by the law for the misuse of fire extinguishers outside our flat, and the young man that Sheila had hired to clean had incurred my wrath and given my game away by throwing out a sacred lump of hash I'd left atop the TV set in an ashtray. 'I thought it was rubbish,' he squealed as I screamed.

I had a nice morning ride from Primrose Hill into Regent's Park, sliding right on to Baker Street, gliding right and burning rubber right again on to Gloucester Place, then four blocks north in my powder-blue Chevy ridden, as opposed to driven, by the ever laughing, ever gay and always criminal Reg. It seemed a perfect world. I had mine and seemed to be in control of it, from Primrose Hill to Regent's Park to the marijuana plants on the walls of my office. Life was co-ordinated!

In late 1963 'I Wanna Be Your Man' had been pressed up for release by

London Records (Decca's American subsidiary) without my consultation. I had demanded that it be withdrawn because it stood no chance of being a hit and I didn't want a flop. I knew my American pop and 'I Wanna Be Your Man' was not it! The subsequent American single release 'Not Fade Away/I Wanna Be Your Man' fared slightly better, just scraping into the Top 30. It appealed to the small movement of American kids, who, after the Beatles, were looking to seize on their own the next big thing from England before the record company foisted it on them. Later I would find out that scraping into the Top 30 meant naught, and that was where the real business began, not ended.

I made film plans in my mind and had them translated into press clippings for the Stones, dropping names like Lionel Bart and Peter Sellers. I had to: the Beatles were already filming. Keith Richards announced to the press, 'Peter O'Toole is going to play our manager.' Keith knew how to please me: Lionel shared office space with Peter O'Toole's manager Jules Buck, so in those days it could all easily have happened. Eric Easton started making trips to New York to line his pockets and line up the first Stones' tour of the States. I didn't pay much attention to this – we hadn't had a hit, the whole idea of America seemed so huge and far away and I had no idea of how to manipulate it.

If we were in town, Friday nights were spent at the *Ready Steady Go!* studios. Mick, Keith and I could regularly be seen sipping free drinks in the Green Room, laughing at the other acts. This would set the standard for another Friday night out on the town.

Vicki Wickham, Editor, *Ready Steady Go!*: Presided over by the slightly bossy Isobel, the Green Room was a feature of *RSG!*. Isobel was in charge of budgets, guest lists and schedules. Despite Isobel's vigilance, the Green Room at either Kingsway or Wembley was *the* place to be on a Friday evening. First there were free drinks, but that was probably secondary to the fact that on any given week the Green Room, with its small black-and-white telly in the corner, was the place *everyone* – managers, agents, publishers, pluggers, friends, faces and artists – mingled, chatted and planned where to go on to, and who was doing what and with whom, and all that. It was always packed, smoky, hot; people came just to be there, even if they had nothing to do with that particular week's show. Marianne Faithfull, Kenny Lynch, Chris Curtis, Dusty Springfield, Martin Wyatt, Ian Ralfini, Kit Lambert, Martha Reeves, Johnny Nash, Dave Davies, Patti LaBelle, Jimi Hendrix, Barbara Huliniki from Biba, Simon Napier Bell, Nico, Keith Moon.

Tony Hall: One of the most enjoyable parts of that whole year was *Ready Steady Go!* on a Friday night; it was a real social hang-out thing for everybody who was trying to take the music scene forward. The American artists who were in town would be on the show, the hippest English artists – there was a great atmosphere, really nice vibe, everybody dug each other.

Vicki Wickham: We were on the air from September 1963 to December 67. The show presented the music that was in the clubs, on the radio and in the record shops, set against Pop Art sets – scaffolds and pop posters and Op designs. We did interviews with 'famous' interesting people – ranging from George Best, Muhammad Ali, Phil Spector and Jerry Ragavoy to Burt Bacharach and Bob Crewe, Terry Stamp, David Bailey, Twiggy, Peter Cook and Lionel Bart, and book writers, poets, actors and actresses we liked – just anyone interesting who had the look.

The inspiration for *Ready Steady Go!* came entirely from Elkan Allen. Elkan was head of Light Entertainment for Rediffusion TV, the independent channel opposite the BBC. He was a short, bearded, red-haired man, probably in his forties, who was going out with my friend, Caroline Webb Carter, a very intellectual, upper-crust, tall and willowy English girl. We had both worked for Anthony Rowe at a publishing company and became friends. After I left BBC Radio I was firmly out of work. No work and no money. Caroline introduced me to Elkan, who promised me that my worst fear of being a secretary would be avoided and that, if I went to work for him, I could go back to being a PA within six months. He was true to his word. When I joined Rediffusion at the corner building on Kingsway and the Aldwych, he was already planning *Ready Steady Go!*

My job was to book artists for the pilot. I had been brought up on Gilbert & Sullivan and *South Pacific*, so I had to turn on the radio, buy records, look at *Disc* and *Melody Maker* and quickly work out who was who. We hadn't even had a television at home, and as I went to boarding school I had never even seen *Oh, Boy!* or any of the pop shows of the day. But my crash course fooled Elkan and the pilot was done. The acts that agreed to do the pilot were also to be booked on subsequent shows and one of the hottest groups we'd presented was the Springfields – Dusty, Tom Springfield and Mike Hurst. Dusty came into the office several weeks after the pilot to say that the group had broken up and they wouldn't be able to do it. Francis Hitching suggested she should host during the period while she made her first solo album and then be on with the first single. She was, and became, an essential member of the *RSG!* family.

I was what was called the 'Editor'. God knows what that title meant, as we were live and there was no editing! What I did do, with the team of Cathy McGowan, Michael Lindsay-Hogg and (at first) Michael Aldred and Francis Hitching, was book the show and write the script which mostly entailed giving Cathy info about the artists with an occasional 'Smashing!' thrown in.

1963 was mimed in the studio in Kingsway. Once we moved to Wembley and went 'live', the show took on another image and very much sorted out the 'real' artists from the also-rans. This is why the black Americans and artists who could *really* sing were such favourites, as well as the groups who played their own instruments – you know the list!

The fashion element evolved over the years also. For the first time teenagers had money and spent it. Clothes were a large part of their expenditure. Haircuts. Clubbing. Records. Drink. We chose the audience by going round clubs all across London and picking the best-looking, and best-dressed, to come to the studio.

It was my job to make sure it all came together. I had to get artists down to the recording area on time, try to stop the dancers pulling musicians off the risers, make sure guests were dragged from the Green Room to the floor, etc., etc. Up-front, Michael and I would try to meet the artists to discuss what numbers they were going to do and, for the Americans, tell them what type of show it was they were on.

Rediffusion was at this time run by ex-navy types, so it was all very formal and proper – until our lot came in! Mostly they left us well alone. The only time we got lumbered with an artist was when someone had overbooked and we had to have the act on *RSG!* When Paul Simon planned to sing the entire five and half minutes of 'I Am a Rock', it was my task to tell him that it had to go down to three minutes. Not a good moment! Nina Simone nearly ate me alive when I had to tell her that she could only do one number, instead of the two she'd planned. But she came back the next week and I lived!

Francis Hitching was a journalist we inherited from some other show. He kept things running and dealt with the budgets and Isobel, along with moral issues, like Donovan being busted for pot – should we or shouldn't we have him on the show? There were several hosts. Francis thought Keith Fordyce was a good, stable bet. He turned out to be stuffy and old. We auditioned hundreds of would-bes and chose Cathy McGowan, because she looked so absolutely right, and Michael Aldred, who knew everything about music and especially about American music. They co-hosted for many months, but fame and Michael didn't mix. He was a true casualty of the 60s – too much drink and drugs and always falling in love with the wrong person on a regular basis. I don't know who made the final decision, but probably Elkan and Francis, so Michael Aldred was out and Cathy became the star.

ALO: Michael Aldred was an early tragedy. 'Don't throw your love away' went the Searchers' ditty. Michael threw his heart away at every opportunity and trampled his good self way too young. None of us knew – we were all too young to know – how to give warning, to understand that Michael would wear himself and his heart out . . . You can't fall in love every Friday. I went out with Michael a couple of times and that was one time too many. He became emotional and demanding of my time, so I whacked him. Problem was that we were in the back seat of my powder-blue Chevy late on a Friday night as *Ready Steady Go!* faded and the weekend began. Poor Michael started to bleed and scream, all over the two-tone leather upholstery.

'Reg, the cunt is bleeding . . . Shut up, Michael.' I rallied forth, more concerned about whether my suede jacket and two-tone upholstery would be soiled.

Reg, pinkie on the wheel, leered back and said, 'Throw him out, Andrew . . .'

'Could you slow down a little?' I asked.

Vicki Wickham: After each show Michael Lindsay-Hogg, Cathy, Francis and I would have a post-mortem. 'Why were only three dancers hit with cameras this week? We were late cueing Gene Pitney, so his entrance was almost in darkness.' The Stones on a live show turned up their amps and gave Glyn Johns a heart attack. The sound 'board' was almost non-existent, a mono system used the rest of the week by Muriel Young and some religious programme. It was a total miracle that the sound was as good and as exciting as it was.

One time Michael tried a 'new' technique, which was to stop the action and freeze certain frames. The only thing he hadn't quite worked out was how to keep the sound going. And on and on. But it has to be remembered that we were all young and totally inexperienced, and really too busy just living to learn or even think about technicalities.

Michael had been working, I think, at the Gate Theatre in Ireland. I honestly don't know if he had ever directed TV, but he got the job and was just magnificent. Apart from the fact that he became my brother and my best friend, he knew everything about style and how to live well outside of your means. We'd go to the Connaught every Friday for breakfast before going out to the studio. We'd eat at the best restaurants, shop at Turnbull & Asser and Mr Fish. His mum was the actress Geraldine Fitzgerald. He could deal with chaos and disorder. He didn't stop it being chaotic but he captured it. Probably by default, but it worked. We would hang out every night watching Jimi Hendrix at the Scotch of St James or Patti LaBelle & the Bluebelles at Blaise's . . .

Michael Lindsay-Hogg: A series of events occurred, Dickensian in their coincidence and drama, which took me from a lowly job in a television company in Ireland to a directing job for a big English station. And within a couple of weeks I had intrigued myself to where I really wanted to be, which was directing the premier rock 'n' roll television show in the world: *Ready Steady Go!*

Vicki Wickham: We booked artists on the show from our heart and not from any commercial expectations. Luckily the ones we liked were the hit acts of the day – the Stones, the Who, Marc Bolan, Jimi Hendrix, the Animals, the Kinks. All the gorgeous Americans: Ike & Tina Turner, Otis Redding, Wilson Pickett, Fontella Bass, John Lee Hooker, Sugar Pie Desanto, Dionne

Warwick, and *all* the Motown artists – Marvin Gaye, the Supremes, the Miracles, the Temptations, Stevie Wonder, Martha & the Vandellas, etc., etc.

We were all besotted with America, collecting every single on Tamla or Motown regardless. But they all were brilliant, so we were right. We'd play each other music over the phone. Run down Oxford Street with a new album proudly displayed under our arm – no plastic bags for us.

It wasn't some great idea we had – it was the 60s on the screen. Young people in the Mod fashion of the day dancing the dances that young people were learning from America to music that was being influenced by America. The Stones and the Who were the epitome of what the show was all about. None of us had any money and yet we were out every night at either a club or a gig. We ate out. We bought clothes and records and if we had problems, which we must have had, I don't remember them!

Michael Lindsay-Hogg: Elvis Presley had changed my life when I was a lonely teenager but now there was something more authentic – if you can use that word about five skinny English kids, some of them barely out of their teens – reaching into the very essence of rock 'n' roll. Authentic for me anyway, because I felt that their roots were urban and not rural, so they were more like me and that made them authentic, even if none of them had yet heard the blues on an American jukebox.

I first met the Rolling Stones on the set of *Ready Steady Go!* They were lounging around the bandstand, but what captured my attention and held it was the big red rooster in charge of this barnyard, if a rooster can be lean, suave and elegant: wedge-toed boots, slim grey trousers, a fastidiously cut tweed jacket, cool glasses, tinted, atop a delicate nose in the middle of a delicate face, with a firm jawline that was still fairly new to shaving. We shook hands and then this person launched his questions, often answering them himself: what kind of lighting would they get; how was I going to shoot them; be sure to get an extra close-up on that one because of band problems that weren't worth talking about.

He took me over to meet his charges, who greeted me politely, diffidently, aloofly, disinterestedly or dismissively according to their natures. I spoke to the slight, almost frail boy in the turtleneck sweater with the face of a Renaissance thug about some ideas I had about how to shoot the songs. 'Talk to Andrew about that,' he said. I told him I had and he said, 'Oh', and walked away. In one of the music papers the next week I read that Andrew Loog Oldham had thought that the new director on *RSG!*, 'Martin' Lindsay-Hogg, had done some interesting things and had the benefit of being the same sort of age as they were.

So, the next time I saw Andrew, emboldened by his praise, I told him my name was 'Michael' and he said that was fine by him, and a friendship began to develop that was like a sparkling light in those bright times.

Vicki Wickham: With the artists came the managers. These were divided into two camps. Simply, the old, which we had nothing to do with, and the young. It really wasn't even an age thing, because as I think about it now some of the managers I thought old were almost certainly younger than me. It was attitude and passion that counted. Kit Lambert and Chris Stamp had plenty of both (who else would literally sell the family heirlooms to pay for Pete and Keith's nightly guitar and drum-kit smashing? And take us to lunch at Wheeler's or San Lorenzo when they didn't have a penny?). So did Andrew Oldham and Jeanie Lincoln.

The first time I met Andrew was outside a pub just round the corner from the studio on Kingsway. The Stones had been on the show and we walked round to the pub. This tall, skinny chap with red hair said 'Hello' and promptly slid down the wall and passed out. From then on, things got better!

Andrew was the first person I knew to have a Mini with tinted windows and a chauffeur. The first person to have his shirts handmade by a chap in Soho – whom I immediately went to! Later Michael Lindsay-Hogg and I went in Andrew's Rolls to see the Stones at Wembley. As we got in the car, trying hard not to show how impressed we were, Andrew handed us a large joint. Michael got out his lighter and we debated which end to light. Shows how sophisticated we weren't!

Andrew had a huge box of colourful sweets in partitions – but of course they were uppers and downers and not sweets. They looked incredible. Andrew hung out at the Revolution surrounded by glass pipes and candles and liquid flowing through it all on the table – being into presentation, I loved it. Andrew was part aloof and snooty, and then totally silly and gossipy and available.

Robert Wace: I first saw Andrew at *Ready Steady Go!* early in 1964. He was a Face. He and his entourage would visit the programme even if he didn't have anyone on. All the hangers-on would fawn around him. We didn't speak in those days but I recall him nodding to me once. He portrayed this ultra-cool image and people laughed at things he said which did not seem funny, for fear of being an outsider or of feeling left out, rather like people at parties who take drugs. They always huddle together in a corner and, if you don't take drugs, you're not one of them. When I got to know Andrew better I saw that this aloofness was a cover for a shy person.

Michael Lindsay-Hogg: At that time the managers of the rock 'n' roll groups were often more interesting companions that the musicians. Certainly the drive and the degree of connivance necessary to storm the battlements of an unwelcoming music industry were good for the character of those who survived it, and even probably those who didn't. At dinner with a band, often the songwriters would be talking about chord progressions, or open frets or pussy, while the manager would have stories of double-dealing, bribery, corruption and the general bad behaviour around the music industry, which tactics the manager would be using for his own ends and being delighted that they were available.

I remember on one occasion Andrew telling some hair-raising story, while Mick and Keith sat opposite him, hanging on every word, like younger brothers in thrall to their daring older brother. In fact, thinking about it, I wonder to what degree Andrew's gangster pose (I suppose that's what it was) and his bravado (you fuck with me at your peril) influenced Mick and Keith as they developed their stage characters, which would then morph with their real selves and vice versa. Not a little. Partly it was Andrew's decisiveness. He was always decisive, whether it was about ordering chicken pot pie at the Hungry Horse or what was the A-side and what the B. If decisiveness sounds too grown-up, one has also to remember that part of his and their make-up was plain daring and can-you-believe-we-got-away-with-that.

Robert Wace: If you look at early footage of them, Jagger's almost apologetic. I'm not saying that he's now become the *éminence grise* of rock, but if you've got a hundred million quid it's quite easy to become anything you want to be, really. You see, the problem is that you create these people and then, sooner or later, you get fed up with them or they get fed up with you, and then the bugger of it is that you can't go on a stage and play a guitar. I mean, they've got the residual.

Without Andrew, the Rolling Stones would have been just another band. Nowadays, when I see Jagger being interviewed, I wonder if he has any conception of the huge debt the Stones owe Andrew.

Philip Norman, author of *The Stones* and *Shout!*: To me, Andrew was one of the true originals, he invented the Stones. But nobody wants to say, 'Yes, I was invented by someone else.' The Beatles and the Stones were mirror-images of each other: the Beatles were rough-edged and slightly delinquent and became sweet and cuddly; the Stones were middle-class, well-brought-up lads who became the anti-Christ. Their identities were so inverted, that's why they were such good friends, they both had to accept another identity.

Andrew peaked ridiculously early; he had an unbelievably magic touch for that brief time, he could not put a foot wrong. It was extraordinary and he should have credit, a lifetime achievement award by the record industry. He is a remarkable figure – a combination of the completely outrageous with the sane and articulate. He would tell you something in extremely literate, reasonable language, but it would be the most outrageous thing you'd ever heard.

He was amazing, stylish to the point of self-destruction, the original young entrepreneur in the pop business in this country, for his own ends obviously – as a manager, he wanted to be as big as the act. He himself pressed the ejector button at such an early age. There's still this edge about the Stones, which is so amazing now they're all doddery old freaks – they still manage to be outrageous. The funny thing is they're still reading the script Andrew wrote . . . not only are they reading the script he wrote, but every other group that comes along is reading the same script. Every other group that comes along, at any press conference, sprawling on the couch being a mixture of charming and rude, that's Andrew's script. He wrote it, he thought in script terms, he saw it as a world of posturing and role-playing, which is exactly what it was.

His ideal was Laurence Harvey in *Expresso Bongo*; he took that cardboard stereotype figure and made it much more wild and colourful. That's the blueprint. It's still going on: every five years another group comes along, people tut-tutting about Oasis. They think they're original, they think they've hit on an original idea, they don't even realise that it's in the bloodstream and that anyone who's a pop musician does the Andrew Oldham number. The Rolling Stones turned themselves into something else. They're not still Andrew Oldham's creation obviously, but in many respects they're still using his lines and ideas . . . He came up with the anti-hero and now they've given it a corporate identity.

ALO: I tried to keep tabs on what Peter Meaden was up to, hearing he was travelling life's highway without brakes and was now promoting a band called the High Numbers. It was not pleasant being the leader of the pack in this instance, leader in so many of the games Peter had showed me the rules to. Peter was starting to paunch out; he'd been in the ring of leapers too many times and was pill-drunk, getting soft and emotional around the edges. I'd find out later for myself that drugs' chaser is panic. With the High Numbers, Peter played his hand off every deal, tried to stand up straight, to get that lithe boy running in the street with his national anthem. He tried so hard, so hard, that even though Peter didn't, the group made it.

They had been called the Who and they would be again, their name would be called out by millions; but, in this moment, Peter was the only one screaming and they were the High Numbers. He had managed to get them a singles deal on Fontana, a Philips division; he had ripped off two blues structures, put his 'Mod-prose-speak' to work for them, and 'I'm the Face' and 'Zoot Suit' were due for release. This is early 64. Grab a hold of that image, those titles and get Meaden's genius. A record deal was hard enough to pull off, but an imprint on the future . . . that must be acknowledged.

Peter asked me out to a dance hall in Islington to see the High Numbers. They were very good; better than that – great. They did Miracles and Temptations stuff with a hard slant; Townshend and Moonie were the riveting two for me that day. So were these two characters sitting in the front of the hall: one was a soft, Wilde-looking man with worried eyes and pursed lips; the other good-looking wild yobbo wolf looked like his minder. The former was Kit Lambert, the latter Chris Stamp, the other bright light in the Stamp collection.

'Peter,' I grinded, for when with Peter – whether on speed or not – you started grinding. He was catchy, a straight-out-to-lunch-pill-popping Oscar Wilde in his own jail. Too many Wildes, and I knew then that one of them had to go. 'Peter,' repeat 'n' grind, 'just who are those two guys in the front?'

'Oh, them,' grinded Peter back, his pupils scoring the jackpot, his teeth gnashing the remains of his nails. 'They're two would-be film-director wankers, they want to manage the High Numbers.'

'Looks like they already do, Peter,' I said.

But Peter didn't hear me. He was too busy listening to himself.

Peter Meaden, in *Sounds*, 1975: The Mod thing was actually a guys' thing: at the time all the little girls were screaming for the Beatles. Drynamil lowered your sex-drive, so you didn't have to be desperately searching for a girl to pull. You were independent. I had this dream of getting a group together that would be the focus, the entertainers for the Mods; a group that would actually be the same people on-stage as the guys in the audience. An actual representation of the people.

Chris Stamp: Kit Lambert and I were assistant film directors on big features and we wanted to make a movie, but at that time rock 'n' roll movies were garbage. It was Elvis Presley and Billy Fury, standing up and singing a song; loads of kids hanging out in a coffee bar and they dance a bit, then there's a song. It was nonsense.

I wanted to make a film that was about the reality. The pills and the Mods and the sweat and the tears . . . the life . . . the actual phenomenon that was going on in the streets. The storyline that Kit and I came up with was: these two guys find a band, follow them as they try to make it, blah blah blah, then they become successful. I had to lean on that knowledge because I'd come from the East End, come through all that scene.

Kit didn't really know about rock 'n' roll. He'd come down from Oxford, but he was terribly interested in the phenomenon of the Beatles. We had to find this incredibly good act to centre our film around. We looked everywhere, we went to the north of England – we did it like film-makers, we took a map and started talking to all these bands. We'd seen this band called the Who, then we didn't see the fly-posters any more, then we see this band, y'know, called the High Numbers. So we check 'em out and, y'know, they are *the* Who. It's quite clear because they're totally not regular, they're fucking ugly, they're dangerous, they're like 'fuck you' and they're already doing weird shit. You didn't go to hear a good bar band when you went to see the Who. You either listened or left. They're this Mod band but they're not really Mods. Peter Meaden had put the Mod thing on them. It didn't really sit comfortably on them, but anyway they were doing it.

Peter Meaden was of that second generation of Mods and he was a total fanatic about it. It was like a religion. I sorta liked that about him. He was a pillhead, right off. I took about two of the shit those Mods were taking and they were rubbish, really chalky dex-amphetamine, a by-product of plastics. Really shit! What it was about was staying up all night and not really feeling the cold. It was only later that Mods started to say, 'Yeah, and I couldn't get a fucking hard-on.' You'd seen them on Wardour Street, five o'clock in the morning, January, sleeveless, just come out of the Scene, thinking they're out there. Meaden was that.

Pete Townshend: The new management knew nothing about the music biz, but they were worldly-wise. Chris was a King's Road looker and Kit was a well-educated, refined homosexual – at the time, bisexual – an extremely clever and unbelievable raconteur. For a moment there we had this triad of Kit, Chris and Peter Meaden. Peter Meaden brought in Phil the Greek to scare Chris and Kit, when he was trying to get control of the band. Kit and Chris cut through all that by the simple expedient of giving Peter some money; they gave him some cash, they offered him £250 in hard cash, in notes, in his hand. He took it and left. He went immediately to the Vagabonds, a Jamaican show band, big band, eight-piece, Jimmy James & the Vagabonds, featuring a guy called the Count, a soul band but they'd come out of Jamaica. I wouldn't have looked twice at the Vagabonds, had it not been for the way that Peter sold them. He used to say, 'The Count's elegant, he's sophisticated, he knows about style and Jimmy's got this voice.'

Chris Stamp and Keith Moon

ALO: So here we are on the eve of the big, three-chord gold rush; the eve of destruction would be a slow train coming, and it wasn't yet the evening of the day. We were all still gargling life's offerings of good fortune, trying them on for size but never placing a final order. Life was very good to us, to me and for the most part to all who sailed with me, and we were good for life. We were singing a different tune and it liked us, and gave us a good slice of itself with a view from an equally nice room at the top. Regardless of that bullshit about 'you've never had it so good' . . . we were having it just fine.

From my first days with the Stones, we had conspired as one against the world as we knew it. America and the rest of the world is another story. We had believed that their musical force would break down the doors of resistance, that their strength would trample over the *schadenfreude* hierarchy and trample the nos into yeahs. We'd got that 'yes' from the world as we knew it – it's still 1964 and the Stones have yet to work abroad. We'd get that 'yes', too. We'd win the war and take our spoils in fame and money.

When I met the Stones, they were already. I didn't fall for puppets, I fell for the real thing. They tapped power from the strength of their musical purpose. Apart from the slight false start when they wore costumes in exchange for equipment, and a change in personnel, I said, 'Don't change a thing . . . you've got everything. I believe in you, just let me use it.' I told them who they were and they became it.

After a kindergarten beginning, we started to find our recording legs. I didn't try to force my Spector Wall of Sound on the group (I saved that for my own extracurricular efforts). I went with their Wall of Noise, the noise that had first nailed me to their wall one Sunday night nigh on a year before in Richmond. I showed Mick and Keith that they could write their own songs, making them dependent on no one, not even me; showed them the way to creative freedom. Nobody, no record company, told them what to play – they arrived at it all by themselves.

Together we'd planned the look of the sound as I tried to control what was seen, and did control what was heard. I attempted to control the image and what was said about it. We were writing our own headlines, we were taking no prisoners and no outsiders ever got inside the walls. We were our own buzzword, the Stones created their own sound-bites, and I'd use any event in passing this message on.

We handled our own dirty laundry at home, we didn't take it outside to the cleaners.

We went out to play and we all knew the game we were playing. Life was really nice, and nice was the word of the day. It wasn't brilliant, it was nice. My idea of a night off was to go over to Alan Freeman's flat and play more records, to talk more shop, or nip up the M1 in my new Mini, with its Philips-made 45-rpm singles player, and Dusty Springfield, playing each other the new American singles we'd copped.

Most of us were aware that we were privileged to be part of this wonderful world and just wanted more, just didn't want this good thing to stop. We were all too busy to mope, and as such we wished each other well – there was plenty of room at the top. While embracing this, I drifted apart from my mother and never developed with Sheila, but I didn't have a choice in this. It's not everybody who gets a chance to telephone the gods and have them take the call.

Later I allowed myself to go mad with vanity, spent too much attention

on my own details and concentrated on being interesting, not interested, nearly ending up a very dead lunatic, and thus almost leaving a disgusting legacy to trample on my name. I would lie down with whores and criminals and recognise my waste in the mirror, but somehow I always managed to wake with the angels, until the end of a slow thirty-year train ride into madness. I got taken up with the business of dying, till I got assisted in the art of surviving.

I know my work with the Stones and the many others whose talent I cherished affected the consciousness and ethic of my time, for good and for bad. Each day I am always fortunate, though sometimes saddened, to witness that the generations that have followed us bear the effects of the causes we made. We are warned never to trust the artist, to trust only the work itself: it would have been imprudent of me at the time to try and define the difference, and so this story includes both warts and haloes.

It may have looked as if all I wanted was to have it our way, but as long ago as that, affinity, reality and communication were what I loved about the screams, the laughs and the dreams, so I'll leave on this clear note:

The view of the River Thames from the Decca Albert Embankment offices was quite brilliant that wonderful spring morning in 1964, when I met the Chairman for the first time, asking for what I wanted and getting what I needed. What I wanted was for Sir Edward Lewis to acknowledge me as the future of the business, as I acknowledged him as its past; what I needed was a cheque to complete my Marianne Faithfull record.

Sir Edward put the acetate for 'As Tears Go By' on his green felt turntable and the oboe floated out of the funnel of the old man's wind-up machine. The cor anglais took the fade, Mr Decca picked up the phone on his desk and got through to Dick Rowe.

'Dick, give the boy the money' was all he said.

London and the Thames looked radiantly alive, and a Polaroid stopped, snapped and smiled at me in a way that always distinguishes those special days when you are at one with the world and you both know it.

· ACKNOWLEDGEMENTS ·

For Esther Farfan Oldham – God gives us all an advantage; you are mine.

For Maximillian Oldham – my greatest production and true manager.

For Sean Oldham – my first hit. I applaud your work at surmounting the example I gave you and look forward to your state of grace.

Tony Calder / Pat Clayton / Derek Johnson / Maurice Kinn / Marc Geubard / Lionel Bart / John Douglas / David Miranda / E.R. Marson / Jet Harris / Tony Meehan / Tony Hall / Jimmy Greaves / Lee Everett / Alan Freeman / Don Arden / Mickie Most / Johnny Jackson* / John Elwick / Tania Gordon / Sheila Klein / Linda Keith / John Paul Jones / Angus McGill / Chris Stamp / Pete Townshend / Susie Aspinall / Philip Townsend / Archie McNair / Mary Quant / Vidal Sassoon / Pete King / Jeremy Paul Solomons / Peter Hope Lumley / Shel Talmy / Charles Blackwell / Bobby Graham / Mark Wynter / Dolly East / Tony King / Percy Dickens / Kenny Lynch / Chris Hutchins / Gene Pitney / Freddy Bienstock / Sean O'Mahony / Ken East / Peter Jones / Linda Leitch / Giorgio Gomelsky / Peter Noone / Roger Savage / Keith Altham / Cynthia Stewart Dillane / Leslie Conn / Nik Cohn / John Fenton / Malcolm Forrester / Dave Berry / Judy Geeson / Adrian Millar* / Philip Norman / Steve Inglis / Vicki Wickham* / Michael Lindsay-Hogg* / Big Jim Sullivan / Clem Cattini / Andy Wickham* and Robert Wace* are all great voices in my life and I thank them for providing such a resounding chorus to this song.

The above were interviewed by Simon Dudfield; those marked * provided their own text; Tony King and Lionel Bart were pre-interviewed by Dave Thompson; and Mr Vidal Sassoon was interviewed by Mr Oldham.

Whether the Rolling Stones were too busy being marathon men or whether they're saving our stories for themselves, their absence as present-time voices is ameliorated by some selected quotes, which ring as true for me as any of our conversations. Marianne Faithfull described me so well in her moving autobiography that I needed not ask her for any more words.

Fred Ulan, Lester Bryman and the Natural Health Improvement Center – thank you for the care and the continued gift and assistance of Contact Reflex Analysis.

Thanks to Jim, Patti and Amy at HealthMed, Sacramento, for clearing the body via the L. Ron Hubbard Purification Rundown and Juan Jaramillo M.D. for the Bogota runup.

L.R.H., the Church of Scientology and Dianetics, for the tech and the great start on the road to clear.

Carter Withey for tracking down the other Andrew Loog; Lou Adler and Johnny Rogan for the literary assists, and Lou Adler especially for always being there, even when I was not; Dave Thompson and the late Tony Secunda for the first run; David Milner for transcending the dustjacket mentality and giving us an honest read; Martin Hotham and Malcolm Forrester for keeping our Dock Green an ethical patch.

Simon Dudfield – Without my consent you made my life your agenda and forced me to make that agenda mine. I therefore thank you for bringing me to the table of words and for your assist in making the voices sing.

Ron Ross – for helping me realise it was impossible to sing this song through the voice of another and helping me find a voice of my own. Thank you.

Thomas 'Doc' Cavalier – thank you for the survival run and the assist in making life clear again.

. . . and to Ruby.

The publishers are grateful for permission to quote from the following works: *Faithfull*, Marianne Faithfull with David Dalton, copyright © Marianne Faithfull 1994, published by Michael Joseph; *Expresso Bongo*, Wolf Mankowitz, copyright © The Estate of Wolf Mankowitz; *Quant*, Mary Quant, copyright © Mary Quant 1967, published by Pan, used by permission of the author; *Starmakers and Svengalis*, Johnny Rogan, copyright © Johnny Rogan 1988, published by Queen Anne Press, used by permission of the author;

Awopbopaloobop Alopbamboom, Nik Cohn, copyright © Nik Cohn 1969, published by Vintage, used by permission of the author; *Art into Pop,* Simon Frith and Howard Horne, copyright © Simon Frith and Howard Horne 1987, published by Routledge; *Phelge's Stones,* James Phelge, copyright © James Phelge, used by permission of the author.

Other sources: *The Rolling Stones in Their Own Words,* compiled by David Dalton and Mick Farren, copyright © Omnibus Books 1980 and 1985, published by Omnibus Press / Music Sales Ltd; *The Stones,* Philip Norman, copyright © Philip Norman 1984 and 1993, first published by Hamish Hamilton 1984, and with an afterword by Penguin Books 1993; *Shout! The Beatles in Their Generation,* Philip Norman, copyright © Philip Norman 1996, published by Simon & Schuster; *Tony Curtis, The Autobiography,* Tony Curtis with Barry Paris, copyright © Tony Curtis 1993, published by Heinemann; *Edie, An American Biography,* Jean Stein, ed. George Plimpton, copyright © Jean Stein and Hadada Inc. 1982, published by Alfred A. Knopf; *The Early Stones,* photographs by Michael Cooper, text by Terry Southern, foreword and commentary by Keith Richards, copyright © 1992 published by Hyperion; *Revolt into Style,* George Melly, copyright © George Melly, *Keith,* Stanley Booth, copyright © Stanley Booth 1994, published by Headline.

Every effort has been made to trace the copyright holders of copyrighted material, and the publishers apologise if any sources inadvertently remain unacknowledged or wrongly acknowledged. Any information that will help the publishers trace copyright holders or correct details of copyright holders will be very gratefully received.

PICTURE CREDITS

229, Gus Carol

231, BBC / Hulton Picture Library

233, Gus Carol

239, Gus Carol

246, Gered Mankowitz

247, Dezo Hoffman

250, Pictorial Press

259, Cecil Beaton / Camera Press

268, Philip Townsend

281, Gus Carol

289, Raul Perrone

297, Tony Gale / Pictorial Press

310, Gered Mankowitz

315, John Cowan / Camera Press

331, Gered Mankowitz

352, Gered Mankowitz

· INDEX ·

374
                                    INDEX

'World Without Love. A' 84. 309
Wyatt. Martin 338
Wyman. Bill 170. 188. 220. 245. 249. *253*,
     322. 332: *see also* Rolling Stones
Wyman. Diane 245
Wynter. Mark **147-8,** *155*, *156:* and Mack-
     ender 143. **143-4;** and ALO 144. 146. 151.
     154. 155-6. **156-7,** 171. **175**

Yardbirds. the 79. 203. 293
'Yes. Tonight Josephine' 19
'You Better Move On' 269
Young. Jimmy 152. 212
Young. Muriel 341
Young Lions, The 40. 44
'You've Lost That Lovin' Feeling'